CW00347058

MOTORCYCLE YEARBOOK
1999–2000

© 1999, Chronosports Editeur, Jordils Park, Chemin des Jordils 40, CH-1025 St-Sulpice, Switzerland
This is a Dempsey Parr Book, Dempsey Parr, 13 Whiteladies Road, Clifton, Bristol BS8 1PB, United Kingdom
ISBN 0-75253-627-3
Printed in France

MOTORCYCLE YEARBOOK
1999–2000

Pictures
Maurice Büla
Roger Lohrer

Foreword
Michel Métraux

Text
Jean-Claude Schertenleib

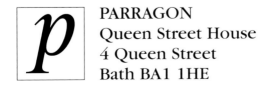

PARRAGON
Queen Street House
4 Queen Street
Bath BA1 1HE

Contents

Foreword

A team sport

Taking a team to victory in the Motorcycle Grands Prix at world level represents a very complex challenge.

The best bike is not enough. The best rider cannot succeed without a top level team.

A team manager must be able to see clearly and watch every detail of his operation like a hawk, so that it runs smoothly. It is essential to concentrate on the technical front and the needs of the riders. A state of permanent evolution in all areas and total quality of the services brought to the team is a motivational force for everyone involved.

The riders are very sensitive to this aspect of a team. The slightest little hiccough in the details of a timetable, quality of food or routines is enough to upset a rider's motivation. Therefore, all these little details must be the subject of permanent attention. In all these areas, the team manager plays a key role. Only when all the small details are in place can success follow. It is a great experience for all those who are ready to sacrifice a lot to compete in the sport at the highest level.

Finally, it is down to an ability to take risks at all levels. Because it is the risks that the riders must take and accept which makes the life of a motorcycle GP team so demanding and complex.

Michel Metraux

- Founder and honorary president of IRTA, the association of GP teams.

- A team manager for over twenty years.

- In charge of the Swissauto project, a Swiss challenge to the technological strength of Japan.

Jurgen Van Den Goorbergh at Brno:
second pole-position

▷

Alzamora, the winner who didn't win

△
Olivier Liégeois

Just one point separated the world champion and his nearest rival. Yet another champion enters the record books without having won a single race on the way to the title. The last lap of the year was nothing if not surprising and while Honda may have dominated the 125 category in 1999, it was no less interesting for that. The winner was Spain's Emilio Alzamora, not exactly Mr. Popular on the track, while losing out was Italy's newest star, Marco Melandri.

Aprilia, who won the previous year's title in the courts, was not in any fit state to defend its crown in 1999. The Noale factory had deliberately changed its plans by entrusting works machinery to outside teams. Honda employed the same strategy to greater effect, dominating its European rival.

Belgian bonanza

The Japanese marque dominated and while it was the team run by Angel Nieto, with technical matters in the hands of Italy's Massimo Matteoni which celebrated winning the championship, the year belonged to the team run by the Belgian, Olivier Liegeois.

The former racer, who turned to preparation several years ago, had already demonstrated his talent last year with Masao Azuma. In 1999, with the dream team of Marco Melandri and the Japanese former double champion, Liegeois, under the Playlife banner, should have emerged victorious. He certainly dominated, taking ten wins, five for Melandri and five for Azuma, proving the team was a cut above the rest.

However, in the face of all this talent, it was consistency which won the day. Emilio Alzamora became the second Spaniard, after Manuel Herreros, the 1989 80 cc world champion, to take a title without winning a race. Azuma had made the perfect start to the season with three wins, the Japanese rider took a terrible knock during the first free practice session in Brno, when he hit a deer which crossed the track in the early morning. It was a big impact and while Azuma was not seriously hurt, it was a big psychological blow as his compatriot Noboru Ueda recalls: "Since the Czech Republic GP, Masao never really got back on top form."

Ill fortune at the start

Azuma's season went downhill, while team-mate Melandri's travelled in the opposite direction, as it started with a triple zero; broken wrist in practice for Malaysia, did not start in Japan and another fall in Jerez. Beaten by a single point,

Melandri paid the penalty for his one real mistake of the year at the Valencia GP where he lost concentration after his team-mate Azuma fell just ahead of him.

Spain's Emilio Alzamora played it safe, climbing onto the podium ten times out of a total of sixteen grands prix. If he had not fallen twice, through no fault of his own - with Ueda in Australia and with his own team-mate Ivan Goi in South Africa, Angel Nieto's rider might well have taken the crown well before the last lap of the last GP of the year when the beaten Marco

---

Return to 1998

An annual, which considers itself a work of reference cannot get by with presenting a profile of a false world champion and we know that is exactly what happened with the 1998-99 edition of "Motorcycle Yearbook." It contained a MAJOR error in that it featured Tomomi Manako instead of Kazuto Sakata in the pages devoted to the 125 cc world champion.

How did it happen? Right from the start of the business surrounding the fuel used by Kazuto Sakata in the Australian GP, we were in daily contact with the FIM at Mies, in Switzerland. Looking back at recent history, we found that in ALL CASES where a second opinion had been demanded by a team which had used a fuel that did not conform to the regulations, the second opinion had confirmed the result of the first. Like most people, we were therefore convinced that Kazuto Sakato would lose his points from Australia and therefore, Tomomi Manako would be the 1998 125 cc world champion. The mistake we made was this: the regulations state that: "the result of the sample analysis to be taken into consideration will be the one which most favours the competitor."

As it was only on 16th November 1998, shortly before 21h00 that the Federation announced its decision, it was too late to react as the "Motorcycle Yearbook, 1998-1999" was in the final stages of production.

Jean-Claude Schertenleib

Melandri tried to lay a pernicious trap for his opponent.

With Honda taking the top three place, the Aprilias were not really in the fight, even though Roberto Locatelli, Gianluigi Scalvini and Arnaud Vincent all scored their first GP wins this season. Also noteworthy was the return of Derbi, who did well thanks to the efforts of Japan's Youichi Ui, who finished on the podium in Australia and eleventh in the championship.

Simone Sanna: rookie of the year

125 at a glance

Outgoing champion:
Kazuto Sakata (J, Aprilia.) Crowned world champion only several weeks after the final race of the season, Kazuto Sakata left the Aprilia team to take up an offer from Honda in the Pileri team. The Japanese company had decorated the wedding cake with promises of post-racing career employment. The close links between Sakata's ancestors and Soichiro Honda also added some weight to the transfer.

The major players
Aprilia: world champions thanks to Sakata, the Italian marque could not use the Number 1 as he left. This was becoming something of a habit. The winter had seen all sorts of changes in Noale, where we now found Gianluigi Scalvini (Inoxmacel Fontana,) Roberto Locatelli (Vasco Rossi,) Gino Borsoi (Semprucci) and the duo of Mirko Giansanti/Manuel Poggiali (Kappa.) France's Arnaud Vincent was entered by Jorge "Aspar" Martinez (CC Valencia,) the German Steve Jenkner stayed faithful to

Marlboro ADAC while the two Frenchmen Frederic Petit and Randy de Puniet used last year's RSV-R.

Honda: the Japanese company picked up the world champion Kazuto Sakata (MTP-Pileri) and the team run by Angel Nieto (Via Digital) with Emilio Alzamora and Nieto Junior (Massimo Matteoni is the technical director and also runs Ivan Goi and Massimiliano Sabbatani, the lightest rider in the field. Other works Honda teams, Belgium's Olivier Liegeois (Playlife Racing Team) with Japan's Masao Azuma on Bridgestone tyres and the youngest winner in GP history, Marco Melandri and the team run by Lucio Cecchinello (Givi Honda LCR) which runs with Japan's Noboru Ueda.

Derbi: The Spanish firm returned to competition under the direction of Austria's Harald Bartol, who designed the engine fitted to a Fabrication Techniques chassis, the English company which also builds the Modenas KR3 and the MuZ- Weber in the 500 class.

The winners:
Masao Azuma (J, Honda, 5,) Marco Melandri (I, Honda, 5,) Roberto Locatelli (I, Aprilia, 2,) Gianluigi Scalvini (I, Aprilia, 2,) Arnaud Vincent (F, Aprilia, 1) and Noboru Ueda (J, Honda, 1.)

The pole positions
Luccio Cecchinello (I, Honda, 3,) Roberto Locatelli (I, Aprilia, 3,) Marco Melandri (I, Honda, 3,) Arnaud Vincent (F, Aprilia, 2,) Masao Azuma (J, Honda, 2,) Gianluigi Scalvini (I, Aprilia, 2) and Noboru Ueda (J, Honda, 1.)

The fastest race laps
Marco Melandri (I, Honda, 4,) Emilio Alzamoro (E, Honda, 3,) Gianluigi Scalvini (I, Aprilia, 2,) Noboru Ueda (J, Honda, 2,) Roberto Locatelli (I, Aprilia, 2,) Kazuto Sakata (J, Honda, 1,) Massimiliano Sabbatani (I, Honda, 1) and Masao Azuma (J, Honda, 1.)

The final classification
1. Emilio Alzamora	E	Honda	227 points
2. Marco Melandr	I	Honda	226
3. Masao Azuma	J	Honda	190

The constructors classification
1. Honda	367 points
2. Aprilia	271
3. Derbi	91
4. Yamaha	11

Rookie of the year
Simone Sanna (I, Honda) 8th in the world championship

Best privateer
Emilio Alzamora (E, Honda) world champion.

New in 1999 Italjet 125

Aprilia are champion, but...

Loris Capirossi
and Valentino Rossi.

Valentino Rossi and Aprilia are the 1999 250 cc world champions. After they were totally dominant in 1998 at the end of a season when the Italian marque found itself embroiled in a battle between its three works riders, everyone felt Rossi would be completely unbeatable this season. And so he was, even if he had to wait a long time before finding himself in the lead in the overall classification.

Why and how? Firstly, because Valentino Rossi was very unlucky in the French GP, when the chain on his Aprilia jumped off the sprocket with just a few hundred metres to go to a victory, which had seemed like his for the taking. Then he had yet another technical problem with the electronic control unit which did not allow him to give it his all in the opening round at Sepang in Malaysia. Finally, because a chink appeared in the armour of this fantastically talented champion: Valentino Rossi does not like getting wet - he finished seventh in Japan and eighth in Valencia.

The surprising Honda

Those were the only weak points in the winner's corner. But the biggest factor keeping Rossi off the number one slot until the German GP was the fact that

the opposition had been given a serious wake-up call after getting soundly thrashed in 1998. Thus, the Honda NSR 250, which had been totally eclipsed twelve months earlier had made serious progress and that situation was helped in no small part by the arrival of the outgoing world champion, Loris Capirossi. Winner of the first GP, Capirossi should have been the main thorn in Rossi's side and indeed he was the only one to have beaten him in a straight fight at Assen and Imola. But a fall in France and then the double zero following the start line incident in Mugello which led to a one race ban after the black flag made an unwelcome appearance, rapidly put the reigning champion out of the running for a second title. It was therefore another Honda rider, Tohru Ukawa who notched up his first two grand prix wins and, mathematically at least posed the biggest threat to the Rossi-Aprilia steamroller.

As well as progress made by Honda, the season marked the official return of Yamaha to the category. It was another step for the marque which had so dominated the 1999 Japanese series with Shinya Nakano on board. As team mate to Olivier Jacque, the Japanese rider soon adopted the mantle of Number One rider in the Tech 3 team, having beaten the Frenchman right from the first race of the season. Winner at home in the rain,

Nakano was too often penalised by a lack of outright power. Jacque's enforced absence after an accident during practice for the Spanish GP, constituted a further handicap for the Herve Poncharal run team. The team did however celebrate a great first, getting two riders on the podium at the Welkom track in South Africa, albeit behind Valentino Rossi.

The revelations

What else was memorable this year? Aprilia only had one real works rider as Marcellino Lucchi the test rider did not finish the season for budgetary reasons and Germany's Ralf Waldmann had a lot of problems with his starts and also had to scratch from the from the first two events after an accident at Sepang and the British rider, Jeremy McWilliams too often paid the penalty for an over- spectacular riding style. So that left the Italian Franco Battaini as the undoubted revelation of the season. He made it to the podium twice after his talent had already been spotted the previous year, riding a standard Yamaha. This year he moved up a notch. Another worthy contender was the Argentinian Sebastian Oscar Porto and the wise men at Yamaha, who entrusted him with the 2000 version of the standard TZ from the Czech GP onwards.

A mention also for a rookie worth keeping an eye on; the young Australian Anthony West, who is Michael Doohan's rider. With his TSR-Honda, he rapidly confirmed himself as the man to watch among the privateers, performing at a similar level to lads who already had a good understanding of the European tracks, like Englishman Jason Vincent and the Italian Luca Boscoscuro.

The 250 key facts

Outgoing champion: Loris Capirossi (I, Aprilia) was still tied contractually to Aprilia for one more year, but he saw his contract rejected by the Italian company. The official reason was that he had "a negative influence on their image." The world champion, with the coveted Number 1 in his pocket had no difficulty finding a home at Honda. There he joined forces with his former 125 team-mate from the days of his two 125 world titles, Fausto Gresini.

The major players

Aprilia: cohabitation having been somewhat strained the previous year, Aprilia returned to a more conventional team structure, with just one official rider taken on by the factory. That man was Valentino Rossi. Test rider Marcellino Lucchi was compensated for his abnegation and was taken on for the whole championship running an "evolution" machine with the Dutch Docshop team. The project was to fizzle out before the end, through lack of funds. In Germany, Ralf Waldmann teamed up once again with his 250 cc mentor, Dieter Stappert and rode an official RSW. Franco Battaini had his own team with Giacomo Guidotti as chief engineer, the son of the factory manager and Jeremy McWilliams, still with QUB was supplied with last year's bikes.

Honda: The humiliation of the previous year had left its mark on Honda, who put a lot of effort into the NSR 250cc project. At the start of the winter, it seemed that only Loris Capirossi (Elf-Axo-Gresini) and Tohru Ukawa (Shell Advance) would be Honda factory riders, but Stefano Perugini managed to find a budget to run an official team, under the technical direction of Tino Villa. The new NSR was as bad as its predecessor at the start of the winter, but Honda reacted quickly.

Yamaha: This was the big novelty of the year. With the YZR, which had dominated the Japanese championship in the hands of Shinya Nakano and Naoki Matsuda, Yamaha came back to the world championship officially, under the banner of the French Chesterfield Tech 3 team run by Hervé Poncharal. The two riders were Olivier Jacque, fed up with Honda, and the young Japanese champion with unusually round eyes, Shinya Nakano. Tomomi Manako the 125 runner up, also made the switch to 250s, with the Kurz team, riding a kitted TZ. On a similar machine was the Argentine Sebastian Oscar Porto with the Semprucci team, who was entrusted with the 2000 version of the TZ from the Czech GP onwards.

TSR Honda: the TSR frame which had shone the previous year, notably in the hands of McWilliams, was the reference point for the privateers. Worthy of note, the performances of the top two in the European championship, Germany's Alexander Hofmann and France's Julien Allemand. After an average year with Aprilia, Luca Boscscuro also rode the British built machine, as did Michael Doohan's young Australian prot?g? Anthony West.

The winners:
Valentino Rossi (I, Aprilia, 9,) Loris Capirossi (I, Honda, 3,) Tohru Ukawa (J, Honda, 2) and Shinya Nakano (J, Yamaha, 1.)

Pole positions:
Valentino Rossi (I, Aprilia, 4,) Shinya Nakano (J, Yamaha, 2,) Loris Capirossi (I, Honda, 2,) Olivier Jacque (F, Yamaha, 2,) Franco Battaini (I, Aprilia, 1,) Marcellino Lucchi (I, Aprilia, 1,) Tohru Ukawa (J, Honda, 1,) Ralf Waldmann (D, Aprilia, 1) and Jeremy McWilliams (GB, Aprilia, 1.)

Fastest race laps:
Valentino Rossi (I, Aprilia, 8,) Loris Capirossi (I, Honda, 3,) Tohru Ukawa (J, Honda, 1,) Shinya Nakano (J, Yamaha, 1,) Stefano Perugini (I, Honda, 1) and Franco Battaini (I, Aprilia, 1.)

The final podium
1. Valentino Rossi	I	Aprilia	309 points
2. Tohru Ukawa	J	Honda	261
3. Loris Capirossi	I	Honda	209

The constructors' classification
1. Aprilia	338 points
2. Honda	326
3. Yamaha	249
4. TSR-Honda	104

Best rookie
Shinya Nakano (J, Yamaha), 4th in the world championship.

Best privateer
Franco Battaini (I, Aprilia), 8th in the world championship.

Anthony West
▽

The king and his heir

Alex Crivillé

The 1999 season marked a turning point in the history of modern motor cycle sport. The accident which befell Michael Doohan effectively eliminated the dominant figure of the Nineties. It was the ideal opportunity to see who could fill the breach. Honda was still in charge with Alex Criville and Tadayuki Okada. Suzuki, thanks to Kenny Roberts, was the sensation of the opening part of the season with Yamaha showing strongly in the final rounds. With two podiums for the Aprilia V twin and Tetsuya Harada and two pole positions for Jurgen Van Den Goorbergh's MuZ-Weber, we witnessed a sensational season with several challengers for top 500 honours.

Before being flown to San Francisco, just over 24 hours after his serious accident in the first practice session at Jerez de la Frontera, Michael Doohan had insisted on abdicating with honour, by nominating his successor, Alex Criville. Although the Spaniard realised his dream, the road to the title was not easy, littered as it was with injuries; a fall at Assen followed by a win a week later in Donington; a fall without injury in Valencia and more seriously at Phillip Island. On top of that the competition was getting hungrier.

The Suzuki surprise

It all started with a more than unusual line up in the 500 cc class. At the magnificent Sepang circuit, for the first Grand Prix of the season, we discovered a front row made up of a privateer Honda (Kocinski,) two Suzukis and a Yamaha. There was not a single HRC-Repsol team rider. Was this some sort of joke? Yamaha had finally got its act together with the dream team of Massimiliano Biaggi and Carlos Checa. It was to be the start of the confirmation of Kenny Roberts, who would dominate the opening two rounds of the season and be a major force throughout the year. He had a few worries, notably with the tyres in Australia and South Africa and the RGV 500 showed occasional but serious signs of weakness, particularly at Donington. Kenny Roberts and the engineer Warren Willing, who had done such a good job over the winter had thus managed to push Suzuki back to the top.

Yamaha lived through a more difficult season. Despite a big budget, the YZR has not yet allowed Max Biaggi to challenge for the championship. On top of that, the Italian was eliminated on three occasions because of crashes. More surprising was the fact Biaggi started bad-mouthing his Yamaha team just as the team scored its first victory since the 1998 British GP, thanks to Regis Laconi, who drove a perfect race in Valencia. This was more than the star of stars could take and Biaggi responded almost immediately with a win at Welkom. After that we had a win for a third Yamaha team and a third rider, with Norifume Abe winning in Rio.

The European poles

Two podiums and a pole position for the Tetsuya Harada Aprilia V2 was proof that the Italian 500 enjoyed a strong period in the middle of the season, although it tailed off badly towards the end. Some people,

most notably Valentino Rossi started to voice doubts about the gamble of running a V2 against the V4s at a time when the Noale company was thinking about its racing future.

Adding to the European tally, the MuZ-Weber with the Swissauto engine took two pole positions in the hands of Dutchman, Jurgen Van Den Goorbergh. However, the team now run by former world side-car champion Rolf Biland still suffered a drought in terms of race results. Nevertheless, the European challenge to Japanese technological supremacy did score a respectable number of points. There is more to come and the Modenas KR4, powered by the same Swissauto power unit was the centre of attention in the paddock, when it was unveiled at Brno.

Three wins for Yamaha, three victories for Suzuki, some sparks from Aprilia and MuZ-Weber, but Honda still dominated its rivals with nine wins. However, customers of the biggest name in bikes in the world did not fair so well and the Sito Pons team with Barros and Borja and the legendary Erv Kanemoto's machine ridden by Kocinski never really shone. There was just one podium apiece for Barros and Kocinski.

Modenas, without a top class rider after Bayle rapidly disappeared from the scene, lived through a difficult year, while the newest team, BSL, was never even capable of getting past the hurdle of qualifying.

Max Biaggi

Kiwi Innovations

The 500 key facts

Outgoing champion:
Michael Doohan (AUS, Honda V4.) The Australian, with five titles in his pocket, continued his career within the same set-up, even if he started the season with some heavy criticism of Honda's strategy. "They are concentrating on the superbike and 250 classes and seem to have completely forgotten about the 500s," he said. As it turned out, Doohan was the only rider to try out a new frame during winter testing, which made its first public appearance in practice for the Japanese GP.

The major players
Honda: The official Repsol team turned out with the same structure as the previous year, with NSRV4 for Michael Doohan, Alex Criville and Tadayuki Okada, as well as an official V2 for Manuel "Sete" Gibernau. The Spaniard would later inherit Doohan's V4 after the Australian's accident. In the MoviStar-Pons outfit, we found Brazilian Alexandre Barros and the Spaniard Juan Batista Borja, while John Kocinski kicked off the year with an Erv Kanemoto prepared 1998 NSR, without any external budget.
Yamaha: The men from Iwata had already announced their ambitions the previous year. Wayne Rainey's last job had been to build up a dream team. The Marlboro Yamaha Team certainly seemed to fit the bill with Massimiliano Biaggi and Carlos Checa. Works YZRs were also available to the Red Bull WCM team with France's Regis Laconi and New Zealand's Simon Crafar both in the saddle, although the Kiwi would soon be replaced by Garry McCoy. The big novelty for this time was its switch from Dunlop to Michelin tyres. A third team entered an official Yamaha, albeit a 1998 model. Run by Luis D'Antin, it was ridden by Japan's Norifume Abe.
Suzuki: In the corridors of power at Hammamatsu, they decided to revive the good old glory days and as far back as the Autumn of '98, they announced a tantalising double signing; Kenny Roberts Junior and race engineer Warren Willing, who had been one of the key figures of the Kenny Roberts Senior organisation, over the past ten years. Alongside Kenny Roberts, Nobuatsu Aoki was also given a ride, while Yukio Kagayama took part in two events thanks to a wild-car ride at the start of the season, before replacing Aoki at the French GP.
Aprilia: 1999 marked the major comeback of the Italian firm. Aprilia had continued development of the V2 500 and returned to the top category after a sabbatical year. Tetsuya Harada was the rider entrusted with the beast

and this move to the blue riband category also allowed the men from Noale to sort out the internal problems encountered in the 250 class in 1998.
Modenas: Officially, Kenny Roberts handed over the reins of his organisation to Chuck Aksland, but the "king" was still around. The KR3 was ridden by Jean-Michel Bayle and the American Mike Hayle, who carried out some of the winter testing, but never made much of an impression. Brett Macleod, the South African who was tragically killed in a supersport race at Kyalami had tried the Modenas in IRTA testing at Jerez. Bayle had to give up due to injury with Jamie Whitham and David De Gea following one another in the saddle of the second Modenas.
MuZ-Weber: the European challenge to the Japanese giants also underwent a serious change. Exit the structure established by France's Serge Rosset, the ROC frame builder. It was the former Swiss rider, Eskil Suter who designed the new bike, with a frame built by Fabrication Techniques in England. This company also produced the Modenas and the 125 Derbi. While the German MuZ marque still had its name on the project, the team was now based in Switzerland, at Burgdorf near Berne. Former side-car king Rolf Biland, winner of 7 world championships and 81 GPs now ran the team. Just before the first round, the bike was officially renamed MuZ-Weber, taking its title from a German company which specialises in engines for the auto industry. After last year's experience with just one rider, MuZ came back in force with two riders; Luca Cadalora, who would quickly head home after the Malaysian GP, giving up on the Japanese race, but returning for Jerez and the Dutchman, Jurgen Van Den Goorbergh, who was the best privateer in 1998. After the divorce from Cadalora, Anthony Gobert was given a shot at it for the last four races.
TSR-Honda: Technical Sports Racing, the business created in England in 1998 by the Japanese Technical Sports firm, expanded its activities. Having notched up some brilliant performance the previous year in the 250 class, it now produced the AC50M

frame to take a Honda V2 engine. The riders were the former 125 double world champion, Haruchika Aoki and Spain's Jose Luis Cardoso.

The winners:
Alex Criville (E, Honda V4, 6,) Kenny Roberts (USA, Suzuki, 3,) Tadayuki Okada (J, Honda V4, 3,) Regis Laconi (F, Yamaha, 1,) Massimiliano Biaggi (I, Yamaha,1) and Norifume Abe (J, Yamaha, 1.)

Pole positions
Kenny Roberts (USA, Suzuki, 4,) Tadayuki Okada (J, Honda V4, 3,) Alex Criville (E, Honda V4, 2,) Jurgen Van Den Goorberg (NL, Muz-Weber, 2,) Massimiliano Biaggi (I, Yamaha, 1,) Tetsuya Harada (J, Aprilia, 1,) John Kocinski (USA, Honda V4, 1) and Regis Laconi (F, Yamaha, 1.)

Fastest race laps
Kenny Roberts (USA, Suzuki, 4,) Michael Doohan (AUS, Honda V4, 2,) Alex Criville (E, Honda V4, 2,) Manuel Gibernau (E, Honda V4, 2,) Tadayuki Okada (J, Honda V4, 2,) Alexandre Barros (BR, Honda V4, 2) and Massimiliano Biaggi (I, Yamaha, 1.)

The final podium

1. Alex Criville	E	Honda V4	267 points
2. Kenny Roberts	USA	Suzuki	220
3. Tadayuki Okada	J	Honda V4	211

The constructors' classification

1. Honda	338 points
2. Yamaha	280
3. Suzuki	231
4. Aprilia	104
5. MuZ-Weber	64
6. TSR-Honda	56
7. Modenas	17

Rookie of the year
Tetsuya Harada (J, Aprilia), 10th in the world championship.

Best privateer of the year
Haruchika Aoki (J, TSR-Honda), 15th in the world championship.

△
The BSL 3 cylinders

Ducati's total domination

The category was superb for other reasons too. From a technical point of view, there were two new bikes: the Yamaha R7 and the Aprilia RSV 1000. Then there was the political rivalry between the four stroke World Championship and Grand Prix racing, as the on track action became more and more exciting, and finally there was the sporting side.

Two cylinders to the fore

Technically speaking, the domination of Ducati typified the current advantages of the two cylinder configuration in superbikes. Following the example of the Bologna manufacturer was its Venetian neighbour, Aprilia, who embarked on the same route. The Japanese took note, and Honda would be launching their own VTR the following year.

But while Ducati dominated, Suzuki made good progress with three wins during the year, two thanks to Pierfrancesco Chili and one with Akira Ryo at Sugo. Kawasaki appeared to stagnate, while Yamaha had a trying year as they race developed a new model.

Politics: spectators vote with their feet

On the political front, the rivalry between the two main motorcycle racing championships continued. The lobbying of the governing body by the boss of SBK International, Maurizio Flammini, considerably delayed the future introduction of four stroke prototypes in the GP1 category. However, the popularity of the class with the spectators increased significantly. There were more spectators at Brands Hatch than there had been for the last Formula One Grand Prix at the circuit. There was a huge crowd at Donington, almost double the number there had been for the Grand Prix at the same circuit.

Monza was a great success with again more spectators than there had been for the Italian Grand Prix, not to mention Imola. Allied to a round in the United States, it was clear that the so-called 'second' championship was actually threatening to become the number one series, certainly in terms of direct earnings from spectators.

Carl Fogarty dominates on track

Ducati's domination on the track went very much hand-in-hand with that of Carl Fogarty. These days, 'Foggy' is perhaps one of Britain's most successful motor sporting heros, perhaps more so than Formula One driver David Coulthard. However, there's only one problem with this; the Superbike championship remains a series promoted by manufacturers for manufacturers. In Britain, the Fogarty phenomenon meant that the category received major publicity, but elsewhere, it was consigned to specialist magazines, and most of the media coverage in daily, even sporting papers went to Grand Prix racing.

△
Ducati's domination

Ducati's record in superbikes was remarkable: 16 wins out of 26 races in the World Championship, including 13 one-twos; national titles in Italy and Great Britain, thanks to Paolo Casoli and Troy Bayliss from Australia. And two riders who battled into the final phase of the American championship, Ben Bostrom and Anthony Gobert. In 1999, the Ducati 996 remained the bike to beat.

▷
The new Yamaha R7

The superbike story

Outgoing champion:

Carl Fogarty from Great Britain on a Ducati. 'Foggy' this time won the title with the Ducati Performance team run by Davide Tardozzi. Virginio Ferrari's ADVF team had been disbanded after the new American owners of the Italian marque showed the fomer World Champion the door

The major players

Ducati 996: why change a winning machine? Even so, Ducati worked hard. They had just one team, that of Ducati Performance run by Davide Tarozzi, and there were a number of technical developments, including new fuel system with twin injectors, new air box, bigger exhaust valves and new Oehlins forks. There were two strong riders too with no doubts that they would keep their rivalry in check: England's Carl Fogarty and Australia's Troy Corser. Two customer teams ran the previous version of the Italian twin, notably for Austria's Andrea Meklau, Italy's Lucio Pedercini and principally Doriano Romboni. The latter was making his debut on a four stroke after almost a year of enforced rest, after fracturing his right wrist for the umpteenth time during practice for the Malaysian Grand Prix in 1998 on a MuZ-Swissauto.

Honda RVF750(RC45): HRC invested heavily in the development of the two cylinder VTRSP1, but the two Castrol Honda riders, New Zealand's Aaron Slight and America's Colin Edwards continued to race the 'old' RC45. The older model had been fitted with new forks, developed specially by Showa. At the European finale at Hockenheim, the Neil Tuxworth-run team announced that they would officially be racing the new two cylinder bike in 2000.

Yamaha YZF-R7: At first glance, the size of the R7 was very impressive because it was so small. The chassis is the same as that of the YZR500 while the swing arm was also derived from that of the GP bike. However, there was a much greater diversity in terms of set-up. A rider could opt for better traction or a lighter front end, depending on his riding style. The Yamaha WSBK team ran the Japanese Noriyuki Haga who used Michelins, and the Italian Vittoriano Guareschi who graduated from supersport. Alessandro Gramigni also had an R7 run by Team Valli Moto.

Kawasaki ZX750: Germany's Harald Eckl was still running the 'green team', where the ZX engine doesn't give much away to those of Honda and Ducati. Instead, the main area of concentration was on the frame with new Oehlin forks and a central shock absorbers. On the riding front, Japan's Akira Yanagawa was still in the team, now joined by the relevation from the previous season, Spain's Gregorio Lavilla.

Suzuki GSXR 750: Three years after its return to Superbikes, the Hamamatsu manufacturer totally revised its competition programme handing the running of both superbikes and supersports to the Coronas-Alstare team run by the Belgian Francis Batta. The new GSXR750 was fully injected with two injectors per cylinder. Much development had also taken place on the suspension. Suzuki did the deal of the year by signing Italy's Pierfrancesco Chili who was backed up by Katsuaki Fujiwara of Japan.

Aprilia RSV 1000 SP: This was the great novelty of the season. It evolved from the 'Mille', the road version which is already considered by all the cogniscenti to be the benchmark in the class.The frame is very sleek and particularly well designed. Furthermore, the engineers could vary the weight distribution by moving the engine. Technology learned in Grand Prix racing was transferred to the superbike, so that the Mille could be considered to be the Grand Prix bike of the future, with a four stroke engine. Rider was the Australian Peter Goddard.

The winners:

Carl Fogarty (GB, Ducati, 11), Colin Edwards (USA, Honda, 5), Troy Corser (AUS, Ducati, 3), Pierfrancesco Chili (I, Suzuki, 2), Noriyuki Haga (J, Yamaha, 1), Anthony Gobert (AUS, Ducati, 1), Ben Bostrom (USA, Ducati, 1), Akira Yanagawa (J, Kawasaki, 1) et Akira Ryo (J, Suzuki, 1).

Pole positions

Troy Corser (AUS, Ducati, 4), Pierfrancesco Chili (I, Suzuki, 1), Carl Fogarty (GB, Ducati, 4), Colin Edwards (USA, Honda, 2), Aaron Slight (NZ, Honda, 1).

Fastest race laps

Troy Corser (AUS, Ducati, 3), Carl Fogarty (GB, Ducati, 2), Colin Edwards (USA, Honda, 2), Aaron Slight (NZ, Honda, 3), Anthony Gobert (AUS, Ducati, 1), Pierfrancesco Chili (I, Suzuki, 1).

Fastest race laps

Carl Fogarty (GB, Ducati, 7), Troy Corser (AUS, Ducati, 6), Colin Edwards (USA, Honda, 3), Pierfrancesco Chili (I, Suzuki, 3), Akira Yanagawa (J, Kawasaki, 2), Aaron Slight (NZ, Honda, 2), Akira Ryo (J, Suzuki, 2) et Anthony Gobert (AUS, Ducati, 1).

The final podium

1. Carl Fogarty	GB	Ducati	489 points
2. Colin Edwards	USA	Honda	361
3. Troy Corser	AUS	Ducati	361

The constructors' classification

1. Ducati	569 points
2. Honda	452
3. Kawasaki	345
4. Suzuki	319
5. Yamaha	261
6. Aprilia	84

△
Pierfrancesco Chili: two wins with Suzuki.

◁
The Aprilia RSW Mille

Yamaha, the beaten bogeyman

The first ever supersport world championship in history was taken by Frenchman Stephane Chambon. The 34 year old drove for the Alstare-Suzuki team run by the Belgian Francis Batta. Fabrizio Pirovano's model teammate in 1998, when the Italian won the world cup in this discipline, Chambon made use of all his experience to beat the bogeyman, the new Yamaha R6.

The bogeyman Yamaha R6

▽

"The arrival of the R6, the first bike in its class to have been built with competition in mind, really moved the goalposts this year as most previous points of reference were no longer valid. From this starting point, the others, all the others had to raise their game to have any chance and that might explain why there were so many fallers among the favourites, very often in the first few hundred metres of the races." This pertinent analysis of the situation came from Switzerland's Yves Briguet, the former European supersport champion, who was forced to quit before the end of the season, through injury..

Stéphane Chambon and Suzuki: champions !

▽

The tyre problem

While the bikes evolved, what can one say about the tyres? Pirelli, who set the standard for several years, lost its main customers one by one this season. The Italian company was no match for its rivals, the two giants, Michelin and Dunlop.
A new and higher level of technology and a level of rider skill which increases every year led to some surprising figures.

Circuit	Pole 1998/Pole 1999	Fastest race lape 1998/1999
Kyalami	1'48"049/**1'47"293**	1'48"646/**1'48"343**
Donington	1'38"286/**1'37"348**	1'38"296/**1'37"565**
Monza	**1'53"235**/1'53"302	1'53"508/**1'53"155**
Albacete	**1'34"841**/1'34"910	rain/1'35"518
Nürburgring	1'45"274/**1'43"927**	rain/1'45"591
Misano	1'37"609/**1'37"915**	**1'38"094**/1'38"746
Laguna Seca	1'30"691/**1'30"227**	**1'30"742**/1'30"807
A1-Ring	**1'35"746**/1'35"835	1'45"853/rain
Assen	2'10"706/**2'09"874**	2'12"031/**2'11"031**

(The figures from Brands Hatch cannot be compared as the track was modified)

The evolution is therefore clear, if Misano, whose surface continues to deteriorate is left out of the equation.

A victory for experience

While the Yamaha R6 was dominant with 6 wins from 11 races, it was nevertheless a Yamaha rider, Stephane Chambon, who emerged as world champion. The Frenchman made full use of the benefits of his great experience, while the Yamaha clan split the big points between six different riders - Bontempi, Mergalli, Xaus, Zeelenberg, Teuchert and Kellner- with the British rider Iain MacPherson being the only Kawasaki representative to fight it out at the front.
Another factor to be taken into consideration was that 1999 was a very tough year for Ducati, the marque which had dominated the category for the previous two years. It finished down in fifth place in the constructors' classification. Its only front runner, Paolo Casoli sat out a major part of the season following an injury in private testing.

Drama at Kyalami

The supersport world championship was hit by the death of 22 year old Brett McLeod, the 1998 South African superbike champion, who had been given a trial on the Modenas KR3 during IRTA testing at Jerez de la Frontera. Originally due to ride a Ducati for the NCR team in the world superbike championship, McLeod had finally opted to run in supersports, defending the Suzuki colours this season.
Second fastest in practice in the opening round in Kyalami, McLeod was in the lead group when he raised an arm to indicate to the other riders that he had a mechanical problem. His bike freewheeled for a few seconds, before picking up again and the rider rejoined the pack. Then he slowed suddenly with dramatic consequences: another bike hit the South African's Suzuki and McLeod was thrown off. Sliding down the middle of the track on his back, he was hit on the neck by the bike of Italian rider, Massimo Meregalli. While the chief medical officer at Kyalami officially recorded the time of death as 16h00 on Sunday 28th March, death had been instantaneous.

Supersport key facts

Outgoing champion:
Fabrizio Pirovano (I, Suzuki.) The Italian had remained faithful to Francis Batta, the Suzuki-Alstare team boss for several years and so the Number 1 that goes with the winner of the 1998 world cup remained stuck on the fairing of a yellow and blue Suzuki.

The major players:
Suzuki GSX 600 RW: The Suzuki, developed in 1997 by Suzuki-Italia and dominant last year in the hands of Pirovano and Chambon is the reference point. The Alstare team lined up the same Pirovano/Chambon duo as last year, while a second team, Endoug Metalsistem, used the official GSX RW with Swiss Yves Briguet and Italian Cristiano Migliorati in the saddle. "Piro" and Chambon were on Dunlops and Briguet and Migliorati used Pirell at the start of the season. But, like many others, the Modena team tore up its Pirelli contract after the American race, where Migliorati had already switched to Michelin.

Yamaha YZF-R6: This was one of the two big novelties of the supersport year. Team Yamaha-Belgarda called up Piergiorgio Bontempi to replace Vittoriano Guareschi, "promoted" to superbikes. Another change in the Italian camp was the switch to Pirelli; a short-lived move as Belgarda also tore up his contract after the first leg of a very difficult first leg in the world championship,

finding success with Michelin boots. Injured at Kyalami, Massimo Meregalli would be replaced by Jamie Whitham who won at Donington. Alongside the Italians arrived with a strong looking team run by Udo Mark. The riders are Jorg Teuchert and Christian Kellner. The Wilco Zeelenberg Team Dee Cee Jeans ran the ebullient Spaniard Ruben Xaus. France's Christophe Cogan with BKM and Belgium's Werner Daemen (Yamaha Belgium) completed the R6 delegation.

Honda CBR 600 F: The new CBR bears no resemblance to its predecessor. The official Castrol Honda team took on Spain's Pere Riba Cabana to ride alongside the young Englishman James Toseland. Another team was put together in France by William Costes, back in the category once more with help from Elf. Alongside him was last year's Nurburgring winner, Sebastien Charpentier. Finally in Spain, that great talent spotter, who discovered a certain Alexandre Barros, Arbizu, started the season with a young David De Gea, who had competed in the 125 class a few years back.

Ducati ZDM 748 SPS: There was a major change for Ducati as the Endoug team had switched to Suzuki. This meant there was only one real factory team, run directly by Ducati Performance for the former winner of the World Cup and twice European champion, Paolo Casoli.

Kawasaki ZX 600 G: The marques official team boss in superbikes, Harald Erkl wanted to have an involvement in supersports. To find the means to match his ambitions, he hired the British rider, Iain MacPherson. Team Kawasaki-Italia lined up with Camillo Mariottini and Luca Conforti.

Bimota YB9 SRI: As the sixth marque

entered in this inaugural supersport world championship, Bimota chose two Italian riders, Norino Brignola and Roberto Panichi.

The winners:
Iain MacPherson (GB, Kawasaki 3,) Stephane Chambon F, Suzuki, 2,) Jorg Teuchert (D, Yamaha, 2,) Jamie Whitham (GB, Yamaha, 1,) Wilco Zeelenberg (NL, Yamaha, 1,) Piergiorgio Bontempi (I, Yamaha, 1) and Ruben Xaus (E, Yamaha, 1.)

Pole positions:
Stephane Chambon (F, Suzuki, 3,) Ruben Xaus (E, Yamaha, 2,) Iain MacPherson (GB, Kawasaki, 2,) Paolo Casoli (I, Ducati, 1,) Piergiorgio Bontempi (I, Yamaha, 1,) Jorg Teuchert (D, Yamaha, 1) and Massimo Meregalli (I, Yamaha 1.)

Fastest race laps:
Iain MacPherson (GB, Kawasaki, 3,) Stephane Chambon (F, Suzuki, 2,) Jamie Whitham (GB, Yamaha, 1,) Pere Riba Cabana (E, Honda, 1,) Christian Kellner (D, Yamaha, 1,) Piergiorgio Bontempi (I, Yamaha, 1,) Paolo Casoli (I, Ducati, 1) and Massimo Meregalli (I, Yamaha 1.)

The final podium:

1. Stephane	Chambon	(F, Suzuki,)	153 points
2. Iain	MacPherson	(GB, Kawasaki)	130
3. Piergiorgio	Bontempi	(I, Yamaha,)	116

The constructors classification

1. Yamaha	235 points
2. Suzuki	191
3. Kawasaki	137
4. Honda	112
5. Ducati	60
6. Bimota	15

◁
Brett MacLeod.

Nürburgring:
Yves Briguet (34),
Iain MacPherson (12),
Wilco Zeelenberg (8)
and Fabrizio Pirovano (1).
▽

Suzuki in the end

▷ Start at Bol d'Or.

Suzuki won the World Constructors' title and its riders, Terry Rymer and Jehan D'Orgeix, clinched the Riders' title by dominating the last Bol d'Or to be run at the Circuit Paul Ricard at Le Castellet. It was the end of a very special season, notable for an overall win in the 24 hours of Oschersleben which wasn't rewarded by a single point.

The opening round of the championship at Le Mans saw Kawasaki head and shoulders above the competition. They led from the start, and set an incredible pace which caused a certain number of retirements. For Yamaha, Brian Morrison pitted after only seven minutes with a broken crank. The second R7 OWO2 disappeared at 01.42 in the morning with a seized big end bearing. Honda's William Costes had a fall early in the race, just after having taken the lead. The World Champion fought back to third place before retiring for good with a holed piston. Only Suzuki remained to challenge Kawasaki, but even they had their problems. Jamie Whitham messed up his start and fell five times, losing all hope of a win.

Privateers at Spa

Former World Champion Christian Lavieille was snapped up by Suzuki for the Spa-Francorchamps 24 hours after losing his Honda-France ride. It was a race that was particularly bad for the factory teams. Hislop's Kawasaki was the first to fall by the wayside with ??pignons de distribution??. Bertrand Stey led on a factory Honda RC45 but stopped at the far end of the circuit with a broken chain. In spite of superhuman efforts, he failed to get the wounded beast back to the pits. Dominique Meliand's team repaired the number one Suzuki's gearbox in 70 minutes, including removal of the engine when it stopped in the early hours of the morning. Lavieille/Rymer/D'Orgeix climbed back up to second place, six laps behind the privateers in the Suzuki-Portugal team, Telmo Pereira and Frenchmen Michel Graziano and Bruno Bonhuil.

Suzuki: an eight hour Grand Prix

It's more important for the Japanese factories to win the Suzuki 8 Hours than the World Championship, so each year the classic long distance race becomes an eight hour Grand Prix. Riders come from all categories. This year, a pair of Grand Prix riders, Tadayuki Okada/Alexandre Barros, beat the superbike pairing of Aaron Slight/Colin Edwards, earning Honda a superb one-two. The world's biggest manufacturer also invited Freddie Spencer to team up with John Kocinski, but unfortunately the three times World Champion fell on the Thursday in practice and broke two fingers.

Stocksport at Oschersleben

The Federation obviously didn't think that a production bike could win a race, otherwise they wouldn't have banned them from scoring points. However, the Franco-Swiss Sylvain Waldmeier with teammates Bernard Cuzin and Jerome Couturier scored a great victory with a Yamaha R1 at Oschersleben, a race boycotted by the factory teams. However, some top riders found seats with privateers in the hope of picking up one or two points.

Suzuku's finale in the Bol d'Or

Forty riders were in contention for the title as they aimed for a prestigious, even historic victory in the last Bol d'Or to take place on the Circuit Paul Ricard. The number one endurance event started off at Grand Prix pace and after eight hours, Honda, Suzuki, Kawasaki and Yamaha were all still wheel to wheel. But then came the deciding moment. Italy's Angelo Conti laid down a long oil slick at the double apex righthander, Beausset after his Laverda suffered an engine failure. Within a few minutes, ten riders had fallen, including the works Honda, MacKenzie's Yamaha, Paillot's Suzuki and Scarnato's Kawasaki. They got back to the pits for repairs, but that left just two manufacturers in contention. Would it be Suzuki or Yamaha? It would be Suzuki because with five hours to go, Deletang's R7 suffered worrying overheating. Terry Rymer and Jehan D'Orgeix clinched the World Championship. Lavieille had the honour of crossing the finishing line of this historic Bol.

△
Kawasaki beaten.

cal side. It was obvious, even before the first race that the R7 would be very quick, but there were concerns about the reliability of the new Yamaha.

Suzuki GSX-R: Dominique Meliand's Suzuki Endurance Racing Team opted for reliability, going for traditional carburettors, while the chassis was the 1997 model as the 1998 version caused a few problems last year.

The winners:
Chris Walker/Bertrand Sebileau/Steve Hislop (GB/F/GB, Kawasaki, 1,) Telmo Pereira/Michel Graziano/Bruno Bonhuil (P/|F/F. Suzuki, 1,) Alexandre Barros/ Tadayuki Okada (BR/J, Honda, 1,) Sylvain Waldmeier/Bernard Cuzin/Jerome Couturier (CH/F/F, Yamaha, 1) and Christian Lavieille/terry Rymer/Jehan D'Orgeix (F/GB/F, Suzuki, 1.)

The final podium:
1. Terry Rymer/
   Jehan D'Orgeix GB/F Suzuki 122 points
3. Christian
   Lavieille F Suzuki 90

The constructors classification
1. Suzuki   180 points
2. Kawasaki   166
3. Honda   111
4. Yamaha   95
5. Ducati   54
6. Aprilia   36

Endurance key facts

Outgoing champions:
Christian Lavieille/Doug Polen (F/USA, Honda.) There was no official explanation given, but there were several frivolous and unprintable ones as to why Honda- France and its world champion Christian Lavieille had gone their separate ways. Doug Polen stayed in the States, while Lavieille turned into a journalist at Le Mans, before jumping back onto the saddle of a Suzuki for the Spa 24 Hours.

The major players:
Honda RVF RC45: A hurrican blew through Honda-France over the winter with the eviction of Christian Lavieille. On the technical front, a new bike arrived from Japan a few days before the Le Mans 24 Hours, but there was nothing revolutionary from the world champions.

Kawasaki ZX-7R: Christian Bourgeois' team stuck with the 7R whose specification is well known; a very powerful engine and

a rather rigid frame. During the winter, some work was carried out on the engine - new head and camshafts and new exhausts.

Yamaha R7 OW02: This was the novelty of the year in both endurance and superbike racings. Yamaha Motor France entrusted the running of its team to Christian Sarron, with Martial Garcia in charge of the techni-

▷
Oscherleben.

The war of the clans

▷
Two stroke ((Klaffenböck/Hänni) and four stroke (Webster/James).
△

Exactly twelve months ago, the term "swan song" was being used to describe the side-car category. The races had actually split into two distinct championships, with different sets of rules. This meant that four stroke machines were not allowed on the track for races which took place during the GP meetings! Twelve months later? No more talk of near death, but instead we had an incredible war of the clans.

The whole thing started over the winter with Rolf Steinhausen determined to retake control of the championship, at a time when the Flammini group was prepared to take the side-cars under its umbrella which already covered the superbike and supersport world championships. There was an ambitious calendar with a structure copied from the solo championships, with teams fixed for the season with wild-card rides at different races. On paper, the Steinhausen project looked good.

With the Number 1

Even better, in order to give the project some credibility, the former world champion had enrolled the services of the top man in the category, England's Steve Webster, who nailed his colours to the four stroke mast.
It seemed ideal, especially as Eurosport ensured that side-cars got more television time than they had ever known before. There was just one little fly in the ointment. While the world cup, running opposing two and four stroke technologies went off without any signs of technical promiscuity, the cham-

pionship was soon transformed into a war of the clans, with a clash between the pro-Steinhausen faction, who were often to be found in the tarmaced part of the paddock and the others, whose main spokesman was the Austrian rider Klaus Klaffenbock and his Swiss passenger Adolf Hanni.

A nice story

These two were pretty much on their own, fighting for the survival of the traditional side-car with two stroke in-line engines. The presence of Swissauto with its famous V4 was far less visible than last year, after the retirement of the Gudel brothers, Paul and Charly. To mount this challenge, Hanni bought up all the remaining stock of engines built and developed by Charles Auf der Maur, including all the spare parts. So, this little garage owner was now the man everyone came to all season long. "My fight must not be pointless. Four stroke motors are very expensive, too

expensive for many people. By paying personally to make sure that two stroke spares would be available, I wanted to show the youngsters that we were still thinking of them," explained the man who started the season with his famous moustache, which he would sacrifice after taking his first win in Germany.

Advantage Webster

Two rival clans and two different philosophies. In the end the big prize went to the big favourites; the English pairing of Steve Webster and David James. In fact, Webster was head and shoulders above the rest all season, in terms of speed, even if he had to wait until the last race of the season to be sure of his seventh major title, after retirements at Donington and Brands Hatch.
With Webster dominant, Klaus Klaffenbock was the only one to beat him fair and square, on two occasions, in Germany and at Misano. He narrowly missed out on a win in front of his home crowd at the A1-Ring after a thrilling end to the race.
So there were no major surprises in this ageing pack. Missing at the end were the Swiss team of Markus Schlosser/Daniel Hauser. After a bad accident in Austria, the Swissauto boys were unable to repair the damage for the final two races. So what of the future? In 2000, the two rival technologies will still be opposing one another, even though it seems that the big 1200 cc four strokes will be in the majority.

△
Ireson.

The side-car key facts

Outgoing Champions:
Steve Webster/David James (GB, LCR-Honda R4.) The English duo who won the first two world cups in this discipline were putting their crown in the arena once again. They decided to go the four stroke route in Rolf Steinhausen's team. The team Webster had been with for several past seasons, run by Markus Bosiger had pulled out of the championship as the boss was now competing in European truck races!

The new regulations:
1999 saw a new set of technical regulations, with two different engine types facing up against one another. The maximum cubic capacity for the four strokes was fixed at 1200 cc and 500 cc for the two strokes which can be used until 31st December 2000. The FIM rules stipulate the following minimum weights: 200 kilos for the two strokes and 215 for the four strokes, with a total minimum of men and machine of 375 kilos. Another new rule banned the use of carbon brakes.

The major players:

Four stroke
LCR-Suzuki 1200: Former world champion Rolf Steinhausen was the man behind the revolution which gave rise to the 1999 World Cup. Not only did one of his companies run the category, but he also formed a team for the reigning champions, Steve Webster/David James and for his son Jorg Steinhausen, who was teamed up with Frank Schmidt. Webster's Suzuki evolution engine pumped out over 200 bhp. Eric Bertschi/Ueli Wafler in Switzerland, Roger Lovelock/Chris Hibberd in England as well as the Belgians Patrick Hanquet/Pascal Legreve also used the Suzuki engines in their LCR chassis.

Two stroke
LCR-HRM-Honda and LCR-ADM-Honda: Swiss garage owner Adolf Hanni, passenger to Austria's Klaus Klafffenbock broke his money box over the winter to buy off Charles Auf der Maur (ADM) the rights to the four cylinder in line engines as well as a huge stock of engine blocks and other spare parts. This was done so that riders who have stayed faithful to this formula can have easy access to spares.

LCR-BRM-Swissauto: the Swiss brothers, Paul and Charly Gudel, who were the Swissauto number one team, at least on paper, last year, had decided to take a year off to be able to take a long cold look at the development of the series. The V4 technology was still very much in evidence with Markus Schlosser/Daniel Hauser (Switzerland,) Benny Jannsen/Frank Geurts van Kessel (Netherlands,) Kurt Liechti/Daniel Locher (Switzerland) and Ian Guy/Andy Peach (Great Britain.)

Windle-Honda: Louis Christen's LCR chassis were definitely in the majority this year even if the British Windle had a weight advantage with Steve Abbot/Jamie Biggs and an ADM in line four cylinder engine. Another English team, Clive Stirrat/Steven English used the same equipment.

Ireson-Suzuki: Trevor Ireson, the former sidecar racer based in the Isle of Man had already built his own chassis for quite a while. Most of his small production of around ten units is sold in the UK and it was the English teams of Stuart Hall/Nick Wood, Tim Rope/Rich Lawrence and Andy Percy/Eddie Kiff who represented the constructor in this season's world cup.

The winners:
Steve Webster/David James (GB, LCR-Suzuki 1200, 6,) Steve Abbott/Jamie Biggs (GB, Windle-Honda, 2,) Klaus Klaffenbock/Adolf Hanni (A/CH, LCR-HRM- Honda, 2.)

Pole positions (superpole)
Steve Webster/David James (GB, LCR-Suzuki 1200, 9,) Klaus Klaffenbock/Adolf Hanni (A/CH, LCR-HRM-Honda, 1.)

Best qualifying times
Steve Abbott/Jamie Biggs (GB, Windle-Honda, 6,) Steve Webster/David James (GB, LCR-Suzuki 1200, 3,) Klaus Klaffenbock/Adolf Hanni (A/CH, LCR-HRM- Honda, 1.)

Fastest race laps
Steve Abbott/Jamie Biggs (GB, Windle-Honda, 4,) Steve Webster/David James (GB, LCR-Suzuki 1200, 3,) Klaus Klaffenbock/Adolf Hanni)A/CH, LCR-HRM- Honda, 3.)

The final podium
1. Steve Webster/ David James   GB   LCR-Suzuki 1200   190 points
2. Klaus Klaffenbock/ Adolf Hanni   A/CH   LCR-HRM Honda   179
3. Steve Abbot/ Jamie Biggs   GB   Windle Honda   139

Constructors classification
1. LCR-Suzuki 1200	212 points
2. LCR-HRM-Honda	179
3. Windle-Honda	142
4. LCR-ADM	117
5. LCR-Swissauto	103
6. LCR-TFR	39
7. Ireson-Suzuki	35
8. LCR-NGK	16
9. Baker-Suzuki	11
10. LCR-Kawasaki	9
11. Windle-Yamaha	7

Steve Abbott (Windle-Honda).
▽

Régis Laconi : as far as it goes (Catalunya)

Aprilia :
two exhausts for one 500
(Paul Ricard)

Alzamora: a winning comeback

▷ *Emilio Alzamora.*

In 1995 and 1996, Spain's Emilio Alzamora was one of the main players in the 125 cc championship, just two years after making his debut in Paolo Pileri's team. Without having won the title in the smallest category, Alzamora decided to try his luck in the 250 class. It was a short-lived affair as he was seriously injured in the Japanese GP. Back in 125, Emilio took two years to make it a winning comeback.

He became one of the rare world champions in the history of the sport to take the title in a year when he won no races, but that didn't bother him too much. Alzamora knows that it's only the top line of a driver's record that counts and that the laws that allow consistency to beat flair are the same for everyone. He knows therefore that his title was not stolen, especially given the circumstances of the final round in Buenos Aires.

"It was a very difficult race," said the world champion. "I knew I had to finish ahead of Melandri or just behind him and that the most important thing was not to make the slightest mistake, because it would cost me dear. Personally, I reckon my opponent's behaviour in the final lap was not professional. But there we have it. I don't want to spoil the pleasure of the moment with politics. I am world champion. I am taking a second 1999 title back home to Spain and it is the greatest day of my life."

IDENTITY CARD

Surname: Alzamora
Name: Emilio
Born: 22nd May 1973
At: Lerida, Spain
First race: 1989
First GP: Malaysia 1994 (125)
Number of GP wins: 2
First GP win: Argentina 1995 (125.)

RACE HISTORY

1989: Catalunya Champion 75 (Honda)
1990: Spanish 75 "Criterium" champion and Catalunya 75 champion (Honda.)
1991: 19th in European 125 championship, 3rd Spanish 125 championship (Honda.)
1992: 7th European 125 championship, 3rd Spanish 125 championship (Honda.)
1993: 21st Spanish 125 open championship, winner of the Spanish Federation 125 Trophy, Spanish supermotard 125 champion (Honda.)
1994: 22nd 125 world championship, Spanish open 125 champion (Honda.)
1995: 3rd 125 world championship, Spanish open 125 champion (Honda.)
1996: 4th 125 world championship (Honda.)
1997: 17th 250 world championship (Honda.)
1998: 21st 125 world championship (Aprilia.)
1999: 125 world champion (Honda.)

A team win

Who do you dedicate this title to?
"To a lot of people, starting with my parents, especially my father who motivated me to take up this career. But also to my team, to my boss Angel Nieto. Also to my manager Dani Amatriain and Massimo Matteoni who built the bike. But I would also like to share this title with Angel Nieto Junior, my team-mate. Because the point he handed me in Australia by stopping on the last lap was worth its weight in gold!"
Tell us about the last race.
"The hardest part was in the opening laps. Melandri was in front and I was stuck behind riders who were hard to pass. Then the Italian group got smaller and Locatelli could not keep up. That was the turning point in the race."
Then there was the final lap and what Melandri did.
"It was slightly absurd behaviour. Today, everyone had a different agenda and Marco worked on his. I have known difficult situations in my career, but this one was particularly complicated as no way could I risk a fall."

When you mention difficult situations are you talking about your unhappy time in 250s?
"Of course, after that and my difficult return to 125 with Aprilia, I was in a strange situation. Angel Nieto had faith in me and I think he was right when he said before this final round that you cannot win a world championship with Number 13 on the fairing."
What about the future?
"I'll start by having a big party, then we can think about next year. The 125s are a great class, always very close. I love it and it seems to suit me. But before taking a definite decision we have to sort out what bike I will ride."

Alzamora at Imola.
▽

The 250 champion

Rossi: the story of a prodigy

▷
Valentino Rossi: a prodigy.

Twenty years old and already a millionaire, twice world champion, on a 125 two years ago and on a 250 this year, Valentino Rossi is "the" star of motorcycle sport as the century comes to an end. He is the darling of the crowds, being more natural than his fellow countryman Massimiliano Biaggi and he has more going for him than his rivals on the tracks of the world. His story is one of a child prodigy.

"Rossimania".
▽

February 1979. Graziano Rossi is at the top of his game and he becomes the father of a little boy called Valentino. Very quickly, the baby gets a taste for the special world of racing, a world that mixes glory and pain, death and victory. He was only three years old when his father had a serious accident at Imola and, having stopped breathing, was saved by Doctor Claudio Costa. Valentino didn't understand. But the years passed and he developed an interest in anything with an engine. A major talent was born; a talent which would not escape the attention of Carlo Pernat, who was then the sporting director at

Aprilia. "You wait and see. The racing world will soon discover a kid who is still an adolescent, whose father was a good GP rider and who will become a phenomenon over the next few years. Soon, he will be more talked about than Massimiliano Biaggi."

First encounter

In 1995, at the age of 16, Valentino Rossi entered the European 125 cc championship. The races were held at the same meetings as the European grands prix and his cheery face soon became familiar in the paddocks, as he trailed around

IDENTITY CARD

Surname: Rossi
Name: Valentino
Date of birth: 16th February 1979 at Urbino/Italy
First race: 1992
First GP: Malaysia 1996 (125)
Number of GP wins: 26 (12/125; 14/250.)
First GP win: Czech Republic, 1996 (125)
World titles: 2 (125/1997; 250/1999.)

RACE HISTORY

1992: Italian minibike endurance champion
1993: 10th in Italian 125 Sport-Production championship (Cagiva)
1994: Italian 125 Sport-Production champion (Cagiva)
1995: 3rd in European 125 championship, 11th in 125 Spanish "open", Italian 125 champion (Aprilia)
1996: 9th in 125 world championship, 10th in European 125 championship (Aprilia)
1997: 125 world champion (Aprilia)
1998: runner-up in 250 world championship (Aprilia)
1999: 250 world champion (Aprilia)

under the affectionate eye of his father Graziano, who was his adviser and is now his manager. In 1996, the young lad tackled his first grands prix, seemingly without a care in the world. He had no problems taking on the opposition, although he made quite a few mistakes. The talent was there, raw and uncut like a diamond and the road he was on suited him just fine. 1996 was a learning year which yielded one win and one year later he won the championship in dominant style, in a way that few had ever done before him. Last year, he moved up a class and right from the first race, at the Johor Bahru circuit in Malaysia, he was good enough to be in front until the final corner, when he made a mistake which allowed Tetsuya Harada to sneak through. It was only a matter of time. Rossimania swept Italy and Valentino's little party pieces after winning were looked forward to with excitement: an inflatable Claudia Schiffer doll at Mugello, a Gaul's helmet in France, the hair dyed in the colours of various nations, his jokes and his verbal attacks, particularly those aimed at Max Biaggi. Nothing could stop him, not even the complaints from the authorities, who felt he went too far at times, notably early in the season, when he stopped to go to a track-side toilet during his lap of honour at Jerez de la Frontera!

A key role

That is what Valentino Rossi is like; a showman at heart, capable of the occasional act of crass stupidity, but also ever more mature. He enjoyed the second half of the season, as much on the track as in his role as the key player in the transfer market. The 250 world champion certainly knew how to manipulate the millions. Aprilia wanted to extend his contract by three years, but he would not look further than the next twelve months. Another offer hit his management's desk, but again Valentino was unhappy, this time because it demanded 45 days of promotional appearances. "Think about it, the races, the testing and 45 days for promotions! Racing would no longer be enjoyable for me. It would become a pain, just like any other job!"

At Aprilia, the suits went back to work, juggling with the millions, while Valentino waited. "First I want to know if I will be world champion, before signing anything for 2000," he said before the end of season trek to faraway shores. Because, waiting in the wings was Michael Doohan and his wish to turn Rossi into his successor as the new Honda star in the 500 category. "Valentino has the potential to be a great champion. His full capacity has not yet been exploited and he will soon be stronger than Max Biaggi," reckoned the five times world champion. Rossi was happy to wait, while enjoying himself in Phillip Island and Welkom, where he handed Aprilia its one hundredth grand prix win. "I cannot follow that," he declared modestly after premiering a great new trick on his lap of honour, when he performed a burn-out standing alongside his bike! It was totally Rossi, totally Valentino. Two weeks later in Rio de Janeiro he was crowned 250 cc world champion after yet another win.

◁
Winner!

Criville's dream come true

At the age of 29, Alex Criville gave Spain its first ever 500 cc world championship title. The consecration of the man from Catalunya was the result of self sacrifice and courage. It also furnished proof that to overcome the perils and pitfalls of a 500 cc machine over the length of a championship, experience is a rider's most valuable ally. In Rio de Janeiro, in between the television interviews and a telephone call with His Majesty, King Juan Carlos, Alex Criville finally poured his heart out.

Alex Crivillé:
dream come true.
▽

What was your initial reaction?
"I have finally achieved my childhood dream. I have wanted this Number 1 for many years, but Michael Doohan was always there. This title is the reward for many years of sacrifice."

Who did you think of as you crossed the line at the end of this decisive Rio GP?
"Of my father, Jose. He was there when I won my first 125 world title, but now he is no longer with us. I would also like to thank all my family and friends and all those who had confidence in me."

At what point did you realise you were world champion? Was it when Tadayuki Okada went out?
"Yes, I knew that in order to give me a hard time for the championship, Tady had to finish in the top two here. So I understood that something had happened, but I was concentrating too much to realise the significance of the moment. I was in the race, up against hard guys like Garry McCoy and

Anthony Gobert. It was a lot of mental pressure, because I knew I could not afford a fall."

The tears of Josep

After that, came the lap of honour and the reunion with your brother, Josep?
"I saw him at the side of the track and he was even happier than me. He was crying and I was crying. Now I am enjoying it. I know this is a special moment and that I have done the most a rider can do. What more can I say?"
Well, what do you have to say to those who reckoned you were mad to move to the 500s after two average seasons on 250s?
"I only have one thing to say to them. I am the 500 world champion."

IDENTITY CARD

Surname: Crivillé
Name: Alex
Date of birth: 4th March 1970, at Seva/Espagne.
First race: 1985.
First GP: Espagne, 1987 (80).
Number of GP wins: 19 (125/5; 500/14).
First GP win: Australie, 1989 (125).
World titles: 2 (125/1989; 500/1999).

RACE HISTORY

1986: winner Critérium Solo Moto in Spain (Honda 80)
1987: 11th 80 World Championship, 3rd 80 European Championship (Derbi)
1988: 2nd 80 World Championship, 32nd 125 World Championship (Derbi)
1989: 125 World Champion (JJ-Cobas)
1990: 11th 250 World Championship (Yamaha)
1991: 13th 250 World Championship (JJ-Cobas)
1992: 8th 500 World Championship (Honda)
1993: 8th 500 World Championship (Honda)
1994: 6th 500 World Championship (Honda)
1995: 4th 500 World Championship (Honda)
1996: 2nd 500 World Championship (Honda)
1997: 4th 500 World Championship (Honda)
1998: 3rd 500 World Championship (Honda)
1999: 500 World Champion (Honda)

If you could wave a magic wand and be somewhere else right now, where would you be?
"In my house in Seva. In my living room, I would lie on the settee and look at the film of this race at Rio to try and realise what I am going through right now."
Whose example have you tried to follow? Who were your heros?
"At first it was Angel Nieto and Giacomo Agostini. Then, as I worked with him, Michael Doohan. By watching him, by trying to keep up with him, I learned a lot from him."
What does this Rio GP mean to Alex Criville?
"I know it will mark my life. It's strange, but I slept well last night. As I have said, the race was harder, because I am an ambitious rider and I do not like finding myself in the middle of the pack. But everyone knew what the problems were and there was no other solution."

The superbike champion

Fogarty, still the King

△
Carl Fogarty:
at Hockenheim.

▷
"Foggymania".

He won 11 of the 26 races, set a new personal record of 489 championship points, and was champion again; England's Carl Fogarty was once again the dominant rider in the World Superbike Championship in 1999. He led the series from the first race at Kyalami, and clinched the title in the final European round at Hockenheim. He left Colin Edwards and his own teammate Troy Corser in the runner-up positions.

Carl Fogarty, you've won everything. Today you're one of the great sporting stars in Britain. Where do you find your motivation?
- Only one thing counts as far as I'm concerned, and that's winning. After 16 years of racing, only the taste of victory motivates me. I don't race for money, nor because I have a contract with a team or with sponsors. No, it's because I love to win and I want to continue racing for a long time so that I can continue to win.

"The Championship continues to improve"

What do think of the development of the superbike series?
- It's a championship that is getting bigger all the time. Each year it's a little better. As long as it caters for well-developed production bikes there won't be a problem. Everyone - particularly race spectators - loves to watch a bike racing that they can use on the road. They like to see what a top rider can do with a machine that is just like theirs. That's the great strength of the championship. You're a great star in Britain, how do you cope with that?
- It's becoming more and more difficult. My life has changed because of my

IDENTITY CARD

Surname: Fogarty
Forename: Carl
Date of birth: 1st July 1966
At: Blackburn, Great Britain
First race: 1983
First GP: Great Britain, 1986 (250)
Number of world superbike championship wins: 59
First world superbike championship win: Donnington Park, 1992
World titles: 7 (*) (TT Formula One, 1988; TT Formula One, 1989; endurance, 1992; superbike 1994, 1995, 1998 and 1999.)
(*): in 1990 the TT Formula One category had lost world championship status, Carl Fogarty won the FIM TT Formula One cup.

RACE HISTORY

1985: winner of the Manx 250 GP, three wins in the English 250 championship (Yamaha)
1986: runner-up in the British TT Formula Two championship, 12 wins (Yamaha)
1987: runner-up in the British Super Two championship, 16 wins (Yamaha)
1988: world TT Formula One champion (Honda)
1989: 45th in world superbike championship, world TT Formula One champion, British superbike champion (Honda)
1990: 18th in 500 world championship, 19th in world superbike championship, winner of FIM TT Formula One cup, winner of the TT Formula One and Senior races at Isle of Man (Honda)
1991: 7th in world superbike championship, 61st in world endurance championship, 3rd in 8 hours at Suzuka, 4th in Transatlantic match (Honda)
1992: 9th in world superbike championship (Ducati) ,world endurance champion (Kawasaki)
1993: 23rd in 500 world championship (Cagiva), runner-up in world superbike championship (Ducati)
1994: world superbike champion (Ducati)
1995: world superbike champion (Ducati)
1996: 4th in world superbike championship, 60th in world endurance championship, 3rd in 8 hours at Suzuka (Honda)
1997: runner-up in world superbike championship (Ducati)
1998: world superbike champion (Ducati)
1999: world superbike champion (Ducati)

popularity. People recognise me, they want to talk to me, they ask me for photographs and autographs It's part of the job and I know that I can't ignore my fans. For these reasons, I don't go out much. When I leave home, it's to go and find somewhere quiet where I can be alone with my family.

What's the best and which is the worst moment of your career?
- The worst time was early in my career when I suffered serious leg injuries in two accidents. The best memory? Surely my wins with Ducati.

Any regrets?
- Yes, when I left Ducati at the end of 1995, and then realising the disappointment that I caused with this decision, to the extent that I would not be entitled to the World Championship in 1997.

What do you think of on the grid?
- I don't know. Or rather yes, I do: I think of nothing! I have only one aim, and that is to make a good start and win the race. Nothing else is important.

Fogarty in 1999.
▽

The supersport champion

Chambon, the jack of all trades

Number 1: △
Stéphane Chambon and Fabrizio Pirovano.

From motocross to superbike via super-motard, France's Stephane Chambon has built himself a career as a motorcycling jack of all trades. World champion in a solo category fifteen years after Christian Sarron (250 cc) and nine years after Raymond Roche (superbike,) this natural talent gave France the first of three titles in 1999, the others being Jehan D'Orgeix in endurance and Fred Bolley in 250 motocross. Here is a thumbnail sketch of the man with the sing-song southern accent and a burning passion.

When he got to the paddock in Hockenheim on the allegedly historic date of the 9th of the 9th 1999, Stephane Chambon learned he was supersport world champion. This was because his only rival, Italy's Piergiorgio Bontempi had to scratch from the event as a result of his first lap crash in the race at Assen.

Thanks to his 21 point lead, Chambon would not need to worry in the final race. "Now I can give my all on Sunday. I want to prove I am not a champion by default." So how did Chambon spend those few strange days which transformed him into the Number One rider in the category? "After Assen, I did all I could to maintain my concentration. It was out of the question to celebrate the championship in advance, because I know that anything can happen in racing."

For example? "After the Dutch race we learned that Bontempi had a broken wrist and shoulder blade. But the miracles of modern science are well known. Deep down, I reckoned he would try and race at Hockenheim with adequate protection. I was still not world champion."

The future? The Number One!

On the eve of the final, Stephane Chambon watched the superbike qualifying with interest. His eyes sparkled with envy. Maybe it would be his future?

"Of course I would love to try superbikes, but the Suzuki bosses have made it clear they would very much like to see me keep the Number One in supersports next season. But who knows? Maybe in 2001."

Then, Chambon was silent, concentrating again on preparing his final assault.

"I would like to end the season on the podium. As for a win, we will have to see, because Ruben Xaus is obviously going well here."

That was Saturday, the day before the race. On Sunday, the champion was in the leading group right from the start, before being caught out at the final braking area at the famous Hockenheim stadium section, by MacPherson and Xaus. "Leading out of the last chicane, I knew I had just lost the race, but I did not have the heart or the courage to ease off the throttle to let the other two past."

▷

No comment...

◁
Stephane Chambon,
the showman.

This time, Stephane Chambon is world champion. On the podium his eyes were lost in the blue skies of Baden-Wurttemburg. "I thought of how far I had come, of the gamble I had taken coming from loose surface to tarmac, to give up my career in supermotard to try the high speed discipline. I thought of everyone who said I was mad, but also of those who helped me reach this point." A tear ran down his face as the lad from Carpentras realised he was on top of the world.

Little man, big talent.
▽

IDENTITY CARD

Surname: Chambon
Forename: Stephane
Date of birth: 10th August 1965
At: Carpentras, France
First race: 1979

Race History

1983: regional motocross champion
1988: French 250 motocross champion
1989: French supermotard champion
1990: French supermotard champion, winner of the Guidon d'Or
1992: French supermotard champion, winner of the Guidon d'Or
1993: French supermotard champion, French 125 promosport champion, French Sound of Single champion
1994: 22nd in the world endurance championship, French supermotard champion, 7th in French superbike championship (Ducati)
1995: 72nd in world endurance championship, 3rd in French superbike championship, 3rd in French superbike championship (Ducati)
1996: 43rd in world superbike championship, French superbike champion, French supersport champion (Ducati)
1997: 4th in world championship cup, 4th in French supersport championship, runner-up in French superbike championship (Ducati)
1998: 3rd in world supersport cup (Suzuki)
1999: world supersport champion (Suzuki)

Rymer-D'Orgeix: the dynamic duo

Endurance champions

△
*Terry Rymer,
Christian Lavieille and
Jéhan D'Orgeix.*

By leaving Kawasaki at the end of the previous year, France's Jehan D'Orgeix was facing a new challenge. Alongside Englishman Terry Rymer, he won his first world title, a crown which he doubled up on this year as he also took top honours in the French superbike series.

Jehan D'Orgeix, how would you rate your team-mate Terry Rymer?

"Terry is a bit quicker than Brian Morrisson, who I rode with in the past, even if Brian was very cunning, no doubt because of his Scottish background. For me, Rymer's presence in the S.E.R.T. (Suzuki Endurance Racing Team) was an important asset when it came to discussions with Dominique Meliand."

How do you prepare for a 24 hour race like the Bol d'Or?

"The bulk of your physical training is done before the start of the season, especially in the area of your arms, which really have to work hard. Psychologically, it is important to spend some time relaxing before every big event."

How can so many different riders work together, especially when it comes to the bike's set-up?

"It's true that you have to find a middle way and everyone has to make some concessions. You have to accept that the bike isn't perfectly set up for your own needs so that it also suits your partners who might be interested in some other aspect of the bike's character."

IDENTITY CARD

Surname: Rymer
Name: Terry
Born: 28th February 1967
At: London/GB
First race: 1984
First GP: Great Britain, 1992, 500 cc

Race History

1988: 10th in world superbike championship, 81st in the world endurance championship (Honda.)

1989: 7th in world superbike championship, runner up in British superbike (Yamaha.)

1990: 7th in world superbike championship, British superbike champion (Yamaha.)

1991: 6th in world superbike championship (Yamaha.)

1992: 17th in 500 cc world championship (Harris-Yamaha,) 32nd in world superbike championship, endurance world champion (Kawasaki.)

1993: 8th in world superbike championship, European superbike champion (Yamaha.)

1994: 10th in world superbike championship, European superbike champion, endurance world champion (Kawasaki.)

1995: runner-up world endurance championship (Kawasaki,) 18th in European superbike championship (Honda.)

1996: 20th in 500 cc world championship, 16th in the world endurance championship (Suzuki.)

1997: 8th in world endurance championship (Kawasaki.)

1998: 53rd in world superbike championship, 6th in world endurance championship, 5th in British superbike championship (Suzuki.)

1999: world endurance champion (Suzuki.)

IDENTITY CARD

Surname: d'Orgeix
Name: Jehan
Born: 30th April 1963
First GP: Spain, 1993, 500 class

Race History

1990: 2nd in Kawasaki Cup.

1991: 15th in world endurance championship, 2nd in French superbike championship (Kawasaki.)

1992: 21st in world superbike championship, 4th in French superbike championship (Kawasaki.)

1993: 16th in the IRTA ranking, 500 (Yamaha.)

1994: 26th in world endurance championship (Kawasaki.)

1995: 5th in world endurance championship, 6th in European supersports, French supersport champion (Kawasaki.)

1996: 19th in world endurance championship, 4th in French supersport championship (Kawasaki.)

1997: 8th in world endurance championship, French supersport champion, 19th in French superbike championship (Kawasaki.)

1998: 5th in world endurance championship, French supersport champion (Kawasaki.)

1999: world endurance champion, French superbike champion (Suzuki.)

◁ Terry Rymer:
world champion!

The *16* Grands

MALAYSIA

JAPAN

SPAIN

FRANCE

ITALY

CATALUNYA

DUTCH

GREAT BRITAIN

GERMANY

CZECH REPUBLIC

IMOLA

VALENCIA

AUSTRALIA

SOUTH AFRICA

RIO

ARGENTINA

Prix

Kenny, father and son

1. Sepang

▷
Kenny Roberts and Suzuki: the sensation of Sepang

After the Grahams, the Paganis and the Rossis, the Roberts, father and son now have the right to put their name in the racing record books. On the new Sepang circuit , for the opening of the 1999 world championship, Kenny "Junior" scored the first major success of his career. Here we tell the tale of a child who did not always have it easy...

"I don't know why my son tries so hard with "Junior", he will never be a big champion. Kurtis? he's something else, he's the best, even more talented than his father was at the same age". Amongst the hills which surround Kenny Roberts' ranch at Hickman near Modesto California, Buster, Grandfather Roberts, desperately tries to get a few apple trees to grow. At the same time he keeps a benevolent eye on the little lad who works out, riding a mini-bike on the ranch's dirt tracks. He is often the victim of mocking laughter from Kenny senior every time he falls off, which happens very often.

It is a winter's day like any other on the Roberts' ranch. Wayne Rainey is there. "Junior" is getting ready for the next season in the USA championships while Kenny Senior is having a whale of a time out on the track while making the occasional barbed remark about the AMA, the American Federation. " This will be the last year that Junior risks his life on circuits which haven't got any security measures in place and in races that are far too short. Next year I'll take

him with me to Europe where he can continue to learn his trade in the open Spanish championship, a much better school than what we have here." It is 1992, Junior has just celebrated his nineteenth birthday and his international career is about to start.

The burden is all in the name

First Grand Prix at Laguna Seca one year later and a place as an official rider in the 250 team built up by Kenny Roberts, who has entrusted the running of it to Wayne Rainey after his paralysing accident. "Junior" is a Grand Prix racer but there is nothing about him that suggests the talent of other American riders who arrive in Europe and win everything in their path.

On the contrary, Kenny "Junior" is having a rather quiet time. He is almost timid as if he is finding it difficult to carve out his own personality in this very family orientated, maybe even too family orientated environment. Some people are already making sarcastic comments about him and all the

remarks have the same theme: " It's lucky his last name is Roberts!". Despite this, Junior makes progress and finishes his first Grand Prix season with three good results including a sixth place in Argentina. Wayne Rainey for one believes in him and when Roberts finishes fourth in the 1995 German Grand Prix those who criticised him in the past begin to show interest. Eighth in the 250 world championship, here he is thrown into the deep end as a factory rider in the 500 class, in his father's team of course. There are more sarcastic remarks and once again progress is steady but slow. Junior hasn't changed. Still reserved, still ready to listen, he is now part of the Modenas project, but still a prisoner of his own family's influence.

The Big Decision

And now we reach the point where he is going to make the most important decision of his career and in the first officially announced transfer for the 1999 season he quickly accepts the offer put on the table by Suzuki, who are looking for a new number one who is capable of reviving the glorious past they enjoyed in the days of Kevin Schwantz. Kenny Roberts Junior thus leaves his father behind, taking with him Warren Willing, one of the top engineers with the team as well as Dean Miller, his physio and trainer. Right from the start of winter testing he was a sensation. Not only had the Suzuki rediscovered a taste for quick lap times, but Roberts seems to be prepared to fight to get the best lap time on every circuit where tests are organised. Were we to be in for a surprise? Once again his critics expressed a few doubts, pointing out that what happens in the winter does not often translate into quick times once the season has started. However, at Sepang, Junior proved them wrong. He went very well in practise despite a spectacular fall and then he had a perfect race topped off with his first win, which was incidently also the first time he had been on the podium. Sixteen years after his father's final victory in the 1983 San Marino Grand Prix, the last race in the career of the man they refer to as the king, another Roberts had put his name on the winner's trophy. "Ever since I joined Suzuki everything has gone fantastically well. I get everything I ask for and I feel totally at home in this team. I know that I've been taken on here because of what I can do and not because my father is the boss. Physically, having spent the winter working hard with Dean Miller, I'm in better shape than ever. Mentally, this first race was easier than I had expected. My goal for the year is to try and win the championship and to become therefore the best rider in the world. Today I honestly believe I was the best." "Junior" had finally joined the seniors.

◁
"Please
don't call me Junior!"

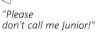

The races

125 cc

Frenchman, Arnaud Vincent, now the Number One rider for the Aprilia team run by Jorge "Aspar" Martinez, was the top man of the weekend. In qualifying, he scored the first pole position of his career, dominating the opposition on both Friday and Saturday. Marco Melandri had to miss the final showdown, having broken his left wrist in the second free practice session. Taking the lead at the start, Vincent tried to go it alone, leading by 0.604 seconds after four laps. He was then joined by Masao Azuma (Honda, but on the same Bridgestone tyres as Vincent) and Emilio Alzamora. The three of them soon found themselves out on their own ahead of Scalvini, fourth but six seconds down after a lousy start. By lap ten, with Vincent back in the lead, after Alzamora made a small mistake which also delayed Azuma, a first French 125 win since Jean-Claude Selini won at Nogaro in 1982 looked on the cards. Sadly, on the next lap, the former European champion fell at the hairpin linking the two straights on the Malaysian track. Victory would be played out between Azuma and Alzamora, the latter risking all on the way to the first ever Sepang official lap record. Despite this, Azuma hung on to the win by 106 thousandths at the line. Scalvini was third with Vincent saving a few points with fourth.

△
Loris Capirossi beats
Aprilia and Rossi:
not easy!

250 cc

Valentino Rossi, who had dominated the second half of the 1998 season, secured his first ever 250 cc pole position, with qualifying run on just one day, Friday, after the Saturday session was washed out by torrential rain. With an Aprilia out in front, everything seemed normal, but the others were closing up. Nakano and Jacque on the new Yamaha YZR and the Honda NSR of world champion Loris Capirossi were also on the front row. There was another bad blow for the previously dominant marque as Aprilia lost one of its key players in the Friday morning session when the engine in Ralf Waldman's engine seized, causing the German to crash and break his right wrist. Capirossi made the best start, with Rossi only seventh at the end of the first lap. There was good reason for it: "After the race, my chief engineer, Rossano Brazzi admitted there had been a major electrical problem on the grid which affected the automatic gear change." In the end it was little Nakano who would stamp his authority on the race. He took the lead on lap 2 and extended it to 1.912s by lap nine. Unfortunately, his YZR engine began to lose power and the two Honda riders, Loris Capirossi and Tohru Ukawa closed the gap, catching him on lap 16 of the 20 lap race. Capirossi left his braking too late at the end of the straight, although he managed to stay on, but it was Ukawa who took the lead on the penultimate lap, before being caught out by the Number 1 at the final corner.

500 cc

Anyone who just turned up in the media centre on Saturday afternoon, for the post qualifying press conference, would have had to rub his eyes in disbelief at the sight of the four fastest qualifiers. On pole was John Kockinski, riding for Erv Kanemoto's impoverished team. Alongside him, Yamaha's Number One, Max Biaggi, followed by the two Suzuki riders, Kenny Roberts and Nobuatsu Aoki. Where were the top men from HRC? Absent, with Criville fifth and Doohan, seventh, having fallen on Friday morning. Okada was twelfth. Were we in for something special? It seemed not, as Doohan restored order by going quickest in the race morning warm-up. It was a mistake: Criville shot into the lead off the second row, with Doohan only eleventh at the end of the first lap. Kenny Roberts took control as from the third lap. One lap later, Kocinski tried an impossibly late braking move and took the unfortunate Norifume Abe with him as he fell. Out in front, Roberts was on his own, at first by eight tenths and then by whole seconds. On lap eleven, when Biaggi retired with electrical problems, the American had a 6.611s lead over the chasing trio of an on-form Checa, Criville and Okada. With five laps to go the gap was at its biggest (9.044s.) "Junior" was heading imperiously for his first GP win. Towards the end of the race, Doohan was on a charge and set the first ever lap record at Sepang for the category. A Suzuki had not led the championship since the 1995 Italian GP, when Beattie had 119 points to Doohan's 95.

...Kenny Roberts Junior's first victory. After the Pegani family (Nello and Alberto,) the Graham clan (Leslie and Stuart) and the Rossis (Graziano and Valentino,) the Roberts (Kenny Leroy Senior and Kenny Lee Junior) have now joined the pantheon of racing families. The "king's" twenty-second and final win came on the 4th September 1983 at Imola, ahead of Spencer and Lawson. Junior's first success was on the 18th April 1999 at Sepang when he beat Checa and Criville.

...The return of Derbi. 10th May 1992: Ezio Gianola leads the Spanish 125 Grand Prix as he comes through the final corner astride the works Derbi. But a mechanical failure stops the Italian at the side of the track and he dissolves in floods of tears. Derbi, the company with 18 world titles, (10 for the riders and 8 for the constructors) is about to retire from the world championships. 18th April 1999 : Youichi Ui and Pablo Nieto debut the new Derbi in a team run by Italt's Giampiero Sacchi. The engine is designed by Austria's Harald Bartol and the chassis built in England by the same company which produces the Modenas and new MuZ-Weber 500s.

...BSL's false start. There was another debut but this one was a complete failure: the BSL 3 cylinder New Zealand machine was pulled out during the final qualifying session as the team decided to give up competing in the Japanese GP. The team came together thanks to a Kiwi millionaire who specialises in the production of electronic chips. Bill Buckley's BSL team was given a place in the world championship under rather strange terms given that the team paid IRTA, rather than being paid by IRTA, the equivalent of what a 500cc rider would be paid who finished every qualifying and race in last place.

Coolheaded Biaggi: really?

...the return of Giacomo Agostini and Carlo Pernat. The Italian racing scene was very vibrant at the moment and two of its biggest names have reappeared in the paddock. Giacomo Agostini, the rider who has won more championships than any other in the history of the sport, now works as a consultant for RAI, Italy's national television station, while Carlo Pernat the ebullient and former sporting director at Aprilia now has a job relaying pit-lane information for the same TV channel. Welcome to the new journalists!

...cool headed Biaggi. Massimiliano Biaggi has never been backward in coming forward when it comes to innovation. In Sepang, the number two rider in the 500cc class had a strange new crash helmet, the interior of which had been replaced with a special fibre material developed by NASA for use in the astronauts' space suits. The aim of the operation was to reduce the internal temperature of the crash helmet by between 5 and 7 degrees which would be a major advantage in the atrocious heat.

Roberts: a front row start followed by a win.

Sepang, Circuit of the Future

The two-sided grandstand: a world first.

Welcome to the future, south-east Asia style. Tomorrow's world has really arrived today. Over a hundred and ten million Swiss francs, and just 30 months between the decision being taken to build the place and the first world championship event taking place, fifteen months of on-site work and the Sepang circuit is ready to show what a sporting venue will look like in the 21ˢᵗ century. Let's go on a guided tour...

Kazhir Ibrahim, our chauffeur almost apologised "Look, we're only 2 kilometres from the airport where we started from but unfortunately there is no direct route to this place and that is why we've made this detour ." The little Proton bus has just gone done an avenue lined with giant palm trees. From the moment we touched down in Malaysia , tomorrow's world has sprung up before our eyes just about everywhere. The moment we left the new international airport of Sepang - the most modern in the world and now the biggest in south-east Asia - we were lounging around in a Jacuzzi in a five star hotel. Just ten minutes by road and we were at Sepang F1 circuit with its huge double grandstand that allows spectators to see over 80% of the track. It also has ultra modern pits above which are small lounges where the riders can relax. The circuit of the future exists and the world motorcycle championship circus discovered it at the first race of the season.

"Malaysia boleh"

Behind this very real glimpse of the future is hidden some equally real politics. Malaysia's Prime Minister since 1981, Datuk Seri Dr Mahathir Mohamad, wanted to show the "Malaysia boleh," the Malaysian ability when it comes to high technology and investment. To assure the long term future of his country, he started by introducing an automobile industry, first in the form of assembling cars for major foreign constructors (for the most part Japanese); and then by creating a national company, Proton, in 1985. What followed was a dream that became reality. "Our next goal was to be able to host as soon as possible a Formula One race," he explained . "Not only to underwrite from a technological point of view our country's automobile industry but also to give a serious boost to tourism. So the Sepang circuit should not just be a centre for mechanical sports for our country, it should be capable of transforming itself rapidly into a unique opportunity for all the governments of the region and for the big teams to one day come and establish themselves in our midst."

We know what happened next: ever more increasing presence at the highest level with Petronas joining forces with Sauber in Formula One, Modenas in the GP class and the Hong Leong group being involved with MuZ-Swissauto also in the 500s. However, Malaysia is today deep in the middle of a serious economic crisis but nevertheless this does not stop it from wanting to win.

KEY DATES

- **June 1996:** the Cabinet asks Malaysia Airports Berhad, the company which runs motorised sports in the country, to obtain the rights to hold the Formula One Grand Prix as soon as possible and to plan an ultra - modern circuit in the same complex which will be home to the future international airport of Sepang.

- **1996:** Malaysian representatives visit Silverstone, Melbourne, Kyalami, Estoril, Nurburgring and the A1-Ring. In September, Prime Minister Mahathir is a guest at the Portuguese Formula One Grand Prix at Estoril.

- **October 1996:** An agreement is reached between the Malaysians and the German group Tilke Engineering who were responsible for building the A1 - Ring, in Austria.

- **13ᵗʰ December 1996:** A first plan is presented to the Prime Minister.

- **September 1997:** the budget to build the track comes to a total of 286 million ringgits (more than 110 million Swiss francs).

- **November 1997:** work begins.

- **November 1998:** first 300 km race counting for the International Proton Cup. F1's race director Charlie Whiting agrees that the track can apply to be homologated.

- **February 1999:** the Malaysian Grand Prix is incorporated into the Formula One world championship calender and the circuit is renamed "Sepang F1 Circuit." Claude Danis president of the FIM's road racing commission approves the circuit for motorcycle racing.

- **9ᵗʰ March 1999:** official opening of the Sepang circuit.

- **18ᵗʰ April 1999:** Malaysian motorcycle Grand Prix opens the 1999 world championship.

- **17ᵗʰ October 1999:** first Formula One Grand Prix to be held in Malaysia.

Young palm trees on natural viewing areas

Fallers

△ Maurice Bolwerk:
the first really bad injury
of the year.

Friday 16th March 1999

125 cc: Bernhard Absmeier (D, Aprilia.)
250 cc: Ralf Waldmann (D, Aprilia,)
Franco Battaini (I, Aprilia) and Shinya
Nakano (J, Yamaha.)
500 cc: Yukio Kagayama (J, Suzuki,)
Michael Doohan (AUS, Honda,) Michael
Rutter (GB, Honda, twice,) Haruchika
Aoki (J, TSR- Honda,) Carlos Checa (E,
Yamaha,) Jean-Michel Bayle (F, Modenas)
and Kenny Roberts Junior (USA, Suzuki.)

Saturday 17th March 1999

125 cc: Marco Melandri (I, Honda) and
Manuel Poggiali (RSM, Aprilia.)
250 cc: Yuzy Shahrol (MAL, Honda) and
Jarno Janssen (NL, TSR-Honda.)
500 cc: Massimiliano Biaggi (I, Yamaha.)

Sunday 18th March 1999

125 cc: Direk Archewong (THA, Honda,)
Lucio Cecchinello (I, Honda, restart,)
Steve Jenkner (D, Aprilia, restart,)
Arnaud Vincent (F, Aprilia, restart,)
Noboru Ueda (J, Honda) and Frederic
Petit (F, Aprilia.)
250 cc: Maurice Bolwerk (NL, TSR-
Honda,) Tomomi Manako (J, Yamaha)
and Yuzy Shahrol (MAL, Honda.)
500 cc: Norifumi Abe (J, Yamaha) and
John Kocinski (USA, Honda V4.).

Ouch!...

1. Ralf Waldmann (fracture to right
wrist.)
2. Jarno Janssen (cuts and bruises to
right hand and right knee.)
3. Marco Melandri (fractured left wrist.)
4. Manuel Poggiali (bruising to knee and
forearm.)
5. Maurice Bolwerk (dislocated right
wrist, concussion.)

Non Starters...

1. Ralf Waldmann (result of fall in
practise, Waldmann went home to
Germany on Friday evening.)
2. Marco Melandri (result of fall in
practise, Melandri underwent surgery at
the circuit hospital.)
3. Maurice Bolwerk (result of fall in
warm-up.)

Retirements...

125 cc: Bernhard Absmeier (D, Aprilia,
piston.)
250 cc: Franco Battaini (I, Aprilia, broken
gear lever.)
500 cc: Luca Cadalora (I, MuZ-Weber,
counter-balance,) Jurgen Van Den
Goorbergh (NL, MuZ-Weber, seized
engine,) Massimiliano Biaggi (I, Yamaha,
electrical problems,) Jose Luis Cardoso
(E, TSR-Honda, suspension) and Michael
Rutter (GB, Honda, gear box.)

Steve Jenkner:
man and machine
▽

A waltz in four time?

2. Motegi

Will two stroke technology like these Yamaha 500 pistons and cylinders soon be replaced...

▷

....by four stroke prototypes like Troy Corser's Ducati?

▷

The Japanese GP, held for the first time on the Motegi circuit, definitely did not want for track action, what with Roberts' dominance, Aprilia's problems and Azuma's faultless 125 performance. Behind the scenes, things were equally busy. The long awaited meeting finally took place between the FIM, represented by its president Francesco Zerbi and managing director Guy Maitre amongst others and the constructors' association, the GPMA. The purpose of the meeting? To discuss the future of the sport.

As was to be expected, the decision was taken not to decide on anything, mainly because of determined opposition from Maurizio Flammini (the world supersport and superbike promoter) and from Ducati. Flammini was understandably wary of his championship becoming a second rate competition, with machines much closer to road bikes. The president of the Federation, Francesco Zerbi was keen to clarify the following point: "We can now consider a switch to four stroke technology for the grands prix, but only on condition that the manufacturers enter genuine prototypes and not 1000 cc machines derived from road bikes. This type of bike will still be catered for in the superbike series."

Opinions on this subject, whether from Europe or Japan, were diametrically opposed. Yamaha's top motor sport man, Toshimitsu Iio reminded everyone that four stroke technology offered greater commercial opportunities. "Manufacturers continue to produce small capacity bikes with two stroke 125 and 250 cc engines and we should continue with those. Today however, the

larger capacity machines are all powered by four strokes and the cost of future prototype development could be partly recovered from production bikes. Another idea we should look at is the restriction of fuel tank capacity and a reduction in consumption which could also prove very useful."

While Yamaha was totally in favour of a switch to four strokes, Heijiro Yoshimura, the president of HRC, Honda's racing arm, was more partial to a technology mix, a view shared by the majority of the GPMA. "We should not fool ourselves. To build a four stroke prototype with the same performance level as a 500 two stroke would be very costly. My ideal solution would be total freedom as to the number of cylinders for the formula of the future, with a minimal cylinder capacity."

Rainey: "who will pay?"

Waye Rainey, the former three times world champion felt that, "Something had to be done. Logic would seem to favour adopting four stroke technology as these are the engines that are available commercially. But the biggest problem lies elsewhere. Developing such a prototype would be very expensive, maybe in the region of fifty million dollars. Who can afford that sort of money when there are not enough sponsors around? At the moment, with a few exceptions, most of the commercial partners are Spanish. To take this further, we have to look at the whole marketing of the operation as soon as possible, because a show like this cannot survive while being totally ignored in an important market like the States. The paddock has a lot of good stories to offer the mainstream media in our part of the world."

European opposition

On the European front, Swissauto engine builder, Urs Wenger was totally opposed to a change in technology. "Changing the type of engine will not produce the magic formula. The system simply lacks a proper marketing and promotional strategy, because the spectacle we can offer deserves far better than the meagre coverage it currently gets in the major media. The balance between the major marques has never been closer, so why turn everything on its head?"

At the moment there is no answer to this question. However, the influence of the major Japanese players is so important, that inevitably the sport will go whichever direction they point it in. The "little" Europeans will be powerless to do anything about it. "When I started the Modenas project I wanted people to realise that there was room for small, independent projects which could still be taken seriously," said Kenny Roberts. Because the desire of the big companies to go for a more complicated engine type will signal the death knell of the lesser teams. "This would not be for technological reasons," maintained Urs Wenger. "It would simply be down to an inability to finance such a project."

V4 Swissauto.

The races

Shinya Nakano, Japan's winning flag bearer.

The heavens opened on Friday evening and it did not stop raining until the end of the weekend with some terrible storms battering the track, However, as the 125 cc prepared to get on the grid, the rain had eased off, although the track was wet. Starting from the first pole position of his long career, Lucio Cecchinello made the best start ahead of fellow countryman, Roberto Locatelli. The two Italians tried to go it alone, pulling out a 3.064 s gap after just one lap, but it wouldn't last. Firstly, because the lightest rider of all time, Massimiliano Sabbatini would charge through from the back, then because the two leaders both hit the deck, Locatelli on lap five and Cecchinello two laps later. Sabbatini led, but winner of the first GP, Masao Azuma took the lead on lap eight, just as one of the leading lights of the season, France's Arnaud Vincent crashed. On lap 14 of the 21 lap race, Sabbatini fell as he tried to stay with Azuma. The featherweight had a hard time picking his bike up, but he managed to finish seventh. Azuma was out on his own at the front, sixteen seconds ahead of the reigning Japanese champion, Hideyuki Nakajoh, a wild card entry and Spain's Emilio Alzamora. Azuma thus took his second win in a row, with Alzamora staying in touch in the points while Youichi Ui giving Derbi a great fourth place in its second GP.

Valentino Rossi: a fine handling Aprilia, but serious doubts in the wet.

250 cc

Franco Battaini, a slippery track specialist, took a sensational pole position in qualifying, but at Motegi it would be the Japanese riders who stole the show. Reigning Japanese champion, Shinya Nakano took his first grand prix win, making the most of his understanding of the new Yamaha YZR. He made the best start and had an eight tenths lead over fellow countryman Naoki Matsudo, also Yamaha mounted, by the end of lap one. Valentino Rossi, who does not like the rain, was down in eleventh place. By lap three, Yamahas occupied the top three places - Nakano, Matsudo and Jacque - but the Frenchman and Italy's Stefano Perugini, who had taken off like a scalded cat would not go much further. On lap seven of 23, Matsudo took the lead only to fall later. That left Nakano with a clear field and he soon built up a substantial lead of 4.259 over the pursuing duo of Battaini and Capirossi by lap 13. Battaini was the only rider to start with an intermediate front tyre and would pay the price in the second half of the race. "I don't understand my team's tyre choice," he would later complain. Capirossi went past him on lap 15, then Ukawa did the same, just as the rain came down hard again. Nakano was faultless out in front, while Tohru Ukawa provided some excitement by closing on Capirossi, riding round the outside of the Malaysian GP winner as if it was the easiest thing in the world on a wet track!

500 cc

The surprise winner in Malaysia, Kenny Roberts recorded the first pole position of his career at Motegi. Just as in Sepang, his race would be perfect. Along with France's Regis Laconi, who had what could have been a serious crash on the second lap, Roberts made the best start and just as the previous week, he was in a class of his own. Harada parked his Aprilia V2, complaining of awful handling, while the Suzuki rider took off on his own, leading by 8.108 s by half distance. The second part kicked off with a fight back from Michael Doohan, who had a hard time shaking off Norifumi Abe. John Kocinski fell on lap 16 and Doohan set the fastest lap to get within 2.717 s of Roberts with just three of the 25 laps remaining, but Kenny stayed in control, pulling away in the last laps. Doohan decided to settle for second. Junior thus confirmed that his Malaysian win had been no fluke. Norifume Abe was on top form, right from the start of the season, although he was brought down by Kocinski in Malaysia and he was now in the lead group in the championship and the best placed Yamaha rider. Max Biaggi had a quiet race, disguised in a plain white Arai helmet as his Bieffe was not keeping the water out! Noriyusa Numata, replacing Luca Cadalora in the MuZ-Weber camp, scored his first points of the season. Therefore, after two races, the seven official factory teams in the GP1 category - the New Zealand BSL outfit missed Japan - had all opened their points account. Suzuki and Kenny Roberts, who no longer wants to be known as "Junior" were the best of the bunch with a perfect score.

Worth nothing...

Yamaha President, Takehiko Hasegawa (on left) and Senior Managing Director, Hitoshi Nagayasu present Wayne Rainey with his 1991 championship winning YZR500.

... the return of MV-Agusta. Would the MV-Agusta F4, of which 300 examples were built, serve as the basis for the company's return to GP racing? Certainly this was the latest brainwave of Cagiva boss, Claudio Castiglioni. The impressive client list included Juan Carlos, King of Spain, the actor Gerard Depardieu and the Sultan of Dubai.

... a gift for Wayne Rainey from Yamaha. On the eve of the Japanese GP, the triple world 500 cc champion, Wayne Rainey was presented with the YZR500 he rode to lead the 1990 world championship. Takehiko Hasegawa, president of Yamaha Motor Company Ltd., wanted to personally honour the champion, whose main occupation at the moment is going to sports events with his son Rex. "He wants to do everything, from football to hockey, including basketball on the way. But luckily not motor cycling."

... the absence of Luca Cadalora. A few hours after the end of the Malaysian GP, Luca Cadalora secretly boarded a plane for Europe. He only informed his team manager, Rolf Biland, two days before qualifying in Japan: "Luca feels he is incapable of motivating himself, given the lack of testing and that he cannot show on the track what our machine can do. He preferred not to take part in the Japanese GP, but he assures us he will be back in Jerez, a track where we already know the basic set-up." At

Motegi, it was Japan's Noriyasu Numatu who took the Swiss bike to thirteenth spot.

... the appearance of Darryl Beattie. He had retired two years ago, but turned up to have a look at Motegi. He arrived with his old chum, Mick Doohan, who was trying to persuade him to make a comeback. Beattie spent half an hour in conversation with team MuZ-Weber boss Rolf Biland. Engineer Urs Wenger, the father of the Swissauto engine had this to say on the subject: "With this type of star, you have to have a clear idea of their motivation. I am concerned that in this case, it is purely financial."

... Biaggi and Checa try Sumo. Japan is a country rich in tradition. One of the oldest is Sumo, the art of wrestling between giants of men, who weigh in at around the 140 kilo mark. Before the weekend, Massimiliano Biaggi, Carlos Checa and Nobuatsu Aoki paid a visit to a Sumo school run by Master Ogurama in Tokyo. Ogurama San's school is for young aspirants aged 15 to 16. To compete professionally you have to be 20 years old. Their daily programme was as follows: training between 6 and 10 in the morning, followed by a two hour meal and two to three hours rest, before having another two hour meal and then bed!

Drying out session for the Givi team of Cecchinello and Ueda.

Honda: new paradise

KEY DATES

March 1988: Honda Motor Co. Ltd. initiates a study for a new project called "Mobility World Motegi."

December 1988: The project goes public.

October 1991: A report is presented to the Tochigi prefecture, outlining its impact on the environment. The plan has to be revised several times before it is finally approved in January 1994, when the "Twin Ring Motegi Co. Ltd." is established.

December 1994: The final plan, featuring the linked road and oval circuits is accepted by the local authorities.

January 1995: Construction begins.

October 1996: Signature of a contract with CART, to host a Formula Indy race.

August 1997: Opening of Twin Ring Motegi.

September 1997: First car race staged; a round of the national Formula Nippon series.

April 1998: First leg of the Japanese motorcycle championship.

November 1998: First NASCAR race.

25th April 1999: First world championship motor cycle grand prix.

△
Twin Ring Motegi: Honda's new temple to motorised sports.

After Suzuka, a grand prix circuit in a leisure complex, we now have Motegi. In a different part of the country, to the north east of Tokyo to be precise, it is more modern, but above all more surprising because of its location in the middle of nowhere in the Japanese countryside. The "Twin Ring Motegi" name refers to the fact that it features two main circuits which run together; a normal road course and a high speed oval for CART and Nascar races. The reason for its remote location is that Honda can safely test new cars and motorcycles far from prying eyes.

"One must work with the belief and enthusiasm of youth," was one of Soichiro Honda's many little homilies, which he was keen to dispense when it came to expressing his philosophy when it came to his work methods. He was more of a visionary than a manager and that is what gave birth to the empire which bears his name. It was a chief principle of his that his workers and partners should enjoy the best possible working conditions so that they could express themselves and therefore be more productive.

A fortified encampment

Motegi actually looks like some sort of fortified encampment. To build the imposing complex, its creators simply made the most of a natural crater hidden among the surrounding hills. Thousands of cubic metres of soil were shifted and this transformation of a natural site did not go down well with local conservationists and ecologists. A bridge was built over the Nakagawa river to link this remote area in the middle of nowhere to the outside world and if the bridge is closed off it gives Honda perfect privacy to test its new and secret machines on the oval ring, hidden from view by giant grandstands. Nothing could be simpler.

The layout has been carefully thought out to meet every possible need, be it for testing new products or for racing. The main road course is 4,801 metres long and can be split into three different loops (north, east and west.) Then there is the high speed oval with banked corners, the karting track, two dirt tracks, Honda's security centre, the fabulous museum collection, which also features European motorcycles and last but not least, a luxury hotel. Motegi is truly the ultimate expression of the Honda way.

A way that began 51 years ago by a blacksmith's son, whose descendents have forgotten just one thing: to build sufficient access roads to the place. Because Route 123, which links Motegi to the two neighbouring small towns of Mito and Utsonomiya, was in a permanent state of chaos during the Japanese GP weekend. Worst affected were the 125 teams, who had to set off from their hotels before five in the morning, to use the shuttle buses provided by the organisers and thus avoid the daily traffic jams!

Fallers

Friday 23rd March 1999

125 cc: Bernhard Absmeier (D, Aprilia) and Lucio Cecchinello (I, Honda.)
250 cc: Taru Sekiguchi (J, Yamaha,) Matias Rios (ARG, Aprilia,) Lucas Oliver (E, Yamaha,) Johan Stigefelt (S, Yamaha) and Alfonso Gonzales-Nieto (E, Yamaha.)
500 cc: Shinichi Itoh (J, Honda,) Jean-Michel Bayle (F, Modenas,) Markus Ober (D, Honda V2,) Manuel Gibernau (E, Honda V2,) Carlos Checa (E, Yamaha) and John Kocinski (USA, Honda V4.)

Saturday 24th March 1999

125 cc: Kazuto Sakata (J, Honda,) Manuel Poggiali (RSM, Aprilia) and Jeronimo Vidal (E, Aprilia.)
250 cc: Marcellino Lucchi (I, Aprilia,) Roberto Rolfo (I, Aprilia,) Olivier Jacque (F, Yamaha,) Takehiko Kurokawa (J, TSR-Honda, twice,) Anthony West (AUS, TSR-Honda,) Matias Rios (E, Aprilia,) Alexander Hofmann (D, TSR-Honda,) Sebastian Porto (ARG, Yamaha,) Tohru Ukawa (J, Honda,) Jarno Janssen (NL, TSR-Honda,) Stefano Perugini (I, Honda) and Luca Boscoscuro (I, TSR-Honda.)
500 cc: Jose Bautista Borja (E, Honda) and Kenny Roberts Junior (USA, Suzuki.)

Sunday 25th March 1999

125 cc: Simone Sanna (I, Honda,) Roberto Locatelli (I, Aprilia,) Noboru Ueda (J, Honda,) Gino Borsoi (I, Aprilia,) Massimiliano Sabbatani (I, Honda, restart,) Ivan Goi (I, Honda, restart,) Arnaud Vincent (F, Aprilia, restart and a second fall!) and Lucio Cecchinello (I, Honda, restart.)
250 cc: Lucas Oliver (E, Yamaha,) Stefano Perugini (I, Honda,) Olivier Jacque (F, Yamaha,) Johan Stigefelt (S, Yamaha,) Naoki Matsudo (J, Yamaha, restart,) Matias Rios (ARG, Aprilia, restart,) Jason Vincent (GB, Honda) and Takehiko Kurokawa (J, TSR-Honda.)
500 cc: Simon Crafar (NZ, Yamaha,) Regis Laconi (F, Yamaha,) Shinichi Itoh (J, Honda V4, restart) and John Kocinski (USA, Honda V4.)

Ouch!...

1. Bernhard Absmeier (bruising to left knee.)
2. Lucio Cecchinello (injured right shoulder.)
3. Markus Ober (fractured little finger right hand, bruising to lower back, bruising to both ankles.)
4. John Kocinski (bruising to little finger, right hand and to right knee.)
5. Kazuto Sakata (bruising to left shoulder.)
6. Lucas Oliver (fractured left ankle.)

Non Starters...

1. Marco Melandri (result of fall in practise for Malaysian GP. Not replaced.)
2. Ralf Waldmann (result of fall in practise for Malaysian GP. Not replaced.)
3. Maurice Bolwerk (result of fall in warm-up for Malaysian GP. Replaced by the Japanese rider Takehiko Kurokawa.)
4. Luca Cadalora (the Italian flew home to Italy on Sunday evening of the Malaysian GP and he didn't warn the team until Wednesday that he was giving up due to lack of motivation. Replaced by the Japanese rider Noriyasu Numata.)

Retirements...

125 cc: Jeronimo Vidal (E, Aprilia, brakes) and Bernhard Absmeier (D, Aprilia, result of Saturday's fall.)
250 cc: Jeremy McWilliams (GB, Aprilia, ignition problems right from the formation lap,) Luca Boscoscuro (I, TSR-Honda, connecting rod) and Julien Allemand (F, TSR-Honda, injury to right knee after hitting an object on the track!)
500 cc: Tetsuya Harada (J, Aprilia, handling,) Jurgen Van Den Goorbergh (NL, MuZ-Weber, electrical problems,) Jean-Michel Bayle (F. Modenas KR3, electrical problems) and Haruchika Aoki (J, TSR-Honda gear selector.)

*Kocinski:
the Honda burns!*
▽

The king and his successor

3. Jerez de la Frontera

Michael Doohan was seriously hurt during the first practise session for the Spanish Grand Prix at Jerez de la Frontera and on race day he was air-lifted to San Francisco to undergo an operation. Before leaving Spain for the United States, via London, the five-times world champion, the absolute kings of the Grands Prix was keen to abdicate in regal fashion. He indicated who his successor should be.

"Alex must make the most of this opportunity," was the message from Michael Doohan, a message which the Spanish media echoed throughout all the Sunday newspapers. It had the feeling of a royal abdication. The young pretender, Alex Criville, would therefore now have to prove that he had nerves of steel and was strong enough to take on his new responsibilities which go with the job of number one rider for the Honda factory team in the 500 cc category.

The tasks that confronted Alex seemed simple almost, maybe too simple. Racing is a building where each stone has to be put in place and every stage of the construction is a new difficulty to be overcome and a problem that needs solving. For Alex Criville that Sunday 9th May 1999, the first problem he had to face was the psychological one : that of being the number one rider. Then he would have to cope with the enormous pressure of being the local hero, of carrying the hopes of 150,000 afficionados who had come to Andalusia to

cheer him on . They had spent the night singing and partying , getting warmed-up for their big moment at the start of "the" race of the year: the 500 cc Spanish Grand Prix.

Biaggi piles the pressure on

Once he had dealt with the psychological problems Alex Criville still had to resolve the technical problems that go with every race. He had to make the right tyre choice, to cope with an ever increasing ambient temperature in practise. He had to keep a little bit in reserve so that he didn't get caught out by the gusts of wind which occasionally blew across the track. Then, and it was obvious that this wasn't going to be an easy task, the Catalan rider would also have to be able to get the upper hand on his opponents: John Kocinski, who made a perfect start, Regis Laconi who looked strong at first but then faded and above all Massimiliano Biaggi. "I knew that Biaggi could use a different line to mine in

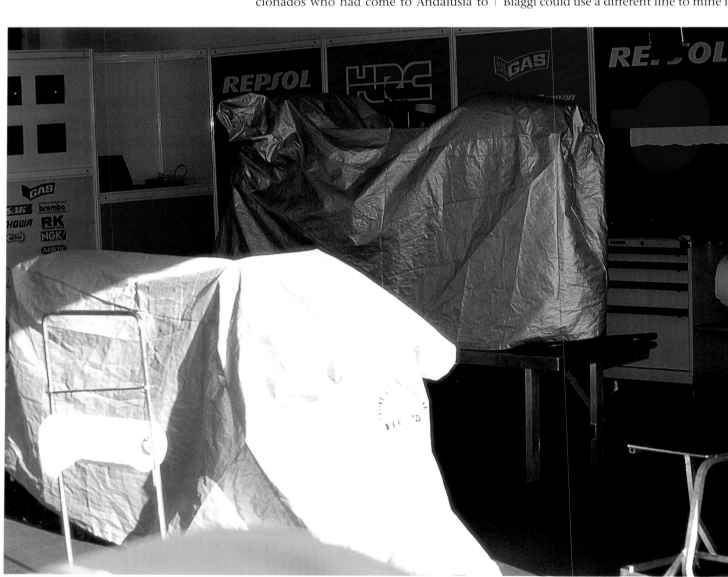

Sunday 9th May 1999 and the Number 1 bikes stand silent.

It was a massive impact.

"Now I'll show'em."

the last corner. So I closed the door on him," said the new world championship leader. He was now the prince of Spain having sat on the throne in front of his loyal subjects who were delighted with the result.

Friday 14h30

In fact Criville was crowned not at the end of the race but two days earlier at exactly half-past two on Friday 7th May 1999. Michael Doohan ,the man who has beaten almost every record, who had won the last five world titles in motorcycle sports top category was on the provisional pole in the first qualifying session. It had rained in the early afternoon but the track was totally dry when the 500 cc riders left the pits. Doohan the king realised that now was the time to put in a quick lap, to remind everyone that he was still the absolute master. His loyal team boss Jeremy Burgess would admit a few hours later that , "as he left the pits Mick gave us a big smile. He said to us "Now I'm going to go out and destroy them."

The number one rider in the world was pushing his machine through one of the key parts of the Andalusian circuit. As the track goes downhill there is a long right-hand bend then an easy left followed by the hardest corner on the Jerez track where the riders are accelerating all the way through it. In order for the trajectory to be absolutely perfect, the rear wheel must dig in to the white line which marks the outer edge of the track.

Unfortunately, the earlier rain had left a few drops and the white paint was suddenly transformed into an unforgiving trap. The rear wheel broke away suddenly and the rider was thrown off his machine, his body flew through the air before stopping abruptly in a barrier made of old tyres which had gone hard with age. The barrier offered no protection as there were Michelin advertising hoardings strapped to the front of it.

For seconds which seemed like hours he lay completely motionless. Then we saw the first signs of life as Doohan managed to move his head, then an arm , and then his left leg. Doohan was alive. His vital functions seemed to be okay. But his right leg did not move. Pain was etched on his face. Doohan's main rivals, Kenny Roberts, Alex Criville and Massimiliano Biaggi, headed back to the pits knowing that they would soon have to go out again on to the track as though nothing had happened. What they did understand was that the career of the greatest rider of modern times had maybe just come to an end. He had broken his right collar bone. He had a deep wound at the back of his right shoulder. He had broken his left wrist and his right leg just above the knee. Michael Doohan was transported to Seville before being flown on to the United States. Would he be back one day? Turn the pages and find out....

Hideyuki Okada, son of Tadayuki and already in the saddle.

500 cc

Everyone present realised the importance of this date. The weekend of the Spanish Grand Prix at Jerez de la Frontera would forever be remembered as the one where five-times world champion Michael Doohan was seriously injured. Alex Criville now carried the heavy burden of responsibility on his shoulders. Although he was quickest in practise, the Spaniard was caught out at the start by John Kocinski who unfortunately was unable to maintain his pace for very long. On lap Criville was in second place ahead of Laconi and Biaggi but Nobuatsu Aoki fell breaking a wrist bone while Kenny Roberts, winner in both Sepang and Motegi, was forced to go straight on through a gravel trap having been hit by his team- mate's motorbike. Criville took the lead when Barros fell and Biaggi was now in second place. The two men fought it out with a gap of just 161 thousandths on lap ten, a gap which increased to 359 thousandths on lap fifteen. Further back Okado, Abe and Gibernau, who was having a very good race with a V2 Honda, caught up and passed Laconi. Kenny Roberts fought back and was in eighth place four laps from the flag but then he again started to drop back as his Suzuki's engine was only running on three cylinders. On the last lap there was a very close fight between Gibernau, Okada and Abe for third place while out ahead of them Criville made sure of his win ahead of Biaggi. The result of all this was that in the championship, the Spaniard now had just a slender one point lead over Kenny Roberts.

125 cc

Emilio Alzamora will remember "his" Jerez grand prix for a very long time. He will remember it even if those memories will leave a bitter taste in his mouth. In practise the man who had dominated the early part of the season, Japan's Masao Azuma, notched up his first pole position and, right from the start of the race all the front runners were where they should be - up at the front: Azuma of course but also Lucio Cecchinello, Emilio Alzamora and the Italians Roberto Locatelli and Gianluigi Scalvini. Unfortunately the timing system had crashed and everyone would have to wait until lap twelve of the twenty-three lap race to have a precise idea of what the gaps were between the riders. It was a spectacular battle for the lead and on the penultimate lap France's Frederic Petit and the young Italian Marco Melandri, who was making his comeback after an injury in the Malaysian Grand Prix when he fractured his left wrist , both fell, while they were fighting it out for ninth place. Then on the last lap Alzamora was obviously ready to take all the risks to close up on Azuma. Breaking for the last hairpin the Spaniard's Honda dived down the inside and Alzamora emerged in the lead with just 120 metres to go before the chequered flag. But he would make a huge mistake trying to break the slip-streaming tow for his persuers. Angel Nieto's rider moved to the side, Azuma tried to make the most of it and the two men touched lightly allowing Cecchinello also to get past the Spaniard by a whisper or to be more precise by just 30 thousanths of a second. Alzamora bashed his fuel tank in anger while Angel Nieto was crying on pit wall and Masao Azuma maintained a perfect score in the championship with 75 points representing a 23 point lead over Alzamora.

250 cc

Shinya Nakano celebrated his first pole position but the team-mate to the Japanese Grand Prix winner, France's Olivier Jacque, had a fall at the start of the final session of practise. He broke the interior and exterior ankle bones of the right foot and an operation was needed. When the lights went green Nakano and Capirossi made the best starts with Battaini continuing his good season and Rossi in close attendance. On lap two Valentinik (Rossi's new nick-name) took the lead. He tried to make a break for it with a 1.011 second advance over Nakano on lap three but the little Japanese Yamaha rider along with Tohru Ukawa (Honda) hung on for grim death. On lap nine while Capirossi was already beaten because of major problems with his rear tyre, Nakano was out with an engine failure. Out in front Rossi and Ukawa were inseparable, the Japanese rider took the lead on lap fourteen but then gave himself a huge fright . Rossi did not bother hanging around to wait for him and started to build up a lead of around 0.888 seconds in just one lap. It would be the decisive moment of the race. Further back Ralf Waldmann was mounting an impressive climb through the field from twenty-first to sixth place. There was also a great tussle going on for eighth place with Perugini, Boscoscuro, Vincent, Rolfo and Stigefelt although the Swede fell with just two laps to go. All that was left now for everyone to wait and see what Valentino Rossi had in mind for his lap of honour this time. He had a new idea in Spain and rushed for a mobile toilet pretending to deal with an urgent need: "I knew there was the podium ceremony and the press conference to come and that I wouldn't have time to go to the toilet first," he explained with a laugh. As far as the championship was concerned it was Ukawa thanks to three second places who was in the now lead ahead of Capirossi and Rossi.

After a first win, it was now time for the first pole in Japan.

Worth noting...

Doctor Costa was no stranger to Michael Doohan. He had already saved his right leg which had been seriously injured in a 1992 accident. "We won't know until he wakes up after his operation if Michael Doohan will be once again the rider who has thrilled us so much with his riding or whether he will have to make do with looking after the baby that his girlfriend, Selina, is carrying at the moment. If he makes a comeback he will be the most amazing hero in the history of the sport. If he decides to stop he will be an even bigger hero".

...Safety is questioned. Mick Doohan's accident prompted a lot of questions. Riders were suddenly confronted with the stark reality of their mortality even more so because of the status of the victim as the best rider of modern times. Kenny Roberts was the first to do something about it and Massimiliano Biaggi who along with Michael Doohan had been the race directors' representatives on the track agreed to take on this responsibility alone from now on. " The moment has come to form a true riders association. Franco Uncini, the safety delegate, is paid by the system so one has to question whether he is really free to make decisions on his own."

...The camera car. Making its debut at Jerez was a new camera car which BMW

◁ With Nutec giving up on the Spanish GP, some teams had carburation problems, just ask Sakata and his seized engine.

had given to the race directors as well as some rapid intervention vehicles. As Switzerland's Leo De Grafenried explained, the thinking behind this camera car was that it would film the first lap of every race.

▷ Massimiliano Biaggi: he wanted what the Australian had and here he was in Doohan's shoes as the Race Director's man on the track.

"Two miniature cameras are on board, one forward facing and one rearward facing."
...The Docshop Viper. The emblem of the Dutch Docshop team, Docshop being a pharmaceutical company, is a red snake on a black background. Maybe it's not the most original but it was pretty close to the truth! Opening one of the packing cases which had come directly from Japan, the mechanics had a nasty surprise when they discovered a live viper inside. The snake was put into a box before being looked after by a representative from the Jerez zoo. The reptile specialist said: "This type of snake does not exist in Japan so I'm ready to bet it had been in the packing case all the way from Malaysia." It's enough to make your skin creep.

Nutec to back down. The American aerospace fuel company which supplies several teams, most notably Suzuki, had to beat a retreat in Jerez. Jean-Francois Balde, Nutec's man in the field, explained why: "every time a new product is introduced, you have to leave a sample footprint with the EMPA laboratory in Switzerland as a control. With the latest fuel we have developed, one of the many parameters measured was outside the prescribed limits. In order not to take any undue risks, we preferred to shut up shop just for one weekend."

Fallers

▷
*Roberto Locatelli:
look out for the gravel.*

Jerez: show!
▽

Friday 7ᵗʰ May 1999

125 cc: Manuel Poggiali (RSM, Aprilia,) Massimiliano Sabbatani (I, Honda,) Emilio Delgado (E, Honda,) Ivan Goi (I. Honda,) Antonio Elias (E, Honda) and Luis Costa (E, Honda.)

250 cc: none
500 cc: Michael Doohan (AUS, Honda V4,) Kenny Roberts Junior (USA, Suzuki) and Jamie Whitham (GB, Modenas.)

Saturday 8ᵗʰ May 1999

125 cc: Kazuto Sakata (J. Honda,) Frederic Petit (F, Aprilia,) Roberto Locatelli (I, Aprilia,) Lucio Cecchinello (I, Honda,) Emilio Delgado (E, Honda,) Bernhard Absmeier (D, Aprilia,) Mirko Giansanti (I, Aprilia,) Masao Azuma (J, Honda) and Arnaud Vincent (F, Aprilia.)
250 cc: Jason Vincent (GB, Honda,) Olivier Jacque (F, Yamaha,) Jeremy McWilliams (GB, Aprilia,) Alex Debon (E, Honda) and Franco Battaini (I, Aprilia.)
500 cc: Michael Rutter (GB, Honda.)

Sunday 9ᵗʰ May 1999

125 cc: Luis Costa (E, Honda,) Frederic Petit (F, Aprilia,) Marco Melandri (I, Honda) and Massimiliano Sabbatani (I, Honda.)
250 cc: Julien Allemand (F, TSR-Honda) and Johan Stigefelt (S, Yamaha.)
500 cc: Nobuatsu Aoki (J, Suzuki,) Alexandre Barros (BR, Honda V4) and Jamie Whitham (GB, Modenas.)

Ouch!..

1. Luis Costa (bruising to left hand and leg.)
2. Michael Doohan (fractured left wrist, fractured right clavicle, puncture wound to right shoulder, fractured right leg including damage to tibia.)
3. Jamie Whitham (bruised right foot.)
4. Kazuto Sakata (bruising to chest and back.)
5. Lucio Cecchinello (bruising to right heel.)
6. Olivier Jacque (fractured both malleolars, right ankle.)
7. Nobuatsu Aoki (fractured scaphoid, left hand.)

Non Starters...

1. Maurice Bolwerk (result of fall in warm-up at Malaysian GP. Replaced by the Japanese rider Naohiro Negishi.)
2. Jean-Michel Bayle (officially, JMB was declared injured with an infection in his thigh following an insect bite! - but off the record the Frenchman doesn't want to ride for Modenas anymore. Replaced by Jamie Whitham.)
3. Michael Doohan (result of fall in practise. The five-times world champion was transferred on Saturday afternoon to a specialist San Francisco hospital where he underwent an operation on his right leg. The two specialists, Doctors Arthur Ting and Kevin Louie, who had already treated him in 1992, were in charge of the operation.)
4. Olivier Jacque (result of fall in practise. The Frenchman was taken on Saturday evening to the Salpetriere hospital in Paris, under the care of Professor Saillant.)

Retirements...

125 cc: Randy De Puniet (F, Aprilia, sparkplug,) Pablo Nieto (E, Derbi, electrical problems) and Youichi Ui (J. Derbi, con-rod.)
250 cc Shinya Nakano (J, Yamaha, engine.)
500 cc: Tetsuya Harada (J, Aprilia, gear box,) Jose Luis Cardoso (E, TSR- Honda, electrical problems) and Sebastien Gimbert (F, Honda V2, electrical problems.)

Youichi Ui and a broken conrod on the Derbi 125.
▽

Thank you Paul Ricard!

4. Le Castellet

▷

Would Alex Criville be the last ever 500 winner at Paul Ricard?

The first winner of a French 500 cc grand prix at Paul Ricard, the circuit surrounded by pine trees, set on top of a plateau in the Sainte-Baume mountains, was called Saarinen. He was the prince of speed, come from a cold country. Twenty six years later, the future king of the 500s was to come from a hot country, but was Alex Criville to be remembered as the last man to have his name engraved on the Ricard trophy? On Sunday night, the 23rd May 1999, nobody knew if we would ever return to this charming part of the world.

In fact, the bombshell had been dropped the previous week. Just before the Monaco Formula 1 Grand Prix, the sport's supremo, the all-powerful Bernie Ecclestone had signed papers, making him the new owner of the Paul Ricard circuit, including all its land, as well as the airfield which runs alongside the track. This was an important day for Daniele Ricard, the eldest daughter of the famous founder of what is today a financial empire. An historic page in the life of the Ricard family had just been turned; a page packed with an overwhelming passion for motor sport.

A visionary

Paul Ricard, who died on 7th November 1997, aged 88, had been a visionary, when at the age of only 29, he opened what was at the time, the most modern racing circuit in the world. Christian Bourgeois, who was a journalist for "Moto Revue" at the time, had been one of the first motorcyclists to try the track. It was an unforgettable moment, described in issue 2000 of the French publication: "Anyone used to a

conventional track cannot help but be surprised here, because the track offers everything one could wish for. The paddock is huge and totally tarmac, the wash rooms are ultra modern and it has a small shopping centre among other attractions. On top of that, the welcome is warm and friendly. Very important in making a success of the circuit, the spectator is not treated as a poor relation or stuck out in remote and uninteresting parts of the track. There are giant grandstands, which can currently house 10,000 spectators along the short pit straight, while a network of roads allows easy access to points of interest. However, a circuit lives or dies on the merits of its layout and it has to be said that, for a motor cycle, the 3.6 km of the Castellet with its numerous corners and turns of varying difficulty and radius, really puts a premium on rider skill."

The inheritance

All that was a long time ago. Today, it is time to split the inheritance and the Ricard family was confronted with a difficult choice. "It was a very emotional moment for all of us," recalled Daniele Ricard. "Sentiment told us not to sell, but Bernie Ecclestone convinced us. Not only did he give us assurances that sport would always be the key element, but he also told us the circuit would always bear our father's name. Over the past thirty years, the Ricard circuit has aged. Despite heavy investment made by our company, it needed modernising and brought up to present day motor sport standards."

What will become of the new Castellet circuit? The keys were handed over to its new owners, on paper a French company, but actually owned by the boss of Formula 1, at the beginning of October. At the moment, Bernie Ecclestone has not revealed his plans for this new acquisition, but one can hazard a guess. It is likely that the revitalised Ricard will host the French Formula 1 Grand Prix from 2001. An oval circuit will be added in order to host CART (Formula Indy) races in Europe.

What about motor bikes?

What will happen to the motor cycle races? After all, the French GP and the Bol d'Or are classics among classics. French GP promoter, Claude Michy has already considered a move to a new home. "My contract with Dorna to organise the French GP is still valid for 2000 and I have an option for a further five years on a French GP, although no circuit is specified. So, why not think about a move to Magny Cours or Le Mans?"

Or why not hope that once the renovation work is completed, the motorbikes could still have a home at Ricard?

RICARD WINNERS

6 wins: Rolf Biland (side cars)
3 wins: Angel Nieto (125 cc)
2 wins: Kent Andersson (125 cc,) Anton Mang (250 cc,) Tetsuya Harada (250 cc,) Johnny Cecotto (250 and 350 cc,) John Ekerold (250 and 350 cc,) Jarno Saarinen (250 and 500 cc,) Giacomo Agostini (350 and 500 cc,) Eddie Lawson (500 cc,) Michael Doohan (500 cc) and Alex Criville (500 cc.)
1 win: Pierpaolo Bianchi, Luca Cadalora, Jorge Martinez, Loris Capirossi, Stefano Perugini, Valentino Rossi, Kazuto Sakata and Roberto Locatelli (125 cc;) Kork Ballington, Carlos Lavado, Jacques Cornu, Loris Reggiani, Massimiliano Biaggi and Tohru Ukawa (250 cc;) Takazumi Katayama (350 cc;) Barry Sheene, Kenny Roberts (Senior,) Marco Lucchinelli, Freddie Spencer and Wayne Rainey (500 cc;) Klaus Enders, Herman Schmid, Alain Michel and Eggbert Streuer (sidecars.)

◁
Ricard,
23 years ago and
the start of the 1976
200 Miles.

The races

125 cc

Aprilia took its first win of the year, making it a one-two finish for the Italian marque, thanks to the best efforts of Roberto Locatelli and Arnaud Vincent. Practice, red flagged on Friday afternoon because the wind had blown down the airfence barriers, was dominated by Luci Cecchinello and championship leader, Masao Azuma. Locatelli took the lead when the lights went out, but he was soon joined by Cecchinello. Trouble started early with a coming together at the Raccordement corner, both Ui and Goi falling. Poggiali was another faller on lap two, while Cecchinello got it all wrong a few kilometres down the road. Melandri poked his nose up front for a look, but it was Locatelli who took command on lap five, before building up a substantial lead of 7.689s after 23 of the 27 laps. The chasing group was at first made up of six riders; Azuma, Ueda, Vincent, Alzamora, Melandri and Scalvini. But it was to be reduced in number of four very exciting final laps. Vincent made a move up to second, while Azuma and the others got in the slipstream to latch onto him again. But the little Frenchman was to have the last word, with Spain's Alzamora surprising the championship leader in the last few metres, to score his fourth podium in as many races.

△
Tetsuya Harada: first podium of 1999 for the V2 Aprilia.

250 cc

Loris Capirossi had a spectacular fall, escaping with concussion, Jeremy McWilliams risked everything on the last lap and hit the deck, Franco Battaini was penalised for having overtaken under waved yellow flags and Valentino Rossi broke down just two kilometres from the chequered flag having been head and shoulders above the rest throughout the race. The 1999 250 cc French Grand Prix would be remembered for a long time to come, not least because Japan's Tohru Ukawa took his maiden grand prix win,

Roberto Locatelli's first world championship success.
▽

which gave him a substantial lead in the championship. Practice served to confirm the current pecking order among the top three factory teams. Rossi and Battaini were quickest on their Aprilias, ahead of the Honda duo of Capirossi and Ukawa. Nakano, who the French had adopted as one of their own, was not far off the pace on his Yamaha. Capirossi and Stefano Perugini made the best start, but Rossi took the lead on lap two, building up the gap at a rate of half a second per lap. Despite his engine not running as sweetly as it should, Capirossi tried to close the gap, while himself being caught by Ukawa, the Japanese rider passing the world champion with eight of the 29 laps remaining. After that, the action intensified: McWilliams forgot to brake as he tried to take third place off Nakano! Then, unbelievable scenes; an aerial shot showed Valentino Rossi stopped at the side of the track. He was kneeling at the side of his Aprilia which had just thrown its chain off the sprocket. The race was run with Ukawa winning at last, Nakano happy to be second and Perugini delighted with third.

500 cc

This was act two in the battle to succeed to the throne and the new king was going to teach his subjects a lesson. Two weeks after events at Jerez, Alex Criville was back on yet another circuit where he had won the previous year, beating Michael Doohan fair and square. It was clear that the French GP would allow the Spaniard to tighten his grip on the title of leader of the pack. However, his main opponents would not be easy meat and both Massimiliano Biaggi and Kenny Roberts were determined to put Criville under pressure. In qualifying, Biaggi recorded his first pole for Yamaha, despite the first of three falls, the second in the warm-up and the third in the race. Biaggi came out fighting at the start, leading Roberts by 608 thousandths at the end of the opening lap and over a second next time round. There would be no lap three for Biaggi as he fell, badly injuring both hands. It was the start of act two. The red was followed by the blue of Roberts' Suzuki. By lap nine the American had a 3.942s lead over Criville, who had just passed Kockinski. Pundits reckoned this was a big enough gap, but they were to be proved wrong. The Spanish rider had cleverly worked out that, running at this sort of pace, the Suzuki's tyres would be taking a pasting. On lap 21 of 31, Criville sailed past Roberts, who was to fall away, after a brief attempt to stay with the leader under the blue skies of Paul Ricard. The new boss had won again. Kocinski was second, but unsure about his future. Tetsuya Harada handed the Aprilia V2 its second ever podium, after Doriano Romboni had scored the first back in 1997 at Assen.

... John Kocinski's future. Second in the French 500 GP, John Kocinski was a figure of pity in the Paul Ricard media centre: "Put yourself in my place. Put yourself in the shoes of someone who likes his job, but doesn't know what he will be doing in a couple of hours. It's a strange feeling."

... the situation at Aprilia. Tetsuya Harada had agreed not to take part in the IRTA test session at Valencia, scheduled to start three days after the Spanish GP and this started the rumour that the V2 project was going to be canned immediately. To shed some light on the situation, a press conference was called for late on Thursday afternoon. The team bosses announced that an extra budget had been freed up for the development of the 500 project. Aprilia's former sporting director, Carlo Pernat had been put in charge of running the project by the Piaggio group.

... A weekend of firsts. First win for Roberto Locatelli - "after five years of grand prix racing, this feels really good," - first win for Tohru Ukawa - "why aren't there more people here for the press conference?"

... Max and Formula 1. Biaggi put the cat among the pigeons with the Italian media. On the eve of the French GP, he let it slip that at the Monaco F1 GP, he had dined with Luca di Montezemolo (the Ferrari president,) Jean Todt, (Ferrari's sporting director) and Bernie Ecclestone, (Formula 1 supremo.) He hinted that a surprise or two might be in the pipeline, which everyone took to mean he might be switching from two to four wheels.

... the fabulous Fulgur. Making the most of the French GP, the creators of the Fulgur, a hand-built French 250 cc, took the opportunity to unveil their beautiful all-carbon baby. One of the project leaders, Didier Langouet confirmed the company intends getting it onto the GP grid in 2000.

... Rossi shrugs off threats. After he was given a stern warning over his lap of honour antics in Jerez, Valentino Rossi was unrepentent. "Motor cycle sport will not become less important or less serious because someone celebrates in style after winning. Personally, I will carry on, although I might try and get Aprilia to pay the fine." However, in France, a chain with a mind of its own robbed him of the chance to try again.

△
Valentino Rossi will do anything for a show.

◁
The French Fulgur - superb!

Fallers

Jean-Michel Bayle: ouch! ▷

*Max Biaggi:
all the violence of a crash
in one shot.*
▽

Friday 21st May 1999

125 cc: Herve Louiset (F, Honda,) Frederic Petit (F, Aprilia,) Gino Borsoi (I, Aprilia,) Mirko Giansanti (I, Aprilia) and Randy De Puniet (F, Aprilia.)
250 cc: Tomomi Manako (J, Yamaha) and Tohru Ukawa (J, Honda.)
500 cc: Haruchika Aoki (J, TSR-Honda,) Markus Ober (D, Honda) and Massimiliano Biaggi (I, Yamaha.)

Saturday 22nd May 1999

125 cc: Gino Borsoi (I, Italy, twice,) Jimmy Petit (F, Honda,) Bernhard Absmeier (D, Aprilia) and Randy De Puniet (F, Aprilia.)
250 cc: Luca Boscoscuro (I, TSR-Honda,) Franco Battaini (I, Aprilia,) Thomas Metro (F, Honda,) Jeremy McWilliams (GB, Aprilia,) Vincent Philippe (F, Honda) and Tomomi Manako (J, Yamaha.)
500 cc: Jean-Michel Bayle (F, Modenas,) Markus Ober (D, Honda,) Jose Luis Cardoso (E, TSR-Honda,) Yukio Kagayama (J, Suzuki) and Carlos Checa (E, Yamaha.)

Sunday 23rd May 1999

125 cc: Youichi Ui (J, Derbi,) Ivan Goi (I, Honda,) Manuel Poggiali (RSM, Aprilia,) Luca Cecchinello (I, Honda,) Massimiliano Sabbatani (I, Honda,) Reinhard Stolz (D, Honda) ans Alessandro Brannetti (I, Aprilia.)
250 cc: Johan Stigefelt (S, Yamaha,) Herve Mora (F, Aprilia,) Jarno Janssen (NL, TSR-Honda,) Loris Capirossi (I, Honda,) Julien Allemand (F, TSR-Honda) and Jeremy McWilliams (GB, Aprilia, restart.)
500 cc: Massimiliano Biaggi (I, Yamaha, twice = warm-up and race,) Regis Laconi (F, Yamaha,) Mike Hale (USA, Modenas,) Jose Luis Cardoso (E, TSR- Honda,) Markus Ober (D, Honda, restart,) Michael Rutter (GB, Honda) and Kenny Roberts (USA, Suzuki.)

Ouch...

1. Haruchika Aoki (bruising to buttocks and left fore-arm.)
2. Markus Ober (fracture to little finger of right hand , cut to left wrist.)
3. Gino Borsoi (abrasions to both hands during fall on Saturday morning, bruising to right hand during the afternoon's fall.)
4. Jean-Michel (bruised abdomen.)
5. Jimmy Petit (fractured tip of fourth toe left foot.)
6. Yukio Kagayama (severe bruising to left side of chest, two broken ribs.)
7. Mike Hale (fractured fifth metacarpal in left hand.)
8. Youichi Ui (fractured left clavicle.)
9. Manuel Poggiali (bruised left shoulder.)
10. Johan Stigefelt (bruising to left foot.)
11. Herve Mora (concussion.)
12. Loris Capirossi (slight concussion.)
13. Massimiliano Biaggi (dislocated fourth and fifth fingers of left hand, injured fifth finger of right hand.)

Non starters...

1. Maurice Bolwerk (result of fall in warm-up for Malaysian GP. Replaced by Rob Filart.)
2. Olivier Jacque (result of fall in practise for Spanish GP. The Frenchman underwent a successful operation in Paris under the care of Professor Saillant. He was present at the Castellet circuit to support his replacement Toshihiko Honma, the development rider of the YZR250.)
3. Michael Doohan (result of fall in practise for Spanish GP. The five-times world champion underwent a successful operation in San Francisco. On the eve of practise for the French GP, he left hospital for an hotel where he stayed for a few days before returning to Europe. Officially, Doohan's return is scheduled for the Czech Republic GP. Not replaced.)
4. Nobuatsu Aoki (result of fall during Spanish GP. Replaced by his compatriot Yukio Kagayama.)
Yukio Kagayama (result of fall in practise. Kagayama was helicoptered to hospital on Marseille, for various checks.)
5. Mike Hale (result of fall during warm-up.)

Retirements...

125 cc: none!
250 cc: Roberto Rolfo (I, Aprilia, fuel supply,) David Garcia (E, Yamaha, electrical problems) and Valentino Rossi (I, Aprilia, chain came off 2 kilometres from the finish when he was comfortably in the lead.)
500 cc: Luca Cadalora (I, MuZ-Weber, broken fairing after a highside,) Jean-Michel Bayle (F, Modenas, ignition) and Jurgen Van Den Goorbergh (NL, MuZ-Weber, ignition.)

Loris Capirossi: sparks at Ricard.
▽

Capirossi: blind passion

▷ *Is this man dangerous?*

No, I just felt something touch the back of my seat and you can see the actual marks, which prove I was ahead of him.
Why did you not stop immediately after being show the black flag? (On lap 9)
Because I did not see it.
Nor did you see your team's pit board calling you into the pits? (On lap 10)
No. Right from the start of the race, I never saw my pit board. My team was set up right next to Tohru Ukawa's and my pit board was hidden by his.

"I know the rules."

The same on the following laps?
Lets not be silly here. I know the rules. I know the black flag means you are out of the race immediately. Under these circumstances, do you honestly believe I would have continued taking risks, knowing that I was out of the running? But on the main straight, we run nose to tail, almost touching, in order to get a tow, so it is impossible to see any pit signals.
Until lap 15?
That was different. An official, along with one of my mechanics was standing pretty much in the middle of the track. I finally saw the flag and I came into the pits as is stipulated in the regulations.

He is the reigning 250 cc world champion, but Aprilia kicked him out the door just weeks after he took the title. Loris Capirossi stands out like a sore thumb when compared with the other Italian riders of the day, who like to play on their star status. He was regarded as the black sheep of the 250 family after his "mugging" of Tetsuya Harada at the final corner of the 1998 Argentine GP. Then at Mugello, he became the outcast of the sport.

Sunday night, 6th June 1999, just after eight o'clock in the evening. Some people were impatiently stuck in traffic, while others were still in the paddock, waiting to hear the results of a meeting of the Stewards and the Race Director. Loris Capirossi came into the media centre at Mugello and was immediately surrounded by a host of inquisitive hacks. It was time for the defendant to be interrogated...
Loris Capirossi, did you see Marcellino Lucchi's motor cycle when you moved over to the left?

Lets go back to the start. What happened? Lucchi got a great start. I stuck to his back wheel and I got the impression he was slowing down, as though he had an engine problem. I went right to avoid him and to try and pass. Then I moved left to get back on the line again. Those who think it was deliberate know nothing about racing!

The accused had thus presented his defence. The accusation was clear for anyone to see, by watching the footage of the start of this 250 cc Italian GP. His victim had this to say: "Even though I am not the sort to bear a grudge, I don't think I will ever forget what happened. Loris was my friend," declared Marcellino Lucchi, the old man of grand prix racing who had so dreamed of winning. He had hoped to triumph and thus dedicate the win to his mate Marco Pantini.

The drama unfolds

What actually happened? On the right of the track, in pole position, the Aprilia factory test rider was attacked by Loris Capirossi. Starting from the second place on the grid, the world champion had moved to the right at the start, slipping between the verge and Lucchi's bike, before moving left again. The two men touched, Lucchi fell in the middle of the chasing pack. The Japanese rider Honma flew over the Aprilia, but by some miracle the rest of the field avoided the fallen rider. A major tragedy had been narrowly avoided.

But there were repercussions. While Valentino Rossi was out on his own, the race director decided to exclude Capirossi and he was shown the black flag. Capirossi ignored this instruction for six laps, before finally riding into his garage. It was the start of a long evening for everyone. The penalty was announced at 20h16. Loris Capirossi was banned for one race, for ignoring the black flag.

THE PENALTIES

The following penalties can be imposed by the Race Director to punish transgressions of the rules (article 3.3.1.3):
- a warning, a fine, a stop-go penalty, a time penalty, exclusion, removal of championship points, a suspension.

Following a penalty, the accused has the right of appeal to the Stewards Commission. If the commission confirms the Race Director's decision, no recourse is possible, apart from taking the matter to the Sport Arbitration Tribunal in Lausanne, Switzerland. If they find in favour of the accused, which did not happen in the case of Capirossi as the Stewards agreed with the Race Director, then he can make a claim to the International Disciplinary Court of the Federation.

◁

Luigi Brenni,
president of the Stewards
at Mugello.

The races

125 cc

It is hard to believe that it was five years already, yes five years since Roberto Locatelli took part in his first grand prix as a wild card rider. At Mugello, the young Italian who had spent most of his racing career to date in enduro racing, had secured pole position, by a whisker, beating all the regular world championship contenders. He did not really understand what he had done, but hired by Aprilia to race their 250, he was about to learn the harsh realities of this strange little world. Locatelli had to bite the bullet and back track to the 125 cc. He was often brilliant in practice, but tended to make too many mistakes in the races. But then, two weeks before this Italian GP, he celebrated his first win in France. It would prove to be a liberating experience. At Mugello, the scene of his debut, Locatelli did the double, winning the race from pole position. It was a very exciting race. With two laps to go, France's Arnaud Vincent was leading and he tried to make a break for it. On the next lap, he led the pack by 0.283s. Would he take his first grand prix win? Not yet, because Locatelli went for it on the final lap. Vincent had a very scary moment at the last corner and it all got too close for comfort on the line. Locatelli won from Melandri and Ueda.

△
Massimiliano Biaggi with Luca Cadalora: a heroic race.

▷
Manuel "Sete" Gibernau: two more cylinders.

250 cc

Marcellino Lucchi, who had won here last year, dominated qualifying and he dedicated his pole position to his mate Marco Pantini, who had been excluded from the Giro d'Italia cycle race, just 36 hours from the finish. Right from the start, this was an action packed race. Capirossi moved over to the right, slipping through between the wall and Lucchi's bike, but as he moved back, the two machines touched with the Aprilia hitting the deck. Marcellino went flying, Honma goes flying, having used the Aprilia as an unwilling launch ramp. It was a miracle that the rest of the pack somehow avoided Lucchi lying in the track, thankfully with nothing more serious than a broken toe on his right foot. Out in front, McWilliams was in charge, ahead of Capirossi and Ukawa. Rossi rapidly closed on the group and took the lead for the first time on lap four. With seven of the 21 laps completed, Rossi stepped up the pace and began to break away, while the start-line incident reared its head. On lap 9 Capirossi was shown the black flag by the Race Director who wanted him in for dangerous riding. Next time round, the world champion's team showed him the "Box" sign on his pit board, but Loris chose to ignore it, finally pitting on lap 16. Not surprisingly, he was up before the Stewards. Meanwhile, back on the track, Rossi seemed to have the race in the bag, but his lap of honour was less than straightforward as his fans invaded the track. Rossi even hit the deck when he hit a Dorna cameraman! Waldmann was second, ahead of Ukawa. The day was far from over: Franco Battaini was fined for brandishing a giant inflatable penis, draped in the Italian flag, during his lap of honour. Tohru Ukawa and Julien Allemand were cleared of overtaking under a waved yellow flag. All these incidents paled into insignificance as everyone waited to hear what would happen to Capirossi after he ignored the black flag. At exactly seven minutes past eight in the evening the verdict finally arrived. The world champion was suspended for one race, the Catalunya GP!

500 cc

Right from the start of practice, a wind of change was blowing through the Tuscan hills. Tetsuya Harada planted the two cylinder Aprilia on pole, setting an outright Mugello circuit lap record for two wheeled vehicles on the way. If proof was needed that the field was levelling out, there were no less than five different marques in the top six on the grid and, just as he did a fortnight earlier in France, Cadalora qualified sixth on the MuZ-Weber. At the start, Biaggi charged through from the mid-grid to take the lead. Abe did not even complete the first lap and Barros fell on lap two. Meanwhile, Harada made a bad start, then his engine started cutting out with an electrical problem in the early laps, before he set out on a thrilling climb through the field. On lap five, championship leader, Alex Criville moved into the lead and formed a breakaway group with Biaggi and Okada. Kenny Roberts gradually dropped back. "Once I lost the tow from the leaders, I could not keep up the same pace." Harada was going quicker and quicker and he passed Gibernau, having his first race with the V4, as well as Laconi and Roberts. Laconi fell five laps from the flag. Criville made a small mistake on lap 19 and Biaggi nipped into the lead, forgetting the pain from his injuries, but Criville got him back to record his third successive win.

Franco Battaini
on his lap of honour:
he was fined
1000 Swiss francs.

... Loris Capirossi's ban. Until now the rule had never been brought into force before. However, the Race Director and Stewards of the Meeting were entitled to ban a rider from one or more races and this time the sanction was applied. Capirossi was to miss the next round for failing to come in when shown the black flag.

... pain and suffering for Max Biaggi. Max was the big hero of the Italian GP in an unfolding drama of heroic proportions. After falling in the French GP, Biaggi had needed an operation in the hospital in Marseille to insert a steel pin to strengthen the articulation in the little finger of his left hand. A few days before the Italian GP, his hand swelled up dramatically and the good Doctor Costa decided to remove the pin on Friday morning before free practice. This was done without the use of anaesthetic. Biaggi fell again on Saturday morning and had to settle for 13th spot on the start grid. He rode a superb race. But afterwards, the pain was so intense that he passed out and had to be helped onto the podium by his team, in order to be cheered by the tifosi.

... Marcellino Lucchi's terrible weekend. Lucchi, who is a big mate of the cyclist Marco Pantani went through a whole range of emotions at Mugello. He had hoped for a double celebration with his mate, who was riding in the Giro d'Italia. But on the Saturday night, he heard that Pantani had been disqualified after a drugs test and he himself went on to be eliminated from his own race within metres of the start.

... Franco Battaini's lap of honour. Battaini had to stump up for a big fine after he rode the slowing down lap brandishing the Italian flag draped over a huge inflatable penis!

... the return of the Paton. It has become something of an Italian tradition that the home-built Paton 500 put in an appearance in Tuscany. It performed well in practice. It was definitely better than that of the New-Zealand BSL, admitted to the grands prix this year, while Giusseppe Patoni, who has done so much for the sport had his request to participate turned down. However, in the race, it did not complete a single lap as Tessari fell off the Italian machine.

... the super cool look of Rossi's Aprilia. "Valentinik peace and love." Valentino Rossi went for way out artwork for the Italian GP, turning up with his Aprilia painted in psychedelic colours. "I like the Seventies and I seem to remember that my dad won a few races back then."

"Valentinik peace and love"
when Rossi proved hippies
are still cool.

WWW.MAXBIAGGI.COM

Roberto Rolfo: why me?

Friday 4ᵗʰ June 1999

125 cc: Gianluigi Scalvini (I, Aprilia.)
250 cc: Valentino Rossi (I, Aprilia) and Alfonso Gonzales-Nieto (E, Yamaha.)

Saturday 5ᵗʰ June 1999

125 cc: none.
250 cc: David Garcia (E, Yamaha,) Sebastian Porto (ARG, Yamaha,) Shinya Nakano (J, Yamaha,) Tohru Ukawa (J, Honda) and Toshihiko Honma (J, Yamaha.)
500 cc: Massimiliano Biaggi (I, Yamaha.)

Sunday 6ᵗʰ June 1999

125 cc: Riccardo Chiarello (I, Aprilia) and Reinhard Stolz (D, Honda.)
250 cc: Marcellino Lucchi (I, Aprilia,) Toshihiko Honma (J, Yamaha,) Ivan Mengozzi (I, Yamaha,) Rob Filart (NL, Honda,) Ivan Clementi (I, Aprilia,) Jarno Janssen (NL, TSR-Honda) and Roberto Rolfo (I, Aprilia.)
500 cc: Paolo Tessari (I, Paton,) Norifumi Abe (J, Yamaha,) Alexandre Barros(BR, Honda) and Regis Laconi (F, Yamaha.)

Ouch!...

1. Toshihiko Honma (bruised right ankle, probable fracture to big toe left foot and slight concussion.)
2. Marcellino Lucchi (bruising to right elbow and shoulder, fracture to a metatarsal bone in right foot.)
3. Ivan Mengozzi (bruising to left hand.)
4. Rob Filart (dislocated left knee.)
5. Jarno Janssen (injury to right hand, open wound to right knee.)

Non starters...

1. Youichi Ui (result of fall in French GP. The Japanese rider decided against having an operation. Not replaced.)
2. Maurice Bolwerk (result of fall in warm-up for Malaysian GP. Replaced by Rob Filart.)
3. Olivier Jacque (result of fall in practise for Spanish GP. Replaced by Toshihiko Honma.)
4. Lucas Oliver (the Spaniard, who was back in the saddle after falling in the Japanese GP - he broke his left ankle - had an operation the day after the French GP. Replaced by Filippo Cotti.)
5. Michael Doohan (result of fall in practise for Spanish GP. The five-times world champion remains in the USA. Not replaced.)

6. Nobuatsu Aoki (result of fall in Spanish GP. Not replaced as Yukio Kagayama was in turn injured during practise for the French GP.)
7. Mike Hale (officially because of his fall in French GP , even though we would not be seeing the American back on the Modenas. Replaced by Jamie Whitham.)

Retirements...

125 cc: Gianluigi Scalvini (I, Aprilia, sparkplug.)
250 cc: Anthony West (AUS, TSR-Honda, clutch.)
500 cc: Jose Luis Cardoso (E, TSR-Honda, piston,) Michael Rutter (GB, Honda, broken left foot-rest,) Jurgen Van Den Goorbergh (NL, MuZ-Weber, piston) Jean-Michel Bayle (F, Modenas, ignition.)

◁
*Biaggi:
the wounded stag...*

MuZ-Weber: the sensation!

▷ *Champagne for Jurgen Van Den Goorbergh and a first pole for the MuZ-Weber.*

Two weeks after the Aprilia V2 secured pole position at Mugello, it was time for another sensation. Dutchman Jurgen Van Den Goorbergh put his MuZ-Weber on the prime spot on the grid. It was a magnificent reward for a project begun five years earlier.

7th March 1994. The Swiss daily paper "Le Matin" visited the Wenko (Swissauto) factory. The following is part of what appeared in the paper under the headline: "A Swiss 500 in GP Racing?"
"A brand new complete side-car outfit, with engine, sells for less than 100,000 Swiss francs. When I learned that ROC and Harris sold their 500s for around 300,000 mainly because of the 150,000 charged by Yamaha for the engines, I realised there was a potential market here." Urs Wenger is not your typical mad professor type. Even though he might spend whole nights leaning on his drawing board, the young Swiss designer also knows how to make the figures add up. "Since 1991, we have been maintaining the engines for Rolf Biland's outfits. This engine, an in-line four, is completely out-dated now and the world champion asked me to build something

totally new. As the development and construction of a completely new engine would require a lot of time and money, I made Biland understand that it was a pipe-dream to think of making something just for the very limited side-car market. We had to envisage its use in a solo frame as well. Just like the Cosworth F1 engine, I wanted to see it made available to constructors who would provide their own frame."

The role of Michel Metraux

In Burgdorf near Berne, development and testing got underway, Michel Metraux, president of the International Racing Team Association (IRTA) can claim a hand in Switzerland's greatest racing moments of recent times, and he could ignore this challenge. He had played a part in the "Parisienne 250" project and he would become involved in 1994.
The adventure begun, there would be all sorts of heartache, joy and disappointment. This is how it evolved, up to the moment of what was surely its greatest triumph - that Catalunya GP pole position.

- **July 1994:** first test session at Magny Cours, fitted to Biland's side-car. The crankshaft gave up the ghost after seven laps.
- **2nd October 1994:** first race and first victory! The Swissauto engine was fitted to the Rolf Biland/Kurt Waltispurg side-car at the little Swiss track at Lignieres.
- **9th October 1994:** first grand prix for the Swissauto engine at the Catalunya circuit. Biland secured pole position but had to retire six laps into the race with a broken ignition.
- **20th May 1995:** five side-car teams took part in the German GP, using the Swissauto engine. All five were forced to retire. After this catastrophe, Michel Metraux signed an exclusive deal with Urs Wenger.
- **10th June 1995:** The Swiss brothers, Paul and Charly Gudel take the Swissauto engine to its first GP win at Mugello.
- **25th June 1995:** The final piece of the jigsaw slots into place at Assen. Under the code name, "Projekt Elf" the Swiss 500 is soon to be born. Serge Rosset, the ROC frame builder enters the equation.

Catalan christening

- **6th October 1995:** Official presentation of the Elf-Swissauto at the Catalunya circuit.
- **7th October 1995:** Switzerland's Adrian Bosshard does a few laps on the Elf 500 during practice.
- **31st March 1996:** First GP for the Elf 500s in Malaysia. Spain's Juan Bautista Borja finishes tenth.
- **3rd August 1997:** best result for the Elf, thanks to Germany's Jurgen Fuchs' sixth place at the Rio GP.
- **1998:** The Malaysian company, Hong Leong, which has bought the German MZ company to create MuZ, makes its grand prix debut. Exit the Elf 500, long live the Muz-Swissauto. Doriano Romboni finishes 12th in the Japanese GP, before being injured in practice for the Malaysian GP. The team's development rider, Switzerland's Eskil Suter replaces him on several occasions, although sometimes the task falls to France's Jean-Philippe Ruggia (Assen) and Italy's Luca Cadalora (Buenos Aires.)
- **19th September 1998:** having retired from competition for over a year, Rolf Biland becomes the boss of the Muz-Swissauto team. Collaboration with Serge Rosset comes to an end and Eskil Suter is put in charge of designing a frame which is to be built in England.
- **Spring 1999:** MuZ-Swissauto becomes MuZ-Weber, taking its name from a new partner, a German company which makes engine blocks for the motor industry.
- **19th June 1999:** Switzerland (Sion 2006) will not host the Winter Olympics, but its technology triumphs thanks to Jurgen Van Den Goorbergh's pole position at the Catalunya GP.

◁
Michael Doohan's chief engineer Jerry Burgess came to congratulate Eskil Suter: the Swiss had succeeded.

The races

"Crivillemania"

125 cc

While Frenchman Arnaud Vincent dominated the first day of practice, it was Roberto Locatelli who ended up on pole. At the start, Marco Melandri and Lucio Cecchinello were quickest out of the blocks. Sabbatini was the first notable retirement when he fell, followed shortly by championship leader, Masao Azuma, whose radiator broke on lap ten. At this point in the race, Vincent was in charge and rather surprised to find himself in the lead: "It's strange, because there were many other times this season when I felt more at ease on the bike and when I felt I was riding better, but there I was." Once again the 125 race saw a very close fight with no less than seven riders, Vincent, Alzamora, Cecchinello, Locatelli, Ueda, Melandri and world champion Kazuto Sakata, all covered by a handkerchief. The race would therefore go down to the wire. On the penultimate lap, Vincent led Alzamora by just a few metres, but the fiery Spaniard closed down the Frenchman and passed him. However, Vincent used all the experience and guile of an old hand, which he is not, to claim it back. "I knew I was very quick under acceleration coming out of the last corner," he explained. "Then I saw that Emilio had come up the inside and I knew it was in the bag for me." Alzamora knocked Masao Azuma off the championship leader's perch by a solitary point.

250 cc

Loris Capirossi was absent and the two Japanese Yamaha riders, Shinya Nakano and Naoki Matsudo had to take all sorts of risks, falling twice in practice, to stay in touch with the fastest man Tohru Ukawa. Valentino Rossi finished up just one thousandth of a second off the pole position time! Ralf Waldmann never got past the first corner. The German had fluffed his start and was trying to make up for it under braking. He ended up taking West and a few local riders, while Ukawa took the lead from Rossi. The shape of the race had already been drawn up, with Ukawa and Rossi out in front. Lucchi and Battaini made up a second pair, soon to be joined by Nakano, who made up for lack of power with riding skills. At the start of lap ten, Rossi passed Ukawa at the end of the straight and tried to break away, pulling out a 1.105s lead, but Ukawa and Lucchi fought back. On lap 17 of 23, the veteran Italian could not avoid a swift trip through the gravel and came back to his pit in a terrible rage, kicking everything in sight! Nakano and Battaini were fighting it out for third place, while out in front, Rossi had the final word in his battle with Ukawa, who thus dropped back by a further five points to his championship rival. It was Franco Battaini's first podium. He made sure he hung onto the flag handed to him by his supporters and after the ceremony, it seemed that his first taste of podium champagne had robbed him of the power of speech. Rossi was trapped by his fans and was having a struggle with a wasp, which had got into his helmet through the ventilation system during the race.

500 cc

The sensation of practice was the pole winning performance of Dutchman Jurgen Van Den Goorbergh. He had a near perfect lap on the backstreet special MuZ- Weber. He was warned he would be in for a hot race, both literally and metaphorically. With his left hand healing nicely, Biaggi made the best start from Abe, Barros, Criville and Van Den Goorbergh in fifth at the end of the first lap. Just as in France, Max tried to make a break for it, but he never managed to lead by more than 1.112s on lap three. By lap eight the Italian Yamaha rider, had been caught by the two HRC-mounted Spaniards, with the boss Alex Criville leading his young friend Manuel Gibernau - a fine performance in only his second race on Doohan's V4. The pace was too much for the chasing pack as they tried to reel in the two works Hondas, which had also been joined by Okada. Alexandre Barros and Massimiliano Biaggi (lap 12,) Morifume Abe and then Regis Laconi (four laps from the flag) were all fallers. Staying upright, Japan's Tadayuki Okada took the lead with a 0.779s advantage over Criville on lap 16, extending it, thanks to a late charge to 1.070s with two laps remaining. Gibernau had to ease up a bit because his rear tyre was giving up. Alex Criville fought back and passed his Japanese team mate, so the atmosphere was tense to say the least. Testuya Harada brought the Aprilia V2 home fourth, leading the chasing pack, which included the revelation of practice, Jurgen Van Den Goorbergh.

Arnaud Vincent ahead of Ueda and Locatelli. A first win for the Frenchman.

◁
"Bring the 500 title back to Spain," says King Juan Carlos to Alex Criville.

... the Swissauto engine's first 500 cc pole position. Thanks to the Swissauto V4, Jurgen Van Den Goorbergh became the sixth man to secure a pole position this season. Five different marques had the honour of starting from the best place on the grid; Honda twice, Yamaha, Suzuki, Aprilia and MuZ-Weber once each.

... the first win for Arnaud Vincent. This was yet another first, after Kenny Roberts in the 500 class, Shinya Nakano and Tohru Ukawa in the 250s and Roberto Locatelli in the 125 class, it was France's Arnaud Vincent who joined the ranks of GP winners, taking top honours on his works Aprilia.

... the royal GP birthday. Fifty years to the day after the first ever GP in the history of the world championship (the Isle of Man Tourist trophy for 250, 350 and 500 cc machines,) a delegation led by FIM president Francesco Zerbi was met by King Juan Carlos of Spain at his Zarzuela palace in Madrid. Also present were Angel Nieto, Alex Criville, Kenny Roberts Junior, Carlos Checa, Masao Azuma and Tohru Ukawa.

... the first divorce of the season. Red Bull Yamaha WCM and Simon Crafar went their separate ways, by common consent. The New-Zealand rider and the team run by his fellow countryman Peter Clifford decided to end their collaboration, as Crafar never got on with the Yamaha, fitted with Michelin tyres.

... the absence of Loris Capirossi. The 250 cc world champion put himself in the history books as the first rider to be given a one race ban, after he ignored the black flag in the Italian GP. Suspended for Catalunya, Capirossi made the most of the break to get on with some work, testing at Misano. He also tried to rescue his tarnished image by visiting a Kosovo refugee camp, with the Italian arm of Amnesty International.
... the track invasion and its consequences. As happened in Italy two weeks earlier, the circuit security was powerless to prevent the spectators invading the track at the end of the races. As a result, the Mugello and Catalunya circuits, whose homologation expires at the end of the year, will have to present new plans to ensure this does not happen again in the future. From now on, a circuit's homologation license could even be suspended by the International Federation in the event of a track invasion.

... the coy dad. On Thursday before the Catalunya GP, Ralf Waldman became the proud father of little Leo. Even the German's nearest and dearest were unaware that "Waldi's" girlfriend, Astrid Grunfelder, was expecting a happy event!

The authorities penalised the organisers over the track invasion after Criville's win.
▽

△

Max Biaggi:
the harder they come....

Friday 18th June 1999

125 cc: Simone Sanna (I, Honda,) Antonio Elias (E, Honda) and Frederic Petit (F, Aprilia.)
250 cc: Jeremy McWilliams (GB, Aprilia,) Masaki Tokudome (J, TSR-Honda) and Jarno Janssen (NL, TSR-Honda.)
500 cc: Juan Bautista Borja (E, Honda.)

Saturday 19th June 1999

125 cc: none.
250 cc: Naoki Matsudo (J, Yamaha, twice,) Jason Vincent (GB, Honda,) Jarno Janssen (NL, TSR-Honda,) Shinya Nakano (J, Yamaha) and David Garcia (E, Yamaha.)
500 cc: Tadayuki Okada (J, Honda,) Jean-Michel Bayle (F, Modenas) and Juan Bautista Borja (E, Honda.)

Sunday 20th June 1999

125 cc: Massimiliano Sabbatani (I, Honda,) Victor Carrasco (E, Honda,) Angel Nieto Junior (E, Honda,) Steve Jenkner (D, Aprilia) and Pablo Nieto (E, Derbi.)
250 cc: Anthony West (AUS, TSR-Honda,) Ralf Waldmann (D, Aprilia,) Alfonso Gonzales-Nieto (E, Yamaha,) Ivan Silva (E, Honda,) Johan Stigefelt (S, Yamaha,) David Garcia (E, Yamaha) and Marcellino Lucchi (I, Aprilia.)
500 cc: Manuel Gibernau (E, Honda V4, warm-up,) Alexandre Barros (BR, Honda V4) Massimiliano Biaggi (I, Yamaha,) Norifumi Abe (J, Yamaha,) Regis Laconi (F, Yamaha) and Jean-Michel Bayle (F, Modenas.)

Ouch!...

1. Antonio Elias (bruised right foot.)
2. Jean-Michel Bayle (bruising to right hand during practise, bruising to right shoulder during race.)
3. Naoki Matsudo (concussion, injury to cervical spinal column.)
4. Massimiliano Sabbatani (small fracture to pubic bone, bruising to right testicle.)
5. Steve Jenkner (fractured scaphoid, left hand.)

Non starters...

1. Loris Capirossi (suspended for one race for failing to comply with a black flag during the Italian GP. Not replaced.)
2. Olivier Jacque (result of fall in practise for the Spanish GP. The Frenchman came out of plaster on the Thursday before the Catalunya GP. The fracture hadn't healed so a new resin cast was fitted. The return of OJ was thus delayed to the German GP. Replaced by Naoki Matsudo.)
3. Maurice Bolwerk (result of fall in warm-up for the Malaysian GP. Not replaced.
4. Michael Doohan (result of fall in practise for the Spanish GP. Doohan came back from the States on the Thursday before the race. From his Monaco apartment he admitted that, unlike in 1992, he would not be rushing his recovery.)
5. Simon Crafar (the New Zealand rider and the Red Bull Yamaha team mutually agreed to end their collaboration. Not replaced.)
6. Mike Hale (officially, the result of a fall in the French GP. Not replaced.)
7. Mark Willis (the BSL team was still incapable of building a competitive bike and withdrew from the Catalunya GP. Willis was in the paddock looking for a better ride.)

Retirements...

125 cc: Youichi Ui (E, Derbi, crankshaft,) Jeronimo Vidal (E, Aprilia, electrical problems,) Masao Azuma (J, Honda, radiator,) Manuel Poggiali (RSM, Aprilia, rear tyre puncture) and Bernhard Absmeier (D, Aprilia, piston.)
250 cc: Julien Allemand (F, TSR-Honda, went off the track on the first lap) and Jason Vincent (GB, Honda, electric gear selection problem.)
500 cc: Luca Cadalora (I, MuZ-Weber, bad tyre choice,) Jamie Whitham (GB, Modenas, clutch) and Michael Rutter (GB, Honda, lack of power.)

Frederic Petit: a big gap.
▽

7. Assen

Criville: the curse continues

▷
Alex Criville, the calm leader of the championship on the eve of the Dutch GP.

Michael Doohan in 1992, Darryl Beattie in 1995, Alex Criville in 1997 and Alex Criville once again this 26th June 1999. The Assen circuit is a historic date on the calendar. It is also a track in urgent need of renovation. And every year it stages one of the key events in the world championship. It is a grand prix that even the greats face with some trepidation as they hope to avoid the curse of the Dutch TT!

Friday evening, the night before the race in the Assen paddock. Having set the fastest time in the first practice session on Thursday, the clear leader of the 500 class championship, Alex Criville had slid down the order to fourth place on the grid. Nevertheless, the Spaniard was as calm as he had been all season long. "We tried some new things today and they did not work. We have nothing to worry about for the race. We have a good base from the settings we ran on Thursday," claimed Criville.

"A logical progression"

Criville was unusually calm as on the eve of an important moment in the year, just prior to the middle of the season. He was a different man ever since the vagaries of racing, in the shape of Michael Doohan's injuries, had promoted him to Number One rider for HRC. He was effectively the boss of the 500 class in the world championship. It did not seem to provoke much change in the man himself. It was just another step for this likeable lad who is always discrete and modest. "Let's say, its just the continuation of a development: the fact I won at Jerez and then in France gave me confidence. Maybe I have changed this year, but I don't think so. We certainly cannot talk about a complete transformation. The explanation is the most common one in competition and it is more down to earth and straightforward as it is a technical one. The 1999 NSR is different to last year's and I find it easier to ride as the power comes in more progressively. It is the bike Doohan was already using last year. We would have liked to have had it, but it wasn't possible. That was mainly because, in 1998, the switch to lead-free fuel had created a few reliability problems and HRC was worried that they would not be able to keep up with the demand for spare parts."

Alex's superstition

Alex Criville is calm, relaxed and determined, even after something has been mentioned which makes him clam up. Someone has mentioned superstition and his immediate future: "I am a believer and that is why I cross myself every time I take to the track. I am also superstitious. There was a time when I always wore the same body suit under my leathers, but I had to pluck up the courage to get rid of it. The future, the title? I don't want to plan anything and we can talk about it later. For now, I want to concentrate on tomorrow's race, then the next one in one week's time at Donington. Racing is like that. The unexpected happens very often."

That was Friday, the day before the race; a race Alex Criville would not finish. On lap four, when he had just come up behind the back wheel of John Kocinski's blue machine, with Okada and Roberts up at the front, the championship leader suffered a high speed fall. The inflatable barriers bounced up, Criville's body was smothered in them before coming to an abrupt halt against a barrier made of old tyres. The Spaniard cried out with the pain and the marshals rushed to his aid as the race carried on.

Reassurance from the doctor

An hour later and the Spaniards in the grand prix camp are in a state of shock. Doctor Claudio Costa came up to the media centre at the "Van Drenthe" circuit to give his preliminary diagnosis. "Alex Criville has displaced the head of the left femur. There are no fractures, but we have found serious damage to the ligaments, to the capsule and the muscles. At the moment, he is planning on being back in time for Donington. If he wants to meet that deadline, he must start physio immediately. As I am not a great mathematician, I will not talk about the percentages of the chances I will give Criville of being there in a week's time. What I will say, is that at the scene of the accident, everyone was very worried, in as much as, for over a minute, his left thigh ended up in a non-functional position. (Criville had been trapped under a pile of tyres.) But at this time, he is already a lot better," said the doctor. In race control everyone breathed a big sigh of relief. Criville was alive and everyone was looking forward to seeing a new and much safer Assen in the third millennium. "The race promoters have listened to our comments and they are planning to increase the size of the run-off areas," explained race director, Roberto Nosetto. The new Assen? We will not have long to wait.

The Assen track proved to be a grassy trap which closed on Alex Criville.

The races

125 cc

There are those who like Assen, like Marco Melandri, Masao Azuma and Noburo Ueda. There are those who discover it for the first time and are not overawed by it, like the surprising Frenchman Randy De Puniet. Then there are those who are happy to leave Holland, having made the best of a bad job. A winner a week earlier in Catalunya, Arnaud Vincent fitted into the latter category. Italy's Lucio Cecchinello took pole, while last year's winner Melandri had a big crash, braking three toes and the race had plenty of excitement in store. Right from lap three, Cecchinello, Azuma and Ueda tried to break away with a 1.613s lead. Roberto Locatelli joined them one lap later and the four men fought it out to the bitter end. Lucio Cecchinello was the big loser. He tried to take the lead by going round the outside three laps from the flag, but he was squeezed hard by Roberto Locatelli. Cecchinello went grass cutting prior to eating dirt! This left three fighting for the lead. There were several changes of position at the front with Masao Azuma coming out on top, which also put him back in the lead of the championship, as Alzamora could do no better than fourth. The happy winner dedicated his latest triumph to the Dutch partners of the team run by the Belgian Olivier Liegeois, who had a very busy weekend. He had to make the run from the track back to his factory in Liege, Belgium, to pick up new crankshafts as Azuma is not officially backed by HRC and uses parts developed by European craftsmen!

Masao Azuma: just a bit pleased with himself!

△
Capirossi - Rossi: vengeance for the Number One.

250 cc

Loris Capirossi was back and he looked even more alone in the world than usual. After events at the Italian GP, even his team manager and former team mate, Fausto Gresini was critical of the category's Number One rider. Practice was dominated by Aprilia with Rossi ahead of McWilliams and Waldmann. The race would belong to the reigning world champion. Once again, Shinya Nakano made the best start, but Capirossi did not wait long before sailing past to lead at the end of the first lap. Once again, Waldmann had fluffed the start and was back in fourteenth spot. Lucchi retired with a broken engine and Waldmann began to fight back. At the front, six riders could not be separated: Capirossi, McWilliams, Rossi, Ukawa, Waldmann and Nakano were all covered by just 0.995s at half-distance. Waldmann was the first to drop back, while Loris Capirossi and Valentino Rossi fought it out at the front; the outcast and the Aprilia rider having an infernal struggle. Rossi's RSW did not seem as sharp as usual, while Capirossi was majestic on his way to his second win of the season. Ukawa was beaten to third place by McWilliams and so the gap between him and Rossi, disgusted with being beaten, increased to seven points. Shinya Nakano gave another riding lesson on his Yamaha, even if the YZR suffered a chronic power shortage as usual.

500 cc

It was the 26th June and Massimiliano Biaggi was celebrating his 28th birthday. Naturally, he was dreaming of his first win for Yamaha, all the more so as Wayne Rainey was in the pits, trying to help those he had wanted to convince that he should rejoin the marque with the three tuning forks for a logo. However, right from the start of practice, it was Honda who ruled the roost. Tadayuki Okada and John Kocinski were the only two riders to get under the 2m 02s barrier at Assen and the Japanese rider seemed so at ease that the race looked in the bag already. "Tady" led from the start and lorded it over the rest of the field, even if Kenny Roberts hung on until lap seven of the twenty lap race, on a Suzuki which was evidently performing better than at Mugello and Catalunya. Criville had a terrible fall on lap four and Checa also hit the dust. Biaggi was incapable of matching the leader's pace. Once again, it was Giberneau who provided a pleasant surprise as he and Alexandre Barros fought back. Okada had the race sewn up with Roberts safe in second from Giberneau, while Barros had disappeared all the way back to tenth, having fallen in a desperate last lap bid to make up a place. With Criville failing to score, Roberts moved up to within 35 points of the leader and Okada was 36 behind. In the Red Bull Yamaha camp, the little Australian Garry McCoy had inherited Simon Crafar's YZR. The MuZ-Weber team was crumbling, just one week after its great performance in Catalunya. Van Den Goorbergh had a bad fall on Thursday which literally pulverised the bike. Luca Cadalora had a mechanical failure and a fall in practice and he scratched after the warm-up. The champagne had been replaced by bitter lemon.

... Alex Criville's injuries. For the fourth time in seven years, the 500 class world championship leader ended the Dutch GP in Doctor Claudio Costa's mobile clinic. Suffering from a displaced left femur, Alex Criville now only had a 35 point lead over the pursuing pack.

... Michael Doohan's visit. Having left the United States one week earlier, the five times 500 world champion turned up in the Assen paddock, where once again he made it clear he had no intention of hurrying back. "During my career (since his 1992 accident) I have made comebacks too early. This time I will wait until I am sure I can give it 100 percent. Will I be back for Brno? Maybe, but I might leave it another two weeks and the Imola GP."

... Loris Capirossi's winning return. Having sat out his one race ban in Catalunya - "I watched the 125s and the 500s, but I could not bring myself to sit in front of the television for the 250s! -

the world champion Loris Capirossi came back in style to win by beating Valentino Rossi's Aprilia in a thrilling duel.

... The popularity of Assen and a foolhardy marshal. 151,600 spectators turned up over the four days. At least 1600 turned up on Wednesday to watch the classic bikes practice! The Dutch TT gad attracted 20,600 more spectators than the previous year. This great success did not prevent the race director from ticking off one of the track marshals. "During the second day of practice, Mr. Harm Dunnik, without informing the race director, took a decision prejudicial to the required safety measures as per the homologation documents." Just what had Mr. Dunnik done? He had quite simply decided to move several straw bales to build a personal protection barrier. The only problem with this was that the bales in question were removed from the exact spot where Marco Melandri crashed, breaking three bones in his right foot!

△
Michael Doohan visited his colleagues before yet another trip across the Atlantic.

... the "Van Drenthe" circuit of the future. The roof of the new grandstand was already in place, as was an ultra-modern building housing a restaurant and VIP areas. New grandstands and a new track layout are on the way. In September, after the world superbike and supersport meeting, work was scheduled to commence at Assen. The first stage is to replace the archaic pits with new ones and new media centre above them in time for 2000. The second phase involves increasing the size of the paddock, modifying the track layout and extending the main grandstand, in order to create a true "stadium" around the track. This should be completed by 2001 or 2002 at the latest.

◁
Giacomo Agostini: a legend can always draw a crowd!

Fallers

A broken MuZ: the provisional end to the love story between Luca Cadalora and the Swiss team.

Thursday 24ᵗʰ June 1999

125 cc: Noboru Ueda (J, Honda.)
250 cc: none
500 cc: Jurgen Van Den Goorbergh (NL, MuZ-Weber,) Alexandre Barros (BR, Honda,) Regis Laconi (F, Yamaha) and Mark Willis (AUS, Modenas.)

Friday 25ᵗʰ June 1999

125 cc: Angel Nieto Junior (E, Honda,) Roberto Locatelli (I, Aprilia) and Marco Melandri (I, Honda.)
250 cc: Naoki Matsudo (J, Yamaha, twice,) Matias Rios (ARG, Aprilia) and Stefano Perugini (I, Honda.)
500 cc; Markus Ober (D, Honda,) Luca Cadalora (I, MuZ-Weber) and Norifumi Abe (J, Yamaha.)

Saturday 26ᵗʰ June 1999

125 cc: Randy De Puniet (F, Aprilia,) Lucio Cecchinello (I, Honda) and Bernhard Absmeier Aprilia.)
250 cc: Matias Rios (ARG, Aprilia,) Roberto Rolfo (I, Aprilia) and Maurice Bolwerk (NL, TSR-Honda.)
500 cc: Alex Criville (E, Honda,) Carlos Checa (E, Yamaha,) Markus Ober (D, Honda) and Alexandre Barros (BR, Honda, restart.)

Ouch!..

1. Angel Nieto Junior (slight concussion, cut to cervical spine.)
2. Marco Melandri (fractures to 1ˢᵗ, 4ᵗʰ, and 5ᵗʰ metatarsals of right foot.)
3. Matias Rios (dislocation of 1ˢᵗ finger of right hand during Friday's fall.)
4. Naoki Matsudo (broken 5ᵗʰ metatarsal of right foot, dislocated left ankle.)
5. Stefano Perugini (slight injury to cervical spine.)
6. Lucio Cecchinello (bruising to right hand.)
7. Bernhard Absmeier (bruising ti back.)
8. Roberto Rolfo (concussion, fractured 4th metacarpal of right hand.)
9. Alex Criville (twisted head of left femur, with damage to the capsule, ligaments and muscles.)

◁
*Still no sign
of the BSL 3 cylinder.*

Retirements...

125 cc: Alessandro Brannetti (I, Aprilia, sparkplug) and Reinhard Stolz (D, Honda, the German stopped thinking his engine was about to seize but the engineers found nothing.)

250 cc: Marcellino Lucchi (I, Aprilia, engine.)

500 cc: Jamie Whitham (GB, Modenas, seized engine) and Michael Rutter (GB, Honda V2, seized engine.)

*The little Australian
Gary McCoy replaced
Simon Crafar.*
▽

Non starters...

1. Steve Jenkner (result of fall in Catalunya GP. Not replaced.)
2. Massimiliano Sabbatani (result of fall in Catalunya GP. Not replaced.)
3. Oliver Jacque (result of fall in practise for Spanish GP. OJ, who had delayed his return, was at Assen on crutches. Replaced by Naoki Matsudo.)
4. Michael Doohan (result of fall in practise for Spanish GP. The five-times world champion was a visitor at Assen. Not replaced.)
5. Simon Crafar (the Red Bull Yamaha team and the New Zealand rider jointly agreed to end their collaboration on the morning of the first practise at the Catalunya GP. Replaced by Australian Garry McCoy.)
6. Jean-Michel Bayle (result of fall on the last lap of the Catalunya GP (torn ligaments of right shoulder.) Replaced by Australian Mark Willis, out of work because of problems encountered by the BSL team.)
7. Mike Hale ("officially", result of fall in French GP. Replaced by Jamie Whitham.)
8. Angel Nieto Junior (result of fall in practise.)
9. Naoki Matsudo (result of fall in practise.)
10. Matias Rios (result of fall in warm-up.)
11. Luca Cadalora (the Italian did not take the start complaining of pain s in his ribs following his fall on Friday afternoon.)

Aprilia: gambling on a V-twin

8. Donington

▷
A V2 ahead of a V4, when Tetsuya Harada (31) passes Alexandre Barros.

By finishing third in the British GP in the unique setting of Donington Park, Japan's Tetsuya Harada and Aprilia proved the worth of a European bet in the 500 class. Namely to show that the manoeuvrability and light weight of a V2 could triumph over the power of the big V4s. On that first weekend in July, the "Apriliona" was back on the turf where it had been conceived.

In the end, the new creation came with 981 thousandths of a second of total happiness. Back home in front of the television, the Dutch engineer Jan Witteveen, who created the racing Aprilia, made sure he did not miss the demonstration put on by his favourite rider, Tetsuya Harada. Witteveen had stayed in Italy to work on the development programme and had to miss the party in England, when his creation came third, within a second of winning its first ever GP in the top category of the sport. It was a surprising reward for a project which took shape in the Dutch engineer's brain six years earlier, exactly here at Donington. "In August 1993, when Jean-Philippe Ruggia had won the British 250 GP on one of our bikes, I started to analyse some of the figures: his average speed (151.257 km/h) was very close to that of the 500 winner (Luca Cadalora at 153.620 km/h.) Over a single lap the best 250 time (1.34.888) was also very close to the quickest 500 time (Doohan in 1.34.289.) That was the day I came up with the idea of the Aprilia 500 V2. If we could preserve the characteristics of the 250, while increasing its capacity and therefore its power, in theory we could pull off

something special in the top category," recalled Jan Witteveen.

From theory to practice

The first drawings and the first steps from theory to practice came at the same time as the governing body introduced new weight limits for the various 500 cc engine configurations: minimum weight for 2 cylinder machines, 100 kilos; 115 kilos for 3 cylinder machines, which would not be seen until later, when first Modenas and then on a lesser scale BSL appeared this year and 130 kilos for the "traditional" V4 powered machinery.

On 8th May 1994, at Jerez de la Frontera, a track which suited the characteristics of the Italian's technical gamble, Loris Reggiani took the seven points which went with ninth place on the Aprilia V2's first outing. The racing world was stunned and this performance in Andalusia would have shock waves that would travel all the way to Japan and Honda rummaged around in the back of its cupboard to produce its own lightweight V2!

There then followed the difficult task of turning theory into practice. The big Aprilia, a 400 cc unit at first, gradually grew in size; first to 480 then its current

*Harada,
just a few metres away
from another exploit.*

500 incarnation. It broke very often, but that was the price to pay as the mechanical components were forced to deal with ever more power.

A sabbatical year

At the end of 1997, Aprilia announced it was retiring "provisionally" from the 500 world championship and everyone thought the bet was off. Everyone was proved wrong when Tetsuya Harada got back in the saddle in 1999. "At the start of the season, we still had a lot of problems," said Mathilde Tomagnini, the Italian company's press spokesperson. "During the Spanish GP weekend at Jerez, we broke down six times in three days! However, we never lost faith in our philosophy and now that the Aprilia is reliable, Harada is having a great time."

When Harada has a great time, everyone was forced to sit up and take notice. He took a historic pole position in the Italian GP at Mugello. He notched up the project's second podium in the French GP at Ricard, followed by this third place in the British GP, at less than a second behind the winner.

A stage completed

More was to come. The Donington performance was simply a stage completed in the Italian firm's V2 project. "Now we are working on improving acceleration coming out of the corners," explained Jan Witteveen. "And before the next GP in Germany, we hope to be carrying out a series of tests at Mugello. While these tests are not definite yet, Tetsuya Harada will certainly be running at Valencia on 27th and 28th July to prepare for the end of the 1999 season and to get ready for 2000," continued the Dutch engineer. Would these tests lead to the ultimate prize? Before the Dutch GP, Mick Doohan had predicted: "Even if, in theory, a V2 should not be able to beat a V4 in a straight fight over a grand prix distance, watch out for Harada at Donington and the Sachsenring!" In Britain it came very close. What would happen in Germany? Turn a few pages for the answer to that question.

*Marcellino Lucchi
and Harada:
two essential pawns in
Aprilia's sporting game.*

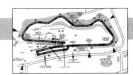

125 cc

While Gianluigi Scalvini notched up his first pole position on an Aprilia, qualifying was notable for a fantastic performance from Youichi Ui riding a Derbi in only its eighth grand prix. Nevertheless, the race, turned into a straight fight between the Honda riders. However, Ui and Roberto Locatelli were quickest off the line, but the Italian rider on the factory Aprilia was unable to make the break, leading by just 0.480s on the second lap. Two laps later, it was Noburu Ueda and then Masao Azuma who took control, with the flying Emilio Alzamora joining them at half distance (lap 13.) The top four could not be separated, but Lucio Cecchinello fell on lap 18 and the race would be decided two laps from the flag. Alzamoro tried a couple of crazy moves which panicked the leading trio. Azuma was in front at the right moment and managed to pull out a 1.361s lead and he rode faultlessly for the final two laps. In the championship, the Belgian team run by Olivier Liegeois now had a twenty point lead over Alzamora and a forty seven point advantage over Locatelli.

Criville comes back and wins! △

250 cc

Loris Capirossi likes Donington. Four times a winner here, including his maiden 125 world championship win in 1990, he did it again the following year, before going on to win twice in the 250 class. He easily dominated practice ahead of Ralf Waldmann. Shinya Nakano, the genial little Japanese rider with the Tech 3 team, had a heavy fall on Friday, but that did not stop him from powering into the lead at the first corner off the second row. Behind him came Tohru Ukawa and Valentino Rossi, as Waldmann had fluffed the start yet again and was way back in eighteenth spot at the end of the first lap! Rossi had a 0.507s lead over a Nakano, Jeremy McWilliams and Tohru Ukawa trio Bt Capirossi fought back and by lap six, Rossi, Nakano and Capirossi were all within 0.332s of one another. The world champion passed the Japanese rider on the next lap before charging up behind the leader. The two Italians fought it out until lap ten, when Rossi moved over and raised an arm to indicate it had just begun to rain and a few seconds later the race was red flagged. At first they announced a "wet" warm-up but that was cancelled as the track was no longer wet! So pretty much the same bunch lined up for another eighteen laps. Ukawa came off the second row so quickly, there were some who thought he deserved a stop-go penalty, but Rossi was in the lead right from the start. But Capirossi was in no mood to let him get away with it and fought back with the fastest lap of the day. He took the lead and the crowd was treated to a superb duel between the two Italians, the gap fluctuating between 137 and 349 thousandths. But from lap 23 to 27, Rossi put the hammer down with some perfect lappery and with the handicap of a tired rear tyre, Capirossi was beaten. Nakano was third, on the podium yet again. Rossi was now only three points behind Tohru Ukawa in the championship standings.

Take the same ingredients and start again: this time Valentino Rossi will have the final word.

▽

500 cc

Injured a week earlier at Assen, the world championship leader, Spain's Alex Criville was back in action. Right from the start of practice, his physical condition seemed incredibly good, even if complained of experiencing difficulty occasionally when he was cranked over. Qualifying was a landmark for the season, as it was the first time this season that a rider notched up a second pole position. That honour fell to Tadayuki Okada and the very on-form Japanese rider made the best start with Kenny Roberts (Suzuki) stuck to his back wheel once again. By lap 3, the two men had a 1.761s lead over the chasing pack, led by Max Biaggi, Regis Laconi and Alex Criville. They caught up to the front three laps later and a superb race was on the menu, with Criville taking the lead on lap 11 of 30. The Spaniard tried to force the pace along, Biaggi hung on, but not for long and then all eyes were on Tetsuya Harada and the V2 Aprilia, as he too joined the fray at the front. With seven laps remaining, Criville still led, with Harada 0.393s down and Okada at 0.652. Victory would go to one of these three. Laconi fell four laps from home having just passed Biaggi and it looked as though the Italian had taken out the worthy Frenchman. Any hope of a first win for the Aprilia V2 went out the window as Criville put the hammer down to lead by 0.730s on the final lap. The race was over and Harada was on the third step of the podium for the second time this season. Roberts was the big loser having made a poor tyre choice and Simon Crafar came home tenth on the MuZ-Weber.

... the birth of Alexia, daughter of Selina Sines and Michael Doohan. Six weeks ahead of schedule Mick Doohan became a father! The five times world champion's girlfriend Selina Sines gave birth on Thursday 1st July at 14h30 to a tiny Alexia, who weighed in at 1.7 kilos.

... the launch of the Michael Doohan biography. "The whole team has done a remarkable job as we did not have much time available." Mick Doohan's official biography, "Thunder From Down Under" written by the English journalist Mat Oxley was officially launched on the eve of the British GP. It has topped the Australian best-seller list, since it went on sale there in the Spring.

... Simon Crafar's move to MuZ-Weber. One week after Luca Cadalora's second act of treason this season, when the Italian walked out after just a few laps of the warm-up, the MuZ-Weber team turned up with a new line-up at Donington. The winner of the 1998 British GP, Simon Crafar was now Jurgen Van Den Goorbergh's new team-mate.

... the interruption of the 250 GP. In Italy, warring factions have been part of the scene for a while now. First we had Biaggi versus Aprilia and at this point in the season there was a clash between Capirossi and the Italian company. Now there would be much discussion about the interruption to the 250 race, instigated by Valentino Rossi, who raised his arm to signal a brief shower, just when Capirossi was closing in on him at a rate of knots. While Rossi naturally claimed he was worried about safety, some of Capirossi's clan were quick to point out that it was supposed to be the reigning world champion's prerogative to "inform" the race director of the changing conditions.

△
MuZ-Weber team manager, Rolf Biland employed last year's winner, Simon Crafar for one race.

... Alex Criville's great return to form. On the day of his Assen crash, he was moved to the Dexeus clinic in Barcelona. There he was treated by Professor Villarubias, who had already looked after him two years ago, when he seriously injured his hand. In England, the Spaniard held his own and more, winning on what was his 100th appearance in the 500 GP category.

... the "Riders For Health" auction. The traditional auction held on the "Day of Champions" raised a record amount for the "Riders For Health" charity, with 112,000 thousand dollars coming into the pot. The helmet that Kenny Roberts wore when he won in Malaysia and Japan fetched an astounding 11,800 dollars.

▷
Michael Doohan: a biography for the five times world champion.

△
*Frederic Petit:
a stylish display
without any physical
consequences.*

Friday 2ⁿᵈ July 1999

125 cc: Mirko Giansanti (I, Aprilia,) Manuel Poggiali (RSM, Aprilia) and Massimiliano Sabbatani (I, Honda.)
250 cc: Paul Jones (GB, Honda,) Franco Battaini (I, Aprilia,) Loris Capirossi (I, Honda,) Jarno Janssen (NL, TSR-Honda,) Shinya Nakano (J, Yamaha,) Sebastian Porto (ARG, Yamaha,) Stefano Perugini (I, Honda) and Alex Hofmann (D, TSR-Honda.)
500 cc: Juan Bautista Borja (E, Honda,) Regis Laconi (F, Yamaha,) Markus Ober (D, Honda,) Sebastien Gimbert (F, Honda,) Nobuatsu Aoki (J, Suzuki) and Jamie Whitham (GB, Modenas.)

Saturday 3ʳᵈ July 1999

125 cc: Alessandro Brannetti (I, Aprilia) and Jeronimo Vidal (E, Aprilia.)
250 cc: Ralf Waldmann (D, Aprilia) and Anthony West (AUS, TSR-Honda.)
500 cc: Garry McCoy (AUS, Yamaha) and Carlos Checa (E, Yamaha.)

Sunday 4ᵗʰ July 1999

125 cc: Manuel Poggiali (RSM, Aprilia,) Bernhard Absmeier (D, Aprilia,) Simone Sanna (I, Honda,) Randy De Puniet (F, Aprilia,) Andi Notman (GB, Honda,) Frederic Petit (F, Aprilia) and Lucio Cecchinello (I, Honda.)
250 cc: Lucas Oliver (E, Yamaha,) Paul Jones (GB, Honda,) Shane Norval (SA, Honda,) Sebastian Porto (ARG, Yamaha,) Jason Vincent (GB, Honda) and Maurice Bolwerk (NL, TSR-Honda.)
500 cc: Manuel Gibernau (E, Honda,) Carlos Checa (E, Yamaha,) Nobuatsu Aoki (J, Suzuki ,) Jamie Whitham (GB, Modenas,) Markus Ober (D, Honda,) Garry McCoy (AUS, Yamaha) and Regis Laconi (F, Yamaha.)

Ouch!..

1. Mirko Giansanti (neck injury.)
2. Sebastien Gimbert (bruising to right hand and right ankle.)
3. Nobuatsu Aoki (concussion.)
4. Shinya Nakano (broken left hand, dislocated right wrist, abrasions to right shoulder.)
5. Sebastian Porto (injuries to three fingers of right hand.)
6. Jeronimo Vidal (concussion.)
7. Manuel Gibernau (dislocated left shoulder.)
8. Simone Sanna (bruising to right foot.)
9. Paul Jones(slight concussion, bruising to left shoulder.)
10. Garry McCoy (fractured 5th metatarsal, right foot.)
11. Regis Laconi (severe bruising to left hip.)

Fallers

Non Starters...

1. Steve Jenkner (result of fall in Catalunya GP. The German took part in practise but withdrew from the race.)
2. Oliver Jacque (result of fall in practise for Spanish GP. Replaced by British rider Jamie Robinson.)
3. Roberto Rolfo (result of fall in Dutch GP. Not replaced.)
4. Michael Doohan (result of fall in practise for Spanish GP. Doohan arrived in the paddock at Donnington on Thursday evening , a few hours after he had attended the birth of his daughter, Alexis. Not replaced.)
5. Luca Cadalora (officially declared injured - a bruised rib after his fall in practise for the Dutch GP. Replaced by Simon Crafar.)
6. Jean-Michel Bayle (result of fall in Catalunya GP when he hurt his shoulder. Not replaced.)
7. Mike Hale (result of fall in French GP. Replaced by Jamie Whitham.)
8. Mark Willis (still no trace of the BSL but this time he did not pick up a ride on the second Modenas.)
9. Manuel Gibernau (result of fall in warm-up. Not replaced.)

Retirements...

125 cc: none.
250 cc: Matias Rios (ARG, Aprilia, sparkplug) and Franco Battaini (I, Aprilia, broken piston.)
500 cc: Jose Luis Cardoso (E, TSR-Honda, following surgery on his forearm the Spaniard suffered chronic tendonitis,) Jurgen Van Den Goorbergh (NL, MuZ-Weber, broken gear lever,) Sebastien Gimbert (F, Honda V2, gear-box) and Haruchika Aoki (J, TSR-Honda, rear brake.)

△
Andi Notman:
a flying wild card.

"Tino" becomes Rossi

Rossi and his shadow.

9. Sachsenring

It took nine races for **Valentino Rossi, the out and out favourite to take the 250 cc crown, to take the lead in the championship for the first time. At the Sachsenring, we saw the real Rossi shine through; playing with his bike the way he likes to play with life.**

Sunday 18th July. For the fifth time this season, Valentino Rossi was on the top step of a GP podium. It was a regular ritual, taking place just a few days from the summer break and it meant the Aprilia rider was leading the world championship at last.

On his head, complete with yet another hairdo, the green hair of Donington making way for a shaved head, was a straw hat bearing the legend: "Nazionale Esportazione senza filtro," national export without filter. "All the riders have a cap with a cigarette brand on it and I also wanted to be a real rider. Impressed with my win, a major sponsor has come on board. Its a new brand with a growing market."

The vital piece

Valentino Rossi laughed heartily. Having been merciless towards Loris Capirossi, he had just had a dig at another of his "enemies," Massimiliano Biaggi, who never goes anywhere, even for the Thursday night football match, without his red and white cap.

Victory and the lead in the championship,

Valentino Rossi was once again the vital piece in the big puzzle; the man who held in his hands the key to the transfer market for the 2000 season. At this point in the year, it was becoming increasing possible, week by week, that the prize ride, the best piece on the board, Michael Doohan's, might be up for grabs.

Valentino Rossi is the most sought after man in the paddock. Not only because he is he the hottest talent around, but also and above all because he has the ideal image which appeals to the greatest cross section of the very large following which the sport attracts. Amongst those who are transfixed by him is Michael Doohan himself, who could become the boss of a new Honda team, backed by Shell and Winfield cigarettes. "At the moment, I have not been approached. I have not seen a contract, had a proposition or discussed budgets. Doohan has never spoken to me about this project. Although I do know he has talked with my father Graziano, who is my personal manager."

Valentino Rossi: a well worn ritual precedes every visit to the track.

There'll be another train after this one

So will Valentino Rossi race for Honda in the 500 class? Or will he do another year in the 250 class with Aprilia? "Of course I am fascinated by the 500s. I also know that one day I am bound to make the move there. It is a given. But and it's a big but, I like the 250 class and I want to win the world championship. It would be too stupid for me to rush in now, and then in a few years time to regret my move and to tell myself that I should have been patient and waited another year before making the big jump. At the moment, there is a sixty percent chance I will stay with Aprilia in the 250 class, thirty percent that I switch to an existing Honda 500 team (Erv Kanemoto's) and ten percent says I join the team Doohan is planning to set up. There is a saying that one should jump on the right train when it comes along, but I reckon that if I continue running at the front, the train will always stop at Rossi station every year! At the end of 1996, some people reckoned I should have moved straight up to the 250 class. I stayed with the 125s, I won the title and I became popular. I am not 36 years old. I know that plenty of opportunities will present themselves in the future, as long as I am still competitive. If I stay in the 250 class and finish thirteenth in the championship next year then neither Aprilia nor Honda, nor even a superbike team or even a motocross outfit would want me for 2001. However, if I win…"

"I like fighting with Capirossi"

This was what Valentino Rossi had to say just before the summer break. On the track, the darling of the crowd had just won again after coming off best in yet another duel with Loris Capirossi. "I love facing up against Loris, because it's always a good fight. Today, he caught me out, coming round the outside on lap four and I got him back the same way. That's racing! Last year with Harada was a lot less fun. He is the kind of rider who follows you all race and then stuffs you by four seconds on the last lap. That was no fun, just like any race whose strategy is pre-planned around a table. Me, I live for racing and the action and for the moment. I adapt to situations. I look for a solution and when I find it, I win. When I lose at this little game I am furious with rage for a little while. But I quickly forget about it."

Marco Melandri gets a kiss for a win.

125 cc

From the moment he arrived at the Sachsenring, a circuit which reminded him of the minibike tracks of his youth, Marco Melandri dominated the opposition. Championship leader Masao Azuma could do no better than ninth place on the third row of the grid. Roberto Locatelli, Melandri and Emilio Alzamoro were quickest on the draw at the start, Melandri leading the field through at the end of the first lap, while Azuma was way back in eleventh spot. The young Italian went for the big break, leading by 1.488s on the second lap, but his main rivals were soon to fight back.

On lap seven of 29, four of them were thus covered by only 1.455s - Melandri, Alzamora, Lucio Cecchinello and Locatelli. Lap 21 saw Melandri back in the lead he had temporarily relinquished to Alzamora. The Playlife rider tried once again to pull away, but it was in vain as Alzamora put on a breathtaking display of late braking. On the final lap, Angel Nieto's prot`"g`" had got with in 182 thousandths of victory. Second wasn't bad for Alzamora as it brought him to with in ten points of Masao Azuma, who could do no better than sixth here in the German GP, in the championship.

250 cc

There were several fallers in practice, including Shinya Nakano. The little Team 3 hero suffered a major puncture wound in his right shoulder, losing a lot of blood and his participation in the race was in doubt right up to a few minutes before the start. The French team which runs the official Yamaha operation welcomed back Olivier Jacque. Although pole had Valentino Rossi's name on it, it was obvious from qualifying that despite a none too serious fall in practice, Loris Capirossi would be a force to be reckoned with. How true that would turn out to be! Rossi, Nakano and Battaini made the best starts, while Jacque fluffed his completely. Rossi took control, leading by 1.692s after one lap. On lap four, Capirossi fought back, passing his fellow countryman with a great move round the outside, while Jason Vincent and championship leader Tohru Ukawa were already out of the running. With Capirossi leading Rossi and Jeremy McWilliams falling, getting back on before retiring, the race would be played out in two sections. On the one hand we had a great fight between the two current kings of the category, Capirossi and Rossi and on the other, we witnessed Waldmann closing in on the wounded beast that was Shinya Nakano. The German in the heat of battle, tried to get past for the first time on lap 12 but he overdid it and came within centimetres of the gravel trap. At the front, the gap between the two leaders varied between 230 and 447 thousandths of a second.

Waldmann tried a second time and got by Nakano on lap 19. Third place was spoken for and Olivier Jacque was also having a great climb through the field which lasted half the race and he was also lapping quicker than anyone else. Now it was a case of which of the two leaders would emerge victorious. It would all be decided on the penultimate lap. Capirossi attacked Rossi, but the Aprilia rider counter attacked with the world champion riding the kerb. This was the decisive move and Rossi won again which put him at the top of the championship table, leading Ukawa, a big loser this weekend, by 18 points and the brave Nakano by 40. Capirossi was 43 points down but we had not seen the last of him.

500 cc

Kenny Roberts and Alexandre Barros clearly dominated practice, although the star of the show was Cadalora who was third on the MuZ. Also dominating the headlines were the problems encountered by the three riders of the HRC-Repsol team: Criville was only tenth, starting from back on row three on a track where it is very difficult to overtake. However, a change of settings on the championship leader's machine completely transformed it for the warm-up and it was clear that Criville would once again be on the pace. Just as at Donington, Giberneau fell on Sunday morning. At the first corner, Roberts led Kocinski and Abe. Biaggi did not finish the first lap, Cadalora was also a faller, in his case on lap two. Roberts had no trouble shaking off Kocinski, but Barros was harder to deal with, fighting back from fourth to challenge the American

by lap ten. Roberts counter attacked, the two men touched, Barros rode into the gravel trap and fell off. The race was not yet over for Kenny. First of all, Okada had a crack at the race leader, but he too was a faller on lap 15 of 31 and then Criville came up to the Suzuki's back

wheel and narrowly missed out on the win. This was Roberts' third victory of the year and Criville again did well in the championship thanks to Okada's fall.

Future winner Kenny Roberts (10) is already in the lead. Cadalora (7) and Biaggi (2) will not go far.

A full Sachsenring is a magic setting.

Biland, "we were once again gathered around a table to decide if Luca would come with us for the four final races outside Europe."

... The long absence of Jean-Michel Bayle. The former world motocross champion had been away for a long time. The Frenchman had missed Assen and Donington and he failed to turn up at the Sachsenring. Would he ever be back in action?

... the huge success of the Sachsenring. 38,500 spectators on Friday, 51,000 on Saturday and 62,200 on Sunday. Doing the sums produces a total of 152,000 spectators over the weekend. The German tradition is alive and well.

Carlo Pernat the former pit man for Italian TV becomes Loris Capirossi's personal manager.

... a record number of fallers. There were 69 fallers over the three days, all in "normal" weather conditions; an amazing record for the second German GP to be held in the new Sachsenring era. How can one explain such carnage? It is probably down to the track layout. The high number of corners means the riders often have to get on the gas while still cranked over. Thus, over 80% of the weekend's fallers involved the rear wheel breaking away very suddenly.

... Valentino Rossi takes control. For the first time this season, Valentino Rossi the nominated favourite to take over from Loris Capirossi after the end of his previous championship, was leading the 250 world championship.

... Marco Melandri's mastery. Last year, he had dominated the German GP right up until half a lap from the flag. This time there were no mistakes and Marco Melandri took the third victory of his grand prix career.

... another zero from Max Biaggi. Mechanical problems in Malaysia, falls in France and Catalunya, Massimiliano Biaggi racked up his fourth no-score of the season, falling on the very first lap in Germany. At the mid-point in the season, the man who had dreamt of winning the title was only ninth in the championship, a massive 103 points behind Alex Criville the leader!

... the return of Luca Cadalora. He left Assen after the warm-up; he was absent from Donington; the Salvatore Dali of the bike world - "like a great artist, I cannot create a masterpiece every Sunday!" - was back for the MuZ-Weber's home race, their factory being twenty kilometres from the circuit. He made a great comeback with third place on the grid, before falling on lap two while lying fourth. After long discussions with the boss of the German-Swiss team, Cadalora agreed to take part in the remaining four grands prix to be run on European soil. "After the Valencia GP," explained Rolf

Fallers

Franco Battaini:
a fall in two scenes.

Friday 16th July 1999

125 cc: Manuel Poggiali (RSM, Aprilia,) Mirko Giansanti (I, Aprilia,) Jarno Muller (D, Honda,) Steve Jenkner (D, Aprilia,) Masao Azuma (J, Honda,) Arnaud Vincent (F, Aprilia,) Pablo Nieto (E, Derbi) and Reinhard Stolz (D, Honda.)

250 cc: Maurice Bolwerk (NL, TSR-Honda,) Matias Rios (ARG, Aprilia,) David Garcia (E, Yamaha,) Stefano Perugini (I, Honda,) Alfonso Gonzales-Nieto (E, Yamaha,) Jeremy McWilliams (GB, Aprilia) and Christian Gemmel (D, Honda.)

500 cc: Markus Ober (D, Honda, twice) Michael Rutter (GB, Honda,) Juan Bautista Borja (E, Honda,) Carlos Checa (E, Yamaha) and Sebastien Gimbert (F, Honda.)

Saturday 17th July 1999

125 cc: Noboru Ueda (J, Honda,) Frederic Petit (F, Aprilia,) Pablo Nieto (E, Derbi,) Lucio Cecchinello (I, Honda,) Youichi Ui (J, Derbi,) Arnaud Vincent (F, Aprilia,) Mirko Giansanti (I, Aprilia,) Simone Sanna (I, Honda,) Jarno Muller (D, Honda) and Roberto Locatelli (I, Aprilia.)

250 cc: Tohru Ukawa (J, Honda,) Jeremy McWilliams (GB, Aprilia,) Mathias Neukirchen (D, Aprilia,) Jason Vincent (GB, Honda,) Shinya Nakano (J, Yamaha,) Roberto Rolfo (I, Aprilia,) Luca Boscoscuro (I, TSR-Honda,) Alexander Hofmann (D, TSR-Honda, twice,) Loris Capirossi (I, Honda,) Jarno Janssen (NL, TSR-Honda) and Lucas Oliver (E, Yamaha.)

500 cc: Carlos Checa (E, Yamaha,) Nobuatsu Aoki (J, Suzuki,) Juan Bautista Borja (E, Honda,) Mark Willis (AUS, Modenas,) Jamie Whitham (GB, Modenas,) David De Gea (E, TSR-Honda) and Tetsuya Harada (J, Aprilia.)

Sunday 18th July 1999

125 cc: Mirko Giansanti (I, Aprilia, warm-up,) Pablo Nieto (E, Derbi,) Alessandro Brannetti (I, Aprilia,) Massimiliano Sabbatani (I, Honda,) Bernhard Absmeier (D, Aprilia) and Jarno Muller (D, Honda.)

250 cc: Jason Vincent (GB, Honda,) Tohru Ukawa (J, Honda,) Johan Stigefelt (S, Yamaha, was shown the black flag to exclude him for having arrived late on the grid,) Franco Battaini (I, Aprilia,) Jeremy McWilliams (GB, Aprilia, starts before going back to the pits) and Mike Baldinger (D, Honda, restart.)

500 cc: Manuel Gibernau (E, Honda, warm-up,) Massimiliano Biaggi (I, Yamaha,) Luca Cadalora (I, MuZ-Weber,) Nobuatsu Aoki (J, Suzuki,) Jamie Whitham (GB, Modenas,) Alexandre Barros (BR, Honda, restart) and Tadayuki Okada (J, Honda.)

Fallers

Ouch!..

1. Manuel Poggiali (bruising and haematoma to right hip.)
2. Steve Jenkner (injury to ring finger on right hand.)
3. Matias Rios (bruising to lower back.)
4. Reinhard Stolz (bruising to right tibia.)
5. Michael Rutter (bruising to cervical spine and to right side.)
6. Juan Bautista Borja (bruising to right side.)
7. Alfonso Gonzales-Nieto (bruising to left hand.)
8. Noboru Ueda (bruised right hand.)
9. Frederic Petit (dislocated right hip.)
10. Pablo Nieto (bruising to right hand and arm.)
11. Jason Vincent (fractured both malleolars right foot.)
12. Shinya Nakano (bruising and puncture wound to right shoulder, fractured third metacarpal of right hand.)
13. Luca Boscoscuro (slight cranial bruising, bruising to left hand.)
14. Arnaud Vincent (dislocated left wrist.)
15. Mirko Giansanti (fractured left foot, bruising to right side of chest.)
16. Johan Stigefelt (left hand injury.)
17. Luca Cadalora (cuts and bruises to left hand and forearm.)

Non starters...

1. Michael Doohan (result of fall in practise for the Spanish GP. The Australian went back to the United States to continue his recovery.)
2. Jean-Michel Bayle (officially, the result of his fall in the Catalunya GP. Replaced by Mark Willis.)
3. Mike Hale (officially, as a result of his fall in practise for the French GP. Replaced by Jamie Whitham.)
4. Jose Luis Cardoso (The Spaniard had an operation on both wrists to try to solve the remaining tendonitis problem. Replaced by his compatriot David De Gea, who we had seen at the start of the season in the world supersport championship.)
5. Frederic Petit (result of fall in practise.)

Retirements...

125 cc: Youichi Ui (J, Derbi, engine.)
250 cc: David Garcia (E, Yamaha, ignition.)
500 cc: Michael Rutter (GB, Honda V2, result of Friday's fall.)

Olivier Jacque is back at last.
▽

The man who wasn't

▷ Fire on the track and the 500 GP is stopped.

The pictures were shown all over the world. It happened on lap two of the Czech Republic 500 GP. Towards the back of the pack, Englishman Jamie Whitham lost control of his Modenas KR3. The rider was thrown clear, but the bike literally exploded as it hit the ground. The petrol caught fire immediately and Spain's Jose Luis Cardoso and France's Sebastien Gimbert both went down on a track which had been transformed into a river of fire. The straw bales and the tyre barriers also started to burn. It was the start of the longest grand prix of the year, coming at the end of a weekend which would have a profound effect on the sport's recent history.

It all began with a surprising image on Friday 20th August 1999. While Kenny Roberts, Alex Criville and Massimiliano Biaggi were fighting it out to the nearest thousandth of a second on the track, the main point of interest in the media centre at Brno was a scheduled flight which was transporting Michael Doohan back to the United States yet again. There were some who had hoped he would be back here in Brno. The man himself dreamed of making a comeback at "his" grand prix at Phillip Island on 3rd October. That way he could quit racing with the perfect scenario, but neither of these options would come true.

Another operation

It was all summed up in a few short lines which did not actually emanate from the five times world champion's team. "Michael Doohan is going back to the United States to undergo a further operation. Its aim is to straighten the bones which have healed badly in his wrist." Doohan added: "I will see how things stand in six weeks." It was a bolt

from the blue and the telephone and fax lines were red hot between the Czech Republic and Australia, via Doohan in Monaco. There were long faces as everyone understood the situation even if they did not dare speak their mind. In six weeks time the championship would have reached Australia and if Doohan was going to speak on the 3rd October, by which time he reckoned he "would have a clearer picture," then that could only mean he would announce his retirement from racing!

What the doctor said

End of a legend? End, above all, of an era; the Nineties which had been totally dominated by Mick Doohan. A few moments later, unconfirmed reports started to filter through that the good Doctor Claudio Costa had indeed had a medical discussion with his favourite patient and yes, Michael Doohan was due to have further surgery on his left wrist. But no, there was no talk of retirement.

The world championship world had just

realised they had been present for a historical moment that 20th August 1999: not on the track but on an airplane, or rather in the heart and soul of a man whose body had been cruelly abused; a man who had become a father to a little girl seven weeks earlier and who now felt he had given enough of himself to racing.

"If Doohan ever races again, he will be the greatest champion of all time, but if he does not make a comeback, then he will be even greater," declared Costa, standing at the foot of the stairs leading to the mobile surgery at Brno. He had said pretty much the same thing after that terrible accident in Jerez. It was as though an echo had taken an eternity to travel from joyous Andalusia to this sad region of the Czech Republic.

Just routine or more serious?

That was the mood on Friday 24th August 1999. One day later and there was another line to add to the story, which could have been called: What is Mick Doohan's real state of health and is there a chance he will ever ride again?" The five times world champion's entourage confirmed most of what had been said. "Mick is going to San Francisco for a routine check up of his injuries. I cannot say if he will need another operation," said Doohan's personal press officer Mike Porter, speaking from Australia. Just routine? More than that. The fact was that Doohan had only recovered 60% of the strength in his left wrist and as soon as he tried any repetitive strengthening exercises, his forearm would swell up alarmingly. Because of this, a metal plate which inhibited the natural movement of the tendons had to be removed. It would be a short operation followed by two weeks rest. The American doctors wanted the rider to undergo a further check up one month later. That meant we would not know before the Australian GP if the world Number One would be able or would want to race again. The news was met with criticism from Doctor Costa. "I said right from the start that the plate should have been removed at the end of July, to enable Mick to make a comeback as soon as possible." But this time, Doohan had decided to let things take their natural progression.

▷
Tadayuki Okada wins...

◁
... but the talk is all of Doohan.

125 cc

Roberto Locatelli had dominated practice with a lead which was rarely seen in this category - 876 thousandths of a second. He was therefore the big favourite for the race and the Aprilia rider was quickest away at the start. He led from Ueda and Melandri, who moved up to second before the end of the opening lap. Cecchinello joined the fray for a few laps, but pretty quickly, Locatelli and Melandri escaped, so that the fight for first was an all-Italian affair. Arnaud Vincent was a strong third until he fell on lap 14, picking up his bike and continuing. Further back, Alzamora got away from championship leader Masao Azuma, who was suffering from the effects of his fall in practice. At the head of the field, Locatelli and Melandri were stuck together and with three laps remaining the gap between them was 246 thousandths of a second. It would all come down to the final lap. Melandri mounted an attack and got past at the second attempt. Then, less than two kilometres from the flag, Locatelli fell, although Melandri was unaware of this as the Playlife rider took his second win of the season and the second in a row at that. Emilio Alzamoro was still looking good for the championship thanks to his sixth place, which brought him to within four points of Masao Azuma who could only finish twelfth.

Marco Melandri: the sky did not fall in on him.

250 cc

Everyone was looking forward to the next round of the Rossi-Capirossi duel. But with the world champion having two harmless falls in practice, the German Ralf Waldmann was going to play a prominent role. The Aprilia rider took his first pole position of the season and it became obvious that the critical part of the race, as far as he was concerned, would happen the moment the lights turned green. "We did some testing during the summer break and I think we have come up with some good solutions." Prophetic words, as while Stefano Perugini had the quickest reactions and led from Capirossi and the surprising Jason Vincent, Waldmann was on the pace

Olivier Jacque is back after a long absence.

right from the start and was lying fourth as they crossed the line for the first time, behind Capirossi, Ukawa and Perugini. Ukawa took control on lap three, then Rossi came back, but it was Waldmann who wanted to be the boss. He went into the lead on lap eight, but Rossi and Ukawa were right there with him. Waldman set the fastest time on lap 15, but Rossi fought back, closing the gap to a tiny 79 thousandths of a second. With two laps remaining, Rossi slipstreamed past across the line and held on. Waldman counter attacked a couple of corners later and the two Aprilias actually touched. Rossi tried again, this time having a look down the outside, but he ran too wide. Waldman was still ahead as the crossed the line to start the final lap, but Rossi was just 57 thousandths down and slipstreamed by and this time he stayed in front. Loris Capirossi, who lost touch around the halfway mark with a engine and handling problems, lost place after place finally picking up a few points for coming seventh. In the championship, Rossi was looking good as he now had a 27 point advantage over Ukawa. The Italian's supporters tried to invade the track, but once again, "Tino" managed to avoid being smothered by the crazy crowd.

500 cc

In the Catalunya GP back on 20th June, Alex Criville had been seen to shut down his team mate Tadayuki Okada to clinch a vital win. Some people thought this end to the race was a classic example of team tactics, which are perfectly valid in this modern age, when there is so much financial interest at stake. In the Czech Republic, we saw the same scenario played out between the same two team-mates, except that this time the roles were reversed. "He is my main rival for the title, not Roberts," insisted Criville these past few days when talking about Okada. It was the Japanese rider doing the hunting this time, while championship leader Criville was the prey. The hunter had the last world at the end of a mesmerising final lap during which Okada took every risk in the book. At the same time, Roberts snaffled third place in a move which Max Biaggi will remember for a long time to come. He was not exactly happy with the American rider's behaviour. The longest race in the history of the sport in modern times had just ended after a fiery opening, two hours earlier when Jamie Whitham fell and his Modenas literally exploded, setting fire to the track, the straw bales and the tyre barrier. The Englishman suffered serious injuries to the pelvis. Race Director Roberto Nosetto inspected the crash scene, along with Criville, Biaggi and Roberts, in order to evaluate the damage to the track. At the time, no one could have guessed that safety worries would now send shock waves running through the paddock.

The autumn novelty was the Modenas KR4.

... Masao Azuma's deer. "I had time to look it straight in the eyes and..." 125 cc championship leader Masao Azuma had a very silly accident on Saturday morning in the opening moments of the free practice session. The Japanese rider was unable to avoid a deer which crossed the track in his path! It was a big impact. The bike flipped over its front wheel and the Honda was a write-off. Azuma got off with multiple bruising and the fright of his life. The telemetry data threw up some remarkable figures. At the moment when the rider spotted the danger, he was travelling at 174 km/h. Azuma was able to break for 86 metres and at the time of the impact he was doing 130 km/h. The deer, killed on the spot, tipped the scales at 38 kilos.

... Manuel Poggiali's appendicitis. The continual drop in the ages of the 125 cc riders often has surprising side effects: Manuel Poggiali, who only turned 16 on 14th February, was forced to pull out of the Brno event because of an acute case of appendicitis.

...the first grand prix for the Italjet 125. Causing people to sit up and take notice in Brno was the debut of the 125 cc Italjet ridden by the Czech Jaroslav Hules. This bike, created the previous year in Italy, is the latest brainchild of the marque established by Leopoldo Taratarini, winner of the 1953 Tour of Italy, riding a Benelli. He started the company building machines with 125 cc Yamaha engines, with which riders like Felice Agostini and Mario Lega won Italian junior championships. After a successful period building trial bikes, the company then specialised in scooters.

...the future of BSL. It was now official. Mark Willis would see out the season riding a Modenas KR3, while the development of the BSL, also a three

cylinder, continued in parallel. "For next year, we aim to line up with two riders; Willis and a New-Zealander," explained Dave Stewart, the team coordinator.

... Red Bull quits. It was a tough blow for the WCM-Yamaha team and the whole world championship scene. On of the grand prix's non-tobacco sponsors, Red Bull, would not continue as a sponsor in 2000. WCM, which still has a contract with Yamaha for the next season, should however find a way to continue.

... the launch of the Modenas KR4. The new Modenas KR4, powered by a Swissauto engine, was unveiled on Sunday morning in Brno. It was fitted with an early 1998 version of the Swiss engine, which puts out around 15 horsepower less than that currently used in the MuZ-Weber. While the chassis might look different from the outside, the geometry is actually identical to the bike which recorded its second pole position of the season at Brno.

First GP for Jaroslav Hules' Italjet 125.

Fallers

Friday 20th August 1999

125 cc: Michael Brezina (CZ, Honda.)
250 cc: Arno Visscher (NL, Aprilia,) Franco Battaini (I, Aprilia,) Lars Langer (D, Yamaha,) Tomomi Manako (J, Yamaha) and Loris Capirossi (I, Honda.)
500 cc: none.

Saturday 21st August 1999

125 cc: Masao Azuma (J, Honda,) Marco Melandri (I, Honda,) Noboru Ueda (J, Honda,) Igor Kalab (CZ, Honda,) Lucio Cecchinello (I, Honda,) Mirko Giansanti (I, Aprilia,) Bernhard Absmeier (D, Aprilia, twice,) Alessandro Brannetti (I, Aprilia,) Gianluigi Scalvini (I, Aprilia,) Massimiliano Sabbatani (I, Honda) and Jakub Smrz (CZ, Honda.)
250 cc: David Garcia (E, Yamaha,) Loris Capirossi (I, Honda,) Scott Smart (GB, Aprilia,) Alexander Hofmann (D, TSR-Honda) and Jeremy McWilliams (GB, Aprilia, twice in the space of 37 minutes!)
500 cc: Carlos Checa (E, Yamaha,) Juan Bautista Borja (E, Honda, twice,) Haruchika Aoki (J, TSR-Honda) and Garry McCoy (AUS, Yamaha.)

Sunday 22nd August 1999

125 cc: Arnaud Vincent (F, Aprilia, restart) and Roberto Locatelli (I, Aprilia.)
250 cc: Johan Stigefelt (S, Yamaha, twice/ warm-up and race,) Alexander Hofmann (D, TSR-Honda,) Maurice Bolwerk (NL, TSR-Honda,) Julien Allemand (F, TSR-Honda) and Sebastian Porto (ARG, Yamaha.)
500 cc: Jamie Whitham (GB, Modenas,) Jose Luis Cardoso (E, TSR-Honda,) Sebastien Gimbert (F, Honda, took the second start,) Carlos Checa (E, Yamaha, gets back on track before retiring to the pits,) and Norifumi Abe (J, Yamaha, gets back on track and does a few laps before retiring.)

▷
Arnaud Vincent fell, but had the good sense to get going again and score a few points.

Fallers

Ouch!..

1. Masao Azuma (bruised back, bruised little finger of right hand.)
2. Gianluigi Scalvini (bruised right ankle.)
3. Jamie Whitham (fractured pelvis.)
4. Jose Luis Cardoso (badly bruised right arm.)

Luca Cadalora: was this the last start for a great champion?

Non starters...

1. Frederic Petit (result of fall in practise for German GP. Not replaced.)
2. Manuel Poggiali (the youngest rider in the championship had an acute attack of appendicitis on the Thursday before the GP.)
3. Marcellino Lucchi (the world champion veteran was told a few days before the GP that, for financial reasons, his world championship had come to an end. Replaced by Scott Smart.)
4. Jean-Michel Bayle (the Frenchman injured himself mountain-biking - an open fracture of his right foot. Replaced by Jamie Whitham.)
5. Markus Ober (the German rider broke his ankle during the Pro Superbike championship at Nurburgring. Replaced by the Spaniard David De Gea, who we had seen at the Sachsenring on Jose Luis Cardoso's bike.)
6. Jamie Whitham (following his fall on the second lap, the Englishman did not take the second start.)
7. Jose Luis Cardoso (result of second lap fall, the Spaniard did not take the second start.)
8. Luca Cadalora (the triple world champion stopped at the end of the first lap complaining that he couldn't feel what the machine was doing; he refused to take the second start.)

Retirements...

125 cc: Randy de Puniet (F, Aprilia, piston) and Kazuto Sakata (J, Honda, electrical problems.)
250 cc: Scott Smart (GB, Aprilia, seized engine.)
500 cc: David De Gea (E, Honda, exhaust,) Michael Rutter (GB, Honda V2, exhaust)
and Sebastien Gimbert (F, Honda V2, due to injury caused by his second lap fall.)

11. Imola

Ciao, Gepetto...

▷ *Giuseppe Pattoni: a life dedicated to racing.*

Flash back to the beginning of August 1997 and the paddock at the Nelson Piquet Circuit at Jacerapagua, outside Rio de Janeiro. Giussepe Pattoni was dripping with sweat and had to sit down for a few moments. He had just learned, albeit unofficially, that the approval of teams for the following season was not going to plan and the selectors were hesitating over his entry. "They can't do this. They cannot forget what I have done for the sport. If they want the scalp of the last of the sport's privateers then I am sure they will get it. But they do not appreciate they are committing hara-kiri by getting rid of all the little constructors." He said all this in short bursts while staring up at the heavens with the green colour of his Paton reflected in his eyes.

"They will kill him..."

By his side, Jean-Louis Millet, the Frenchman who ran another of the private teams, was almost in tears. "They will kill him if they refuse his entry..." End of flashback.

Giuseppe Pattoni, who had turned seventy three on 7th July, died on 29th August 1999, as he was returning from the track, as he was preparing to load his truck in the Via San Vittore, Milan, in preparation for a departure to yet another race track. While Gepetto dreamed of giving life to a small wooden

Giussepe Pattoni's heart, generous as it was, played a sad trick on him on the night of Sunday 29th August 1999. He was returning from Mugello, where he had attended a test session for his latest creation, the 1999 Paton 500, which Paolo Tessari was due to ride at Imola. He walked into his offices at a brisk pace, but he was carried out, having breathed his last. Pattoni, the Gepetto of racing, died a few days before what would undoubtedly be the last ever motorcycle grand prix on the Imola circuit. It was a symbolic ending.

▷ *Paolo Tessari did a lap in honour of the Gepetto of the grands prix.*

Giuseppe and Roberto Pattoni with the Paton fitted with the first ever 2 stroke V4. It was 1980.

puppet called Pinnochio, for his part, "Peppino" Pattoni devoted his life to racing motor cycles. After the war, with the help of his brother Giovanni, he converted military motorcycles for civilian use. One of the regulars at the Via San Vittore workshop was Count Giuseppe Boselli, one of the owners of Mondial. He was impressed by Pattoni's ability and took him on in his company's racing department. When Cecil Sandford won the 250 world title in 1957, his chief mechanic was a young man who was already carrying a bit of weight. It was Pattoni.

"Give me the equipment..."

However, Mondial and Gilera and Moto Guzzi too, were to retire from the championship at the end of the 1957 season and along with plenty of others, Giuseppe Pattoni found himself out of work. But he was a man of ideas. Rather than take the redundancy money on offer after his contract was cancelled, Pattoni asked to be paid with equipment. Thus the first Paton, the name taken from the initials of PAttoni and Lino TONti, Mondial's engine designer, was born. There was a 125 and a 175 twin cam, followed by 250, 350 and 500 twin cylinder machines. A swarm of Italian riders as well as foreigners were all employed by this surprising set-up, which had a workshop in a barn, situated next to the family home. The motorbikes had to be brought in and out with an ingenious winch.

A rider by the name of Mike Hailwood

In 1958, a rider by the name of Mike Hailwood finished seventh at the Tourist Trophy, riding a Paton 125. It was the first step in a remarkable history. In 1964, Alberto Pagani was third in the 250 TT and in 1967, the team owner could celebrate his first championship title when Angello Bergamonti was crowned Italian 500 cc champion. Added to that, Fred Stevens came sixth in the world championship.

In the world championship, it was the era of the Hannah-Paton team, underwritten by an enthusiastic Englishman, who entered Stevens and Billie Nelson with some success; Nelson finishing fourth in the 1969 500 championship.

The years went by and two stroke technology evolved. The Pattonis, Giuseppe and his second son Roberto embarked on a major project, building the first 500 V four two stroke. Virginio Ferrari was the rider and Pattoni kept updating the engine, even including a big-bang system in its final version. Marco Papa, who was the test rider for much of this development work, died ten days after Giuseppe Pattoni in a traffic accident.

This genius of design got very little recognition for his efforts. For two years, the Patons were only allowed to compete on an occasional basis, thanks to the wild-card system. At Imola, on 5th September 1999, the green machine was not fired up. Its father and creator was already comfortably installed in motorcycle heaven.

The V4 Paton from 1980-1981.

The races

125 cc

Marco Melandri, complete with orange and blue hair decorated with his number 13, was head and shoulders above the opposition throughout the weekend. Although only 17, "Macio" showed remarkable maturity and did not panic a bit when rain began to fall during the first opening lap of the day. In the lead, acting like an old pro, he simply raised an arm. The red flag was shown and there was a new start a few minutes later. This time Lucio Cecchinello charged into the lead off the second row of the grid, but Melandri was in front by the end of the first lap. That was the last the rest of the field would see of him. A lead of 1.303s after four laps was extended to 2.850s four laps after that and the young Italian could not be beaten. All eyes therefore turned to the battle for second place and what a battle it was! Sabbatini, Scalvini and Sakata were already out and Cecchinello also got it wrong on lap 11 of 21. Then came a remarkable fight back from Roberto Locatelli who moved into second place with three laps remaining. However, just as at Brno, the Italian would throw it all away almost within sight of the chequered flag. He had to console himself with a few points for eleventh place, leaving the podium to Melandri, the very talented Sanna and France's Arnaud Vincent. Spain's Emilio Alzamora was fourth and for the second time this season, he took the championship lead. Despite three early season no-scores, twice he did not start and once he fell at Jerez, Melandri was now only 30 points behind the leader and he had certainly not given up on the title.

250 cc

Olivier Jacque was back on form and on a circuit where he has always felt comfortable, the Frenchman took his first pole position of the season. Until then, Capirossi had been the dominant force in practice, but had to miss the final qualifying shoot-out for the strangest of reasons. The world champion suffered an allergic reaction after being stung by a wasp and was forced to return to his garage where he needed medical help to keep breathing. Rossi was also suffering on this track, but in his case it was for technical reasons. OJ made a complete mess of the start, unlike Capirossi who would finish the first lap leading by 1.756s from Rossi, Perugini and Nakano. It was obvious that the reigning world champion was unbeatable that day and he was putting in fastest lap after fastest lap. By half distance he had a nine second lead over Valentino Rossi, who had managed to break free from the pursuing group, which was held up by Perugini for a long time. Jacque fought back to fifth, while Tohru Ukawa, Rossi's biggest threat for the title, fell on lap 12. The Japanese rider got back on the track to take four points for twelfth place. The end of the race saw a titanic struggle between Perugini and Jacque. The Frenchman had the final word at the end of a thrilling last lap. Although he was badly beaten, Rossi was still looking good in the championship thanks to Ukawa's fall.

Following Loris Capirossi is a difficult task. Just ask Julien Allemand. ▽

500 cc

Regis Laconi and his girlfriend Aurelia. Things are looking up! ▽

Alex Criville had never won at Imola and it soon became clear that he intended correcting that little mistake this time around. Practice was marked by a few spectacular incidents. Tadayuki Okada, who had taken a great win in the Czech Republic, suffered a huge high-side accident in Friday morning's free practice session. Landing on the fuel tank and handlebars the Japanese rider suffered serious injuries to the thorax. His injuries were further complicated by the fact he had been suffering from a bad case of bronchitis for the past few days. Another victim was Carlos Checa who fell on his third qualifying lap. A quick visit to Doctor Costa's clinic revealed a broken ring finger of the left hand, but that didn't stop him getting out on the track again before the end of the session. On Saturday, the Yamaha rider felt well enough to set a time which would see him line up on the front row of the grid. Roberts and Criville were first away at the start of what turned up to be a very close fought race. Carlo Checa would not be part of it for long, as his engine let go on lap three. Out in front, Roberts, Okada and Criville all took turns to lead and at half distance, eight riders were covered by less than two seconds. It was a rare treat. Then it all changed. Roberts began to drop back with rear tyre problems and Criville and Barros managed to pull away from the rest with Norifume Abe following along at a distance that would remain constant until the penultimate lap. Then things really hotted up as Barros was stuck to Criville's rear wheel but he made a small error and that allowed Criville to consolidate his position and Abe was a faller. Criville and his Honda had finally corrected this unusual omission from his curriculum vitae, taking his first ever win at the historic Imola track.

Giancarlo Fisichella pays
Marco Melandri a visit:
"long live freedom!"

Look out,
its Loris Capirossi.

...the Aprilia-Capirossi court case. The bank accounts had been frozen and shares in a Dutch company with offices in Switzerland were seized. Five million dollars was the figure being bandied around as the Aprilia-Capirossi divorce had to be settled in the courts.

...the 250 reigning champion's near-death experience.
The final 250 cc qualifying session turned into an episode of "Casualty." The patient was Loris Capirossi. Just as he was trying to steal pole position off Olivier Jacque, the world Number One felt a terrible pain in his neck. He pitted immediately, realising what had happened to him. Allergic to wasp stings, Capirossi immediately started experiencing breathing difficulties. Doctor Claudio Costa was called in to sort out the problem. "Loris can have a fatal reaction to wasp stings," said the Italian doctor.

...the divorce between MuZ-Weber and Luca Cadalora. Bernard Garcia was back at Imola, the first time the Frenchman had been in a paddock since 1995. The younger of the Garcia brothers had drifted off the scene, not through any lack of talent, but because he had not managed to convince his employers to keep him on at the beginning of the Swiss company's adventure into the world of motor cycle engines. But now he was back again, as Rolf Biland had called him in to replace Luca Cadalora at the controls of the MuZ- Weber, after the three times world champion had been shown the door the day after the Czech Republic GP.

...Giancarlo Fisichella pays a visit. The Benetton Formula 1 driver Giancarlo Fisichella appeared in the paddock on Saturday morning to visit the company's two riders in the 125 cc class, Marco Melandri and Masao Azuma. "I like coming to see the bikes as the riders seem free to wander around the paddock. I would love Formula 1 to be like this again. Sadly, the pace is too frenetic in our sport and so it is almost impossible to stroll around."

...an NSR500 for the year 2000. For the first time in history, HRC made a public presentation of what the NSR500 would look like in 2000. During testing at Brno which followed the grand prix, Tadayuki Okada tried a seriously modified machine: frame, swing arm, seat and fuel tank. The frame had been substantially modified and now closely resembled that of the V-twin to try and improve its agility. A more flexible swing arm was used during Friday's testing at Imola by both Okada and Alex Criville. On Saturday, the HRC president Yasuo Ikenoya stated that next year, a maximum of seven riders would have the use of the Honda NSR500 with a further four NSR250s being entered.

Bernard Garcia replaced
Luca Cadalora.

Fallers

▷
Tohru Ukawa:
an expensive mistake.

Friday 3ʳᵈ September 1999

125 cc: Angel Nieto Junior (E, Honda,) Pablo Nieto (E, Derbi) and Massimiliano Sabbatani (I, Honda.)
250 cc: Stefano Perugini (I, Honda,) Ivan Clementi (I, Aprilia) and Franco Battaini (I, Aprilia.)
500 cc: Alexandre Barros (BR, Honda) and Carlos Checa (E, Yamaha.)

Saturday 4ᵗʰ September 1999

125 cc: Christian Magnani (I, Aprilia,) Reinhard Stolz (D, Honda,) Diego Giugovaz (I, Aprilia) and Youichi Ui (J, Derbi.)
250 cc: Ivan Clementi (I, Aprilia) and Tohru Ukawa (J, Honda.)
500 cc: Bernard Garcia (F, MuZ-Weber.)

Sunday 5ᵗʰ September 1999

125 cc: Massimiliano Sabbatani (I, Honda,) Angel Nieto Junior (E, Honda,) Gianluigi Scalvini (I, Aprilia, restart,) Kazuto Sakata (J, Honda,) Bernhard Absmeier (D, Aprilia,) Lucio Cecchinello (I, Honda,) Alex De Angelis (RSM, Honda) and Roberto Locatelli (I, Aprilia, restart.)
250 cc: David Garcia (E, Yamaha,) Julien Allemand (F, TSR-Honda,) Jason Vincent (GB, Honda,) Maurice Bolwerk (NL, TSR-Honda,) Tohru Ukawa (J, Honda, restart) and Jeremy McWilliams (GB, Aprilia, restart.)
500 cc: Bernard Garcia (F, MuZ-Weber) and Juan Bautista Borja (E, Honda.)

Fallers

Ouch!..

1. Ivan Clementi (dislocated left ankle.)
2. Carlos Checa (fractured ring finger, left hand.)
3. Christian Magnani (bruised coccyx.)
4. Reinhard Stolz (bruising right hand.)
5. Diego Giugovaz (fractured fifth meta-carpal of right hand.)
6. Bernhard Absmeier (bruising to left hip.)
7. Alex De Angelis (broken left foot.)
8. Jason Vincent (injured left knee.)
9. Bernard Garcia (bruised right wrist.)
10. Juan Bautista Borja (bruised left hand.)

Non Starters...

1. Michael Doohan (result of fall in prac-tise for the Spanish GP. The five times world champion is in the USA for another operation to his left wrist to remove a metal plate. Not replaced.)
2. Luca Cadalora (the Italian was sacked by Rolf Biland, the MuZ-Weber boss. Replaced by Frenchman Bernard Garcia.)
3. Jean-Michel Bayle (result of an accident on a mountain-bike. Not replaced, becau-se Jamie Whitham was seriously injured in an accident on the second lap of the Czech Republic GP, suffering multiple frac-tures to his pelvis.)
4. Markus Ober (result of a fall sustained during a race in the German Pro Superbike championship. Replaced by Spaniard David De Gea.)
5. Diego Giugovaz (result of fall in free practise on Saturday morning.)

Retirements...

125 cc: Randy De Puniet (F, Aprilia, the Frenchman missed his breaking for the last chicane and was forced to use the pit lane and was disqualified) and Gino Borsoi (I, Aprilia, engine.)
250 cc: Jarno Janssen (NL, TSR-Honda, result of a coming-together with Roberto Rolfo on the first lap,) Scott Smart (GB, Aprilia, broken rear mud-guard) and Matias Rios (ARG, Aprilia, battery failure.)
500 cc: Carlos Checa (E, Yamaha, engine,) Michael Rutter (GB, Honda, result of col-liding with another rider,) David De Gea (E, Honda, went off the track) and Jose Luis Cardoso (E, TSR-Honda, went off the track.)

◁
Roberto Locatelli was a follower when a podium finish awaited him.

Regis Laconi: with all his heart!

12. Valencia

▷
Regis Laconi: a victory from the heart.

Regis Laconi is one of the nicest of the 500 riders and he took his first win in the category in atrocious conditions. Here we meet a lad who does not make much of a noise in the paddock and has a totally different approach to racing from his peers.

The first thing he did was to kiss his girlfriend and accomplice in all things, Aurelie. Then he cried a few tears. But then his boss Peter Clifford took him away in a hurry. When you meet the royals it is best not to be late! Regis Laconi looked like a man who did not really understand the enormity of what he had just done, but he stuck to the protocol. First there was the official interview, in his own version of the English language. Then back to the spectators, his spectators. The top rung of the podium was followed by a jump for joy and an air of respect as he accepted the trophy from His Majesty, King Juan Carlos of Spain. All these images were jumbled around in his head and then they played the Marseillaise and Regis Laconi sobbed and sobbed.

"I thought of him"

"At least he won't be able to tell me off for never winning," he said with a lump in his throat. His big smile gave way to a sad expression. "He" is his brother Alban, killed in a car crash a few years ago. "He made me what I am today. He was my mechanic when I started and he taught me everything about life. When he died I swore one thing: I want to be world champion to be able to dedicate the title to him. Today, I can start by offering him this win."

Regis Laconi is not like the other stars. He is not like all those riders he dominated on the new Cheste circuit, near Valencia, in extremely difficult conditions. He had to ride as though on egg shells on a drying line no wider than thirty centimetres. "The force that moves me is different to what drives the others, but I insist on being true to myself. I just want people to understand that motorcycling is great and in this business you can find people who listen to their heart. I always knew I could be a front runner, that I was worthy of a podium. I was never the sort to complain. I have tackled the obstacles I have encountered by facing them head on, but it's true I've had more than my share of bad luck. This weekend, everything came good at the same time. On the grid, when I had done the formation lap with an intermediate rear tyre, I was playing double or quits. Everyone around me wanted to play safe, but I could feel that my team thought that the slick tyre would be the best choice. In the end, I made my decision, because that is what I do. In life, you have to gamble everything to win everything!"

A perfect race

What followed was a delight. The perfect race for Regis Laconi. "After a few laps I could no longer hear the other engines. I turned round once and I begun to understand. Then, when a few drops started to fall again, I made a big effort and that is when I won the race."

He talks like an old campaigner does Regis Laconi, but in his own words. "On the last lap, I told myself, 'don't be stupid. No way am I going to pull a wheelie before the finish line, because you could still flip over and end up on the deck. It was only later that it sunk in." What sunk in was that he had just passed an important test. Before the season, he had spoken of his hopes. "I am about to start my second season riding a works 500 and I know it could be decisive. At this level of competition, experience is the most important asset. Some people might forget that I was only twenty three when I got a factory ride, while guys like Doohan, Rainey and Schwantz (still his hero) were at least thirty."

Is thirty the ideal age? "Some people think so. Apparently, at that age you take less risks and that seems to be the best way to go quickly! A young rider might compensate for his lack of experience by some dodgy moves, but he hasn't really got a choice. If you want to beat the old ones, you have to."

That was in February 1999. In September of the same year, a young Frenchman had beaten all those racing oldies.

◁
On slicks on a damp track: it took courage.

The races

125 cc

France's Arnaud Vincent was playing at home on this circuit, designed by his employer, Jorge Martinez. The winner in Barcelona dominated practice and was enjoying himself. "I love to make my bike slide and with so much dust on the track these are the ideal conditions for me." He therefore set the pole time, but rain on race day morning wiped the grin off his face. However, the Frenchman managed to make the best start ahead of Alzamora and led across the line for the first time from Azuma and Scalvini. Then, very soon after, the Japanese and Italian riders took control and they were soon joined by Melandri on lap 5 of 25. Japan's Ui on the Derbi, was the first to be caught out by the slippery conditions. Three laps later, Cecchinello was a faller, along with Goi and Pablo Nieto, the youngest member of the family who was a surprising third quickest in qualifying on his Derbi. Vincent was unable to stay on the pace and Azuma really pushed himself hard to claim a sizeable lead just before half distance. Then, the incredible happened: the Japanese rider clipped a white line and was thrown off his machine. At the same time, his team mate Melandri also fell. This left Emilio Alzamora in the lead without having to worry about the two other title contenders. Behind him was Gianluigi Scalvini on the Aprilia. Much further back, one of the championship babies, Manuel Poggiali was fighting it out with Noboru Ueda, while Arnaud Vincent was scrapping over fifth with the German Steve Jenkner. Poggiali had to stop four laps from the finish so that everyone behind moved up one. Scalvini had a scary moment before celebrating his first GP win, as the German Absmeier fell just in front of him as he was being lapped. Alzamora had done his championship chances a lot of good and despite not having won a race this season, the Spaniard had a 23 point lead over Azuma.

The first corner in the 125 race: watch out for a slippery track!

250 cc

There were three different manufacturers represented on the front row. Little Shinya Nakano was on pole position, ahead of out-going champion Loris Capirossi, so it looked like a good 250 cc race in prospect, but here also, the weather would turn the race on its head. Firstly and most importantly, because championship leader Valentino Rossi does not like riding in the wet and secondly, because right from the first corner, Olivier Jacque, who qualified third, was going to get it wrong. It was to be the day of the Japanese and Tohru Ukawa, the big loser at the previous race at Imola took control of the race right from the green light. Following him at first was Nakano, but he soon lost touch, dropping 2.148s behind by lap four. Jacque fell at the first corner, only to pick the bike up and keep going, retiring when he had got back to fifteenth place. The Frenchman clipped Rossi as he fell, forcing Valentino to miss out on the action at the front and he eventually finished eighth. Out in front, Ukawa was riding a perfect race, fighting off Jeremy McWilliams, who fell five laps from home, and Ralf Waldmann, who also fell, to win from Franco Battaini and Loris Capirossi. Rossi now had to cope with the fact that Ukawa was now just 26 points behind him in the championship.

Jeremy McWilliams (9) and Ralf Waldmann (6) close on Tohru Ukawa, but neither Aprilia rider would finish the race.

500 cc

Regis Laconi secured the first pole position of his career, at the end of a fascinating qualifying session. Alex Criville made a mistake and Max Biaggi was only sixteenth on Friday night, demanding to use the old chassis for the following day. The Roman used it to good effect to secure a front row position and have a dig at Laconi. "Pole is one thing, the race is another matter." Biaggi was wrong. As the rain stopped after the 250 cc race, the 500 riders lined up on the grid. Laconi, McCoy and Okada took a gamble and started with slick rear tyres and Laconi went into the lead on lap 2, never to be seen again. By lap 14 he led by almost six seconds from Okada, who was going at it wheel to wheel with McCoy, one of the spectacular stars of the weekend. Further back, Criville and Roberts fought it out with intermediate rear tyres, but the championship leader got it wrong with five laps to go. Laconi thus won his first grand prix and Roberts had to be very aggressive to see off McCoy. In the championship, Criville now led by "only" 46 points, while the mood in the Biaggi camp was black, as he finished worst of the five Yamaha riders.

Gianluigi Scalvini's mascot: first win!

.... this was the first grand prix to be held on the Cheste circuit. Braving the elements, His Majesty King Juan Carlos of Spain officially inaugurated the latest Spanish circuit, by unveiling a plaque which read: "His Majesty, King Juan Carlos I officially opened the circuit of the Community of Valencia, Ricardo Tormo, on the 19th September 1999."

....a first for Gianluigi Scalvini. The Italian rider had to wait until his 79th grand prix start to take top honours for the first time. France's Regis Laconi, who also notched up his first grand prix victory, got there slightly quicker as this glorious day of September 1999 was his 64th start.

....Alex Criville's fall. "I made a mistake. That's all there is to it. People who never take risks never make mistakes. I was pushing hard to catch up to Okada, when I found myself on a more slippery part of the track. When races are run in these conditions they can often turn into a lottery."Just like his King and all his people, Criville dreamed of taking a decisive step on the path to the first Spanish 500 title. Instead, he lost his footing.

....this Autumn's Italian novella. Marco Melandri tried Stefano Perugini's Honda 250. Valentino Rossi was still refusing to sign his contract with Aprilia, because there was a clause stipulating he should dedicated 45 days per year to promotional activities. Loris Capirossi had been offered a colossal amount of money to ride for Ducati in the Superbike world championship. The stories surrounding the transfer market are always fascinating in Italy at this time of year.

....Claudio Costa's depression. The GP Doc had been in touch with Mika Doohan, who was not in Valencia, choosing to spend time with his girlfriend and their daughter. He was suffering from complications to his right knee. "As soon as Mick puts in some effort in training, he is in terrible pain. He told me he might only be 34 years old, but he feels 50. At the moment, I don't think he will ever race again."

....the 105, 000 brave spectators. As dawn broke on the Cheste circuit, some people could not believe their eyes, because despite the threat of bad weather, the grandstands were already jam-packed. "Several times during the night, I was woken up by a loud noise. I was sure it was already the morning," admitted Arnaud Vincent.

....an injury for a double world champion. The Japanese rider, Haruchika Aoki, who has two 125 cc titles to his name, was the first victim of the new Valencia circuit. Hit by Alexandre Barros' bike, the Brazilian having fallen just behind him, "Haru" was carried away with a broken right shoulder-blade. He very quickly got on a plane home to Japan to undergo surgery.

There was a lot of talk about chassis around Max Biaggi in Valencia.

Aspar's legacy

▷
The "Circuit de la Comunitat Valenciana Ricardo Tormo" was built in record time.

With four world championships to his name in the tiny capacity class, in the days before it was removed from the world championship programme. Jorge "Aspar" Martinez is a legend in the province of Valencia. During IRTA testing back in May and even more so during the September weekend for the inaugural GP of the Community of Valencia, he showed off his "legacy;" the new Cheste circuit.

Flash back. It is the eve of the Spanish GP at Jerez de la Frontera, six days before the first day of IRTA tests planned to take place at the new Valencia track. Jorge Martinez is more nervous than when he had to get on a bike and race. "I did a few laps yesterday for the first time. The pits and the media centre will be operational and there will already be enough seats to accommodate 12000 spectators. But God, I'm scared. What will the riders say? Will they like the layout?"

Jorge Martinez: worried about this major premiere.
▽

"A knife to the throat"

That same Tuesday 11th May 1999: Lucio Cecchinello, Noboru Ueda and a few others congratulated him publicly for his creation, Aspar could barely contain himself. "We have done all this in four and a half months. Give us until the end of July and everything will be ready." There was a moment of silence, before Martinez continued: "We worked with a knife to the throat, day and night. There is very strong political support here of course and major resources have been put at our disposal, but that would not have mattered without the dedication of the workers these past few weeks. It was a passion and a strong desire that did it. It was that desire that mattered. Everyone wanted this circuit."
The Circuit de la Communitat Valenciana Ricardo Tormo would set a standard for future new tracks: "I think it is the first layout thought out with the spectators in mind. They can see everything from the outside and the complex is like a giant arena with grandstands which can accommodate 100,000 spectators around the track. It's a new concept, designed for the future," explained the master of ceremonies. "Today, a promoter cannot entice people to a race and then stick them all around just one corner."

First plan

The circuit was created in record time, rising from the ashes of a previous 1991 project, which had more modest aims. The final version had a paddock in the centre of the track and several corners differed from the original design. The first contact wsith the Valencian authorities took place three years ago. Then came the political agreement, the work started, it was inaugurated in May and then came this fantastic September party. It was a major success. "This circuit illustrates the passion for the sport that exists in this region, not just for motorcycles but for motor sport as well," claimed Councillor Marcela Miro, representing the political interests in the track. "But this facility must also play the role of producing fresh talent," continued Martinez. "If we want to have a regular date on the world championship calendar, we also want local riders to reach the highest level of the sport." These were not idle words, because Jorge "Aspar" Martinez, along with another former rider, Julian Miralles had created a racing school for 8 to 14 year olds to ride Aprilia 50 cc mini-bikes. It was a great legacy from a happy king.

Fallers

Friday 17th September 1999

125 cc: Antonio Elias (E, Honda,) David Mico (E, Aprilia) and Kazuto Sakata (J, Honda.)
250 cc: Ralf Waldmann (D, Aprilia,) Stefano Perugini (I, Honda) and Loris Capirossi (I, Honda.)
500 cc: Haruchika Aoki (J, TSR-Honda,) Alexandre Barros (BR, Honda,) Michael Rutter (GB, Honda) and Alex Criville (E, Honda.)

Saturday 18th September 1999

125 cc: Randy De Puniet (F, Aprilia, twice... in 23 minutes,) Manuel Poggiali (RSM, Aprilia,) Alessandro Brannetti (I, Aprilia) and Gino Borsoi (I, Aprilia.)
250 cc: Masaki Tokudome (J, TSR-Honda, twice, free practise and qualifying,) Julien Allemand (F, TSR-Honda,) David Garcia (E, Yamaha,) Stefano Perugini (I, Honda,) Jeremy McWilliams (GB, Aprilia, twice, free practise and qualifying,) Franco Battaini (I, Aprilia,) Ismael Bonilla (E, Honda,) Roberto Rolfo (I, Aprilia) and Matias Rios (ARG, Aprilia.)
500 cc: Carlos Checa (E, Yamaha) and Manuel Gibernau (E, Honda.)

Sunday 19th September 1999

125 cc: Youichi Ui (J, Derbi, twice, warm-up and race,) Ivan Goi (I, Honda,) Pablo Nieto (E, Derbi,) Lucio Cecchinello (I, Honda,) Frederic Petit (F, Aprilia,) Massimiliano Sabbatani (I, Honda,) Marco Melandri (I, Honda,) Masao Azuma (J, Honda,) Ivan Martinez (E, Aprilia) and Bernhard Absmeier (D, Aprilia.)
250 cc: Daniel Ribalta (E, Yamaha,) Olivier Jacque (F, Yamaha, got going again but had to retire,) Tomomi Manako (J, Yamaha,) Johan Stigefelt (S, Yamaha,) David Ortega (E, TSR-Honda,) Ralf Waldmann (D, Aprilia,) Maurice Bolwerk (NL, TSR- Honda) and Jeremy McWilliams (GB, Aprilia.)
500 cc: Michael Rutter (GB, Honda,) Jose Luis Cardoso (E, TSR-Honda,) Carlos Checa (E, Yamaha,) Mark Willis (AUS, Modenas,) Juan Bautista Borja (E, Honda) and Alex Criville (E, Honda.)

Ouch!..

1. Haruchika Aoki (fractured right clavicle.)
2. Marco Melandri (dislocated left shoulder.)
3. Ralf Waldmann (concussion and various bruises.)

Non Starters...

1. Michael Doohan (result of fall in practise for the Spanish GP. The Australian suffered complications at right knee level. Not replaced.)
2. Bernard Garcia (result of fall at Imola GP. The Frenchman only did a few laps on Friday before giving up because his wrist hurt.)
3. Jean-Michel Bayle (result of a fall from his mountain-bike. Replaced by Spanish rider David De Gea.)
4. Markus Ober (result of a fall during a German Pro Superbike race. Replaced by Frenchman Marc Garcia.)
5. Haruchika Aoki (result of a fall in Friday's practise.)

Retirements...

125 cc: Mirko Giansanti ((I, Aprilia, lack of motivation,) Jeronimo Vidal (E, Aprilia, plug cap) and Manuel Poggiali (RSM, Aprilia, broken plug.)
250 cc: Julien Allemand (F, TSR-Honda, went off the track) and Matias Rios (ARG, Aprilia, electrical problems.)
500 cc: Jurgen Van Den Goorbergh (NL, MuZ-Weber, crankshaft) and Jose Luis Cardoso (E, TSR-Honda, result of fall in warm-up.)

◁
Alex Criville had a big fright at Valencia.

The day when Criville....

13. Phillip Island

Michael Doohan: a photo for the history books? △

....realised he was going to be the 500 cc world champion. He finished fifth in a grand prix that began full of doubt, but in which the Spaniard pushed Destiny into making a decision at Phillip Island. Criville was one of three key players that historic Sunday 3rd October 1999. Another was Michael Doohan, who did three flat chat demonstration laps which would forever be a memorable moment in the history of the sport.

"If there is sufficient time, Michael Doohan will do a lap of honour for his fans." This bit of news was confirmed on the Friday, much to the delight of all the Aussie race fans, who had come to the island to see their hero, who had dominated the local newspapers for the past few days.

On Friday, 1st October, Doohan had faced a barrage of questions in the circuit media centre, looking tired and drawn. "Physically, I could probably be back in action next week in South Africa. But what would my chances be? Maybe I could finish tenth or twelfth. Mentally, I am not yet ready to get on the bike just to cruise around in the middle of the pack. Doing that would hurt everyone; not just me, but Honda and the sponsors as well. No, I prefer to wait a bit longer."

Until when?

Wait how much longer though? "My injuries are taking a lot longer to heal than I had expected. The weeks and the months have gone by. I would not say I have changed my mind about competing, but...I have to say that, today, I really don't know if I will ever be able to get back to doing this job I love, but that I am not capable of doing right now."

It was half past one in the afternoon on Friday 1st October. Before leaving the stage, the five times world champion still had a few comments to make, notably some aimed at his most likely successor, Alex Criville, who was busy getting ready for qualifying one floor down in the garages. It was to be a catastrophic session for the Spaniard, as he broke one of the eight bones (the pisiform) in his left wrist. He did it thanks to a high speed fall at a corner which, only two days earlier had been christened Doohan Corner. Alex Criville was now the main topic of conversation, except among his own Spanish press, who were struck dumb, as if the sky had

just fallen in on them. "The fracture will not stop Criville riding on Saturday and Sunday, but he will be in great pain," confirmed Dr. Claudio Costa after making an initial examination. Another race against time had just begun and the cameras all turned to another subject: Kenny Roberts. Criville's main rival for the title was setting fastest laps on his Suzuki and was crushing the opposition. Was the race already won? Had the balance of power in the championship just shifted completely? As the paddock woke up on Sunday morning under menacing black clouds, everyone thought so.

We'll take the same ones

It was time for another parade for the three principal players of the weekend in the order, Michael Doohan, Alex Criville and Kenny Roberts.
11h35: Photographers, cameramen and the nosy had gathered in front of the HRC-Repsol team garage like a giant swarm of ants, all crawling around one

bike and one man with a helmet on, who was about to go out onto the track. Mick Doohan looks serious. He shuts his visor and at last he is alone with his thoughts; alone against the moment. One flying lap. He doesn't stop. Another at high speed and the crowd goes wild. Then he is back to where he started from and the helmet comes off. He goes out again, trying to ease the pain in his left arm, by using it to wave to the crowd as a thank you, but also as a farewell. The image that follows is one of terrible pain, of a man in leathers limping badly down the pit lane. Doohan is back with his entourage and the races can start, without the greatest champion of the second half of the Nineties.

Then the cameras switch to the track, where Roberts seems unbeatable, in the lead from the start, until four laps from home. Criville digs deep despite the pain and fights off the attack of his own team-mate Manuel Gibernau, who is under threat of a penalty for a jumped start. Could Roberts win? Would he make up a big part of the gap to the championship lead? No, because with four laps to go, he suddenly slows and raises an arm to show he is slowing down. Bits of rubber are flying off his rear tyre. Okada wins, Criville is fifth and the Spaniard gets even closer to the crown.

◁

The usual gesture, but this 3rd October 1999 it had a very special significance.

The races

▷ Alzamora picks up his machine: has the title gone out the window?

125 cc

While the Givi team run by Cecchinello took the two top places on the grid, it was definitely Melandri who seemed to be the strong man of the category, putting in solid rides all through practice, while Alzamora fell on Saturday morning. The race was frantic, mainly thanks to Youichi Ui, who led at the end of the first lap on his Derbi. Also providing the spectacle, Melandri, Locatelli, Cecchinello and Ueda, the four different leaders on the day. So, with four laps to the flag, five of them - Cecchinello, Ueda, Alzamora, Melandri and Ui - were all covered by just 0.291s. Then things started to happen: it was only a miracle that kept Ui upright and that moment, Ueda and Alzamora fell. Both Honda riders tried to get going again, but Ueda soon realised it was futile. Not Alzamora though, who was in 16th spot after his fall and would salvage a point for 15th place thanks to team-mate Angel Nieto Junior whose father manager made him stop on the final lap! Cecchinello and Melandri had it all to themselves and then set about one another on the final lap. It ended with "Macio" taking another win and to put himself back in the frame for the title, just like his team-mate Azuma, who was fifth after a catastrophic qualifying. Alzamora now only had a 13 point lead over Azuma, 26 over Melandri with 75 still to play for. The Honda one-two meant the Japanese firm had won its first title of 1999, that of the 125 cc constructors.

250 cc

There was a surprise in qualifying with a first career pole position for McWilliams, who made the most of his factory Aprilia RSW, even if he did not enjoy the same support as Valentino Rossi. The championship leader had a wake-up call when he fell on Friday, without serious injury, apart from a cut to his neck. The Yamahas were doing well, especially Jacque; the Frenchman being particularly fond of this track. Only seventh in qualifying, Rossi reacted in the warm-up by setting a time, four tenths of a second quicker than pole. The cards had been redistributed for the race. McWilliams hung onto his pole advantage with Ukawa, Capirossi, Jacque and Nakano in his wheel tracks. However, the Englishman had a short race, falling at high speed on the second lap and breaking the third and fourth

▽ Juan Bautista Borja in a unique setting.

metacarpals of his left hand. As usual, Waldman messed up his start but was now climbing through the field. Four men formed a breakaway group - Ukawa, Jacque, Rossi and Nakano. Capirossi had engine problems and was unable to keep up. At the front, the positions were changing every corner and the gap between the top four varied from 0.339s on lap 6 and 0.377 on the penultimate lap. Jacque was glued to Rossi's rear wheel and the Frenchman tried all he knew to get past, but Rossi rode a perfect lap, setting a new lap record on the final lap. Nakano had previously caught Ukawa unawares but was passed on the line for third place. In the championship, Rossi made up for his bad weekend in Valencia and now had a 35 point lead over Ukawa, but Capirossi now had no chance.

500 cc

He was on pole position after dominating every session, he was quickest in the warm-up; it looked as though Roberts would be unbeatable in this crucial round of the 500 championship. A few hours earlier, Doohan had ridden three parade laps on his Honda with the Number 1 on it and the American knew that this was the race he would have to beat Criville, if he wanted that number for himself. Criville had fallen on Friday afternoon and was riding with a broken left wrist. It seemed that only an earthquake could stop Roberts and it did, in the form of a poor choice of rear tyre, which also affected Barros and Borja, who both

stopped to change tyres. On lap 23 of 27, Roberts, who had built up a 5 second lead, despite giving himself a big fright on lap 2, had to give best, when chunks of rubber came off the tyre carcass. Biaggi, Okada and Laconi had been roped together since the half distance and would fight it out for the win. Making the most of the misfortunes of others, Criville bravely came home fifth despite his injuries. Before the race, he led Roberts by 46 points. Now he led team-mate Okada by 41 and was 51 points in front of the Suzuki rider. Biaggi just beat Laconi who took his second podium finish of the year.

....the return of Anthony Gobert. Australia's Anthony Gobert, who was kicked out of the grand prix scene by Suzuki back in 1997, was back at Phillip Island with the MuZ-Weber that Luca Cadalora had ridded at the beginning of the season. Third in the USA Superbike championship this year on a Ducati, he behaved himself in practice only to throw it away on the opening lap.

....Michael Doohan Corner. On the day before practice started, Turn 1 at Phillip Island was dedicated to the honour of Michael Doohan. "This new Doohan Corner reflects the character of the champion," stated Peter Henderson, President of Phillip Island Sports Pty. Ltd. It was at this infamous Turn 1, that Doohan lost out to Wayne Gardner in 1990 after his foot slipped off the peg. It was also the corner where Doohan suffered a high speed fall back in 1997 and finally it was also the site of a masterfully controlled slide a year ago, when he beat Simon Crafar.

....Kenny Roberts' tyres. Michelin's motor sport boss, Jacques Morelli had put out a warning: "While our teams are given specific tyres to cope with the characteristics of a particular circuit, to deal with things like lots of left hand high speed turns where tyre temperatures go up considerably, the rider must still be responsible for looking after his tyres in the race." While some made the most of it, others, notably Kenny Roberts had all sorts of problems, finishing the race at walking pace.

....the odd start to the 500 race. "I was on the front row and rather than keep my eye on the red light, I started to watch the flashing orange light on top of the lighting gantry. When the green light came on, I hesitated." Frenchman Regis Laconi was one of the riders caught out by this strange start. What happened? "As I was about to press the button to signal the start, an Australian official accidentally pressed the one that operates the flashing orange light," explained the new race director, Paul Butler. "If we had dished out stop-go penalties to those who jumped the start (like Criville) then they could easily have turned over the penalty because of the abnormal start procedure. We could have stopped everyone with a red flag, but we felt the incident had not really affected the way the race got underway."

....two of the world championships are decided. Two of the six championships up for grabs in the road racing world championship (grand prix) were settled here, with Honda taking top constructors' honours in the 125 and 500 classes.

△
Carlos Checa:
red and white bike on
azure blue background.

▷
Anthony Gobert:
the enfant terrible
is back.

Fallers

Friday 1st October 1999

125 cc: Michael Teniswood (AUS, Honda,) Steve Jenkner (D, Aprilia,) Andrew Willy (AUS, Honda,) Randy De Puniet (F, Aprilia) and Alessandro Brannetti (I, Aprilia.)

250 cc: Shaun Geronimi (AUS, Yamaha,) Valentino Rossi (I, Aprilia,) Lucas Oliver (E, Yamaha) and Roberto Rolfo (I, Aprilia.)

500 cc: Manuel Gibernau (E, Honda,) Mark Willis (AUS, Modenas,) David De Gea (E, Modenas,) Steve Martin (AUS, Honda) and Alex Criville (E, Honda.)

Saturday 2nd October 1999

125 cc: Manuel Poggiali (RSM, Aprilia,) Emilio Alzamora (E, Honda,) Arnaud Vincent (F, Aprilia,) Robin Harms (DK, Aprilia) and Michael Teniswood (AUS, Honda.)

250 cc: Jay Taylor (AUS, Honda, twice) and Jarno Janssen (NL, TSR-Honda.)

500 cc: Nobuatsu Aoki (J, Suzuki.)

Sunday 3rd October 1999

125 cc: Michael Teniswood (AUS, Honda,) Noboru Ueda (J, Honda) and Emilio Alzamora (E, Honda, restart.)

250 cc: Jeremy McWilliams (GB, Aprilia,) Maurice Bolwerk (NL, TSR-Honda,) Shaun Geronimi (AUS, Yamaha) and Jay Taylor (AUS, Honda.)

500 cc: Jose Luis Cardoso (E, TSR-Honda,) Anthony Gobert (AUS, MuZ-Weber) and Sebastien Gimbert (F, Honda.)

△
Jay Taylor at Phillip Island: mind out.

◁
Jeremy McWilliams was on pole for the first time, but his race would soon be over.

Ouch!..

1. Steve Jenkner (fractured tip of fourth finger of right hand.)
2. Mark Willis (bruising to right shoulder.)
3. David De Gea (bruising to left shoulder.)
4. Alex Criville (fractured bone in left hand.)
5. Lucas Oliver (broken left knee.)
6. Roberto Rolfo (fracture to left ankle.)
7. Jose Luis Cardoso (severe bruising to left side of abdomen.)
8. Jeremy McWilliams (fractured third and fourth metacarpals of left hand.)
9. Shaun Geronimi (bruising to left side of chest.)
10. Anthony Gobert (bitten tongue.)

Non Starters...

1. Bernhard Absmeier (was sacked by the Mayer-Rubatto team. Replaced by Robbin Harms of Denmark.)
2. Michael Doohan (result of fall in practise for the Spanish GP. The five times world champion attended Phillip Island where the first corner was named after him. On Sunday before the race he did three demonstration laps; for the first two at race pace he wore a helmet. On the following Tuesday Doohan returned to the United States to be checked out by the doctors who operated on him.)

3. Luca Cadalora (sacked by the MuZ-Weber team boss after the Czech Republic GP. Replaced by the Australian Anthony Gobert.)
4. Jean-Michel Bayle (result of falling off his mountain-bike. Replaced by David De Gea of Spain.)
5. Markus Ober (result of fall in the German Pro Superbike championship. Replaced by Steve Martin, Australian superbike champion ,1999)
6. Lucas Oliver (result of fall in practise.)
7. Roberto Rolfo (result of fall in practise.)

Retirements...

125 cc: Massimiliano Sabbatani (I, Honda, faulty cut-out) and Arnaud Vincent (F, Aprilia, engine.)
250 cc: Scott Smart (GB, Aprilia, rear tyre) and Julien Allemand (F, TSR-Honda, faulty front tyre.)
500 cc: Michael Rutter (GB, Honda, front tyre,) Mike Hale (USA, Modenas, exhaust valve control,) Jose Luis Cardoso (E, TSR-Honda, result of fall in warm-up,) Alexandre Barros (BR, Honda, poor tyre choice) and Tetsuya Harada (J, Aprilia, engine.)

14. Welkom

Built on gold

▷
*Not everyone struck gold
at Welkom.*

The promoters of "Phakisa Freeway" were certainly prepared to take a gamble. What else do you call building a modern facility for motorised sports in the middle of the desert and then running a decisive round of the most important motorcycle championship in the world. Also taking a gamble on a track where straying off the narrow racing line was like riding on marbles, was Alex Criville, riding with a very painful left wrist. Staging an incredible come back to finish eighth was proof that Valentino Rossi was hungry for gold.

The "Phakisa Freeway" in the Welkom district is about twenty kilometres from Allanridge. It was here, in 1896, that an Englishman by the name of Allan Roberts discovered the first traces of gold. Legend has it that, in 1904, the boat that was bringing proof of his research, curtailed through lack of funds,

back to England sunk off the coast of France. Despite this, the rumour quickly spread that the land in this part of South Africa was rich in gold and in 1932 new searches begun. Large amounts of gold were discovered just a hundred metres below where poor Roberts had been forced to give up his search.

▷
*The weekend got off
to a slow start....*

A serious economic crisis

Today, Goldfields in the Welkom region is the biggest producer of gold in the world. However, the crisis and drop in price of the precious metal has had a dramatic effect on the area. 10% of the one million unemployed in South Africa come from the Free State of Welkom, which is the crime capital of the state these days. "A few years ago, the mines sacked most of their workers to employ piece workers," explained a spokesperson. "Now the miners drink their pay and return to work when they run out of money." Out of this rotten environment, a dream was born to rebuild the economy on the basis of a race circuit, with a road race track and a high speed oval for Indy and Nascar racing. Only time will tell if it will be a success. The first event certainly proved popular with 35,000 spectators turning up and feeling that something new was taking place in the area, or at least that was the opinion of the locals.

The ingots

A circuit to combat misery. It would be several years before it could be judged a success or not. At least on the sporting front everything ran pretty much to plan. There were several crashes with every move off-line paid for with a visit into the earth where the grass had yet to grow, or a gravel trap or even a diversion onto the oval track.
While Allan Roberts lost out at the beginning of the century in his search for gold, others were to lose out in the fight for the championship on that 10th October 1999. Kenny Roberts chose the wrong tyres yet again and Tadayuki

... and finished with a colourful spectacle.
◁

Okada was incapable of matching Max Biaggi's pace and even worse, that set by Alex Criville. The 500s were racing on a golden road which would lead to the title a few weeks further down the road.
It was the same situation in the 250 class. Tohru Ukawa, who had posed the biggest threat in practice, was powerless against Valentino Rossi. In South Africa, the young Italian proved his maturity, remaining calm when practice did not go his way and the Aprilia rider was forced to start off the second row. He then had to fight for several laps with lads like Anthony West and Tomomi

Manako and was full of panache in the second half of the event when he thought the race could still be won.
A gold ingot for Max Biaggi's great return to form, another for Alex Criville, with the title in his sights and another for Valentino Rossi. The honours were shared in the 125 class which would stay undecided to the bitter end; Alzamora fell, triple error for Masao Azuma and another podium for Marco Melandri meant that the smallest, but not the least thrilling category had provided the most surprises.

the races

125 cc

Ueda was quickest on Friday on a track which was liberally covered with sand, blown across by the strong wings. However, in qualifying, it was Valencia winner Scalvini (Aprilia) who took pole and dominated the warm-up. Melandri was first away while Azuma ended up at the back of the pack after an off track excursion. The man who dominated the early part of the series would go off two more times before the end of the race. Melandri led from Scalvini, Sanna, Locatelli and Vincent. On lap 10 of 24, these five riders are all within 1.163s, with Vincent lapping quickest. It is about to get even more exciting. The television picture captured Goi and team-mate Alzamora in the gravel: the Spaniard was on his back and apparently in pain.

What happened? The two men touched, Goi unable to avoid his team leader, who had been in trouble right from the start with big tyre problems. Alzamora limped back to the pits with a sulky expression on his face. Melandri looked to be the main beneficiary from all this excitement. By lap 20, Locatelli and Sanna were beaten and only three riders are in with a chance of a win. Then, the Benetton Playlife team waved at Melandri to tell him Alzamora was out. Although Melandri wanted to fight for the win, it was Scalvini who would have the last word, surprising Vincent with two laps to go. It was all happening in the title race with Melandri now only 10 points behind Alzamora.

Lucio Cecchinello, rider and team owner.

▷

250 cc

Right from the start of practice, it was obvious that Honda and Yamaha were evenly matched with Capirossi ahead of Nakano, Ukawa and Jacque. It was also good to see that, in certain grip levels, the privateers, Manako and Porto were also looking good. The Aprilia men seemed to be riding on egg shells, with Rossi no better than sixth. Were we about to witness a slaughter in this category as well. No, because right from the start, Nakano and Ukawa set the pace

The Biaggi we know and love: unbeatable!

▽

while Olivier Jacque was down in seventh. Waldmann's race ended on the grid, after colliding with Boscoscuro. By some miracle, no one ran over his prone body. Out it front it was Nakano and Ukawa with Capirossi being closed down by Rossi and Jacque a bit further back. On lap 14 of 26, Rossi took second place and closed on Ukawa, who was in trouble with his tyres. Two laps from the end the Japanese rider ended up in the gravel trap, leaving Rossi to win. "This

weekend, I am pleased with myself, because I dealt with my problems." Olivier Jacque was quickest in the closing stages and it was thanks to him that the Tech 3 team run by Herve Poncharal had something to celebrate as it was the first time in the team's history that it had ever got two riders on the same podium, albeit behind Rossi, who was now just three points short of another world championship title.

500 cc

There was a storm brewing in the Marlboro-Yamaha team as Max Biaggi had demanded that most of his technical crew be changed for the following year. His engineer Mike Sinclair simply decided to quit grand prix racing! On the track, Criville was still in pain with his broken left wrist and on top of that, he also had a dose of 'flu. Okada took control of the situation, just pipping Biaggi to pole position, with Roberts also looking very comfortable on the Welkom track. It was the Roman who shot off the line into the lead with his Yamaha and rode a perfect race, leading from start to finish, just like the good old days. Criville had rocketed off the second row and was well placed with fellow

countryman Gibernau stuck to his rear wheel. On lap four, Roberts, who had made the wrong tyre choice went off the track to rejoin in 12th place and definitely out of the title race. The race now seemed all but over with an unbeatable Biaggi out in front. Gibernau passed Criville who had to slow down from around the half distance. Gibernau did appear to close on Biaggi in the last lap until he ran very wide and onto the dirt. Okada was beaten, while Roberts was forced to pit for a new tyre and did not score a single point. The championship looked all but over, even if Criville was not mathematically assured of the crown just yet.

....the first GP at the Welkom circuit. As often happens in exotic locations, the weekend started with everyone moaning. While the Continental Circus was impressed with the track and the quality of the organisation, the wind was blowing whole dunes of sand onto the track and tensions were running high the day before practice. The Italian riders led the protest while the South Africans were evidently poorly equipped to clean the track. However, there was a minor miracle on Friday as the wind dropped and the track improved throughout the weekend which ended in glory for the irate Italians who won all three races. All that excitement in front of 35,000 spectators.

....misery for the challengers. Ukawa, who nearly lost it all trying to keep up with Valentino Rossi in the 250s; Alex Criville, still suffering, beat Tadayuki

Okada and made the most of problems affecting Kenny Roberts in the 500 class; the title challengers were having a tough time. The only exception was Marco Melandri. Thanks to mistakes from his team-mate Masao Azuma and a fall for championship leader Emilio Alzamora, the young Italian came out of it smiling.

....a visit from Mauro Benetton. With the titles up for grabs and plans for the future being finalised, Mauro Benetton, the Italian company's motorcycle boss turned up in Welkom, where he confirmed his company intended to have a long term involvement in the sport. "We have a strategy for several years, which should allow Marco Melandri to one day fight for the most important championship in the 500 class."

....golden wins. The winners of the three race; Scalvini in 125, Rossi in 250 and

Valentino Rossi scores the decisive victory.

Biaggi in 500, as well as one of the riders who started from pole (Okada was picked at random) were presented with a 99.9% pure gold ingot, weighing 117 grammes. With Welkom being in the centre of the Goldfields area, the mining industry had played a major part in the creation of the Phakisa circuit.

....cash penalties. For safety reasons, a strict rule was enforced prohibiting practice race starts. On Saturday, Anthony Gobert was first rider caught at it and during the Sunday warm-up the race director caught 15 riders, including Alzamora and Scalvini (125,) Capirossi and Rossi (250) and Biaggi, Checa, Abe and Barros (500.) At a thousand Swiss france a piece it was a tidy sum.

Max Biaggi: an ingot and a return to the winner's circle.

the country

Name: South Africa
Type: Republic. Federal state made up of the former British colonies of the Cape, Natal, Orange and Transvaal.
Language: Afrikaans and English.
Capital: Pretoria.
The circuits:
1. Phakisa Freeway. In the suburbs of Welkom, a mining town in the Free State. A new complex with a 4242 metre long road circuit and a high speed oval for indy and Nascar races.
2. Kyalami. To the north west of Johannesburg. The circuit has been modified several times and has hosted a South African Grand Prix in 1983, 1984, 1985 and 1992. For the past two years, it has also hosted a round of the world superbike series. It is the true centre of motor sports in the country. Over the years it has been modified several times: it measured 4104 metres up to 1985. The direction of racing was reversed in 1992 (4260 metres) and the 1999 track measures 4267 metres.

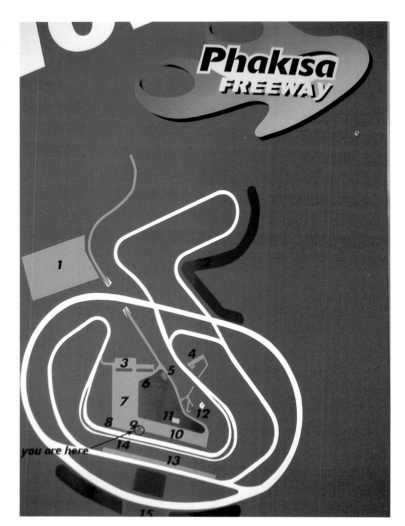

Phakisa Freeway is a project for the future of an △

The Free State is a natural paradise plunged into a serious economic crisis.
▽

the region

Name: Free State. Third biggest state in the Republic of South Africa.
Capital: Bloomfontein.
Social situation: One tenth of South Africa's million unemployed lives in the Goldfields area. For several years, the mine owners have sacked many workers to make way for piece workers. This workforce is not allowed to join a union. The drop in market value of gold has also forced production to drop. It was in an attempt to stop the area from self-destructing through amongst other things, alcoholism that the Free State government decided to finance the Welkom circuit to give the local economy a boost.

Fallers

Friday 8th October 1999

125 cc: Robbin Harms (DK, Aprilia.)
250 cc: David Garcia (E, Yamaha.)
500 cc: Regis Laconi (F, Yamaha) and Juan Bautista Borja (E, Honda.)

Saturday 9th October 1999

125 cc: Robbin Harms (DK, Aprilia,) Massimiliano Sabbatani (I, Honda) and Pablo Nieto (E, Derbi.)
250 cc: Jarno Janssen (NL, TSR-Honda.)
500 cc: Jose Luis Cardoso (E, TSR-Honda, twice, free practise and qualifying.)

Sunday 10th October 1999

125 cc: Ivan Goi (I, Honda,) Emilio Alzamora (E, Honda) and Noboru Ueda (J, Honda.)
250 cc: Ralf Waldmann (D, Aprilia) and Julien Allemand (F, TSR-Honda.)
500 cc: David De Gea (E, Modenas, restart.)

Ouch!...

1. David Garcia (broken right wrist.)
2. Ralf Waldmann (injured left hand.)

Non Starters...

1. Jeremy McWilliams (result of fall in the Australian GP. Replaced by the British rider Adrian Coates.)

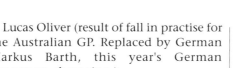
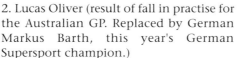
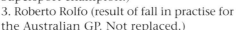

2. Lucas Oliver (result of fall in practise for the Australian GP. Replaced by German Markus Barth, this year's German Supersport champion.)
3. Roberto Rolfo (result of fall in practise for the Australian GP. Not replaced.)
4. Michael Doohan (result of fall in practise for the Spanish GP. The five times world champion underwent further surgery in San Francisco, notably on his left knee which had ligament problems. Not replaced.)
5. Luca Cadalora (sacked by the MuZ-Weber team after the GP of the Czech Republic. Replaced by the Australian Anthony Gobert.)
6. Jean-Michel Bayle (result of a mountain-bike accident. Replaced by Spaniard David De Gea.)
7. Markus Ober (result of fall during a round of the German Pro Superbike championship. Replaced by Steve Martin of Australia.)
8. David Garcia (result of fall in practise.)

Retirements...

125 cc: Manuel Poggiali (I, Aprilia, uncompetitive bike,) Randy De Puniet (F, Aprilia, engine,) Robbin Harms (DK, Aprilia, piston) and Mirko Giansanti (I, Aprilia, lack of power.)
250 cc: Scott Smart (GB, Aprilia, gear box,) Matias Rios (ARG, Aprilia, went off the track and Jarno Janssen (NL, TSR-Honda, rear tyre.)
500 cc: Michael Rutter (GB, Honda, front tyre) and Mike Hale (USA, Modenas, front fork.)

Not many fallers but plenty of off track excursions. Alexandre Barros and Anthony Gobert were two of the many victims of this slippery track.

15. Jacarepagua

Europe wins!

△
Alex Crivillé and his chief mechanic, Gilles Bigot

The first two titles, those of the two most prestigious classes of the world championship, were decided at the Jacarepagua Circuit in Rio de Janeiro. Both crowns reflected the rise to power of the European forces in racing. Whether it is the riders, like Spain's Alex Criville and Italy's Valentino Rossi, or the machinery, the Aprilia RSW250, Europe emerged victorious at the highest level in 1999. It was a cause for rejoicing even if there were a few hiccoughs on the way, which merit closer inspection.

It had taken seventeen years. Seventeen years since European motorcycle sport, which had given birth to the championship in 1949, had waited for one of its own to pick off the jewel in the crown, the 500 cc title. Seventeen years after Franco Uncini, it was the turn of a Spaniard, Alex Criville who pulled off the masterstroke, joining those other great names like, Freddie Spencer, Eddie Lawson, Wayne Gardner, Wayne Rainey, Kevin Schwantz and Michael Doohan.

A long apprenticeship

There will be some for whom Criville's title will be tainted by what happened to Michael Doohan. But remember that Kevin Schwantz won his championship after Wayne Rainey's terrible accident and Rainey won in 1992 because Doohan was out of action after his crash at Assen. But Criville's title shows that, in order to dominate in the 500 category you have to count on a whole range of factors and a full range of talents which only mature after a long apprenticeship. Alex Criville moved up to the 500s in 1992 and he won at Assen in his first year with the kings. He grew up with the same bike, the Honda

NSR, first in the team run by Sito Pons and then in the official HRC team. He developed mainly in the shadow of the dominant force of the second part of the decade, Michael Doohan. "It's true that through being with him and following him and then being in the same garage, I learned a whole barrel of things," the new world champion admitted willingly. The crowning of a European rider involved other factors. First off, there was a commercial desire to take a Spaniard to the top and once Respol replaced Elf on the works Honda fairings it was evident that the Spanish oil company wanted to see one of its own as world champion.

Finally, and it is worth taking a longer look at it, there was the question of technical evolution. While the countries that have provided the previous two world champions, the United States and Australia are now pretty much centred on two four stroke categories (supersport and superbike) the majority of European countries and Japan have still kept at least two two stroke classes (125 and 250 cc) which allows their best riders to get used to grand prix machinery.

The new scale

Because these are no longer the days when a Kenny Roberts could arrive from the USA and dominate the Europeans on their own patch. These are the days when as rider starts off in the smallest category, as Alex Criville was 125 world champion, then moves up a grade, although it has to be said the Spaniard did not shine in 250s, before taking time to learn the ropes in the 500 class.

At the same time, the new Americans and Australians, with the exception of Anthony West who might go against the trend in the next few seasons, have a greater tendency to make a career out of superbikes, in a strongly developed championship. It is currently dominated by English speakers with the notable exception of Pierfrancesco Chili.

The case of Rossi

If we look at the most recent examples, four times 250 world champion, Massimiliano Biaggi did not take long to became a front runner in the top category and it seems almost certain that the same will apply very soon to Valentino Rossi, who became 125 and 250 champion in consecutive seasons, learning to deal with adversity on the way this year.

Although further off, Marco Melandri is another possible. The big question surrounds the sponsors. None of these career paths can be built without them, but how many will have the patience to wait; to wait from 1992 to 1999 in the case of Criville, to see a return on their investment? Because, even if the 500 class evolves and if the bikes are slightly less difficult to control, patience remains a primary virtue for a rider in the blue riband event. Because if he is not patient, then like Icarus, who flew too close to the sun, there is a constant risk of burning his wings.

Valentino Rossi and his angel.
▽

125 cc

Melandri was head and shoulders above everyone else in practice, beating the next man, his own team-mate Azuma, by 8 tenths of a second. The championship leader Alzamora was in trouble, but his engineers sorted it out in time for the race morning warm-up. Melandri, Locatelli, Ui and Scalvini lead the field away with Alzamora down in tenth place. Cecchinello fell on lap 2 but kept going and the first of the championship contenders was out of the running, when Scalvini dropped it two laps later. At the same time, with Melandri still leading, Ueda on the Givi-Honda was on a charge, setting the race fastest lap and Alzamora was now up to sixth and the race was getting spectacular. By half distance, Melandri, Locatelli, Ueda, Giansanti, Poggiali, Borsoi and Alzamora were all in a bunch. Ueda took the lead with three laps remaining, but Melandri took control again on the penultimate lap, setting another lap record. But Ueda threw in a fantastic last lap to take the win, with Alzamora staging an aggressive comeback to take third. In the championship, the gap between the two front runners was now down to six places, with Azuma, sixth in Rio, 17 points down on Alzamora.

Tomomi Manako. △

Abé, Biaggi and Roberts.
▽

250 cc

Olivier Jacque was the man in Rio, the circuit where he scored his first win, before doing the double in 1997. With the best qualifying lap, the Tech 3 team rider was one of the big favourites, along with Rossi, the second Yamaha rider Nakano and Capirossi. Indeed the two silver YZR machines did indeed lead over the first few metres, thanks to a bad start from Rossi, Jacque crossing the line on lap one 0.805s ahead of Perugini. Nakano lost any chance he had next time round when he fell. But he got going again to salvage a point from 15th place. Meanwhile Rossi started to come back while the leaders squabbled and slowed. On lap 16 of 22, Ukawa, Perugini, Rossi, Capirossi and Jacque are all covered by just 1.161s, with the first three pulling away slightly over the next three laps. Rossi led on lap 20 and then set the fastest lap next time around, with a 1.336s lead over Capirossi who was toughing it out with Ukawa and Perugini. That was it for this race and Rossi was the new world champion, celebrating with yet another win before putting on an end of season show with the help of a group of around twenty friends who hit the city of Rio.

500 cc

It had been raining for five days when the Continental Circus set up camp in the Jacarepagua paddock. On Friday, on a wet track, the Sito Pons team riders, Barros and Borja seemed the most at ease. On Saturday, when the sun came out Roberts was also on the pace, although Criville, who could not afford the slightest mistake, was down in eleventh place, but the Spaniard did not panic. The race was the first one of the day to fit in with the time difference and it was run in sunny conditions. It would be the craziest and most exciting of the season. Okada and Barros got away best, even though Roberts tried to make a break right from the opening lap (0.660 in the lead.) Criville was tenth. Okada, who was the Spaniard's only rival for the title, caught up with the American by lap nine and one lap later, Biaggi and Abe joined the leading duo. Two laps later and the championship looked all but over. At exactly 11h38 and 23s, an over-anxious Okada ran into the back wheel of fellow countryman Abe on the Yamaha. Okada had to finish in the top two to have a tiny chance of beating Criville but now he was tenth. It was the start of another race: Abe, Roberts and Biaggi in front with Barros and Gibernau fighting for fourth. Criville was caught up in a fierce battle, exactly what he did not want, between McCoy, Gobert and Aoki and was trying not to put a foot wrong. On the penultimate lap, Biaggi mounted his first attack, Abe on the Luis D'Antin machine fought back and then it all happened in the very last corner when Biaggi tried a mad move, going round the outside of the Japanese rider, but it did not come off, even though the two men touched. Abe won the race and Criville won the championship, while Biaggi and Roberts were all smiles having contributed to the most spectacular afternoon of the series.

Anthony Gobert.

...Criville's first 500 title and Rossi's first 250 crown. In their time, both men were the youngest world champions in history. Moving up to the 500s in 1992, Alex Criville learned his trade in the shadow of Doohan, before adopting the Number One mantle this season. Rossi's career has been more meteoric: a year to learn then a year to win in 125 and one year to learn, winning several races and another to take the 250 crown.

....a 500 victory for a third Yamaha rider. After Laconi in Valencia and Biaggi at Welkom, Abe offered Yamaha its third 500 win of the season with a third team sharing the spoils. It was also the very first win for the Luis D'Antin team.

...Melandri's future plans. Two weeks earlier, in South Africa, he seemed tied in to the Benetton group. Then, in Rio, Marco Melandri let it be known that: what Aprilia has offered me, especially on the technical side is much more solid than my offer from Benetton." Mauro Benetton immediately announced that he felt "betrayed" and there was even talk of him pulling out of the sport.

....Rolf Biland's strange calculations. Relations between the MuZ-Weber boss and Anthony Gobert are never better. In Rio, the "Go Show" had a good scrap with world champion Alex Criville. "I had a bit of fun with a calculator: today all the 500 V4s weigh 129 kilos and put out 200 ps. All kitted up, Criville tips the scales at 66 kilos against Gobert's 88. To compensate, the Swissauto engine ought to put out 28ps more than the NSR Honda," said Biland. Translated as, Get on a diet Gobert!

....Rossi's guardian angel. The new 250 world champion rode his lap of honour with his guardian angel. "I had organised a trip to Rio for twenty of my mates from Tavullia. A few days before we left, my guardian angel appeared, thinking I would need him in Brazil. I had to explain to him that all the seats on the flight were already booked, but he laughed and replied that he could get there under his own steam."

....Josep and Alex Criville reunited. He had been Alex's manager at the start of his career. It was him who had faked their father's signature to allow Alex to get his first license. Josep Criville had not worked for his brother for several seasons after the two men had fallen out. Then, in Rio, given the importance of the occasion, the man with the black moustache was back for a very emotional reunion with the new 500 cc world champion.

The old woman and the champion: Alexandre Barros.

Fallers

*Ralf Waldmann:
after the crash.*

Friday 22nd October 1999

125 cc: none
250 cc: Alexander Hofmann (D, TSR-Honda,) Masaki Tokudome (J, TSR-Honda,) Luca Boscoscuro (I, TSR-Honda,) Anthony West (AUS, TSR-Honda,) Jason Vincent (GB, Honda,) Maurice Bolwerk (NL, TSR-Honda) and Franco Battaini (I, Aprilia.)
500 cc: Massimiliano Biaggi (I, Yamaha.)

Saturday 23rd October 1999

125 cc: Cristiano Vieira (BR, Honda,) Steve Jenkner (D, Aprilia,) Simone Sanna (I, Honda) and Alessandro Brannetti (I, Aprilia.)
250 cc: Ralf Waldmann (D, Aprilia.)
500 cc: Haruchika Aoki (J, TSR-Honda) and Juan Bautista Borja (E, Honda.)

Sunday 24th October 1999

125 cc: Lucio Cecchinello (I, Honda, restart) and Gianluigi Scalvini (I, Aprilia.)
250 cc: Maurice Bolwerk (NL, TSR-Honda) and Shinya Nakano (J, Yamaha, restart.)
500 cc: Carlos Checa (E, Yamaha.)

Norifumi Abé's helmets.

△
*Noboru Ueda:
first win since
his accident during
French GP 1998.*

Ouch!..

1. Masaki Tokudome (slight concussion.)
2. Alessandro Brannetti (broken left wrist.)
3. Maurice Bolwerk (broken fourth metatarsal, right foot.)

Non Starters...

1. Lucas Oliver (result of fall in practise for the Australian GP. Replaced by German Markus Barth.)
2. Michael Doohan (result of fall in practise for the Spanish GP. Not replaced.)
3. Luca Cadalora (sacked by the MuZ-Weber team after the Czech Republic GP. Replaced by Anthony Gobert.)
4. Jean-Michel Bayle (result of a mountain-bike accident. Replaced by David De Gea.)
5. Markus Ober (result of a fall during a round of the German Pro Superbike championship. Replaced by Steve Martin.)
6. Masaki Tokudome (result of fall on Friday. The Japanese rider was declared fit by the medical team but he preferred not to ride on Saturday.)
7. Alessandro Brannetti (result of fall in practise.)
8. Maurice Bolwerk (result of fall in warm-up.)

Retirements...

125 cc: Pablo Nieto (E, Derbi, suspension.)
250 cc: David Garcia (E, Yamaha, spark-plug,) Franco Battaini (I, Aprilia, result of twice going off the track,) Jeremy McWilliams, (GB, Aprilia, seized engine,) Anthony West (AUS, TSR-Honda, ignition) and Markus Barth (D, Yamaha, engine vibration.)
500 cc: Steve Martin (AUS, Honda, stuck throttle,) Michael Rutter (GB, Honda, clutch,) Mike Hale (USA, Modenas, crankshaft,) Jurgen Van Den Goorbergh (NL, MuZ-Weber, electrical problems) and Juan Bautista Borja (E, Honda, following his fall in practise the Spaniard was suffering from cramps.)

Melandri: guilty or innocent?

16. Buenos Aires

▷
Emilio Alzamora: second World title for Spain.

The final corner of the 1998 Argentinian 250 GP: Loris Capirossi versus Tetsuya Harada. Start of the 1999 Italian 250 GP: Capirossi versus Marcellino Lucchi. The two final laps of the 1999 Argentinian 125 GP: Marco Melandri versus Emilio Alzamora and once again a decisive race was played out in controversial fashion. Once again a few basic questions needed to be asked. Can riders do what they like? Can the intensity of a race where a championship is at stake justify behaviour which gets close to the bounds of what is decent? Does the money and investment involved justify bending the rules? The 125 cc 1999 world championship certainly ended in explosive fashion.

On the left, Marco Melandri, 17 years old and last year, the youngest ever winner in the history of GP racing. He is the flag carrier for the internationally famous Benetton group and he is already a star, when he is too young to know much about life. He is the outstanding 125 rider in the second half of the season. At the beginning of the year he fell in practice in Malaysia, he did not start in Japan and fell again in Jerez and Valencia. Now he had closed the gap to just six points. Melandri is the major strength of the moment and by far the quickest on the track for the past few months. He also has the best bike, the Honda prepared by the Belgian Olivier Liegeois.

The sums

On the right, Emilio Alzamora. Ten years older, plenty of experience but also a major character, something which comes out on the track where he has been known to use his elbows. He is not much liked in the 125 pack, maybe because he is fighting with a machine which is not the quickest in the category and that he has to make up for it one way or another and maybe because he is beginning to feel out of place in a class filled with baby riders. He leads the championship, without having won a single race and has a six point advantage over Melandri coming into the final round. He knows therefore, as does everyone else, that if the young Italian wins, he will be crowned champion by one little point if he finishes second.

In the lead from the start, Melandri does what he must. He is in control and is going to win. But behind him, Alzamora has also done what he has to do, taking this very significant second place and shaking off his pursuers, notably the Italian posse who are unable to match their Phillip Island form of 1990, when

Marco Melandri

Masao Azuma

they all forgot they were riding for different teams and marques and all rode for Loris Capirossi! It was enough to make him world champion for the first time in his life.

Innocent or guilty?

It was at this point that things got out of hand. On the Playlife-Benetton pit wall there was a lot of waving going on. Melandri looked over his shoulder. He had got the message. He slowed down tempting his rival into a game of double bluff. Not only was Alzamora in direct contact with the Italian and with all the risks this situation entailed. Better still, it meant the Spaniard was coming under threat from Roberto Locatelli, who until then, had been unable to match the pace of the two leaders. Now, if Locatelli could get past, Melandri would be world champion. He would not pass and good for him he was behaving in a more sporting fashion than Melandri who tried some dangerous intimidating moves. It was in vain. Emilio Alzamora made no mistakes and came home as world champion. Melandri is beaten and has also lost a lot of his support.

Guilty? Fined 10,000 Swiss francs by the race director for unsporting behaviour, was Melandri the orchestrator of this Machiavellian plot played out on the limits of grip? It's hard to believe. And if he was responsible for his own actions, despite his tender years, then he was also the innocent victim of a scenario written for him by people who should have known better and who control the golden future of the young champion. They evidently knew just what a world title is worth.

Even if, twelve months earlier, Loris Capirossi had been "forced" to try a risky move on Tetsuya Harada and later absolved of any guilt by the Federation tribunal, Marco Melandri must have learned just what it can take to win a title and that it is not always achieved by entirely fair means. Sometimes one has to do something different to triumph in adversity. Playing by the rules seems to get harder to do, as each year, the championship takes on more importance and more money is invested in the discipline.

125 cc

Right from the start of the weekend, it was a war of nerves between Melandri and Alzamora. And when, after just a few minutes of the Friday morning free practice session, the championship leader got it wrong on the wet track, everyone was saying the Spaniard would have his work cut out fighting off the young Italian. Azuma had not said his piece yet and he went out and took pole to ensure life would be exciting during the race. With the three title contenders, in all the wrong order on the front row of the grid, battle could commence. Melandri and Locatelli tore away at the green light with Alzamora a little further back. Azuma made a total mess of things and crossed the line in fourteenth place at the end of the opening lap and was eliminated next time round. There were now only two riders in the title hunt. While Locatelli tried his luck with a 0.539s lead on lap four, Melandri fought back, passing his compatriot to take the lead. Things were tough further back. Alzamora was a prisoner in a group which included Cecchinello and Ueda and could only ride and watch. Cecchinello attacked Melandri on lap 8, fell and just missed hitting his opponent by a matter of centimetres! At half distance, Melandri was still in the lead with a 3.310s advantage over Alzamora, Locatelli and Ueda, although the Japanese rider soon dropped back. Melandri did what he had to, easily leading the race, but Alzamora had done nothing wrong, as he was second which he made safe over the last few laps. It was now that the talking point of the weekend took place, when the Italian deliberately slowed the race, allowing Alzamora and Locatelli to catch up. He was sailing very close to the wind, trying to force his rival into making a mistake. It was in vain. Locatelli did not want to get involved in the scrap and although he won, Melandri was beaten in the championship. Worse than that, he lost a lot of support and sympathy for his behaviour, which was in fact reprimanded with a 10,000 Swiss franc fine from the race director.

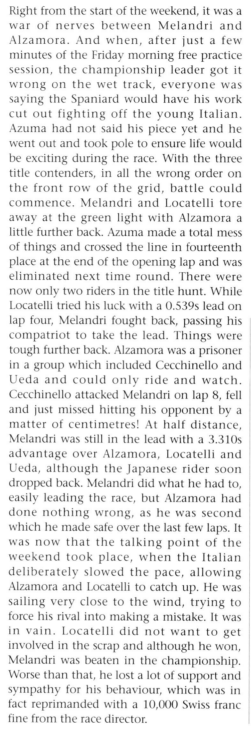

Olivier Jacque unbeatable

▷

Baiggi before Roberts

▽

250 cc

The rain on the first day of practice provoked some surprises as, come Saturday morning, Valentino Rossi was not qualified! In the afternoon, order was restored when the young Italian took pole, by 2 thousandths of a second from Olivier Jacque. The other surprise came from Sebastian Porto, the young local rider claiming a front row position on his Yamaha TZ in fourth place. At the start, Jacque, Rossi and Shinya Nakano who started from third place were best away. The Frenchman dominated the race from the first to the last kilometre with 3.637s of a lead after 12 laps and 6.345s on lap 14, Rossi having made a bad tyre choice. The struggle for fourth place was thrilling with a dice between Perugini, Porto, Nakano and Capirossi, last year's champion suffering a mechanical failure with six laps to go. At the same time, Tohru Ukawa had closed on Rossi and passed him to take second place. But Valentino's third was good enough to give Aprilia its fourteenth world championship, the 250 constructors' trophy.

500 cc

Kenny Roberts took pole from Okada, Criville and Biaggi. Right from the start, the American and Italian cleared off with a 0.898s lead over the chasing pack by lap two. Behind them came Norifume Abe, Carlos Checa and world champion Alex Criville. Jurgen Van Den Goorbergh was a strong sixth on the MuZ-Weber in the early laps but he would drop back during the rest of the race. Nobuatsu Aoki was the first notable retirement, falling on lap six and in front, Biaggi was glued to Roberts' back wheel. Okada closed on Criville in lap ten, but he fell a little bit later. Abe managed to shake off Checa and closed on the leaders. It looked as though all the ingredients were now in place for a fireworks finale to the season. Biaggi tried once, going round the outside on lap 22 of 27. Checa passed Criville on lap 24 and then we had a great battle between Roberts and Biaggi for the last three laps, which ended with an acrobatics display from Biaggi in the last few hundred metres. "I just gave it too much throttle. At first I thought I could control the rear wheel slide but then I had to get out of the saddle. I went over the handlebars and I hurt my shoulder when I came down again. In the circumstances, saving second place is not so bad," confided Max. He dismissed claims he had made a mistake. "When you do this sort of thing trying to win, it is not a mistake, it is just part of the game."

Sebastian Oscar Porto

....a champion who didn't win. After the side-car men George O'Dell (1977,) Bruno Holzer (B2B 1979,) and Werner Schwarzel (1982,) as well as Spain's Manuel Herreros (80 cc, 1989,) Emilio Alzamora became the fifth world champion in the history of the sport to be crowned without winning a single grand prix in his championship season. He does have two wins to his credit: Argentina 1995 and Holland 1996.

....Marco Melandri's fine. "On Sunday 31st October 1999, on the final lap of the 125 cc race, rider Marco Melandri drove in an irresponsible manner, putting the rider Emilio Alzamora in a dangerous position. For this reason, the race director decided to fine the rider responsible a sum of 10,000 Swiss francs." The 1999 championship had just ended in similar circumstances to the previous one.

.... another 500 podium with no Hondas. After the GPs in Valencia (Laconi, Roberts, McCoy,) Rio (Abe, Biaggi, Roberts,) came the Buenos Aires podium (Roberts, Biaggi, Abe.) The second half of the season was more difficult for the giant Honda in the 500 class, who were nowhere to be seen on three times in the last five races. We might be in for some surprises in 2000.

....Aprilia's fourteenth title. Valentino Rossi's third place was enough to assure Aprilia of the 250 cc constructors' championship, the fourteenth top honour for the company from Noale, which started racing in 1985. Loris Reggiani was their first rider with a first win on 30th August 1987 at Misano in the 250 cc race. Nine riders titles, from Alessandro Gramigni to Valentino Rossi, five constructors, two 125, three 250. Aprilia was now present in four of the top five disciplines: 125, 250, 500 and superbike.

....Anthony Gobert's illness. On Friday, the MuZ-Weber team boss Rolf Biland was dreaming of a bright future with Anthony Gobert. On Sunday afternoon, his rider did not turn up at the track as he was suffering from stomach pains. The former side car champion was a sorry sight. Today there is only a one percent chance that Gobert will be in our team next year. For that to happen, he must move to Switzerland, so we can keep an eye on him twenty four hours a day!"

....probably the last grand prix in Argentina. While the Argentinian GP was down as "to be confirmed" on the 2000 calendar, it seemed that the Autodromo Oscar Galvez in Buenos Aires had hosted its last motorcycle grand prix that October weekend. This meant that the sale of the Argentinian oil company, YPF to the Spanish giant Repsol was confirmed.

Repsol and YPF: same family

Fallers

Friday 29th October 1999

125 cc: Noboru Ueda (J, Honda,) Franco Lessio (ARG, Yamaha) and Jeronimo Vidal (E, Aprilia.)

250 cc: Gabriel Borgmann (ARG, Yamaha, twice in the space of five minutes!,) Sebastian Porto (ARG, Yamaha,) Olivier Jacque (F, Yamaha,) Roger Buffa (ARG, Yamaha,) Leandro Giuggia (ARG, Yamaha,) Matias Rios (ARG, Aprilia) and Franco Battaini (I, Aprilia.)

500 cc: Kenny Roberts (USA, Suzuki,) Norifumi Abe (J, Yamaha,) Carlos Checa (E, Yamaha,) David De Gea (E, Modenas,) Sebastien Gimbert (F, Honda) and Garry McCoy (AUS, Yamaha.)

Saturday 30th October 1999

125 cc: Emilio Alzamora (E, Honda,) Kazuto Sakata (J, Honda,) Masao Azuma (J, Honda,) Jason Di Salvo (USA, Honda,) Simone Sanna (I, Honda,) Lucio Cecchinello (I, Honda,) Arnaud Vincent (F, Aprilia,) Mirko Giansanti (I, Aprilia,) Manuel Poggiali (RSM, Aprilia) and Youichi Ui (J, Derbi.)

250 cc: Valentino Rossi (I, Aprilia,) Roger Buffa (ARG, Yamaha,) Shinya Nakano (J, Yamaha,) Jeremy McWilliams (GB, Aprilia,) Matias Rios (ARG, Yamaha) and Jason Vincent (GB, Honda.)

500 cc: Mike Hale (USA, Modenas,) Sebastien Gimbert (F, Honda,) Juan Bautista Borja (E, Honda, twice in 18 minutes!,) Alex Criville (E, Honda,) and Carlos Checa (E, Yamaha.)

Sunday 31st October 1999

125 cc: Jason Di Salvo (USA, Honda,) Lucio Cecchinello (I, Honda,) Steve Jenkner (D, Aprilia,) Noboru Ueda (J, Honda,) Manuel Poggiali (RSM, Aprilia) and Reinhard Stolz (D, Honda.)

250 cc: Markus Barth (D, Yamaha,) Franco Battaini (I, Aprilia,) Luca Boscoscuro (I, TSR-Honda,) Diego Pierluiggi (ARG, Honda) and Gabriel Borgmann (ARG, Yamaha.)

500 cc: Nobuatsu Aoki (J, Suzuki,) Tadayuki Okada (J, Honda) and David De Gea (E, Modenas.)

Tadayuki Okada
▽

Fallers

△ Jason Di Salvo

Ouch!..

1. Norifumi Abe (bruising to left hand.)
2. Youichi Ui (bruising to both heels.)
3. Roger Buffa (fractured left clavicle.)
4. Jeremy McWilliams (cut with injury to tendon of little finger of right hand.)
5. Matias Rios (twisted left ankle.)
6. Lucio Cecchinello (cracked bone, left ankle.)
7. Tadayuki Okada (abrasions to right hand.)

Non Starters...

1. Alessandro Brannetti (result of fall in practise for the Rio GP. Not replaced.)
2. Lucas Oliver (result of fall In practise for the Australian GP. Replaced by German Markus Barth.)
3. Michael Doohan (result of his fall in practise for the Spanish GP. Not replaced.)
4. Luca Cadalora (sacked by the bosses of the MuZ-Weber team after the Czech Republic GP. Replaced by Anthony Gobert.)

5. Jean-Michel Bayle (result of a mountain-bike accident. Replaced by David De Gea.)
6. Markus Ober (result of fall during a round of the German Pro Superbike championship. Replaced by Steve Martin.)
7. Youichi Ui (result of fall in practise.)
8. Jeremy McWilliams (result of fall in practise.)
9. Roger Buffa (result of fall in practise.)

Retirements...

125 cc: Masao Azuma (J, Honda, left the track,) Kazuto Sakata (J, Honda, lack of motivation,) Jeronimo Vidal (E, Aprilia, broken exhaust,) Angel Nieto Junior (E, Honda, result of a coming-together with Di Salvo on the first lap) and Arnaud Vincent (F, Aprilia, broken wheel.)
250 cc: Matias Rios (ARG, Aprilia, broken exhaust after a coming-together with David Garcia,) Julien Allemand (F, TSR-Honda, rear tyre,) David Garcia (E, Yamaha, went off the track) and Loris Capirossi (I, Honda, cylinder.)
500 cc: none.

Loris Capirossi
▽

The star :
Roger Kellenberger

Fifth in the second leg of the world superbike championship at the A1-Ring in Austria, Roger Kellenberger allowed himself the luxury during much of the race of fending off His Majesty King Carl Fogarty himself. At Hockenheim, at the end of September, his season ended rather more painfully.

The talent confirmed :
Marco Tresoldi

By finishing eighth in the European 125 cc championship, Marco Tresoldi did the necessary on the sporting front for a Swiss to once again find a place in GP racing. The Swiss racer is on the right road, via the Italian championship. Now it remains to be seen if the weight of years...

The nice surprise :
Supermotard

Switzerland has once again discovered a championship that works; supermotard. Heavy participation, both in terms of quality and quantity and above all a big success with the crowds, which numbered around 5000 spectators per race. Sometimes even when it was raining...

The black sheep :
Yves Briguet

The bad run continued for Yves Briguet. Entered in the world supersport championship, as ever under the Endoug banner, but this year with a Suzuki, the former European champion did not finish the season, having suffered a major injury to his right shoulder at Misano...

The star :
Stephane Chambon

A year ago, he had done everything in the service of his team-mate Fabrizio Pirovano. 1999 was to be his year: Stephane Chambon became the first supersport world champion in history. He did it with panache, consistency and style.

The talent confirmed :
Arnaud Vincent

Last year's nice surprise has become a talent confirmed. Promoted to official Aprilia 125 cc rider in the Jorge Martinez team, Arnaud Vincent took his first GP win in Barcelona. Despite a few errors, he fought it out with the championship contenders all the way to South America.

The nice surprise :
Regis Laconi

It's wonderful when emotion overflows. For the French speakers of the Continental Circus, Sunday 19th September 1999 will always be engraved in the memory. By winning the Valencia GP, fourteen years after the last French victory in the 500 class, Regis Laconi entered the court of the greats.

The black sheep :
Randy De Puniet

The looks of a star, a surprising start to the season without any worries, Randy De Puniet could just as well have been this year's nice surprise. Unfortunately he switched to the black sheep award in the second part of the championship, as his equipment let him down too often.

The star :
Ralf Waldmann

After an experience that was rich in lessons but not very rewarding in the 500 class, Ralf Waldmann returned to his favourite category. He had a few problems adapting to his Aprilia, particularly the race starts, he was still the German star.

The talent confirmed :
Klaus Nohles

Last year's 125 European runner-up, European champion in 1999. Klaus Nohles also scored his first world championship points this season. He is the result of all the training efforts taking place in Germany over the past few years.

The German perspective...

The nice surprise :
Jorg Teuchert

Two wins, Albacete and Nurburgring, and a fourth place overall in the world supersport championship, Jorg Teuchert was one of the key players in the series, riding one of the Yamaha R6 which turned the balance of supersport power on its head.

The black sheep :
Bernhard Absmeier

The leap from national to world championship is huge. Bernard Absmeier, runner up in the German 125 championship last year is not the first to learn that to his cost. His nightmare was actually ended prematurely when his contract was broken.

The star :
Carl Fogarty

He totally dominated the world superbike championship. 125,000 fans turned out at Brands Hatch just for him; 60,000 at Donington, 40,000 of his fellow countrymen made the trip to Assen. Carl Fogarty, with yet another title is unique.

The talent confirmed :
Iain MacPherson

One remembered him from the days of the Thunderbike Trophy. This year he was Stephane Chambon's main rival in the race for the supersport world championship. With three wins to his name, Iain MacPherson was actually the best performer of the season.

The nice surprise :
Karl Harris

Only twenty years old, but already a long career on the motocross tracks behind him and a meteoric arrival on the road racing scene. At home, Karl Harris is already considered as Carl Fogarty's natural successor. European superstock champion, he also shone in supersports with a fourth place at Hockenheim.

The black sheep :
Jeremy McWilliams

Honda had not wanted to give him a works NSR 250, so Jeremy McWilliams turned to Aprilia. In Australia he scored the first pole position of his career, before crashing out of the race while leading the big names. His injuries meant he had to miss out on the South African GP.

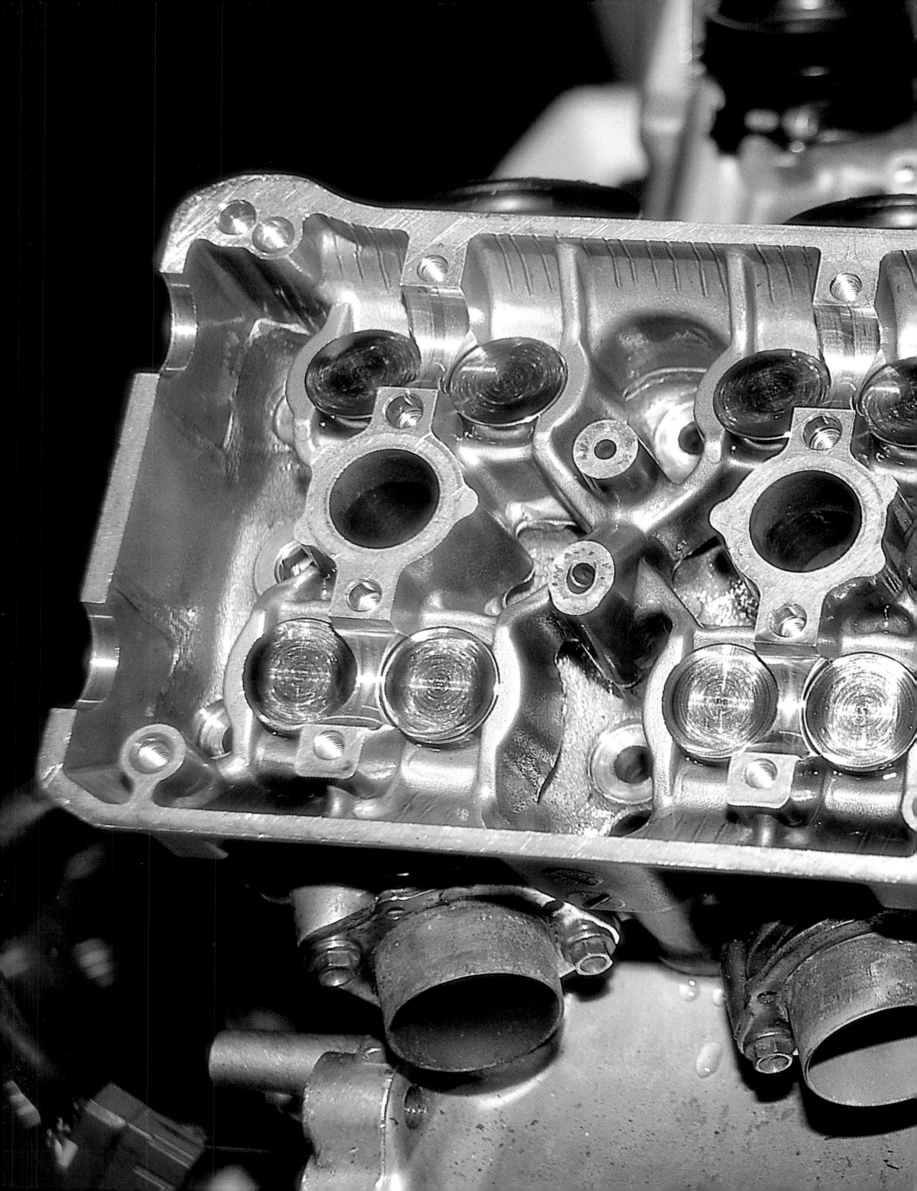

Statistics...

18th April - Malaysia - Sepang

Pole position: A. Vincent (F, Aprilia), 2'17"052 (145.731 km/h).

1. M. Azuma (J, Honda), 19 laps in 43'55"438 (143.992 km/h); 2. E. Alzamora (E, Honda), at 0"106; 3. G. Scalvini (I, Aprilia), at 10"509; 4. A. Vincent (F, Aprilia), at 12"909; 5. J. Vidal (E, Aprilia), at 20"695; 6. S. Sanna (I, Honda), at 27"184; 7. G. Borsoi (I, Aprilia), at 27"208; 8. I. Goi (I, Honda), at 27"351; 9. M. Giansanti (I, Aprilia), at 27"507; 10. K. Sakata (J, Honda), at 27"514; 11. M. Sabbatani (I, Honda), at 27"734; 12. M. Poggiali (RSM, Aprilia), at 37"922; 13. Y. Ui (J, Derbi), at 38"264; 14. A. Nieto Junior (E, Honda), at 38"344; 15. S. Jenkner (D, Aprilia), at 41"962. 22 finishers.

Fastest lap: E. Alzamora (E, Honda), 2'16"868 (145.927 km/h). New record (new track).

25th April - Japan - Motegi

Pole position: L. Cecchinello (I, Honda), 2'00"785 (143.093 km/h).

1. M. Azuma (J, Honda), 21 laps in 46'17"752 (130.665 km/h); 2. H. Nakajoh (J, Honda), at 21"903; 3. E. Alzamora (E, Honda), at 32"523; 4. Y. Ui (J, Derbi), at 35"700; 5. K. Uezu (J, Yamaha), at 36"781; 6. L. Cecchinello (I, Honda), at 36"903; 7. M. Sabbatani (I, Honda), at 38"296; 8. K. Sakata (J, Honda), at 40"169; 9. K. Kubo (J, Yamaha), at 40"956; 10. M. Nakamura (J, Honda), at 48"719; 11. A. Nieto Junior (E, Honda), at 49"059; 12. G. Scalvini (I, Aprilia), at 54"125; 13. S. Jenkner (D, Aprilia), at 1'29"946; 14. I. Goi (I, Honda), at 1'32"451; 15. R. De Puniet (F, Aprilia), at 1'43"423. 21 finishers.

Fastest lap: M. Sabbatani (I, Honda), 2'10"519 (132.422 km/h). New record (new track).

9th May - Spain - Jerez de la Frontera

Pole position: M. Azuma (J, Honda), 1'48"983 (146.103 km/h).

1. M. Azuma (J, Honda), 23 laps in 42'25"263 (143.884 km/h); 2. L. Cecchinello (I, Honda), at 0"099; 3. E. Alzamora (E, Honda), at 0"129; 4. G. Scalvini (I, Aprilia), at 0"357; 5. R. Locatelli (I, Aprilia), at 1"470; 6. J. Vidal (E, Aprilia), at 1"950; 7. S. Sanna (I, Honda), at 16"948; 8. N. Ueda (J, Honda), at 21"074; 9. M. Poggiali (RSM, Aprilia), at 27"613; 10. A. Vincent (F, Aprilia), at 28"855; 11. I. Goi (I, Honda), at 28"959; 12. G. Borsoi (I, Aprilia), at 29"264; 13. M. Giansanti (I, Aprilia), at 30"006; 14. A. Brannetti (I, Aprilia), at 33"254; 15. K. Sakata (J, Honda), at 34"282(*). 21 finishers.

Fastest lap: M. Azuma (J, Honda), 1'49"395 (145.553 km/h).

Record: T. Manako (J, Honda), 1'49"360/1998.

(*): A. Nieto Junior (E, Honda), qui avait passé la ligne d'arrivée en 15e position, a été pénalisé de 30 secondes pour dépassement sous drapeau jaune.

23rd May - France - Le Castellet

Pole position: L. Cecchinello (I, Honda), 1'28"864 (153.943 km/h).

1. R. Locatelli (I, Aprilia), 27 laps in 40'23"904 (152.382 km/h); 2. A. Vincent (F, Aprilia), at 6"124; 3. E. Alzamora (E, Honda), at 6"401; 4. M. Azuma (J, Honda), at 6"567; 5. N. Ueda (J, Honda), at 7"015; 6. M. Melandri (I, Honda), at 7"090; 7. G. Scalvini (I, Aprilia), at 9"163; 8. S. Jenkner (D, Aprilia), at 14"240; 9. K. Sakata (J, Honda), at 14"996; 10. S. Sanna (I, Honda), at 15"487; 11. R. De Puniet (F, Aprilia), at 15"490; 12. A. Nieto Junior (E, Honda), at 15"865; 13. M. Giansanti (I, Aprilia), at 19"043; 14. J. Vidal (E, Aprilia), at 34"498; 15. F. Petit (F, Aprilia), at 36"391. 22 finishers.

Fastest lap: G. Scalvini (I, Aprilia), 1'28"891 (153.896 km/h).

Record: T. Manako (J, Honda), 1'28"383/1997.

6th June - Italy - Mugello

Pole position: R. Locatelli (I, Aprilia), 2'00"254 (157.017 km/h).

1. R. Locatelli (I, Aprilia), 20 laps in 40'52"672 (153.970 km/h); 2. M. Melandri (I, Honda), at 0"271; 3. N. Ueda (J, Honda), at 0"295; 4. S. Sanna (I, Honda), at 0"343; 5. A. Vincent (F, Aprilia), at 0"442; 6. E. Alzamora (E, Honda), at 0"588; 7. M. Azuma (J, Honda), at 1"188; 8. K. Sakata (J, Honda), at 1"193; 9. L. Cecchinello (I, Honda), at 1"260; 10. G. Borsoi (I, Aprilia), at 1"338; 11. M. Giansanti (I, Aprilia), at 1"429; 12. J. Vidal (E, Aprilia), at 2"269; 13. M. Poggiali (RSM, Aprilia), at 8"436; 14. S. Jenkner (D, Aprilia), at 10"382; 15. I. Goi (I, Honda), at 10"541. 25 finishers.

Fastest lap: K. Sakata (J, Honda), 2'00"648 (156.504 kmh).

Record: N. Ueda (J, Honda), 2'00"555/1997.

20th June - Catalunian - Catalunya

Pole position: R. Locatelli (I, Aprilia), 1'52"491 (151.276 km/h).

1. A. Vincent (F, Aprilia), 22 laps in 41'47"749 (149.288 km/h); 2. E. Alzamora (E, Honda), at 0"011; 3. M. Melandri (I, Honda), at 0"340; 4. N. Ueda (J, Honda), at 0"547; 5. L. Cecchinello (I, Honda), at 1"262; 6. R. Locatelli (I, Aprilia), at 1"625; 7. K. Sakata (J, Honda), at 2"097; 8. S. Sanna (I, Chonda), at 20"426; 9. R. De Puniet (F, Aprilia), at 20"595; 10. G. Scalvini (I, Aprilia), at 20"859; 11. A. Brannetti (I, Aprilia), at 20"959; 12. G. Borsoi (I, Aprilia), at 22"768; 13. F. Petit (F, Aprilia), at 22"812; 14. M. Giansanti (I, Aprilia), at 29"025; 15. I. Goi (I, Honda), at 42"860. 18 finishers.

Fastest lap: N. Ueda (J, Honda), 1'52"813 (150.844 km/h). New record.

Old record: M. Giansanti (I, Honda), 1'53"142/1998.

26th June - The Netherlands - Assen

Pole position: L. Cecchinello (I, Honda), 2'12"853 (163.913 km/h).

1. M. Azuma (J, Honda), 17 laps in 38'09"395 (161.701 km/h); 2. N. Ueda (J, Honda), at 0"317; 3. R. Locatelli (I, Aprilia), at 0"343; 4. E. Alzamora (E, Honda), at 8"842; 5. G. Scalvini (I, Aprilia), at 9"204; 6. Y. Ui (J, Derbi), at 9"540; 7. A. Vincent (F, Aprilia), at 9"741; 8. M. Melandri (I, Honda), at 9"748; 9. G. Borsoi (I, Aprilia), at 10"095; 10. K. Sakata (J, Honda), at 11"838; 11. I. Goi (I, Honda), at 25"683; 12. M. Giansanti (I, Aprilia), at 25"881; 13. M. Poggiali (RSM, Aprilia), at 37"303; 14. S. Sanna (I, Honda), at 37"526; 15. F. Petit (F, Aprilia), at 37"868. 20 finishers.

Fastest lap: N. Ueda (J, Honda), 2'13"225 (163.455 km/h). New record.

Old record: T. Manako (J, Honda), 2'14"378/1998.

4th July - Great Britain - Donington Park

Pole position: G. Scalvini (I, Aprilia), 1'39"614 (145.389 km/h).

1. M. Azuma (J, Honda), 26 laps in 43'21"690 (144.733 km/h); 2. N. Ueda (J, Honda), at 1"783; 3. E. Alzamora (E, Honda), at 2"010; 4. R. Locatelli (I, Aprilia), at 2"380; 5. M. Melandri (I, Honda), at 10"516; 6. G. Scalvini (I, Aprilia), at 10"615; 7. Y. Ui (J, Derbi), at 11"195; 8. G. Borsoi (I, Aprilia), at 20"969; 9. A. Vincent (F, Aprilia), at 27"809; 10. M. Giansanti (I, Aprilia), at 32"981; 11. I. Goi (I, Honda), at 33"839; 12. P. Nieto (E, Derbi), at 34"250; 13. K. Sakata (J, Honda), at 43"194; 14. R. Stolz (D, Honda), at 44"396; 15. J. Vidal (E, Aprilia), at 46"529. 20 finishers.

Fastest lap: R. Locatelli (I, Aprilia), 1'39"103 (146.138 km/h). New record.

Old record: V. Rossi (I, Aprilia), 1'39"236/1997.

18th July - Germany - Sachsenring

Pole position: M. Melandri (I, Honda), 1'30"280 (139.884 km/h).

1. M. Melandri (I, Honda), 29 laps in 44'13"126 (138.039 km/h); 2. E. Alzamora (E, Honda), at 0"182; 3. L. Cecchinello (I, Honda), at 0"720; 4. R. Locatelli (I, Aprilia), at 1"449; 5. N. Ueda (J, Honda), at 19"138;

6. M. Azuma (J, Honda), at 19''267; 7. G. Scalvini (I, Aprilia), at 21''524; 8. G. Borsoi (I, Aprilia), at 23''276; 9. S. Sanna (I, Honda), at 23''652; 10. A. Vincent (F, Aprilia), at 23''897; 11. M. Poggiali (RSM, Aprilia), at 24''086; 12. I. Goi (I, Honda), at 20''091; 13. M. Giansanti (I, Aprilia), at 30''875; 14. K. Nöhles (D, Honda), at 31''576; 15. R. De Puniet (F, Aprilia), at 32''348. 23 finishers.
Fastest lap: E. Alzamora (E, Honda), 1'30''159 (140.072 km/h). New record. Old record: T. Manako (J, Honda), 1'30''838/1998.

22nd August - Czech Republik - Brno
Pole position: R. Locatelli (I, Aprilia), 2'09''384 (150.333 km/h).
1. M. Melandri (I, Honda), 19 laps in 41'23''897 (148.784 km/h); 2. N. Ueda (J, Honda), at 11''672; 3. L. Cecchinello (I, Honda), at 11''717; 4. G. Scalvini (I, Aprilia), at 11''785; 5. Y. Ui (J, Derbi), at 21''012; 6. E. Alzamora (E, Honda), at 24''598; 7. S. Jenkner (D, Aprilia), at 24''739; 8. S. Sanna (I, Honda), at 24''801; 9. G. Borsoi (I, Aprilia), at 24''979; 10. A. Vincent (F, Aprilia), at 40''513; 11. I. Goi (I, Honda), at 41''599; 12. M. Azuma (J, Honda), at 41''706; 13. K. Nöhles (D, Honda), at 41''740; 14. R. Stolz (D, Honda), at 41''771; 15. M. Giansanti (I, Aprilia), at 42''289. 23 finishers.
Fastest lap: M. Melandri (I, Honda), 2'09''617 (150.063 km/h). New record.
Old record: M. Azuma (J, Honda), 2'10''899/1998.

5th September - San Marino - Imola
Pole position: M. Melandri (I, Honda), 1'58''141 (150.227 km/h).
1. M. Melandri (I, Honda), 21 laps in 42'26''648 (146.352 km/h); 2. S. Sanna (I, Honda), at 1''244; 3. A. Vincent (F, Aprilia), at 1''535; 4. E. Alzamora (E, Honda), at 2''211; 5. N. Ueda (J, Honda), at 2''276; 6. I. Goi (I, Honda), at 12''586; 7. S. Jenkner (D, Aprilia), at 12''701; 8. M. Poggiali (RSM, Aprilia), at 13''112; 9. Y. Ui (J, Derbi), at 14''186; 10. M. Azuma (J, Honda), at 15''188; 11. R. Locatelli (I, Aprilia), at 26''791; 12. W. De Angelis (RSM, Honda), at 33''998; 13. M. Giansanti (I, Aprilia), at 48''189; 14. R. Stolz (D, Honda), at 48''758; 15. A. Brannetti (I, Aprilia), at 48''819. 20 finishers.
Fastest lap: R. Locatelli (I, Aprilia), 1'59''606 (148.387 km/h).
Record: V. Rossi (I, Aprilia), 1'58''490/1997.

19th September - Valencia - Cheste
Pole position: A. Vincent (F, Aprilia), 1'42''237 (141.025 km/h).
1. G. Scalvini (I, Aprilia), 25 laps in 47'46''994 (126.164 km/h); 2. E. Alzamora (E, Honda), at 7''957; 3. N. Ueda (J, Honda), at 28''360; 4. A. Vincent (F, Aprilia), at 32''455; 5. S. Jenkner (D, Aprilia), at 39''038; 6. G. Borsoi (I, Aprilia), at 1'09''267; 7. S. Sanna (I, Honda), at 1'34''477; 8. R. Locatelli (I, Aprilia), at 1'35''606; 9. D. Mico (E, Aprilia), at 1'35''921; 10. R. De Puniet (F, Aprilia), at 1'39''107; 11. A. Brannetti (I, Aprilia), at 1'39''479; 12. K. Sakata (J, Honda), at 1'50''845; 13. R. Stolz (D, Honda), at 1 lap; 14. A. Elias (E, Honda); 15. A. Nieto Junior (E, Honda). 17 finishers.
Fastest lap: E. Alzamora (E, Honda), 1'51''830 (128.927 km/h).
Record: J. Vidal (E, Aprilia), 1'44''2 (Spanish Championship).

3rd October - Australia - Phillip Island
Pole position: N. Ueda (J, Honda), 1'38''600 (162.401 km/h).
1. M. Melandri (I, Honda), 23 laps in 38'07''081 (161.032 km/h); 2. L. Cecchinello (I, Honda), at 0''035; 3. Y. Ui (J, Derbi), at 0''179; 4. G. Scalvini (I, Aprilia), at 1''043; 5. M. Azuma (J, Honda), at 1''259; 6. R. Locatelli (I, Aprilia), at 1''898; 7. J. Vidal (E, Aprilia), at 10''207; 8. G. Borsoi (I, Aprilia), at 11''845; 9. M. Poggiali (RSM, Aprilia), at 12''890; 10. S. Jenkner (D, Aprilia), at 16''527; 11. M. Giansanti (I, Aprilia), at 17''731; 12. S. Sanna (I, Honda), at 16''837; 13. K. Sakata (J, Honda), at 36''339; 14. I. Goi (I, Honda), at 36''408; 15. E. Alzamora (E, Honda), at 49''941. 24 finishers.
Fastest lap: M. Melandri (I, Honda), 1'38''118 (163.199 km/h). New record.
Old record: M. Melandri (I, Honda), 1'40''296/1998.

10th October - South Africa - Welkom
Pole position: G. Scalvini (I, Aprilia), 1'43''404 (147.684 km/h).
1. G. Scalvini (I, Aprilia), 24 laps in 41'41''665 (146.505 km/h); 2. A. Vincent (F, Aprilia), at 0''660; 3. M. Melandri (I, Honda), at 0''844; 4. R. Locatelli (I, Aprilia), at 8''084; 5. G. Borsoi (I, Aprilia), at 17''277; 6. S. Sanna (I, Honda), at 17''667; 7. Y. Ui (J, Derbi), at 22''769; 8. L. Cecchinello (I, Honda), at 23''794; 9. A. Brannetti (I, Aprilia), at 24''187; 10. J. Vidal (E, Aprilia), at 35''785; 11. S. Jenkner (D, Aprilia), at 38''565; 12. P. Nieto (E, Derbi), at 39''264; 13. A. Nieto Junior (E, Honda), at 50''228; 14. M. Azuma (J, Honda), at 53''917; 15. K. Sakata (J, Honda), at 54''458. 19 finishers.
Fastest lap: G. Scalvini (I, Aprilia), 1'43''324 (147.799 km/h). New record (new track).

24th October - Rio de Janeiro - Jacarepagua
Pole position: M. Melandri (I, Honda), 1'59''490 (148.621 km/h).
1. N. Ueda (J, Honda), 21 laps in 42'14''647 (147.134 km/h); 2. M. Melandri (I, Honda), at 0''131; 3. E. Alzamora (E, Honda), at 0''977; 4. M. Giansanti (I, Aprilia), at 1''055; 5. G. Borsoi (I, Aprilia), at 1''297; 6. M. Azuma (J, Honda), at 1''457; 7. M. Poggiali (RSM, Aprilia), at 1''689; 8. R. Locatelli (I, Aprilia), at 2''025; 9. S. Sanna (I, Honda), at 2''280; 10. Y. Ui (J, Derbi), at 20''470; 11. I. Goi (I, Honda), at 24''150; 12. J. Vidal (E, Aprilia), at 24''424; 13. A. Vincent (F, Aprilia), at 29''529;

Final classification

1. Emilio Alzamora	E	Honda	227 points
2. Marco Melandri	I	Honda	226
3. Masao Azuma	J	Honda	190
4. Roberto Locatelli	I	Aprilia	173
5. Noboru Ueda	J	Honda	171
6. Gianluigi Scalvini	I	Aprilia	163
7. Arnaud Vincent	F	Aprilia	155
8. Simone Sanna	I	Honda	123
9. Lucio Cecchinello	I	Honda	108
10. Gino Borsoi	I	Aprilia	106

11. Y. Ui (J, Derbi), 84; 12. M. Giansanti (I, Aprilia), 66; 13. I. Goi (I, Honda), 61; 14. K. Sakata (J, Honda), 56; 15. S. Jenkner (D, Aprilia), 54; 16. J. Vidal (E, Aprilia), 47; 17. M. Poggiali (RSM, Aprilia), 46; 18. R. De Puniet (F, Aprilia), 26; 19. M. Sabbatani (I, Honda), 21; 20. H. Nakajoh (J, Honda), 20; 21. A. Brannetti (I, Aprilia), 20; 22. A. Nieto Junior (E, Honda), 16; 23. P. Nieto (E, Derbi), 15; 24. K. Uezu (J, Yamaha), 11; 25. F. Petit (F, Aprilia), 9; 26. R. Stolz (D, Honda), 9; 27. K. Kubo (J, Yamaha), 7; 28. D. Mico (E, Aprilia) 7; 29. M. Nakamura (J, Honda), 6; 30. K. Nöhles (D, Honda), 5; 31. W. De Angelis (RSM, Honda), 4; 2. R. Harms (DK, Aprilia), 2; 33. A. Elias (E, Honda), 2. 33 finishers.

250 World Championship

18th April - Malaysia - Sepang

Pole position: V. Rossi (I, Aprilia), 2'08"956 (154.880 km/h).

1. L. Capirossi (I, Honda), 20 laps in 43'29"305 (153.089 km/h); 2. T. Ukawa (J, Honda), at 0"111; 3. S. Nakano (J, Yamaha), at 0"787; 4. O. Jacque (F, Yamaha), at 14"894; 5. V. Rossi (I, Aprilia), at 24"569; 6. M. Lucchi (I, Aprilia), at 30"774; 7. J. McWilliams (GB, Aprilia), at 34"877; 8. N. Matsudo (J, Yamaha), at 35"294; 9. S. Perugini (I, Honda), at 52"956; 10. R. Rolfo (I, Aprilia), at 58"656; 11. L. Boscoscuro (I, TSR-Honda), at 1'05"383; 12. J. Vincent (GB, Honda), at 1'05"385; 13. M. Tokudome (J, Honda), at 1'21"549; 14. A. West (AUS, Honda), at 1'22"318; 15. S. Porto (ARG, Yamaha), at 1'22"741. 23 finishers.

Fastest lap: L. Capirossi (I, Honda), 2'09"381 (154.371 km/h). New record (new track).

25th April - Japan - Motegi

Pole position: F. Battaini (I, Aprilia), 2'06"752 (136.357 km/h).

1. S. Nakano (J, Yamaha), 23 laps in 48'52"950 (135.536 km/h); 2. T. Ukawa (J, Honda), at 2"697; 3. L. Capirossi (I, Honda), at 9"260; 4. F. Battaini (I, Aprilia), at 11"895; 5. D. Katoh (J, Honda), at 13"793; 6. T. Yamaguchi (J, Honda), at 14"264; 7. V. Rossi (I, Aprilia), at 21"092; 8. T. Manako (J, Yamaha), at 24"485; 9. M. Lucchi (I, Aprilia), at 45"594; 10. A. West (AUS, Honda), at 49"724; 11. N. Matsudo (J, Yamaha), at 1'07"293; 12. R. Rolfo (I, Aprilia), at 1'11"813; 13. D. Garcia (E, Yamaha), at 1'15"851; 14. A. Gonzalez-Nieto (E, Yamaha), at 1'17"806; 15. T. Kayo (J, TSR-Honda), at 1'18"400. 21 finishers.

Fastest lap: T. Ukawa (J, Honda), 2'05"726 (137.470 km/h). New record (new track).

9th May - Spain - Jerez de la Frontera

Pole position: S. Nakano (J, Yamaha), 1'44"738 (152.025 km/h).

1. V. Rossi (I, Aprilia), 26 laps in 46'04"289 (149.764 km/h); 2. T. Ukawa (J, Honda), at 4"439; 3. L. Capirossi (I, Honda), at 14"096; 4. F. Battaini (I, Aprilia), at 24"221; 5. M. Lucchi (I, Aprilia), at 28"614; 6. R. Waldmann (D, Aprilia), at 35"373; 7. J. McWilliams (GB, Aprilia), at 40"182; 8. S. Perugini (I, Honda), at 45"096; 9. R. Rolfo (I, Aprilia), at 45"483; 10. L. Boscoscuro (I, TSR-Honda), at 45"762; 11. J. Vincent (GB, Honda), at 46"147; 12. S. Porto (ARG, Yamaha), at 52"082; 13. M. Tokudome (J, TSR-Honda), at 1'00"476; 14. T. Manako (J, Yamaha), at 1'04"989; 15. A. Hofmann (D, TSR-Honda), at 1'09"322. 26 finishers.

Fastest lap: S. Nakano (J, Yamaha), 1'44"875 (151.826 km/h). New record.

Old record: L. Capirossi (I, Aprilia), 1'45"250/1998.

23rd May - France - Le Castellet

Pole position: V. Rossi (I, Aprilia), 1'23"366 (164.095 km/h).

1. T. Ukawa (J, Honda), 29 laps in 40'50"340 (161.904 km/h); 2. S. Nakano (J, Yamaha), at 10"940; 3. S. Perugini (I, Honda), at 20"696; 4. R. Waldmann (D, Aprilia), at 21"219; 5. J. Vincent (GB, Honda), at 21"421; 6. F. Battaini (I, Aprilia), at 26"021 (*); 7. S. Porto (ARG, Yamaha), at 29"172; 8. A. Hofmann (D, TSR-Honda), at 35"011; 9. A. West (AUS, TSR-Honda), at 35"916; 10. T. Honma (J, Yamaha), at 38"122; 11. J. McWilliams (GB, Aprilia), at 43"060; 12. A. Gonzalez-Nieto (E, Yamaha), at 52"963; 13. M. Tokudome (J, TSR-Honda), at 52"970; 14. L. Boscoscuro (I, TSR-Honda), at 53"198; 15. M. Lucchi (I, Aprilia), at 56"805. 20 finishers.

Fastest lap: V. Rossi (I, Aprilia), 1'23"635 (163.567 km/h).

Record: L. Capirossi (I, Aprilia), 1'23"559/1997.

(*): F. Battaini (I, Aprilia), qui avait passé la ligne d'arrivée en quatrième position, a été pénalisé de 5 secondes pour dépassement sous le drapeau jaune.

6th June - Italy - Mugello (*)

Pole position: M. Lucchi (I, Aprilia), 1'54"376 (165.087 km/h).

1. V. Rossi (I, Aprilia), 21 laps in 40'52"837 (161.658 km/h); 2. R. Waldmann (D, Aprilia), at 2"643; 3. T. Ukawa (J, Honda), at 2"684; 4. J. McWilliams (GB, Aprilia), at 11"333; 5. S. Nakano (J, Yamaha), at 11"684; 6. F. Battaini (I, Aprilia), at 12"447; 7. J. Vincent (GB, Honda), at 21"184; 8. S. Perugini (I, Honda), at 21"721; 9. S. Porto (ARG, Yamaha), at 40"911; 10. L. Boscoscuro (I, TSR-Honda), at 45"815; 11. M. Tokudome (J, TSR-Honda), at 53"891; 12. J. Stigefelt (S, Yamaha), at 54"066; 13. T. Manako (J, Yamaha), at 54"096; 14. J. Allemand (F, TSR-Honda), at 1'18"330; 15. D. Garcia (E, Yamaha), at 1'21"272. 19 finishers.

Fastest lap: V. Rossi (I, Aprilia), 1'55"254 (163.829 km/h).

Record: M. Biaggi (I, Aprilia), 1'54"925/1996.

(*): L. Capirossi (I, Honda), a été mis hors course pour non observation du drapeau noir.

20th June - Catalunian - Catalunya

Pole position: T. Ukawa (J, Honda), 1'48"199 (157.276 km/h).

1. V. Rossi (I, Aprilia), 23 laps in 41'47"806 (156.070 km/h); 2. T. Ukawa (J, Honda), at 0"258; 3. F. Battaini (I, Aprilia), at 12"755; 4. S. Nakano (J, Yamaha), at 13"085; 5. R. Rolfo (I, Aprilia), at 25"429; 6. J. McWilliams (GB, Aprilia), at 29"320; 7. S. Perugini (I, Honda), at 45"343; 8. N. Matsudo (J, Yamaha), at 45"563; 9. S. Porto (ARG, Yamaha), at 50"947; 10. L. Boscoscuro (I, TSR-Honda), at 51"482; 11. A. Hofmann (D, TSR-Honda), at 51"673; 12. T. Manako (J, Yamaha), at 51"742; 13. M. Tokudome (J, TSR-Honda), at 1'11"473; 14. L. Oliver (E, Yamaha), at 1'26"093; 15. J. Janssen (NL,

TSR-Honda), at 1'37"071. 18 finishers.

Fastest lap: V. Rossi (I, Aprilia), 1'48"278 (157.162 km/h).

Record: V. Rossi (I, Aprilia), 1'47"585/1998.

26th June - The Netherlands - Assen

Pole position: V. Rossi (I, Aprilia), 2'05"018 (174.186 km/h).

1. L. Capirossi (I, Honda), 18 laps in 38'04"730 (171.563 km/h); 2. V. Rossi (I, Aprilia), at 0"180; 3. J. McWilliams (GB, Aprilia), at 0"534; 4. T. Ukawa (J, Honda), at 0"537; 5. S. Nakano (J, Yamaha), at 0"742; 6. R. Waldmann (D, Aprilia), at 7"019; 7. F. Battaini (I, Aprilia), at 20"889; 8. S. Perugini (I, Honda), at 20"891; 9. J. Vincent (GB, Honda), at 21"310; 10. A. West (AUS, TSR-Honda), at 26"816; 11. A. Hofmann (D, TSR-Honda), at 26"933; 12. S. Porto (ARG, Yamaha), at 27"054; 13. T. Manako (J, Yamaha), at 27"903; 14. M. Tokudome (J, TSR-Honda), at 33"161; 15. J. Janssen (NL, TSR-Honda), at 56"248. 24 finishers.

Fastest lap: V. Rossi (I, Aprilia), 2'05"696 (173.246 km/h). New record.

Old record: O. Jacque (F, Honda), 2'06"047/1997.

4th July - Great Britain - Donington Park

Pole position: L. Capirossi (I, Honda), 1'34"277 (153.619 km/h).

1. V. Rossi (I, Aprilia), 27 laps in 42'54"311 (151.899 km/h); 2. L. Capirossi (I, Honda), at 1"261; 3. S. Nakano (J, Yamaha), at 8"162; 4. T. Ukawa (J, Honda), at 9"000; 5. S. Perugini (I, Honda), at 14"131; 6. J. McWilliams (GB, Aprilia), at 17"368; 7. M. Lucchi (I, Aprilia), at 23"720; 8. R. Waldmann (D, Aprilia), at 25"636; 9. M. Tokudome (J, TSR-Honda), at 46"825; 10. L. Boscoscuro (I, TSR-Honda), at 48"712; 11. A. West (AUS, TSR-Honda), at 52"790; 12. J. Robinson (GB, Yamaha), at 53"854; 13. A. Hofmann (D, TSR-Honda), at 1'01"522; 14. T. Manako (J, Yamaha), at 1'03"660; 15. J. Allemand (F, TSR-Honda), at 1'14"867. 19 finishers.

Fastest lap: L. Capirossi (I, Honda), 1'34"448 (153.341 km/h).

Record: T. Harada (J, Aprilia), 1'34"137/1997.

18th July - Germany - Sachsenring

Pole position: V. Rossi (I, Aprilia), 1'27"913 (143.651 km/h).

1. V. Rossi (I, Aprilia), 30 laps in 44'49"622 (140.861 km/h); 2. L. Capirossi (I, Honda), at 0"148; 3. R. Waldmann (D, Aprilia), at 9"030; 4. S. Nakano (J, Yamaha), at 12"295; 5. S. Perugini (I, Honda), at 18"391; 6. A. West (AUS, TSR-Honda), at 18"553; 7. S. Porto (ARG, Yamaha), at 19"201; 8. O. Jacque (F, Yamaha), at 19"637; 9. A. Hofmann (D, Honda), at 22"149; 10. L. Boscoscuro (I, TSR-Honda), at 35"995; 11. J. Allemand (F, TSR-Honda), at 44"097; 12. R. Rolfo (I, Aprilia), at 45"011; 13. M. Lucchi (I, Aprilia), at 45"254; 14. T. Manako (J,

Yamaha), at 47"452; 15. M. Tokudome (J, TSR-Honda), at 47"559. 24 finishers.
Fastest lap: L. Capirossi (I, Honda), 1'28"662 (142.437 km/h).
Record: T. Harada (J, Aprilia), 1'28"625/1998.

22nd August - Czech Republic - Brno
Pole position: R. Waldmann (D, Aprilia), 2'04"158 (156.661 km/h).
1. V. Rossi (I, Aprilia), 20 laps in 41'48"114 (155.102 km/h); 2. R. Waldmann (D, Aprilia), at 0"700; 3. T. Ukawa (J, Honda), at 2"833; 4. S. Nakano (J, Yamaha), at 6"206; 5. O. Jacque (F, Yamaha), at 11"776; 6. S. Perugini (I, Honda), at 11"989; 7. L. Capirossi (I, Honda), at 20"421; 8. J. McWilliams (GB, Aprilia), at 21"842; 9. J. Vincent (GB, Honda), at 30"956; 10. F. Battaini (I, Aprilia), at 34"465; 11. R. Rolfo (I, Aprilia), at 40"974; 12. M. Tokudome (J, TSR-Honda), at 54"621; 13. L. Boscoscuro (I, TSR-Honda), at 54"787; 14. T. Manako (J, Yamaha), at 59"356; 15. A. West (AUS, TSR-Honda), at 1'02"158. 21 finishers.
Fastest lap: V. Rossi (I, Aprilia), 2'04"469 (156.270 km/h). New record.
Old record: L. Capirossi (I, Aprilia), 2'04"614/1998.

5th September - San Marino - Imola
Pole position: O. Jacque (F, Yamaha), 1'51"929 (158.564 km/h).
1. L. Capirossi (I, Honda), 23 laps in 43'23"269 (156.804 km/h); 2. V. Rossi (I, Aprilia), at 8"248; 3. O. Jacque (F, Yamaha), at 9"971; 4. S. Perugini (I, Honda), at 11"758; 5. S. Nakano (J, Yamaha), at 17"488; 6. F. Battaini (I, Aprilia), at 21"322; 7. R. Waldmann (D, Aprilia), at 23"134; 8. M. Lucchi (I, Aprilia), at 24"194; 9. S. Porto (ARG, Yamaha), at 36"966; 10. R. Rolfo (I, Aprilia), at 37"617; 11. L. Boscoscuro (I, TSR-Honda), at 39"093; 12. T. Ukawa (J, Honda), at 56"984; 13. J. McWilliams (GB, Aprilia), at 1'05"262; 14. T. Manako (J, Yamaha), at 1'06"453; 15. A. West (AUS, TSR-Honda), at 1'11"239. 21 finishers.
Fastest lap: S. Perugini (I, Honda), 1'52"138 (158.269 km/h).
Record: T. Harada (J, Aprilia), 1'51"872/1997.

19th September - Valencia - Cheste
Pole position: S. Nakano (J, Yamaha), 1'37"258 (148.244 km/h).
1. T. Ukawa (J, Honda), 27 laps in 49'50"449 (130.176 km/h); 2. F. Battaini (I, Aprilia), at 5"125; 3. L. Capirossi (I, Honda), at 10"224; 4. S. Nakano (J, Yamaha), at 14"848; 5. S. Perugini (I, Honda), at 34"042; 6. S. Porto (ARG, Yamaha), at 37"495; 7. J. Vincent (GB, Honda), at 44"911; 8. V. Rossi (I, Aprilia), at 1'01"011; 9. A. West (AUS, TSR-Honda), at 1'10"352; 10. A. Hofmann (D, TSR-Honda), at 1'18"683; 11. L. Boscoscuro (I, Aprilia), at 1'20"847; 12. L. Oliver (E, Yamaha), at 1'23"051; 13. R. Rolfo (I,

Aprilia), at 1'24"329; 14. M. Tokudome (J, TSR-Honda), at 1'26"837; 15. A. Gonzalez-Nieto (E, Yamaha), at 1'45"669. 19 finishers.
Fastest lap: F. Battaini (I, Aprilia), 1'47"987 (133.516 km/h).
Record: A. Gonzalez-Nieto (E/Yamaha), 1'40"8 (during a Spanish Championship race).

3rd October - Australia - Phillip Island
Pole position: J. McWilliams (GB, Aprilia), 1'33"919 (170.495 km/h).
1. V. Rossi (I, Aprilia), 25 laps in 39'28"278 (169.034 km/h); 2. O. Jacque (F, Yamaha), at 0"103; 3. T. Ukawa (J, Honda), at 0"729; 4. S. Nakano (J, Yamaha), at 13"097; 5. R. Waldmann (D, Aprilia), at 13"133; 6. L. Capirossi (I, Honda), at 25"831; 7. S. Perugini (I, Honda), at 25"831; 8. F. Battaini (I, Aprilia), at 25"994; 9. S. Porto (ARG, Yamaha), at 35"124; 10. A. West (AUS, TSR-Honda), at 36"446; 11. T. Manako (J, Yamaha), at 49"725; 12. J. Vincent (GB, Honda), at 50"949; 13. A. Hofmann (D, TSR-Honda), at 59"357; 14. L. Boscoscuro (I, TSR-Honda), at 59"373; 15. M. Tokudome (J, TSR-Honda), at 1'06"163. 21 finishers.
Fastest lap: V. Rossi (I, Aprilia), 1'33"556 (171.157 km/h). New record.
Old record: T. Harada (J, Aprilia), 1'35"253/1998.

10th October - South Africa - Welkom
Pole position: L. Capirossi (I, Honda), 1'38"287 (155.373 km/h).
1. V. Rossi (I, Aprilia), 26 laps in 42'57"870 (154.022 km/h); 2. S. Nakano (J, Yamaha), at 1"913; 3. O. Jacque (F, Yamaha), at 3"862; 4. T. Ukawa (J, Honda), at 4"131; 5. L. Capirossi (I, Honda), at 19"739; 6. S. Porto (ARG, Yamaha), at 23"224; 7. S. Perugini (I, Honda), at 26"461; 8. L. Boscoscuro (I, TSR-Honda), at 28"366; 9. A. West (AUS, TSR-Honda), at 37"644; 10. F. Battaini (I, Aprilia), at 42"837; 11. J. Vincent (GB, Honda), at 45"558; 12. T. Manako (J, Yamaha), at 51"489; 13. A. Hofmann (D, TSR-Honda), at 57"309; 14. M. Tokudome

(J, TSR-Honda), at 57"544; 15. A. Gonzalez-Nieto (E, Yamaha), at 1'35"573. 20 finishers.
Fastest lap: V. Rossi (I, Aprilia), 1'37"624 (156.428 km/h). New record (new track).

24th October - Rio de Janeiro - Jacarepagua
Pole position: O. Jacque (F, Yamaha), 1'54"072 (155.680 km/h).
1. V. Rossi (I, Aprilia), 22 laps in 42'17"893 (153.944 km/h); 2. T. Ukawa (J, Honda), at 1"328; 3. L. Capirossi (I, Honda), at 1"944; 4. O. Jacque (F, Yamaha), at 2"342; 5. S. Perugini (I, Honda), at 2"395; 6. S. Porto (ARG, Yamaha), at 13"031; 7. R. Waldmann (D, Aprilia), at 15"483; 8. T. Manako (J, Yamaha), at 16"222; 9. R. Rolfo (I, Aprilia), at 41"230; 10. L. Boscoscuro (I, TSR-Honda), at 43"002; 11. J. Vincent (GB, Honda), at 43"012; 12. A. Hofmann (D, TSR-Honda), at 54"010; 13. J. Allemand (F, TSR-Honda), at 1'12"641; 14. S. Smart (GB, Aprilia), at 1'12"746; 15. S. Nakano (J, Yamaha), at 1'12"791. 19 finishers.
Fastest lap: V. Rossi (I, Aprilia), 1'54"230 (155.465 km/h). New record.
Old record: O. Jacque (F, Yamaha), 1'54"267/1997.

31st October - Argentina - Buenos Aires
Pole position: V. Rossi (I, Aprilia), 1'45"844 (147.953 km/h).
1. O. Jacque (F, Yamaha), 25 laps in 44'34"817 (146.365 km/h); 2. T. Ukawa (J, Honda), at 9"236; 3. V. Rossi (I, Aprilia), at 17"573; 4. S. Porto (ARG, Yamaha), at 21"735; 5. S. Nakano (J, Yamaha), at 26"791; 6. S. Perugini (I, Honda), at 33"162; 7. R. Rolfo (I, Aprilia), at 33"673; 8. A. West (AUS, TSR-Honda), at 40"963; 9. T. Manako (J, Yamaha), at 44"523; 10. A. Hofmann (D, TSR-Honda), at 50"445; 11. R. Waldmann (D, Aprilia), at 52"881; 12. J. Vincent (GB, Honda), at 1'10"078; 13. S. Smart (GB, Aprilia), at 1'10"268; 14. A. Gonzalez-Nieto (E, Yamaha), at 1'10"481; 15. M. Tokudome (J, TSR-Honda), at 1'11"156. 20 finishers.
Fastest lap: O. Jacque (F, Yamaha), 1'45"734 (148.107 km/h).
Record: V. Rossi (I, Aprilia), 1'45"473/1998.

Final classification

1.	Valentino Rossi	I	Aprilia	309 points
2.	Tohru Ukawa	J	Honda	261
3.	Loris Capirossi	I	Honda	209
4.	Shinya Nakano	J	Yamaha	207
5.	Stefano Perugini	I	Honda	151
6.	Ralf Waldmann	D	Aprilia	131
7.	Olivier Jacque	F	Yamaha	122
8.	Franco Battaini	I	Aprilia	121
9.	Sebastian Porto	ARG	Yamaha	98
10.	Jeremy McWilliams	GB	Aprilia	83

11. J. Vincent (GB, Honda), 70; 12. A. West (AUS, TSR-Honda), 66; 13. L. Boscoscuro (I, TSR-Honda), 66; 14. R. Rolfo (I, Aprilia), 62; 15. T. Manako (J, Yamaha), 52; 16. A. Hofmann (D, TSR-Honda), 51; 17. M. Lucchi (I, Aprilia), 49; 18. M. Tokudome (J, TSR-Honda), 37; 19. N. Matsudo (J, Yamaha), 21; 20. D. Katoh (J, Honda), 11; 21. J. Allemand (F, TSR-Honda), 11; 22. T. Yamaguchi (J, Honda), 10; 23. A. Gonzalez-Nieto (E, Yamaha), 10; 24. T. Honma (J, Yamaha), 6; 25. L. Oliver (E, Yamaha), 6; 26. S. Smart (GB, Aprilia), 5; 27. J. Stigefelt (S, Yamaha), 4; 28. J. Robinson (GB, Yamaha), 4; 29. D. Garcia (E, Yamaha), 4; 30. J. Janssen (NL, TSR-Honda), 2; 31. T. Kayo (J, TSR-Honda), 1. 31 finishers.

18ᵗʰ April - Malaisie - Sepang

Pole position: J. Kocinski (USA, Honda V4), 2'06"848 (157.454 km/h).

1. K. Roberts (USA, Suzuki), 21 laps in 44'56"033 (155.572 km/h); 2. C. Checa (E, Yamaha), at 4"279; 3. A. Crivillé (E, Honda V4), at 4"780; 4. M. Doohan (AUS, Honda V4), at 4"902; 5. T. Okada (J, Honda V4), at 7"269; 6. A. Barros (BR, Honda V4), at 13"202; 7. R. Laconi (F, Yamaha), at 23"724; 8. J.-B. Borja (E, Honda V4), at 23"811; 9. N. Aoki (J, Suzuki), at 25"156; 10. M. Gibernau (E, Honda V2), at 31"548; 11. Y. Kagayama (J, Suzuki), at 35"205; 12. J.-M. Bayle (F, Modenas KR3), at 42"405; 13. T. Harada (J, Aprilia), at 46"749; 14. S. Crafar (NZ), at 50"732; 15. H. Aoki (J, TSR-Honda V2), at 51"667. 18 finishers.

Fastest lap: M. Doohan (AUS, Honda V4), 2'07"213 (157.002 km/h). New record (new track).

25ᵗʰ April - Japan - Motegi

Pole position: K. Roberts (USA, Suzuki), 1'50"826 (155.952 km/h).

1. K. Roberts (USA, Suzuki), 25 laps in 51'54"386 (138.740 km/h); 2. M. Doohan (AUS, Honda V4), at 3"841; 3. N. Abé (J, Yamaha), at 21"758; 4. A. Crivillé (E, Honda V4), at 23"610; 5. M. Gibernau (E, Honda V2), at 23"984; 6. C. Checa (E, Yamaha), at 37"480; 7. S. Itoh (J, Honda V4), at 50"582; 8. A. Barros (BR, Honda V4), at 52"008; 9. M. Biaggi (I, Yamaha), at 53"524; 10. N. Aoki (J, Suzuki), at 1'05"068; 11. J.-B. Borja (E, Honda V4), at 1'08"314; 12. Y. Kagayama (J, Suzuki), at 1'13"299; 13. N. Numata (J, MuZ-Weber), at 1'19"245; 14. J.-L. Cardoso (E, TSR-Honda), at 1'26"998; 15. T. Okada (J, Honda V4), at 1'30"225. 19 finishers.

Fastest lap: M. Doohan (AUS, Honda V4), 2'02"889 (140.643 km/h). New record (new track).

9ᵗʰ May - Spain - Jerez de la Frontera

Pole position: A. Crivillé (E, Honda V4), 1'44"674 (153.585 km/h).

1. A. Crivillé (E, Honda V4), 27 laps in 47'38"667 (150.390 km/h); 2. M. Biaggi (I, Yamaha), at 0"157; 3. M. Gibernau (E, Honda V2), at 6"102; 4. T. Okada (J, Honda V4), at 6"609; 5. N. Abé (J, Yamaha), at 6"764; 6. J. Kocinski (USA, Honda V4), at 17"724; 7. R. Laconi (F, Yamaha), at 24"037; 8. L. Cadalora (I, MuZ-Weber), at 28"827; 9. J.-B. Borja (E, Honda V4), at 31"290; 10. C. Checa (E, Yamaha), at 31"308; 11. J. Van Den Goorbergh (NL, MuZ-Weber), at 54"233; 12. H. Aoki (J, TSR-Honda), at 59"081; 13. K. Roberts (USA, Suzuki), at 1'10"457; 14. S. Crafar (NZ, Yamaha), at 1'13"792; 15. M. Ober (D, Honda V2), at 1'22"765. 18 finishers.

Fastest lap: A. Crivillé (E, Honda V4), 1'44"657 (152.142 km/h).

Record: K. Schwantz (USA, Suzuki), 1'44"168/1994.

23ʳᵈ May - France - Le Castellet

Pole position: M. Biaggi (I, Yamaha), 1'20"969 (168.953 km/h).

1. A. Crivillé (E, Honda V4), 31 laps in 42'35"648 (165.938 km/h); 2. J. Kocinski (USA, Honda V4), at 11"398; 3. T. Harada (J, Aprilia), at 13"657; 4. M. Gibernau (E, Honda V2), at 4"370; 5. C. Checa (E, Yamaha), at 14"409; 6. N. Abé (J, Yamaha), at 16"639; 7. J.-B. Borja (E, Honda V4), at 21"224; 8. R. Laconi (F, Yamaha), at 21"245; 9. T. Okada (J, Honda V4), at 26"063; 10. A. Barros (BR, Honda V4), at 27"625; 11. S. Crafar (NZ, Yamaha), at 1'02"754; 12. S. Gimbert (F, Honda V2), at 1'12"210; 13. H. Aoki (J, TSR-Honda), at 1'15"698; 14. M. Ober (D, Honda V2), at 1 lap. 14 finishers.

Fastest lap: K. Roberts (USA, Suzuki), 1'21"487 (167.879 km/h). New record.

Old record: M. Doohan (AUS, Honda V4), 1'21"674/1997.

6ᵗʰ June - Italy - Mugello

Pole position: T. Harada (J, Aprilia), 1'52"454 (167.908 km/h).

1. A. Crivillé (E, Honda V4), 23 laps in 44'05"522 (164.158 km/h); 2. M. Biaggi (I, Yamaha), at 0"283; 3. T. Okada (J, Honda V4), at 6"052; 4. T. Harada (J, Aprilia), at 6"849; 5. K. Roberts (USA, Suzuki), at 12"674; 6. M. Gibernau (E, Honda V2), at 12"714; 7. C. Checa (E, Yamaha), at 21"341; 8. J. Kocinski (USA, Honda V4), at 29"800; 9. J.-B. Borja (E, Honda V4), at 29"801; 10. L. Cadalora (I, MuZ-Weber), at 46"742; 11. H. Aoki (J, TSR-Honda), at 1'07"293; 12. S. Crafar (NZ, Yamaha), at 1'14"550; 13. S. Gimbert (F, Honda V2), at 1'20"353; 14. J. Whitham (GB, Modenas), at 1'27"761; 15. M. Ober (D, Honda V2), at 1'45"918. 15 finishers.

Fastest lap: K. Roberts (USA, Suzuki), 1'53"889 (165.793 km/h).

Record: M. Doohan (AUS, Honda V4), 1'53"342/1998.

20ᵗʰ June - Catalunian - Catalunya

Pole position: J. Van Den Goorbergh (NL, MuZ-Weber), 1'46"076 (160.424 km/h).

1. A. Crivillé (E, Honda V4), 25 laps in 44'55"701 (157.817 km/h); 2. T. Okada (J, Honda V4), at 0"061; 3. M. Gibernau (E, Honda V4), at 4"467; 4. T. Harada (J, Aprilia), at 20"216; 5. J.-B. Borja (E, Honda V4), at 21"087; 6. K. Roberts (USA, Suzuki), at 22"006; 7. C. Checa (E, Yamaha), at 23"637; 8. J. Van Den Goorbergh (NL, MuZ-Weber), at 23"711; 9. J. Kocinski (USA, Honda V4), at 23"899; 10. H. Aoki (J, TSR-Honda), at 29"845; 11. N. Aoki (J, Suzuki), at 37"387; 12. J.-L. Cardoso (E, TSR-Honda), at 1'08"539; 13. M. Ober (D, Honda V2), at 1'08"712; 14. S. Gimbert (F, Honda V2), at 1'08"840. 14 finishers.

Fastest lap: M. Gibernau (E, Honda V4), 1'46"858 (159.250 km/h).

Record: A. Barros (BR, Honda V4), 1'46"810/1998.

26ᵗʰ June - The Netherlands - Assen

Pole position: T. Okada (J, Honda V4), 2'01"564 (179.135 km/h).

1. T. Okada (J, Honda V4), 20 laps in 41'12"732 (176.132 km/h); 2. K. Roberts (USA, Suzuki), at 7"316; 3. M. Gibernau (E, Honda V4), at 7"404; 4. N. Aoki (J, Suzuki), at 10"941; 5. M. Biaggi (I, Yamaha), at 10"980; 6. N. Abé (J, Yamaha), at 16"271; 7. J. Kocinski (USA, Honda V4), at 17"348; 8. J.-B. Borja (E, Honda V4), at 25"950; 9. H. Aoki (J, TSR-Honda), at 26"114; 10. A. Barros (BR, Honda V4), at 31"131; 11. T. Harada (J, Aprilia), at 36"038; 12. R. Laconi (F, Yamaha), at 41"016; 13. J. Van Den Goorbergh (NL, MuZ-Weber), at 41"097; 14. S. Gimbert (F, Honda V2), at 1'04"683; 15. G. McCoy (AUS, Yamaha), at 1'10"481. 17 finishers.

Fastest lap: T. Okada (J, Honda V4), 2'02"471 (177.808 km/h).

Record: K. Schwantz (USA, Suzuki), 2'02"443/1991.

4ᵗʰ July - Great Britain - Donington Park

Pole position: T. Okada (J, Honda V4), 1'32"597 (156.406 km/h).

1. A. Crivillé (E, Honda V4), 30 laps in 47'06"290 (153.729 km/h); 2. T. Okada (J, Honda V4), at 0"536; 3. T. Harada (J, Aprilia), at 0"981; 4. M. Biaggi (I, Yamaha), at 10"020; 5. A. Barros (BR, Honda V4), at 21"316; 6. N. Abé (J, Yamaha), at 21"491; 7. J.-B. Borja (E, Honda V4), at 21"959; 8. K. Roberts (USA, Suzuki), at 22"230; 9. J. Kocinski (USA, Honda V4), at 1'01"073; 10. S. Crafar (NZ, MuZ-Weber), at 1'06"969; 11. M. Rutter (GB, Honda V2), at 1 lap. 11 finishers.

Fastest lap: A. Crivillé (E, Honda V4), 1'33"348 (155.148 km/h).

Record: S. Crafar (NZ, Yamaha), 1'32"661/1998.

18ᵗʰ July - Germany - Sachsenring

Pole position: K. Roberts (USA, Suzuki), 1'27"318 (144.629 km/h).

1. K. Roberts (USA, Suzuki), 31 laps in 45'59"732 (141.858 km/h); 2. A. Crivillé (E, Honda V4), at 0"338; 3. N. Abé (J, Yamaha), at 5"669; 4. C. Checa (E, Yamaha), at 5"737; 5. J. Kocinski (USA, Honda), at 20"316; 6. H. Aoki (J, TSR-Honda), at 27"848; 7. T. Harada (J, Aprilia), at 31"016; 8. A. Barros (BR, Honda V4), at 35"425; 9. M. Gibernau (E, Honda V4), at 35"909; 10. J.-B. Borja (E, Honda V4), at 37"124; 11. G. McCoy (AUS, Yamaha), at 42"252; 12. J. Van Den Goorbergh (NL, MuZ-Weber), at 44"278; 13. R. Laconi (F, Yamaha), at 45"020; 14. S. Gimbert (F, Honda V2), at 46"454; 15. D. De Gea (E, TSR-Honda), at 1'05"990. 17 finishers.

Fastest lap: A. Barros (BR, Honda V4),

1'28"072 (143.391 km/h). New record. Old record: A. Barros (BR, Honda V4), 1'28"381/1998.

22nd August - Czech Republic - Brno

Pole position: J. Van Den Goorbergh (NL, MuZ-Weber), 2'01"572 (159.994 km/h).
1. T. Okada (J, Honda V4), 22 laps in 45'18"066 (157.434 km/h); 2. A. Crivillé (E, Honda V4), at 0"240; 3. K. Roberts (USA, Suzuki), at 1"858; 4. M. Biaggi (I, Yamaha), at 2"205; 5. T. Harada (J, Aprilia), at 3"827; 6. N. Aoki (J, Suzuki), at 4"032; 7. A. Barros (BR, Honda V4), at 9"815; 8. G. McCoy (AUS, Yamaha), at 17"181; 9. R. Laconi (F, Yamaha), at 17"408; 10. M. Gibernau (E, Honda V4), at 17"593; 11. J. Van Den Goorbergh (NL, MuZ-Weber), at 32"221; 12. J.-B. Borja (E, Honda V4), at 34"519; 13. H. Aoki (J, TSR-Honda), at 37"566; 14. J. Kocinski (USA, Honda V4), at 48"323; 15. M. Hale (USA, Modenas), at 1'10"496. 16 finishers.
Fastest lap: T. Okada (J, Honda V4), 2'02"661 (158.573 km/h).
Record: A. Crivillé (E, Honda V4), 2'02"335/1998.

5th September - San Marino - Imola

Pole position: A. Crivillé (E, Honda V4), 1'48"750 (163.200 km/h).
1. A. Crivillé (E, Honda V4), 25 laps in 46'05"244 (160.456 km/h); 2. A. Barros (BR, Honda V4), at 0"265; 3. M. Biaggi (I, Yamaha), at 6"383; 4. T. Okada (J, Honda V4), at 8"987; 5. R. Laconi (F, Yamaha), at 10"449; 6. K. Roberts (USA, Suzuki), at 12"366; 7. N. Aoki (J, Suzuki), at 14"948; 8. J. Kocinski (USA, Honda V4), at 17"719; 9. G. McCoy (AUS, Yamaha), at 28"910; 10. M. Gibernau (E, Honda V4), at 29"015; 11. N. Abé (J, Yamaha), at 34"810; 12. H. Aoki (J, TSR-Honda), at 53"188; 13. T. Harada (J, Aprilia), at 1'01"810; 14. J. Van Den Goorbergh (NL, MuZ-Weber), at 1'07"100; 15. M. Hale (USA, Modenas), at 1'11"127. 17 finishers.
Fastest lap: A. Barros (BR, Honda V4), 1'49"339 (162.320 km/h). New record.
Old record: M. Doohan (AUS, Honda V4), 1'49"436/1997.

19th September - Valencia - Cheste

Pole position: R. Laconi (F, Yamaha), 1'36"132 (149.981 km/h).
1. R. Laconi (F, Yamaha), 30 laps in 53'23"825 (135.007 km/h); 2. K. Roberts (USA, Suzuki), at 3"548; 3. G. McCoy (AUS, Yamaha), at 4"609; 4. T. Okada (J, Honda V4), at 6"155; 5. C. Checa (E, Yamaha), at 22"031; 6. N. Abé (J, Yamaha), at 22"144; 7. M. Biaggi (I, Yamaha), at 36"985; 8. J. Kocinski (USA, Honda V4), at 37"198; 9. M. Gibernau (E, Honda V4), at 43"376; 10. A. Barros (BR, Honda V4), at 43"420; 11. T. Harada (J, Aprilia), at 1'09"478; 12. N. Aoki (J, Suzuki), at 1'12"741; 13. S. Gimbert

(F, Honda V2), at 1'26"833; 14. D. De Gea (E, Modenas), at 1'43"106; 15. M. Hale (USA, Modenas), at 1 lap. 17 finishers.
Fastest lap: K. Roberts (USA, Suzuki), 1'42"473 (140.700 km/h). New record (new track).

3rd October - Australia - Phillip Island

Pole position: K. Roberts (USA, Suzuki), 1'32"319 (173.450 km/h).
1. T. Okada (J, Honda V4), 27 laps in 42'09"271 (170.936 km/h); 2. M. Biaggi (I, Yamaha), at 0"085; 3. R. Laconi (F, Yamaha), at 0"124; 4. C. Checa (E, Yamaha), at 9"497; 5. A. Crivillé (E, Honda V4), at 9"811; 6. M. Gibernau (E, Honda V4), at 10"691; 7. G. McCoy (AUS, Yamaha), at 12"135; 8. N. Aoki (J, Suzuki), at 25"028; 9. J. Kocinski (USA, Honda V4), at 25"219; 10. K. Roberts (USA, Suzuki), at 41"652; 11. H. Aoki (J, TSR-Honda), at 47"628; 12. J. Van Den Goorbergh (NL, MuZ-Weber), at 47"670; 13. D. De Gea (E, Modenas), at 1'22"997; 14. S. Martin (AUS, Honda V2), at 1'23"305; 15. M. Willis (AUS, Modenas), at 1'35"980. 17 finishers.
Fastest lap: K. Roberts (USA, Suzuki), 1'32"743 (172.657 km/h). New record.
Old record: S. Crafar (NZ, Yamaha), 1'33"868/1998.

10th October - South Africa - Welkom

Pole position: T. Okada (J, Honda V4), 1'35"930 (159.191 km/h).
1. M. Biaggi (I, Yamaha), 28 laps in 45'24"602 (156.938 km/h); 2. M. Gibernau (E, Honda V4), at 4"822; 3. A. Crivillé (E, Honda V4), at 5"138; 4. T. Okada (J, Honda V4), at 10"432; 5. J.-B. Borja (E, Honda V4), at 14"187; 6. C. Checa (E, Yamaha), at 14"282; 7. N. Aoki (J, Suzuki), at 22"636; 8. G. McCoy (AUS, Yamaha), at 33"224; 9. N. Abé (J, Yamaha), at 41"357; 10. J. Kocinski (USA, Honda V4), at 44"052; 11. A. Barros (BR, Honda V4), at 56"083; 12. H. Aoki (J, TSR-Honda), at 56"443; 13. J. Van Den Goorbergh (NL, MuZ-Weber), at 57"117; 14. R. Laconi (F, Yamaha), at 59"166; 15. T. Harada (J, Aprilia), at 59"290. 22 finishers.
Fastest lap: M. Gibernau (E, Honda V4), 1'36"554 (158.162 km/h). New record (new track).

24th October - Rio de Janeiro - Jacarepagua

Pole position: K. Roberts (USA, Suzuki), 1'52"227 (158.239 km/h).
1. N. Abé (J, Yamaha), 24 laps in 45'24"308 (156.447 km/h); 2. M. Biaggi (I, Yamaha), at 0"161; 3. K. Roberts (USA, Suzuki), at 0"257; 4. A. Barros (BR, Honda V4), at 4"442; 5. M. Gibernau (E, Honda V4), at 4"631; 6. A. Crivillé (E, Honda V4), at 21"254; 7. T. Okada (J, Honda V4), at 21"525; 8. G. McCoy (AUS, Yamaha), at 22"394; 9. N. Aoki (J, Suzuki), at 23"089; 10. A. Gobert (AUS, MuZ-Weber), at 30"275; 11. R. Laconi (F, Yamaha), at 41"314; 12. T. Harada (J, Aprilia), at 41"648; 13. J. Kocinski (USA,

Honda V4), at 42"757; 14. D. De Gea (E, Modenas), at 43"380; 15. H. Aoki (J, TSR-Honda), at 45"652. 18 finishers.
Fastest lap: M. Biaggi (I, Yamaha), 1'52"869 (157.339 km/h).
Record: T. Okada (J, Honda V4), 1'51"928/ 1997.

31st Octobre - Argentina - Buenos Aires

Pole position: K. Roberts (USA, Suzuki), 1'44"354 (150.066 km/h).
1. K. Roberts (USA, Suzuki), 27 laps in 47'23"710 (148.686 km/h); 2. M. Biaggi (I, Yamaha), at 2"033; 3. N. Abé (J, Yamaha), at 2"631; 4. C. Checa (E, Yamaha), at 4"340; 5. A. Crivillé (E, Honda V4), at 4"451; 6. M. Gibernau (E, Honda V4), at 24"878; 7. J. Kocinski (USA, Honda V4), at 25"338; 8. A. Barros (BR, Honda V4), at 26"387; 9. J.-B. Borja (E, Honda V4), at 31"868; 10. J. Van Den Goorbergh (NL, MuZ-Weber), at 37"536; 11. T. Harada (J, Aprilia), at 38"553; 12. R. Laconi (F, Yamaha), at 47"953; 13. G. McCoy (AUS, Yamaha), at 48"083; 14. M. Willis (AUS, Modenas), at 52"512; 15. H. Aoki (J, TSR-Honda), at 53"237. 20 finishers.
Fastest lap: K. Roberts (USA, Suzuki), 1'44"781 (149.454 km/h).
Record: T. Okada (J, Honda V4), 1'44"122/ 1998.

Final classification

1. Alex Crivillé	E	Honda V4	267 pts
2. Kenny Roberts	USA	Suzuki	220
3. Tadayuki Okada	J	Honda V4	211
4. Massimiliano Biaggi	I	Yamaha	194
5. Manuel Gibernau	E	Honda V2/V4	165
6. Norifumi Abé	J	Yamaha	136
7. Carlos Checa	E	Yamaha	125
8. John Kocinski	USA	Honda V4	115
9. Alexandre Barros	BR	Honda V4	110
10. Tetsuya Harada	J	Aprilia	104

11. R. Laconi (F, Yamaha), 103; 12. J.-B. Borja (E, Honda V4), 92; 13. N. Aoki (J, Suzuki), 78; 14. G. McCoy (AUS, Yamaha), 65; 15. H. Aoki (J, TSR-Honda), 54; 16. J. Van Den Goorbergh (NL, MuZ-Weber), 40; 17. M. Doohan (AUS, Honda V4), 33; 18. S. Crafar (NZ, Yamaha/MuZ-Weber), 19; 19. S. Gimbert (F, Honda V2), 16; 20. L. Cadalora (I, MuZ-Weber), 14; 21. S. Itoh (J, Honda V4), 9; 22. Y. Kagayama (J, Suzuki), 9; 23. D. De Gea (E, TSR-Honda/Modenas), 8; 24. M. Ober (D, Honda V2), 7; 25. A. Gobert (AUS, MuZ-Weber), 6; 26. J.-L. Cardoso (E, TSR-Honda), 6; 27. M. Rutter (GB, Honda V2), 5; 28. J.-M. Bayle (F, Modenas), 4; 29. N. Numata (J, MuZ-Weber), 3; 30. M. Willis (AUS,

28th March - South Africa - Kyalami
Pole position (superpole): T. Corser (AUS, Ducati), 1'42"943 (149.220 km/h). Fastest Qualifying lap: T. Corser (AUS, Ducati), 1'43"255 (148.769 km/h).
Race I: 1. C. Fogarty (GB, Ducati), 25 laps in 43'35"637 (146.821 km/h); 2. T. Corser (AUS, Ducati), at 5"257; 3. A. Slight (NZ, Honda), at 9"779; 4. N. Haga (J, Yamaha), at 13"181; 5. C. Edwards (USA, Honda), at 14"535; 6. A. Yanagawa (J, Kawasaki), at 16"547; 7. P. Chili (I, Suzuki), at 32"857; 8. G. Lavilla (E, Kawasaki), at 37"099; 9. D. Romboni (I, Ducati), at 45"691; 10. R. Ulm (A, Kawasaki), at 54"185; 11. K. Fujiwara (J, Suzuki), at 54"424; 12. V. Guareschi (I, Yamaha), at 1'09"588; 13. A. Meklau (A, Ducati), at 1'09"938; 14. L. Isaacs (SA, Ducati), at 1'11"106; 15. A. Gramigni (I, Yamaha), at 1'26"836. 19 finishers.
Fastest lap: C. Edwards (USA, Honda), 1'43"800 (147.988 km/h).
Race II: 1. C. Fogarty (GB, Ducati), 25 laps in 43'41"963 (146.467 km/h); 2. A. Slight (NZ, Honda), at 6"073; 3. T. Corser (AUS, Ducati), at 7"279; 4. C. Edwards (USA, Honda), at 12"401; 5. A. Yanagawa (J, Kawasaki), at 15"632; 5. G. Lavilla (E, Kawasaki), at 19"634; 7. P. Goddard (AUS, Aprilia), at 21"521; 8. P. Chili (I, Suzuki), at 25"508; 9. D. Romboni (I, Ducati), at 25"660; 10. K. Fujiwara (J, Suzuki), at 31"415; 11. R. Ulm (A, Kawasaki), at 46"765; 12. L. Pedercini (I, Ducati), at 52"192; 13. V. Guareschi (I, Yamaha), at 1'03"311; 14. L. Isaacs (SA, Ducati), at 1'22"799; 15. I. Jerman (SLO, Kawsaki), at 1'26"729. 17 finishers.
Fastest lap: C. Fogarty (GB, Ducati), 1'43"477 (148.450 km/h).

18th April - Australia - Phillip Island
Pole position (superpole)(*): T. Corser (AUS, Ducati), 1'32"193 (173.570 km/h). Fastest Qualifying lap: T. Corser (AUS, Ducati), 1'32"623 (172.764 km/h).
Race I: 1. T. Corser (AUS, Ducati), 22 laps in 34'28"167 (170.220 km/h); 2. C. Fogarty (GB, Ducati), at 3"801; 3. C. Edwards (USA, Honda), at 18"269; 4. A. Slight (NZ, Honda), at 18"538; 5. A. Yanagawa (J, Kawasaki), at 18"558; 6. N. Haga (J, Yamaha), at 18"564; 7. D. Romboni (I, Ducati), at 38"684; 8. C. Connell (AUS, Ducati), at 46"788; 9. K. Fujiwara (J, Suzuki), at 55"040; 10. A. Meklau (A, Ducati), at 58"477; 11. S. Giles (AUS, Suzuki), at 1'06"034; 12. I. Jerman (SLO, Kawasaki), at 1'13"911; 13. V. Guareschi (I, Yamaha), at 1'13"916; 14. R. Ulm (A, Kawasaki), at 1'15"583; 15. J. Mrkyvka (CZ, Ducati), at 1'31"056. 19 finishers.
Fastest lap: C. Fogarty (GB, Ducati), 1'33"333 (171.450 km/h).
Race II: 1. T. Corser (AUS, Ducati), 22 laps in 34'24"328 (170.537 km/h); 2. C. Fogarty (GB, Ducati), at 0"005; 3. C. Edwards (USA, Honda), at 15"247; 4. A. Slight (NZ, Honda), at 15"327; 5. N. Haga (J, Yamaha), at 15"330; 6. A. Yanagawa (J, Kawasaki), at 29"350; 7. S. Martin (AUS, Ducati), at 36"363; 8. D. Romboni (I, Ducati), at 36"891; 9. C. Connell (AUS, Ducati), at 43"242; 10. K. Fujiwara (J, Suzuki), at 51"160; 11. A. Meklau (A, Ducati), at 51"218; 12. S. Giles (AUS, Suzuki), at 56"982; 13. P. Chili (I, Suzuki), at 1'03"133; 14. L. Pedercini (I, Ducati), at 1'15"981; 15. V. Guareschi (I, Yamaha), at 1'17"146. 21 finishers.
Fastest lap: T. Corser (AUS, Ducati), 1'33"019 (172.029 km/h).
(*): the superpole was declared "wet", with each rider having 12 laps at his disposal.

2nd May - Great Britain - Donington Park
Pole position (superpole): P. Chili (I, Suzuki), 1'33"356 (155.096 km/h). Fastest Qualifying lap: C. Fogarty (GB, Ducati), 1'33"212 (155.336 km/h).
Race I: 1. C. Fogarty (GB, Ducati), 25 laps in 39'19"856 (153.391 km/h); 2. A. Slight (NZ, Honda), at 3"430; 3. C. Edwards (USA, Honda), at 16"483; 4. C. Walker (GB, Kawasaki), at 20"942; 5. A. Yanagawa (J, Kawasaki), at 21"424; 6. T. Corser (AUS, Ducati), at 24"487; 7. J. Reynolds (GB, Ducati), at 27"092; 8. S. Hislop (GB, Kawasaki), at 28"978; 9. S. Emmett (GB, Ducati), at 34"962; 10. N. Haga (J, Yamaha), at 37"757; 11. D. Romboni (I, Ducati), at 39"017; 12. N. MacKenzie (GB, Yamaha), at 39"325; 13. K. Fujiwara (J, Suzuki), at 1'02"626; 14. I. Jerman (SLO, Kawasaki), at 1'17"563; 15. F. Protat (F, Ducati), at 1'34"368. 17 finishers.
Fastest lap: C. Fogarty (GB, Ducati), 1'33"700 (154.527 km/h).

16th May - Spain - Albacete
Pole position (superpole): C. Fogarty (GB, Ducati), 1'31"457 (139.304 km/h). Fastest Qualifying lap: C. Edwards (USA, Honda), 1'31"326 (139.504 km/h).
Race I: 1. N. Haga (J, Yamaha), 26 laps in 40'09"482 (137.478 km/h); 2. A. Yanagawa (J, Kawasaki), at 0"498; 3. C. Fogarty (GB, Ducati), at 6"172; 4. A. Slight (NZ, Honda), at 13"017; 5. P. Chili (I, Suzuki), at 13"091; 6. G. Lavilla (E, Kawasaki), at 13"216; 7. T. Corser (AUS, Ducati), at 31"773; 8. K. Fujiwara (J, Suzuki), at 31"798; 9. V. Guareschi (I, Yamaha), at 40"100; 10. P. Goddard (AUS, Aprilia), at 40"182; 11. I. Jerman (SLO, Kawasaki), at 42"564; 12. A. Meklau (A, Ducati), at 48"284; 13. R. Ulm (A, Kawasaki), at 49"331; 14. A. Gramigni (I, Yamaha), at 1'17"049; 15. L. Pedercini (I, Ducati), at 1 lap. 18 finishers.
Fastest lap: A. Yanagawa (J, Kawasaki), 1'31"592 (139.099 km/h).
Race II: 1. C. Edwards (USA, Honda), 26 laps in 40'15"529 (137.134 km/h); 2. A. Yanagawa (J, Kawasaki), at 0"115; 3. C. Fogarty (GB, Ducati), at 0"302; 4. G. Lavilla (E, Kawasaki), at 7"134; 5. P. Chili (I, Suzuki), at 7"308; 6. T. Corser (AUS, Ducati), at 13"250; 7. A. Slight (NZ, Honda), at 15"024; 8. K. Fujiwara (J, Suzuki), at 15"203; 9. V. Guareschi (I, Yamaha), at 35"329; 10. P. Goddard (AUS, Aprilia), at 37"307; 11. A. Meklau (A, Ducati), at 37"412; 12. I. Jerman (SLO, Kawasaki), at 37"850; 13. R. Ulm (A, Kawasaki), at 45"615; 14. A. Gramigni (I, Yamaha), at 1'13"924; 15. L. Pedercini (I, Ducati), at 1 lap. 19 finishers.
Fastest lap: C. Edwards (USA, Honda), 1'31"843 (138.719 km/h).

30th May - Italia - Monza
Pole position (superpole): C. Edwards (USA, Honda), 1'46"365 (195.289 km/h). Fastest Qualifying lap: C. Edwards (USA, Honda), 1'46"694 (194.687 km/h).
Race I: 1. C. Fogarty (GB, Ducati), 18 laps in 32'13"009 (193.427 km/h); 2. C. Edwards (USA, Honda), at 0"120; 3. P. Chili (I, Suzuki), at 0"547; 4. T. Corser (AUS, Ducati), at 11"131; 5. A. Slight (NZ, Honda), at 13"953; 6. N. Haga (J, Yamaha), at 14"937; 7. A. Yanagawa (J, Kawasaki), at 15"256; 8. G. Lavilla (E, Kawasaki), at 26"127; 9. P. Goddard (AUS, Aprilia), at 26"245; 10. A. Meklau (A, Ducati), at 26"835; 11. V. Guareschi (I, Yamaha), at 32"407; 12. I. Jerman (SLO, Kawasaki), at 44"295; 13. L. Pedercini (I, Ducati), at 55"336; 14. R. Ulm (A, Kawasaki), at 55"429; 15. L. Isaacs (SA, Ducati), at 1'23"758. 22 finishers.
Fastest lap: T. Corser (AUS, Ducati), 1'46"533 (194.981 km/h).
Race II: 1. C. Fogarty (GB, Ducati), 18 laps in 32'18"285 (192.900 km/h); 2. C. Edwards (USA, Honda), at 0"005; 3. P. Chili (I, Suzuki), at 0"544; 4. T. Corser (AUS, Ducati), at 8"263; 5. A. Yanagawa (J, Kawasaki), at 12"449; 6. N. Haga (J, Yamaha), at 12"478; 7. G. Lavilla (E, Kawasaki), at 12"764; 8. A. Meklau (A, Ducati), at 28"721; 9. K. Fujiwara (J, Suzuki), at 28"800; 10. V. Guareschi (I, Yamaha), at 42"273; 11. P. Goddard (AUS, Aprilia), at 1'04"172; 12. A. Gramigni (I, Yamaha), at 1'17"755; 13. A. Antonello (I, Aprilia), at 1'21"877; 14. L. Isaacs (SA, Ducati), at 1'23"867; 15. M. Lucchiari (I, Yamaha), at 1'25"965. 17 finishers.
Fastest lap: P. Chili (I, Suzuki), 1'46"547 (194.956 km/h).

13th June - Germany - Nürburgring
Pole position (superpole): C. Fogarty (GB, Ducati), 1'38"843 (165.935 km/h). Fastest Qualifying lap: A. Slight (NZ, Honda), 1'39"202 (165.335 km/h).
Race I: 1. C. Fogarty (GB, Ducati), 21 laps in 35'12"037 (163.081 km/h); 2. A. Slight (NZ, Honda), at 7"262; 3. T. Corser (AUS, Ducati), at 30"178; 4. G. Lavilla (E, Kawasaki), at 35"116; 5. P. Goddard (AUS, Aprilia), at 36"359; 6. K. Fujiwara (J, Suzuki), at 37"463; 7. V. Guareschi (I, Yamaha), at 48"594; 8. A. Meklau (A, Ducati), at 59"878; 9. C. Lindholm (S, Yamaha), at 1'11"069; 10. J. Schmid (D, Kawasaki), at 1'11"374; 11. L. Pedercini (I, Ducati), at 1'11"759; 12. A. Gramigni (I, Yamaha), at 1'24"325; 13. G. Bussei (I, Suzuki), at 1'28"715; 14. J. Ekerold (SA, Kawasaki), at 1'31"515; 15. F. Protat (F, Ducati), at 1'32"908. 20 finishers.
Fastest lap: C. Fogarty (GB, Ducati), 1'39"705 (164.501 km/h).
Race II: 1. T. Corser (AUS, Ducati), 21 laps in 35'06"897 (163.479 km/h); 2. A. Slight (NZ, Honda), at 0"113; 3. A. Yanagawa (J, Kawasaki), at 1"087; 4. C. Edwards (USA, Honda), at 12"862; 5. P. Chili (I, Suzuki), at 12"962; 6. N. Haga (J, Yamaha), at 15"037; 7. K. Fujiwara (J, Suzuki), at 24"298; 8. P. Goddard (AUS, Aprilia), at 25"911; 9. V. Guareschi (I, Yamaha), at 37"931; 10. A. Meklau (A, Ducati), at 38"171; 11. R. Ulm (A, Kawasaki), at 47"636; 12. I. Jerman (SLO, Kawasaki), at 48"991; 13. L. Pedercini (I, Ducati), at 1'00"178; 14. C. Lindholm (S, Yamaha), at 1'02"361; 15. C. Fogarty (GB, Ducati), at 1'07"467. 25 finishers.
Fastest lap: T. Corser (AUS, Ducati), 1'39"318 (165.142 km/h).

27th June - San Marino - Misano
Pole position (superpole): C. Fogarty (GB, Ducati), 1'33"995 (155.497 km/h). Fastest Qualifying lap: T. Corser (AUS, Ducati), 1'34"161 (155.223 km/h).
Race I: 1. C. Fogarty (GB, Ducati), 25 laps in 39'57"687 (152.397 km/h); 2. T. Corser (AUS, Ducati), at 0"126; 3. A. Yanagawa (J, Kawasaki), at 10"935; 4. P. Chili (I, Suzuki), at 16"366; 5. A. Slight (NZ, Honda), at 20"205; 6. C. Edwards (USA, Honda), at 21"549; 7. G. Lavilla (E, Kawasaki), at 21"721; 8. N. Haga (J, Yamaha), at 30"606; 9. V. Guareschi (I, Yamaha), at 43"326; 10. P. Goddard (AUS, Aprilia), at 43"536; 11. L. Pedercini (I, Ducati), at 1'02"348; 12. L. Isaacs (SA, Ducati), at 1'03"749; 13. M. Lucchiari (I, Yamaha), at 1'06"635; 14. K. Fujiwara (J, Suzuki), at 1'08"789; 15. I. Jerman (SLO, Kawasaki), at 1'09"855. 19 finishers.
Fastest lap: A. Slight (NZ, Honda), 1'35"042 (153.784 km/h).
Race II: 1. C. Fogarty (GB, Ducati), 25 laps in 39'52"554 (152.724 km/h); 2. T. Corser (AUS, Ducati), at 6"496; 3. A. Yanagawa (J, Kawasaki), at 10"664; 4. A. Slight (NZ, Honda), at 17"337; 5. G. Lavilla (E, Kawasaki), at 18"557; 6. P. Chili (I, Suzuki), at 22"503; 7. C. Edwards (USA, Honda), at 27"111; 8. V. Guareschi (I, Yamaha), at 32"415; 9. K. Fujiwara (J, Suzuki), at 55"033; 10. R. Ulm (A, Kawasaki), at 55"671; 11. M. Lucchiari (I, Yamaha), at 57"682; 12. I. Jerman (SLO, Kawasaki), at 59"537; 13. A. Gramigni (I, Yamaha), at 1'05"165; 14. L. Pedercini (I, Ducati), at 1'06"483; 15. L. Isaacs (SA, Ducati), at 1'06"663. 19 finishers.
Fastest lap: T. Corser (AUS, Ducati), 1'34"758 (154.245 km/h).

11th July - United States - Laguna Seca
Pole position (superpole): T. Corser (AUS, Ducati), 1'26"194 (150.442 km/h). Fastest Qualifying lap: A. Gobert (AUS, Ducati), 1'25"185 (152.223 km/h).
Race I: 1. A. Gobert (AUS, Ducati), 28 laps in 41'01"775 (147.488 km/h); 2. B. Bostrom (USA, Ducati), at 3"151; 3. A. Yanagawa (J, Kawasaki), at 3"382; 4. C. Edwards (USA, Honda), at 13"405; 5. C. Fogarty (GB, Ducati), at 13"709; 6. T. Corser (AUS, Ducati), at 14"134; 7. P. Chili (I, Suzuki), at 14"320; 8. J. Hacking (USA, Yamaha), at 23"168; 9. A. Slight (NZ, Honda), at 26"888; 10. E. Bostrom (USA, Honda), at 32"774; 11. K. Fujiwara (J, Suzuki), at 40"375; 12. G. Lavilla (E, Kawasaki), at 50"111; 13. I. Jerman (SLO, Kawasaki), at 56"620; 14. L. Isaacs (SA, Ducati), at 1'10"215; 15. A. Gramigni (I, Yamaha), at 1'10"647. 17 finishers.
Fastest lap: A. Gobert (AUS, Ducati), 1'27"366 (148.423 km/h).
Race II: 1. B. Bostrom (USA, Ducati), 28 laps in 40'58"346

(147.693 km/h); 2. T. Corser (AUS, Ducati), at 3"012; 3. P. Chili (I, Suzuki), at 6"310; 4. C. Fogarty (GB, Ducati), at 10"622; 5. C. Edwards (USA, Honda), at 13"993; 6. A. Slight (NZ, Honda), at 16"120; 7. E. Bostrom (USA, Honda), at 8"153; 8. G. Lavilla (E, Kawasaki), at 29"302; 9. P. Goddard (AUS, Aprilia), at 37"081; 10. N. Haga (J, Yamaha), at 39"455; 11. K. Fujiwara (J, Suzuki), at 41"285; 12. A. Yanagawa (J, Kawasaki), at 52"483; 13. J. Hacking (USA, Yamaha), at 1'01"566; 14. F. Protat (F, Ducati), at 1'04"647; 15. A. Gramigni (I, Yamaha), at 1'05"263. 17 finishers.
Fastest lap: T. Corser (AUS, Ducati), 1'27"020 (149.04 km/h).

1st August - Europe - Brands Hatch
Pole position (superpole)(*): C. Fogarty (GB, Ducati), 1'26"758 (175.149 km/h). Fastest Qualifying lap: P. Chili (I, Suzuki), 1'27"553 (173.558 km/h).
Race I: 1. C. Edwards (USA, Honda), 25 laps in 36'51"715 (171.763 km/h); 2. A. Slight (NZ, Honda), at 1"429; 3. P. Chili (I, Suzuki), at 7"879; 4. J. Reynolds (GB, Ducati), at 11"774; 5. T. Corser (AUS, Ducati), at 14"226; 6. A. Yanagawa (J, Kawasaki), at 14"298; 7. N. Haga (J, Yamaha), at 16"612; 8. N. MacKenzie (GB, Yamaha), at 16"927; 9. J. Haydon (GB, Suzuki), at 29"339; 10. C. Walker (GB, Kawasaki), at 33"810; 11. A. Meklau (A, Ducati), at 34"690; 12. P. Goddard (AUS, Aprilia), at 36"042; 13. I. Jerman (SLO, Kawasaki), at 44"535; 14. K. Fujiwara (J, Suzuki), at 45"959; 15. V. Guareschi (I, Yamaha), at 46"324. 24 finishers.
Fastest lap: T. Corser (AUS, Ducati), 1'27"744 (173.181 km/h).
Race II: 1. C. Edwards (USA, Honda), 25 laps in 36'52"981 (171.664 km/h); 2. A. Slight (NZ, Honda), at 0"087; 3. N. Haga (J, Yamaha), at 9"268; 4. C. Fogarty (GB, Ducati), at 11"358; 5. A. Yanagawa (J, Kawasaki), at 15"083; 6. S. Emmett (GB, Ducati), at 17"493; 7. N. MacKenzie (GB, Yamaha), at 17"618; 8. J. Reynolds (GB, Ducati), at 18"904; 9. P. Goddard (AUS, Aprilia), at 19"330; 10. G. Lavilla (E, Kawasaki), at 24"534; 11. J. Haydon (GB, Suzuki), at 24"883; 12. A. Meklau (A, Ducati), at 26"605; 13. T. Corser (AUS, Ducati), at 28"067; 14. V. Guareschi (I, Yamaha), at 35"268; 15. K. Fujiwara (J, Suzuki), at 44"548. 23 finishers.
Fastest lap: A. Slight (NZ, Honda), 1'27"832 (173.007 km/h).
(*): after getting under way as usual, the superpole was interrupted during the ninth rider, Chris Walker's run, because of a rain shower. Il was restarted under the "wet" regulations; each rider having 12 laps available in a 50 minute period.

29th August - Austria - A1-Ring
Pole position (superpole)(*): C. Edwards (USA, Honda), 1'31"068 (170.733 km/h). Fastest Qualifying lap: C. Fogarty (GB, Ducati), 1'31"114 (170.647 km/h).
Race I: 1. C. Edwards (USA, Honda), 25 laps in 43'03"055 (150.485 km/h); 2. C. Fogarty (GB, Ducati), at 20"964; 3. V. Guareschi (I, Yamaha), at 1'12"145; 4. R. Ulm (A, Kawasaki), at 1'40"332; 5. G. Lavilla (E, Kawasaki), at 2'05"348; 6. B. Morrison (GB, Yamaha), at 1 lap; 7. M. Lucchiari (I, Yamaha), at 1 lap; 8. A. Gramigni (I, Yamaha); 9. F. Protat (F, Ducati); 10. L. Pedercini (I, Ducati), at 2 laps; 11. J. Mrkyvka (CZ, Ducati); 12. A. Rechberger (A, Suzuki); 13. C. Macias (COL, Ducati), at 3 laps. 13 finishers.
Fastest lap: P. Chili (I, Suzuki), 1'36"290 (161.474 km/h).
Race II: 1. P. Chili (I, Suzuki), 25 laps in 46'40"235 (138.813 km/h); 2. T. Corser (AUS, Ducati), at 17"746; 3. A. Slight (NZ, Honda), at 38"188; 4. C. Fogarty (GB, Ducati), at 1'11"822; 5. R. Kellenberger (CH, Honda), at 1'17"294; 6. G. Bussei (I, Suzuki), at 1'29"050; 7. A. Meklau (A, Ducati), at 1'30"559; 8. C. Edwards (USA, Honda), at 1'41"560; 9. M. Lucchiari (I, Yamaha), at 1'45"434; 10. B. Morrison (GB, Yamaha), at 1'52"503; 11. R. Ulm (A, Kawasaki), at 1 lap; 12. I. Jerman (SLO, Kawasaki); 13. F. Protat (F, Ducati); 14. V. Karban (SVK, Suzuki), at 2 laps; 15. L. Isaacs (SA, Ducati). 17 finishers.
Fastest lap: P. Chili (I, Suzuki), 1'49"537 (141.946 km/h).
(*): the superpole was declared "wet", with each rider having the laps available in a 50 minute period.

5th September - The Netherlands - Assen
Pole position (superpole): T. Corser (AUS, Ducati), 2'03"119 (176.872 km/h). Fastest Qualifying lap: A. Slight (NZ, Honda), 2'03"641 (176.126 km/h).
Race I: 1. C. Fogarty (GB, Ducatu), 16 laps in 33'19"369 (174.266 km/h); 2. T. Corser (AUS, Ducati), at 4"443; 3. A. Slight (NZ, Honda), at 5"827; 4. P. Chili (I, Suzuki), at 7"466; 5. C. Edwards (USA, Honda), at 12"636; 6. A. Yanagawa (J, Kawasaki), at 13"383; 7. N. Haga (J, Yamaha), at 28"491; 8. A. Meklau (A, Ducati), at 28"801; 9. G. Lavilla (E, Kawasaki), at 29"084; 10. C. Walker (GB, Kawasaki), at 29"418; 11. I. Jerman (SLO, Kawasaki), at 51"765; 12. K. Fujiwara (E, Suzuki), at 1'03"766; 13. V. Guareschi (I, Yamaha), at 1'05"251; 14. R. Ulm (A, Kawasaki), at 1'05"729; 15. A. Gramigni (I, Yamaha), at 1'08"032. 25 finishers.
Fastest lap: C. Fogarty (GB, Ducati), 2'03"914 (175.738 km/h).
Race II: 1. C. Fogarty (GB, Ducati), 16 laps in 33'22"315 (174.009 km/h); 2. T. Corser (AUS, Ducati), at 6"319; 3. A. Slight (NZ, Honda), at 14"592; 4. A. Yanagawa (J, Kawasaki), at 14"645; 5. C. Edwards (USA, Honda), at 14"771; 6. P. Chili (I, Suzuki), at 15"359; 7. G. Lavilla (E, Kawasaki), at 18"858; 8. N. Haga (J, Yamaha), at 25"253; 9. A. Meklau (A, Ducati), at 31"799; 10. C. Walker (GB, Kawasaki), at 34"593; 11. I. Jerman (SLO, Kawasaki), at 38"235; 12. K. Fujiwara (J, Suzuki), at 55"922; 13. M. Malatesta (I, Ducati), at 1'02"900; 14. A. Gramigni (I, Yamaha), at 1'08"543; 15. L. Pedercini (I, Ducati), at 1'08"727. 23 finishers.
Fastest lap: C. Fogarty (GB, Ducati), 2'04"113 (175.456 km/h).

12th September - Germany - Hockenheim
Pole position (superpole): A. Slight (NZ, Honda), 2'00"280 (203.285 km/h). Fastest Qualifying lap: A. Slight (NZ, Honda), 2'00"408 (203.069 km/h).
Race I: 1. C. Fogarty (GB, Ducati), 13 laps in 26'19"818 (201.204 km/h)(*); 2. A. Slight (NZ, Honda), at 0"227; 3. A. Yanagawa (J, Kawasaki), at 5"106; 4. C. Edwards (USA, Honda), at 5"408; 5. N. Haga (J, Yamaha), at 10"198; 6. G. Lavilla (E, Kawasaki), at 22"903; 7. K. Fujiwara (J, Suzuki), at 23"297; 8. P. Goddard (AUS, Aprilia), at 23"584; 9. I. Jerman (SLO, Kawasaki), at 23"648; 10. V. Guareschi (I, Yamaha), at 26"564; 11. M. Malatesta (I, Ducati), at 36"967; 12. A. Gramigni (I, Yamaha), at 37"128; 13. R. Ulm (A, Kawasaki), at 37"281; 14. L. Pedercini (I, Ducati), at 56"131; 15. F. Protat (F, Ducati), at 56"271. 23 finishers.
Fastest lap: C. Fogarty (GB, Ducati), 2'00"428 (203.035 km/h).
Race II: 1. P. Chili (I, Suzuki), 14 laps in 28'26"624 (200.581

km/h); 2. C. Fogarty (GB, Ducati), at 0"342; 3. A. Slight (NZ, Honda), at 0"423; 4. A. Yanagawa (J, Kawasaki), at 0"459; 5. C. Edwards (USA, Honda), at 1"162; 6. A. Meklau (A, Ducati), at 5"990; 7. T. Corser (AUS, Ducati), at 13"825; 8. G. Lavilla (E, Kawasaki), at 17"078; 9. N. Haga (J, Yamaha), at 17"135; 10. K. Fujiwara (J, Suzuki), at 17"377; 11. M. Malatesta (I, Ducati), at 24"923; 12. V. Guareschi (I, Yamaha), at 28"869; 13. J. Schmid (D, Kawasaki), at 41"019; 14. A. Gramigni (I, Yamaha), at 41"335; 15. L. Isaacs (SA, Ducati), at 59"738. 22 finishers.
Fastest lap: A. Yanagawa (J, Kawasaki), 2'00"783 (202.439 km/h).
(*): the race was stopped on the last lap, after an accident involving Peter Goddard (AUS, Aprilia) and Igor Jerman (SLO, Kawasaki). The race result was then calculated from the order at the end of the preceding lap. Carl Fogarty (GB, Ducati) was thus declared the winner, ahead of Aaron Slight (NZ, Honda), whose overtaking move on Foggy on the final lap had therefore counted for nothing.

10th October - Japan - Sugo
Pole position (superpole): T. Corser (AUS, Ducati), 1'29"910 (149.629 km/h). Fastest Qualifying lap: C. Fogarty (GB, Ducati), 1'30"064 (149.373 km/h).
Race I: 1. A. Ryo (J, Suzuki), 25 laps in 37'59"744 (147.530 km/h); 2. C. Fogarty (GB, Ducati), at 2"828; 3. A. Yanagawa (J, Kawasaki), at 2"932; 4. K. Kitagawa (J, Suzuki), at 7"688; 5. W. Yoshikawa (J, Yamaha), at 8"682; 6. T. Serizawa (J, Kawasaki), at 11"537; 7. P. Chili (I, Suzuki), at 13"037; 8. T. Corser (AUS, Ducati), at 13"307; 9. C. Edwards (USA, Honda), at 15"183; 10. M. Tamada (J, Honda), at 15"223; 11. S. Itoh (J, Honda), at 15"856; 12. N. Haga (J, Yamaha), at 17"967; 13. T. Tsujimura (J, Yamaha), at 21"158; 14. G. Lavilla (E, Kawasaki), at 30"828; 15. Y. Takeda (J, Honda), at 31"065. 23 finishers.
Fastest lap: A. Ryo (J, Suzuki), 1'30"210 (149.132 km/h).
Race II: 1. A. Yanagawa (J, Kawasaki), 25 laps in 38'03"761 (147.270 km/h); 2. A. Ryo (J, Suzuki), at 0"139; 3. K. Kitagawa (J, Suzuki), at 0"574; 4. N. Haga (J, Yamaha), at 5"087; 5. C. Fogarty (GB, Ducati), at 5"641; 6. W. Yoshikawa (J, Yamaha), at 7"083; 7. P. Chili (I, Suzuki), at 9"258; 8. T. Serizawa (J, Kawasaki), at 11"892; 9. C. Edwards (USA, Honda), at 12"411; 10. M. Tamada (J, Honda), at 12"441; 11. S. Takeishi (J, Kawasaki), at 14"854; 12. T. Tsujimura (J, Yamaha), at 14"867; 13. A. Slight (NZ, Honda), at 16"071; 14. T. Corser (AUS, Ducati), at 16"366; 15. H. Izutsu (J, Kawasaki), at 16"495. 21 finishers.
Fastest lap: A. Ryo (J, Suzuki), 1'30"519 (148.622 km/h).

Final classification

1. Carl Fogarty	GB	Ducati	489 points
2. Colin Edwards	USA	Honda	361
3. Troy Corser	AUS	Ducati	361
4. Aaron Slight	NZ	Honda	323
5. Akira Yanagawa	J	Kawasaki	308
6. Pierfrancesco Chili	I	Suzuki	251
7. Noriyuki Haga	J	Yamaha	196
8. Gregorio Lavilla	E	Kawasaki	156
9. Katsuaki Fujiwara	J	Suzuki	119
10. Vittoriano Guareschi	I	Yamaha	99

11. A. Meklau (A, Ducati), 94; 12. P. Goddard (AUS, Aprilia), 84; 13. R. Ulm (A, Kawasaki), 59; 14. I. Jerman (SLO, Kawasaki), 56; 15. A. Ryo (J, Suzuki), 45; 16. B. Bostrom (USA, Ducati), 45; 17. D. Romboni (I, Ducati), 44; 18. J. Reynolds (GB, Ducati), 39; 19. A. Gramigni (I, Yamaha), 37; 20. L. Pedercini (I, Ducati), 35; 21. C. Walker (GB, Kawasaki), 31; 22. K. Kitagawa (J, Suzuki), 29; 23. N. MacKenzie (GB, Yamaha), 27; 24. A. Gobert (AUS, Ducati), 25; 25. M. Lucchiari (I, Yamaha), 25; 26. W. Yoshikawa (J, Yamaha), 21; 27. N. Serizawa (J, Kawasaki), 18; 28. S. Emmett (GB, Ducati), 17; 29. B. Morrison (GB, Yamaha), 16; 30. F. Protat (F, Ducati), 16; 31. L. Isaacs (SA, Ducati), 16; 32. E. Bostrom (USA, Honda), 15; 33. S. Hislop (GB, Kawasaki), 15; 34. C. Connell (AUS, Ducati), 15; 35. G. Bussei (I, Suzuki), 13; 36. M. Malatesta (I, Ducati), 13; 37. J. Haydon (GB, Suzuki), 12; 38. M. Tamada (J, Honda), 12; 39. R. Kellenberger (CH, Honda), 11; 40. J. Hacking (USA, Yamaha), 11; 41. S. Martin (AUS, Ducati), 9; 42. C. Lindholm (S, Yamaha), 9; 43. J. Schmid (D, Kawasaki), 9; 44. S. Giles (AUS, Suzuki), 9; 45. T. Tsujimura (J, Yamaha), 7; 46. J. Mrkyvka (CZ, Ducati), 6; 47. N. Manz (D, Suzuki), 5; 48. S. Itoh (J, Honda), 5; 49. T. Rechberger (A, Suzuki), 4; 50. C. Macias (COL, Ducati), 3; 51. A. Antonello (I, Aprilia), 3; 52. M. Craggill (AUS, Suzuki), 3; 53. V. Karban (SVK, Suzuki), 2; 54. J. Ekerold Junior (SA, Kawasaki), 2; 55. H. Izutsu (J, Kawasaki), 1; 56. Y. Takeda (J, Honda), 1. 56 finishers.

28th March - South Africa - Kyalami

Pole position: R. Xaus (E, Yamaha) 1'47"293 (143.170 km/h).

1. I. MacPherson (GB, Kawasaki), 23 laps in 41'52"104 (140.642 km/h); 2. S. Chambon (F, Suzuki), at 12"515; 3. J. Teuchert (D, Yamaha), at 21"145; 4. C. Kellner (D, Yamaha), at 22"500; 5. R. Wood (SA, Yamaha), at 27"675; 6. J. Toseland (GB, Honda), at 29"166; 7. P. Casoli (I, Ducati), at 30"043; 8. W. Zeelenberg (NL, Yamaha), at 38"618; 9. D. De Gea (E, Honda), at 39"640; 10. W. Costes (F, Honda), at 41"919; 11. Y. Briguet (CH, Suzuki)(*), at 44"139; 12. G. Van Breda (SA, Honda), at 48"728; 13. R. Teneggi (I, Ducati), at 51"091; 14. P. Bontempi (I, Kawasaki), at 1'04"227; 15. P. Riba Cabana (E, Honda), at 1'06"117. 23 finishers.

Fastest lap: I. MacPherson (GB, Kawasaki), 1'48"343 (141.783 km/h).

(*): B. Anassis (SA, Kawasaki), qui avait passé la ligne d'arrivée en onzième position, a été mis hors course pour utilisation d'un liquide de refroidissement interdit.

2nd May - Great Britain - Donington Park

Pole position: P. Casoli (I, Ducati), 1'37"348 (148.736 km/h).

1. J. Whitham (GB, Yamaha), 23 laps in 37'51"458 (146.611 km/h); 2. S. Chambon (F, Suzuki), at 4"004; 3. I. MacPherson (GB, Kawasaki), at 12"342; 4. J. Teuchert (D, Yamaha), at 15"572; 5. W. Costes (F, Honda), at 16"370; 6. P. Bontempi (I, Yamaha), at 17"190; 7. C. Migliorati (I, Suzuki), at 26"363; 8. J. Toseland (GB, Honda), at 28"476; 9. J. Crawford (GB, Suzuki), at 30"860; 10. R. Panichi (I, Bimota), at 31"859; 11. C. Kellner (D, Yamaha), at 33"776; 12. I. Simpson (GB, Honda), at 40"798; 13. C. Mariottini (I, Kawasaki), at 42"356; 14. R. Teneggi (I, Ducati), at 42"576; 15. V. Iannuzzo (I, Yamaha), at 43"036. 24 finishers.

Fastest lap: J. Whitham (GB, Yamaha), 1'37"565 (148.405 km/h).

16th May - Spain - Albacete

Pole position: I. MacPherson (GB, Kawasaki), 1'34"910 (134.236 km/h).

1. J. Teuchert (D, Yamaha), 26 laps in 41'59"211 (131.490 km/h); 2. P. Bontempi (I, Yamaha), at 0"488; 3. P. Riba Cabana (E, Honda), at 3"164; 4. S. Chambon (F, Suzuki), at 10"142; 5. F. Pirovano (I, Suzuki), at 10"686; 6. C. Kellner (D, Yamaha), at 10"927(*); 7. Y. Briguet (CH, Suzuki), at 11"972; 8. W. Costes (F, Honda), at 15"814; 9. V. Iannuzzo (I, Yamaha), at 20"236; 10. C. Migliorati (I, Suzuki), at 24"128; 11. J. Toseland (GB, Honda), at 25"831; 12. R. Panichi (I, Bimota), at 26"608; 13. J. Rodriguez (E, Yamaha), at 26"782; 14. C. Cogan (F, Yamaha), at 28"765; 15. W.

Tortoroglio (I, Suzuki), at 33"076. 23 finishers.

Fastest lap: P. Riba Cabana (E, Honda), 1'35"618 (133.242 km/h).

(*): C. Kellner (D, Yamaha), qui avait passé la ligne d'arrivée en quatrième position, a été pénalisé de 5 secondes pour non respect du drapeau jaune.

30th May - Italy - Monza

Pole position: P. Bontempi (I, Yamaha), 1'53"302 (183.333 km/h).

1. W. Zeelenberg (NL, Yamaha), 16 laps in 30'31"260 (181.488 km/h); 2. R. Xaus (E, Yamaha), at 0"016; 3. P. Bontempi (I, Yamaha), at 0"064; 4. M. Meregalli (I, Yamaha), at 0"118; 5. F. Pirovano (I, Suzuki), at 0"200; 6. W. Costes (F, Honda), at 0"663; 7. C. Migliorati (I, Suzuki), at 1"629; 8. Y. Briguet (CH, Suzuki), at 3"482; 9. J. Toseland (GB, Honda), at 10"207; 10. P. Riba Cabana (E, Honda), at 10"219; 11. C. Kellner (D, Yamaha), at 10"365; 12. S. Chambon (F, Suzuki), at 10"421; 13. V. Ianuzzo (I, Yamaha), at 11"669; 14. N. Brignola (I, Bimota), at 12"686; 15. D. De Gea (E, Honda), at 13"688. 24 finishers.

Fastest lap: C. Kellner (D, Yamaha), 1'53"155 (183.571 km/h).

13th June - Germany - Nürburgring

Pole position: J. Teuchert (D, Yamaha), 1'43"927 (157.818 km/h).

1. P. Bontempi (I, Yamaha), 21 laps in 37'40"271 (152.386 km/h); 2. F. Pirovano (I, Suzuki), at 9"782; 3. W. Costes (F, Honda), at 11"715; 4. C. Kellner (D, Yamaha), at 24"420; 5. C. Cogan (F, Yamaha), at 24"834; 6. W. Tortoroglio (I, Suzuki), at 25"820; 7. G. Fiorillo (I, Suzuki), at 39"564; 8. S. Chambon (F, Suzuki), at 42"234; 9. S. Scheschowitsch (D, Suzuki), at 44"051; 10. I. MacPherson (GB, Kawasaki), at 56"768; 11. F. Monaco (I, Ducati), at 1'19"191; 12. M. Barth (D, Suzuki), at 1'29"794; 13. J. Toseland (GB, Honda), at 1'30"428; 14. W. Zeelenberg (NL, Yamaha), à 1'46"059; 15. M. Borciani (I, Honda), at 2 laps. 20 finishers.

Fastest lap: P. Bontempi (I, Yamaha), 1'45"591 (155.331 km/h).

27th June - San Marino - Misano

Pole position: M. Meregalli (I, Yamaha), 1'37"915 (149.272 km/h).

1. R. Xaus (E, Yamaha), 17 laps in 28'14"050 (146.673 km/h)(*); 2. P. Casoli (I, Ducati), at 1"569; 3. M. Meregalli (I, Yamaha), at 2"220; 4. F. Pirovano (I, Suzuki), at 2"274; 5. S. Chambon (F, Suzuki), at 2"765; 6. J. Teuchert (D, Yamaha), at 11"468; 7. P. Bontempi (I, Yamaha), at 11"744; 8. V. Iannuzzo (I, Yamaha), at 12"059; 9. C. Mariottini (I, Kawasaki), at 12"495; 10. W. Zeelenberg (NL, Yamaha), at 13"006; 11. C. Kellner (D, Yamaha), at 17"295; 12. W. Costes (F, Honda), at 18"346; 13. J. Toseland

(GB, Honda), at 18"786; 14. C. Migliorati (I, Suzuki), at 20"697; 15. W. Tortoroglio (I, Suzuki), at 20"838. 27 finishers.

Fastest lap: P. Casoli (I, Ducati), 1'38"746 (148.016 km/h).

(*): la course a été arrêtée au 18e tour, en raison d'une averse violente.

11th July - USA - Laguna Seca

Pole position: S. Chambon (F, Suzuki), 1'30"227 (143.717 km/h).

1. S. Chambon (F, Suzuki), 25 laps in 38'19"719 (140.965 km/h); 2. I. MacPherson (GB, Kawasaki), at 4"083; 3. P. Casoli (I, Ducati), at 10"315; 4. M. Meregalli (I, Yamaha), at 12"329; 5. F. Pirovano (I, Suzuki), at 13"594; 6. P. Bontempi (I, Yamaha), at 18"423; 7. C. Migliorati (I, Suzuki), at 21"165; 8. W. Zeelenberg (NL, Yamaha), at 23"073; 9. C. Kellner (D, Yamaha), at 23"239; 10. W. Costes (F, Honda), at 37"106; 11. J. Toseland (GB, Honda), at 38"984; 12. W. Daemen (B, Yamaha), at 44"897; 13. B. Parriott (USA, Honda), at 45"147; 14. C. Cogan (F, Yamaha), at 46"095; 15. M. Malatesta (I, Ducati), at 52"808. 23 finishers.

Fastest lap: S. Chambon (F, Suzuki), 1'30"807 (142.799 km/h).

1st August - Europe - Brands Hatch

Pole position: S. Chambon (F, Suzuki), 1'31"088 (166.823 km/h).

1. S. Chambon (F, Suzuki), 23 laps in 35'25"212 (164.454 km/h); 2. R. Xaus (E, Yamaha), at 4"908; 3. C. Migliorati (I, Suzuki), at 5"077; 4. P. Bontempi (I, Yamaha), at 7"097; 5. M. Meregalli (I, Yamaha), at 7"178; 6. C. Kellner (D, Yamaha), at 8"242; 7. J. Toseland (GB, Honda), at 11"298; 8. F. Pirovano (I, Suzuki), at 15"190; 9. S. Charpentier (F, Honda), at 15"347; 10. G. Richards (AUS, Yamaha), at 18"425; 11. C. Cogan (F, Yamaha), at 24"923; 12. W. Costes (F, Honda), at 31"554; 13. R. Panichi (I, Bimota), at 32"014; 14. D. De Gea (E, Honda), at 37"868; 15. W. Zeelenberg (NL, Yamaha), at 38"169. 21 finishers.

Fastest lap: S. Chambon (F, Suzuki), 1'31"255 (166.517 km/h).

29th August - Austria - A1-Ring

Pole position: R. Xaus (E, Yamaha), 1'35"835 (162.241 km/h).

1. J. Teuchert (D, Yamaha), 23 laps in 44'52"385 (132.824 km/h); 2. C. Kellner (D, Yamaha), at 8"992; 3. W. Zeelenberg (NL, Yamaha), at 13"615; 4. I. MacPherson (GB, Kawasaki), at 15"031; 5. P. Bontempi (I, Yamaha), at 16"593; 6. W. Daemen (B, Yamaha), at 16"621; 7. P. Riba Cabana (E, Honda), at 20"509; 8. A. Giachino (I, Suzuki), at 20"998; 9. M. Sanchini (I, Suzuki), at 34"150; 10. S. Charpentier (F, Honda), at 36"026; 11. M. Wohner (A,

Yamaha), at 52"421; 12. M. Malatesta (I, Ducati), at 1'23"639; 13. L. Pegram (USA, Ducati), at 1'26"881; 14. I. Antonelli (I, Yamaha), at 1'28"268; 15. C. Migliorati (I, Suzuki), at 1'47"865. 17 finishers.
Fastest lap: M. Meregalli (I, Yamaha), 1'54"348 (135.974 km/h).

5th September - Pays-Bas - Assen
Pole position: I. MacPherson (GB, Kawasaki), 2'09"874 (167.673 km/h).
1. I. MacPherson (GB, Kawasaki), 12 laps in 26'26"707 (164.691 km/h)(*); 2. C. Migliorati (I, Suzuki), at 3"032; 3. R. Xaus (E, Yamaha), at 3"310; 4. K. Muggeridge (AUS, Honda), at 3"587; 5. S. Chambon (F, Suzuki), at 5"542; 6. P. Riba Cabana (E, Honda), at 6"416; 7. J. Toseland (GB, Honda), at 6"813; 8. J. Teuchert (D, Yamaha), at 7"182; 9. W. Costes (F, Honda), at 7"377; 10. W. Zeelenberg (NL, Yamaha), at 7"571; 11. K. Harris (GB, Suzuki), at 8"936; 12. L. Pegram (USA, Ducati), at 16"782; 13. C. Cogan (F, Yamaha), at 17"095; 14. S. Charpentier (F, Honda), at 17"420; 15. D. Checa-Carrera (E, Ducati), at 25"798. 25 finishers.
Fastest lap: I. MacPherson (GB, Kawasaki), 2'11"031 (166.192 km/h).
(*): course arrêtée au 13e des 16 tours en raison de présence d'huile sur la piste. Le classement est celui du douzième passage.

12th September - Germany - Hockenheim
Pole position: S. Chambon (F, Suzuki), 2'07"391 (191.938 km/h).
1. I. MacPherson (GB, Kawasaki), 14 laps in 30'05"421 (189.605 km/h); 2. R. Xaus (E, Yamaha), at 0"446; 3. S. Chambon (F, Suzuki), at 0"494; 4. K. Harris (GB, Suzuki), at 1"264; 5. J. Teuchert (D, Yamaha), at 1"401; 6. F. Pirovano (I, Suzuki), at 4"811; 7. C. Migliorati (I, Suzuki), at 5"296; 8. P. Riba Cabana (E, Honda), at 5"621; 9. W. Zeelenberg (NL, Yamaha), at 7"420; 10. C. Kellner (D, Yamaha), at 7"572; 11. S. Charpentier (F, Honda), at 8"041; 12. C. Cogan (F, Yamaha), at 13"573; 13. W. Tortoroglio (I, Suzuki), at 20"024; 14. V. Iannuzzo (I, Yamaha), at 20"361; 15. W. Costes (F, Honda), at 20"430. 28 finishers.
Fastest lap: I. MacPherson (GB, Kawasaki), 2'07"197 (192.230 km/h).

Iain MacPherson: debut win.

Final classification

1. Stéphane Chambon	F	Suzuki	153 points
2. Iain MacPherson	GB	Kawasaki	130
3. Piergiorgio Bontempi	I	Yamaha	116
4. Jörg Teuchert	D	Yamaha	108
5. Ruben Xaus	E	Yamaha	101
6. Christian Kellner	D	Yamaha	94
7. Fabrizio Pirovano	I	Suzuki	84
8. C. Migliorati	I	Suzuki	81
9. Wilco Zeelenberg	NL	Yamaha	79
10. William Costes	F	Honda	73

11. J. Toseland (GB, Honda), 59; 12. M. Meregalli (I, Yamaha), 53; 13. P. Riba Cabana (E, Honda), 50; 14. P. Casoli (I, Ducati), 45; 15. C. Cogan (F, Yamaha), 27; 16. J. Whitham (GB, Yamaha), 25; 17. Y. Briguet (CH, Suzuki), 22; 18. V. Iannuzzo (I, Yamaha), 21; 19. S. Charpentier (F, Honda), 20; 20. K. Harris (GB, Suzuki), 18; 21. W. Tortoroglio (I, Suzuki), 15; 22. W. Daemen (B, Yamaha), 14; 23. K. Muggeridge (AUS, Honda), 13; 24. R. Panichi (I, Bimota), 13; 25. R. Wood (SA, Yamaha), 11; 26. D. De Gea (E, Honda), 10; 27. C. Mariottini (I, Kawasaki), 10; 28. G. Fiorillo (I, Suzuki), 9; 29. A. Giachino (I, Suzuki), 8; 30. M. Sanchini (I, Suzuki), 7; 31. S. Scheschowitsch (D, Suzuki), 7; 32. J. Crawford (GB, Suzuki), 7; 33. L. Pegram (USA, Ducati), 7; 34. G. Richards (AUS, Yamaha), 6; 35. M. Wohner (A, Yamaha), 5; 36. F. Monaco (I, Ducati), 5; 37. M. Malatesta (I, Ducati), 5; 38. R. Teneggi (I, Ducati), 5; 39. M. Barth (D, Suzuki), 4; 40. I. Simpson (GB, Honda), 4; 41. G. Van Breda (SA, Honda), 4; 42. B. Parriott (USA, Honda), 3; 43. J. Rodriguez (E, Yamaha), 3; 44. I. Antonelli (I, Yamaha), 2; 45. N. Brignola (I, Bimota), 2; 46. D. Checa-Carrera (E, Ducati), 1; 47. M. Borciani (I, Honda), 1. 47 finishers.

10th-11th April - Le Mans 24 Hours - France
1. C. Walker/B. Sebileau/S. Hislop (GB/F/GB, Kawasaki), 787 laps in 24 h.01'13"0 (141.049 km/h); 2. P. Dobé/A. Van Den Bossche/T. Paillot (F, Suzuki), at 7 laps; 3. T. Rymer/J. Whitham/J. D'Orgeix (GB/GB/F, Suzuki), at 27 laps; 4. J.-F. Cortinovis/C. Guyot/A. Lussiana (F, Kawasaki), at 34 laps; 5. J. Couturier/B. Cuzin/J. Marchand (F, Yamaha)(*), at 44 laps; 6. C. Haquin/J.-Y. Mounier/M. Amalric (F, Kawasaki), at 48 laps; 7. X. Brichet/P. Colin/S. Fredix (F, Honda), at 55 laps; 8. G. Jolivet/S. Neff/F. Herfort (F, Kawasaki)(*); 9. J.-P. Leblanc/J.-L. Buffard/E. L'Herbette (F, Kawasaki), at 58 laps; 10. M. Graziano/J. Nogueira/T. Pereira (F/P/P, Suzuki); 11. S. Coutelle/F. Cristobal/G. Lindner (F/E/D, Suzuki), at 60 laps; 12. P. Chapuis/C. Bernard/P. Denis (F, Yamaha)(*), at 67 laps; 13. F. Girardot/E. Lentaigne/D. Marzloff (F, Honda); 14. X. Pommier/D. Emonet/T. Joulin (F, Yamaha)(*), at 68 laps; 15. F. Lethin/P. Guittet/L. Béguelin (F, Honda)(*).

10th-11th July -
Spa-Francorchamps 24 Hours - Belgium
1. T. Pereira/M. Graziano/B. Bonhuil (P/F/F, Suzuki), 516 laps in 24 h.00'11"2 (169.792 km/h); 2. C. Lavieille/T. Rymer/J. D'Orgeix (F/GB/F, Suzuki), at 6 laps; 3. S. Gabrieli/E. Mizera/D. Morillon (F, Yamaha), at 10 laps; 4. P. Carrara/T. Pochon/C. Desmaris (I/F/F, Yamaha)(*), at 13 laps; 5. B. Pister/D. Drieghe/D. Schildermans (F/B/B, Aprilia)(*), at 20 laps; 6. X. Fabra/D. Fuchs/D. Bonvicini (F, Kawasaki)(*), at 22 laps; 7. A. Trappehl/A. Palmer/A. Benitz (D, Yamaha)(*), at 27 laps; 8. B. Destoop/P. Guittet/C. Laurent (F, Honda)(*), at 28 laps; 9. L. Dubus/T. Beaumont/O. Herriberry (F, Yamaha)(*), at 28 laps; 10. A. Legrand/B. Scheiff/M. Weynard (B, Yamaha)(*), at 29 laps; 11. M. Arrighi/E. Lepetit/E. Monot (F, Yamaha)(*), at 29 laps; 12. S. Waldmeier/F. Méller/J. Le Noxais (F, Yamaha)(*), at 29 laps; 13. S. Strauch/T. Roethig/D. Winterbottom (D/D/GB, Kawasaki)(*), at 31 laps; 14. L. Albrecht/J. Plaschka/N. Schmassmann (D/D/CH, Suzuki), at 32 laps; 15. M. Wauters/D. Jadoul/T. Van Wezemael (B, Kawasaki)(*), 34 laps.

25th July - Suzuka 8 Hours - Japan
1. A. Barros/T. Okada (BR/J, Honda), 213 laps in 8 h.01'59"918 (155.48 km/h); 2. A. Slight/C. Edwards (NZ/USA, Honda), at 1 lap; 3. A. Yanagawa/H. Izutsu (J, Kawasaki); 4. N. Haga/R. Laconi (J/F, Yamaha), at 3 laps; 5. T. Serizawa/S. Takeishi (J, Kawasaki), at 4 laps; 6. R. Tsuruta/O. Nishijama (J, Kawasaki); 7. Y. Takeda/J. Kocinski (J/USA, Honda), at 5 laps; 8. M. Tamada/J. Kato (J, Honda); 9. Y. Nukumi/K. Nashimoto (J, Honda), at 6 laps; 10. T. Tsujimura/W. Yoshikawa (J, Yamaha), at 7 laps; 11. T. Suzuki/K. Nakamura (J, Honda), at 11 laps; 12. H. Noda/T. Kimura (J, Honda); 13. I. Asai/M. Hayashi (J, Yamaha), at 12 laps; 14. N. Fujiwara/J. Hacking (J/USA, Yamaha), at 13 laps; 15. Y. Haraguchi/Y. Korogi (J, Honda).

14th-15th August - Oschersleben 24 Hours - Germany
1. S. Waldmeier/B. Cuzin/J. Couturier (F, Yamaha)(*), 769 laps in 24 h.00'41"388 (117.441 km/h); 2. H. Graf/M. Rieder/C. Kénzi (CH, Kawasaki), at 3 laps; 3. T. Heiler/M. Galinski/U. Mark (D, Yamaha)(*), at 6 laps; 4. A. Steinmacher/M. Scherrer/P. Rink (D, Suzuki)(*), at 14 laps; 5. P. Carrara/T. Pochon/C. Desmaris (F, Yamaha)(*), at 17 laps; 6. A. Trappehl/A. Palmer/A. Benitz (F, Yamaha)(*); 7. K. Schulz/J. Martensen/F. Schulz (D, Yamaha)(*), at 21 laps; 8. B. Scheeder/J. Schmidt/J. Vesper (D, Suzuki)(*), at 23 laps; 9. T. Klink/R. Kleiner/U. Kaltwasser (D, Yamaha)(*); 10. A. Bronec/F. Coing-Belley/J.-F. Gleyse (F, Yamaha)(*), at 24 laps; 11. S. Meyer/P. Meyer/J. Hantschmann (D, Aprilia)(*); 12. N. Schmassmann/J. Plaschka/M. Kiok (CH/D/D, Suzuki), at 25 laps; 13. X. Fabra/D. Fuchs/D. Bonvicini (F, Kawasaki)(*), at 26 laps; 14. C. Tigges/P. Eickelmann/J. Gutsche (D, Suzuki)(*), at 27 laps; 15. H. Platacis/R. Seefeldt/M. Méller (D, Aprilia)(*), at 28 laps.

11th-12th Septembee - Bol d'Or 24 Hours (Le Castellet) - France
1. T. Rymer/J. D'Orgeix/C. Lavieille (GB/F/F, Suzuki), 685 laps in 24 h. 01'08"547 (165.26 km/h); 2. J.-M. Delétang/F. Foret/C. Lindholm (F/F/S, Yamaha), at 1 lap; 3. S. Scarnato/S. Plater/E. Korpiaho (F/GB/SF, Kawasaki), at 2 laps; 4. M. Amalric/O. Ulmann/C. Haquin (F, Kawasaki), at 17 laps; 5. B. Bonhuil/M. Graziano/T. Pereira (F/F/P, Suzuki), at 24 laps; 6. J.-P. Guinand/M. Garcia/F. Gebelin (F, Honda), at 31 laps; 7. B. Sebileau/L. Holon/S. Hislop (F/F/GB, Kawasaki), at 32 laps; 8. L. Béguelin/J.-C. Hatchikian/B. Fourcadet (F, Honda), at 36 laps; 9. G. Giabbani/Y. Le Gaudu/F. Moreira (F, Kawasaki)(*), at 38 laps; 10. D. Heal/S. Smith/G. Richards (GB, Yamaha)(*), at 41 laps; 11. D. Thomas/T. Rees/S. Mertens (AUS/GB/B, Suzuki), at 42 laps; 12. J.-P. Leblanc/J.-L. Buffard/E. L'Herbette (F, Kawasaki), at 42 laps; 13. F. Coing-Belley/A. Kempener/J.-F. Gleyze (F/B/F, Yamaha)(*), at 47 laps; 14. P. Carrara/T. Pochon/C. Desmaris (F, Yamaha)(*), at 49 laps; 15. T. Varlet/C. Bernard/P. Denis (F, Yamaha)(*), at 55 laps.

(*): Those teams entered in Stocksport or in Supersport are not eligible to score points in the World Championship.

Final classification

1. Terry Rymer and Jéhan D'Orgeix	GB/F	Suzuki	122
3. Christian Lavieille	F	Suzuki	90
4. Bruno Bonhuil	F	Suzuki	90
5. Michel Graziano and Telmo Pereira	F/P	Suzuki	88

7. S. Hislop (GB, Kawasaki), 80; 8. B. Sebileau (F, Kawasaki), 68; 9. N. Schmassmann and J. Plaschka (CH/D, Suzuki), 62; 11. F. Girardot (F, Honda), 54; 12. M. Rieder, H. Graf and C. Kénzi (CH, Kawasaki), 50; 15. C. Walker (GB, Kawasaki), 50; 16. B. Fourcadet (F, Honda), 48; 17. E. Lentaigne (F, Honda), 48; 18. C. Haquin and M. Amalric (F, Kawasaki), 48; 20. T. De Almeida, C. Suty and G. Munsch (F, Ducati), 46; 23. S. Scarnato (F, Kawasaki), 44; 24. C. Guyot (F, Kawasaki), 44; 25. J.-M. Delétang, F. Foret and C. Lindholm (F/F/S, Yamaha), 40; 28. M. Kiok (D, Suzuki), 40; 29. P. Dobé, A. Van Den Bossche and T. Paillot (F, Suzuki), 40; 32. S. Plater and E. Korpiaho (GB/SF, Kawasaki), 32; 34. E. Mizera, S. Gabrieli and D. Morillon (F, Yamaha), 32; 37. J. Whitham (GB, Suzuki), 32; 38. J.-P. Leblanc, J.-L. Buffard and E. L'Herbette (F, Kawasaki), 30; 41. F. Cristobal and G. Lindner (E/D, Suzuki), 28; 43. O. Ulmann (F, Kawasaki), 26; 44. B. Pister, D. Schildermans and D. Drieghe (B, Aprilia), 26; 47. J.-F. Cortinovis and A. Lussiana (F, Kawasaki), 26; 49. A. Barros and T. Okada (BR/J, Honda), 25; 51. F. Willems, M. Kehrmann and H. Ruroth (D, Honda), 22; 54. L. Albrecht (D, Suzuki), 22; 55. J.-Y. Mounier (F, Kawasaki), 22; 56. J.-P. Guinand, M. Garcia and F. Gebelin (F, Honda), 20; 59. D. Spriet, M. Fissette and A. Aerts (B, Suzuki), 20; 62. A. Slight and C. Edwards (NZ/USA, Honda), 20; 64. X. Brichet, P. Colin and S. Fredix (F, Honda), 20; 67. S. Coutelle (F, Kawasaki), 20; 68. L. Holon (F, Kawasaki), 18; 69. P. Linden and M. Lindner (S/D, Suzuki), 18; 71. H.-R. Portmann, W. Graf and P. Knutti (CH, Kawasaki), 18; 74. C. Charles-Artigues (F, Ducati), 18; 75. L. Béguelin and J.-C. Hatchikian (F, Honda), 16; 77. P. Hecker, F. Penningsfeld and M. Boschung (D, Suzuki), 16; 80. A. Yanagawa and H. Izutsu (J, Kawasaki), 16; 82. R. De Backer, M. Goffinghs and C. Goffinghs (B, Suzuki), 16; 85. J. Nogueira (P, Suzuki), 16; 86. D. Thomas, T. Rees and S. Mertens (AUS/GB/B, Suzuki), 14; 89. M. Barth (D, Suzuki), 14; 90. P. Ettel, Y. Fousse and D. Stefani (F, Honda), 14; 93. N. Haga and R. Laconi (J/F, Yamaha), 13; 95. T. De Maegt, M. Vanlandschoot and G. Roelens (B, Suzuki), 12; 98. D. Marzloff (F, Honda), 12; 99. T. Serizawa and S. Takeishi (J, Kawasaki), 11; 101. A. Bronec and F. Chénais (F, Honda), 10; 103. F. Méller, J. Le Noxaic and H. Sevault (F, Yamaha), 10; 106. R. Tsuruta and O. Nishijama (J, Kawasaki), 10; 108. R. Almet and T. Morel (F, Aprilia), 10; 110. Y. Takeda and J. Kocinski (J/USA, Honda), 9; 112. R. Sanchez-Alvarez and P. Durand (E/F, Ducati), 8; 114. O. Brandt, R. Klemmer and T. Bréring (D, Suzuki), 8; 117. M. Tamada and J. Kato (J, Honda), 8; 119. R. Rodrigues, H. Teixeira and C. Nogueira (F, Suzuki), 8; 122. Y. Nukumi and K. Nashimoto (J, Honda), 7; 124. N. Dussauge (F, Kawasaki), 6; 125. T. Tsujimura and W. Yoshikawa (J, Yamaha), 6; 127. T. Suzuki and K. Nakamura (J, Honda), 5; 129. H.-C. Law and S. Sou (HGK/CHN, Honda), 4; 131. H. Noda and T. Kimura (J, Honda), 4; 133. I. Asai and M. Hayashi (J, Yamaha), 3; 135. N. Fujiwara and J. Hacking (J/USA, Yamaha), 2; 137. Y. Haraguchi and Y. Korogi (J, Honda), 1. 138 classified.

Stocksport European Championship

1. Thierry Pochon and Claude Desmaris	F	Yamaha	136
3. Patrick Carrara	F	Yamaha	110

4. J. Couturier and B. Cuzin (F, Yamaha), 100; 6. S. Waldmeier (F, Yamaha), 92; 7. X. Fabra and D. Bonvicini (F, Kawasaki), 82; 9. F. Coing-Belley and J.-F. Gleyze (F, Yamaha), 76; 11. D. Fuchs (F, Kawasaki), 66; 12. C. Bernard (F, Yamaha), 66; 13. P. Denis (F, Yamaha), 54; 14. E. Monot (F, Kawasaki), 54; 15. T. Beaumont and O. Herriberry (F, Yamaha), 52; 17. G. Giabbani, F. Moreira and T. Le Gaudu (F, Kawasaki), 50; 20. J. Marchand (F, Yamaha); 21. F. Méller and J. Le Noxaic (F, Yamaha), 50; 23. D. Heal, G. Richards and S. Smith (GB/AUS/GB, Yamaha), 40; 26. S. Neff, F. Herfort and G. Jolivet (F, Kawasaki), 30; 29. V. Klett and K.-H. Lemberg (F, Suzuki), 34; 31. A. Kempener (B, Yamaha), 32; 32. A. Bronec (F, Yamaha), 32; 33. L. Dubus (F, Yamaha), 32; 34. P. Chapuis (F, Yamaha), 32; 35. P. Bondu and Y. Parage (F, Aprilia), 32; 37. H. Gres (D, Suzuki), 30; 38. M. Blug (D, Suzuki), 28; 39. P. Carrara (I, Yamaha), 26; 40. B. Scheiff, A. Legrand and M. Weynard (B, Yamaha), 26; 43. X. Pommier, D. Emonet and T. Joulin (F, Yamaha), 26; 46. J. Smolders (B, Suzuki), 24; 47. T. Varlet (F, Yamaha), 22; 48. A. Reinmann and J. Méller (D, Kawasaki), 22; 50. M. Arrighi and E. Lepetit (F, Yamaha), 22; 52. S. Willermoz (F, Yamaha), 20; 53. C. Beck, S. Steinebach, T. Warnke and T. Roth (D, Suzuki), 20; 57. R. Treffort (F, Aprilia), 18; 58. E. Delarbre and D. Beauvais (F, Kawasaki), 18; 60. D. Jadoul, M. Wauters and T. Van Wezemael (B, Kawasaki), 18; 63. A. Heiler (D, Suzuki), 18; 64. R. Robin, T. Carbonnier and P. Chanain (F, Yamaha), 16; 67. E. Nolden (D, Suzuki), 16; 68. R. Colombain, G. Marchat and R. Kesler (F, Yamaha), 16; 71. P. Robert (F, Kawasaki), 16; 72. E. Parisse (F, Aprilia), 16; 73. B. Vecchioni, C. Bayle and C. Dambel (F, Yamaha), 14; 76. R. Ternes (D, Suzuki), 14; 77. S. Watts, M. Davidson and J. Roach (AUS/GB/GB, Yamaha), 14; 80. D. Umbdenstock and P. Richard (F, Aprilia), 14; 82. R. Dernoncourt, Y. Thomas and J. Roig (F, Kawasaki), 12; 85. G. Vermeulen and R. Van Looy (B, Suzuki), 12; 87. M. Deleersnijder and T. Van Loon (B, Suzuki), 12; 89. P. Ettel (F, Yamaha), 12; 90. E. Resmond, M. Perez and M. Martin (F, Yamaha), 10; 93. K. Katoch, K. Angerhofer and P. Resch (A, Aprilia), 10; 96. F. Julien and D. Roy (F, Aprilia), 10; 98. J.-M. Christen, B. Hien and F. Gremion (F, Yamaha), 10; 101. P. Guittet, B. Destoop and C. Laurent (F, Honda), 8; 104. H. Sevault (F, Yamaha), 8; 106. R. Leh (D, Suzuki), 8; 106. N. Boyer, X. Albertini and D. Pardon (F, Yamaha), 6; 109. A. Schrauwen (B, Yamaha), 6; 110. H. Omlor (D, Suzuki), 6; 111. T. Traccan, D. Dumain and E. Célis (F, Yamaha), 4; 114. L. Gyssrechts and S. Casaer (B, Yamaha), 4; 116. B. Pister, D. Schildermans and D. Rouquart (B, Aprilia), 2; 119. G. Bachels, O. Hofmann and I. Koenen (D, Yamaha), 1. 121 classified.

Supersport European Championship

1. Pascal Guittet	F	Honda	160
2. Alex Palmer and Achim Trappehl	D	Yamaha	134

4. A Benitz (D, Yamaha), 114; 5. B. Destoop and C. Laurent (F, Honda), 110; 7. M. Scherrer (D, Suzuki), 108; 8. A. Steinmacher (D, Suzuki), 86; 9. P. Rink (D, Suzuki), 82; 10. F. Gilles, E. Labussiére and N. De Dieuleveult (F, Kawasaki), 80; 13. M. Galinski, A. Heiler and U. Mark (D, Yamaha), 50; 16. L. Béguelin and F. Lethin (F, Honda), 50; 18. B. Sika and J. Cauchard (F, Honda), 48; 20. P. Petitjean, O. Carlier and I. Vlassenbroeck (B, Kawasaki), 38; 23. S. Strauch, D. Winterbotton and T. Roethig (D/GB/D, Kawasaki), 32; 26. V. Bocquet, F. Renault and L. Brian (F, Honda), 32; 29. A. Raskin and E. Lefebvre (B, Kawasaki), 32; 31. F. Helwig, P. Meynle and L. Engel (F, Kawasaki), 26; 34. T. Klink, R. Kleiner and U. Kaltwasser (D, Yamaha), 26; 37. S. Bray (F, Honda), 26; 38. D. Beauvais (F, Suzuki); 39. T. Labeye (B, Kawasaki), 26; 40. F. Tauziede (F, Suzuki), 22; 41. H. Herber, A. Wanninger and F. Schéller (D, Kawasaki), 22; 44. F. Delanoue (F, Honda), 22; 45. S. Nebel (D, Yamaha), 20; 46. J. Neate, D. Mabbutt and A. Hitchcok (GB, Honda), 18; 49. P. Jansen, Y. Bollaerts and J. Rosch (NL/B/NL, Laverda), 16; 52. J. Mergny (B, Kawasaki), 14; 53. A. Van Dijk, C. Schmid and M. Westra (NL/B/B, Honda), 12; 56. G. Valtulini, L. Pedersoli and A. Pizagalli (I, Laverda), 10; 59. P. Panier (B, Kawasaki), 8. 59 classified.

18th April - Australia - Phillip Island

Pole position (superpole): Webster/James (GB, LCR-Suzuki 1200), 1'38"266 (162.843 km/h).

Fastest lap in qualifying: Abbott/Biggs (GB, Windle-Honda), 1'38"972 (161.682 km/h).

1. Webster/James (GB, LCR-Suzuki 1200), 22 laps in 37'12"688 (157.678 km/h); 2. Klaffenböck/Hänni (A/CH, LCR-HRM-Honda), at 11"173; 3. Abbott/Biggs (GB, Windle-Honda), at 12"704; 4. Gray/Pointer (GB, LCR-ADM), at 1 lap; 5. Liechti/Locher (CH, LCR-Swissauto); 6. Bertschi/Wäfler (CH, LCR-Suzuki); 7. Fagan/Rous (AUS, LCR-Kawasaki), at 2 laps; 8. Pickett/Pickett (AUS, LCR-Kawasaki); 9. Steenbergen /Steenbergne (NL, LCR-ADM); 10. Guy/Peach (GB, LCR-Swissauto); 11. Soutar/Partridge (AUS, LCR-Honda), at 4 laps; 12. Spence/Winders (AUS, LCR-Kawasaki). 12 finishers.

Fastest lap: Webster/James (GB, LCR-Suzuki 1200), 1'38"726 (162.084 km/h).

2nd May - Great Britain - Donington Park

Pole position (superpole): Webster/James (GB, LCR-Suzuki 1200), 1'37"905 (147.890 km/h).

Fastest lap in qualifying: Abbott/Biggs (GB, Windle-Honda), 1'38"332 (147.248 km/h).

1. Abbott/Biggs (GB, Windle-Honda), 23 laps in 38'24"807 (144.490 km/h); 2. Janssen/Van Kessel (NL, LCR-Swissauto), at 50"401; 3. Schlosser/Hauser (CH, LCR-Swissauto), at 57"404; 4. Steinhausen /Schmidt (D, LCR-Suzuki 1200), at 1'22"506; 5. Guy/Peach (GB, LCR-Swissauto), at 1 lap; 6. Soutar/Partridge (AUS, LCR-Honda); 7. Gällros/Berglund (S, NGK); 8. Fleury/Fleury (NZ, LCR-TFR); 9. Phillips/Pocklincton (GB, Windle-Yamaha 1100); 10. Schröder/Helbig (CH/D, LCR-Honda), at 2 laps; 11. Klaffenböck/Hänni (A/CH, LCR-HRM-Honda); 12. Stirrat /English (GB, Windle-Honda); 13. Muldoon/Woodhead (GB, LCR-ADM); 14. Lovelock/Hibberd (GB, LCR-Suzuki), at 3 laps; 15. Bertschi/Wäfler (CH, LCR-Suzuki 1200), at 4 laps. 15 finishers.

Fastest lap: Abbott/Biggs (GB, Windle-Honda), 1'38"307 (147.285 km/h).

16th May - Spain - Albacete

Pole position (superpole): Webster/James (GB, LCR-Suzuki 1200), 1'34"818 (134.366 km/h).

Fastest lap in qualifying: Abbott/Biggs (GB, Windle-Honda), 1'35"748 (133.061 km/h).

1. Webster/James (GB, LCR-Suzuki 1200), 19 laps in 30'49"817 (130.860 km/h)(*); 2. Abbott/Biggs (GB, Windle-Honda), at 0"406; 3. Klaffenböck/Hänni (A/CH, LCR-HRM-Honda), at 0"813; 4. Schlosser/Hauser (CH, LCR-Swissauto), at 8"192; 5. Soutar/Partridge (AUS, LCR-Honda), at 41"514; 6. Muldoon/Woodhead (GB, LCR-ADM), at 44"744; 7. Guy/Peach (GB, LCR-Swissauto), at 56"422; 8. Lovelock/Hibberd (GB, LCR-

Suzuki), at 1 lap; 9. Steenbergen/Steenbergen (NL, LCR-ADM); 10. Liechti/Locher (CH, LCR-Swissauto); 11. Schröder/Helbig (CH/D, LCR-Honda), at 3 laps. 11 finishers.

Fastest lap: Abbott/Biggs (GB, Windle-Honda), 1'35"472 (133.446 km/h).

(*): The race, which was scheduled for 26 laps, was red flagged after 20, following an accident between Steinhausen/Schmidt (D, LCR-Suzuki 1200) and Janssen/Van Kessel (NL, LCR-Swissauto). The final classification is taken from the lap prior to the incident.

30th May - Italy - Monza

Pole position (superpole): Webster/James (GB, LCR-Suzuki 1200), 1'53"977 (182.247 km/h).

Fastest lap in qualifying: Abbott/Biggs (GB, Windle-Honda), 1'56"495 (178.308 km/h).

1. Webster/James (GB, LCR-Suzuki 1200), 16 laps in 31'24"630 (176.349 km/h); 2. Schlosser/Hauser (CH-LCR-Swissauto), at 4"678; 3. Klaffenböck/Hänni (A/CH, LCR-HRM-Honda), at 14"464; 4. Galbiati/Sala (I, LCR-Suzuki 1200), at 56"283; 5. Gray/Pointer (GB, LCR-ADM), at 1'56"514; 6. Hall/Wood (GB, Ireson-Suzuki 1200), at 1 lap; 7. Hanquet/Legräve (B, LCR-Suzuki 1200); 8. Rope/Lawrence (GB, Ireson-Suzuki 1200); 9. Schröder/Helbig (CH/D, LCR-Honda); 10. Steenbergen/Steenbergen (NL, LCR-ADM); 11. Fleury/Fleury (NZ, LCR-TFR); 12. Ozimo/Armanino (I, LCR-Suzuki 1200), at 2 laps; 13. Whittington/Laidlow (GB, LCR-ADM), at 3 laps; 14. Liechti/Locher (CH, LCR-Swissauto). 14 finishers.

Fastest lap: Webster/James (GB, LCR-Suzuki 1200), 1'54"779 (180.973 km/h).

13th June - Germany - Nürburgring

Pole position (superpole): Webster/James (GB, LCR-Suzuki 1200), 1'45"187 (155.928 km/h).

Fastest lap in qualifying: Webster/James (GB, LCR-Suzuki 1200), 1'44"542 (156.890 km/h).

1. Klaffenböck/Hänni (A/CH, LCR-HRM-Honda), 21 laps in 37'32"794 (152.892 km/h); 2. Webster/James (GB, LCR-Suzuki 1200), at 0"322; 3. Muldoon/Woodhead (GB, LCR-ADM), at 1'12"851; 4. Soutar/Darby (AUS, LCR-Honda), at 1'35"814; 5. Van De Velde/Gries (B/D, LCR-Suzuki 1200), at 1'44"909; 6. Whittington/Laidlow (GB, LCR-Honda), at 1 lap; 7. Gray/Pointer (GB, LCR-ADM); 8. Bertschi/Wäfler (CH, LCR-Suzuki 1200); 9. Eilers/Eilers (D, LCR-Suzuki 1200); 10. Hanquet/Legräve (B, LCR-Suzuki 1200); 11. Hall/Wood (GB, Ireson-Suzuki 1200); 12. Steenbergen/Steenbergen (NL, LCR-ADM); 13. Fleury/Fleury (NZ, LCR-TFR), at 2 laps; 14. Stirrat/English (GB, Windle-Honda); 15. Rope/Lawrence (GB, Ireson-Suzuki 1200). 16 finishers.

Fastest lap: Klaffenböck/Hänni (A/CH, LCR-HRM-Honda), 1'45"085 (156.079 km/h).

27th June - San Marino - Misano

Pole position (superpole): Klaffenböck

/Hänni (A/CH, LCR-HRM-Honda), 1'37"215 (150.347 km/h).

Fastest lap in qualifying: Klaffenböck/Hänni (A/CH, LCR-HRM-Honda), 1'37"758 (149.512 km/h).

1. Klaffenböck/Hänni (A/CH, LCR-HRM-Honda), 23 laps in 38'10"733 (146.751 km/h); 2. Webster/James (GB, LCR-Suzuki 1200), at 14"927; 3. Schlosser/Hauser (CH, LCR-Swissauto), at 22"088; 4. Abbott/Biggs (GB, Windle-Honda), at 23"349; 5. Guy/Peach (GB, LCR-Swissauto), at 46"855; 6. Steinhausen/Schmidt (D, LCR-Suzuki 1200), at 1'16"437; 7. Soutar/Partridge (AUS/GB, LCR-ADM), at 1'19"306; 8. Lovelock/Hibberd (GB, LCR-Suzuki 1200), at 2'25"791(*); 9. Gray/Pointer (GB, LCR-ADM), at 1 lap; 10. Fleury/Fleury (NZ, LCR-TFR); 11. Hanquet/Legräve (B, LCR-Suzuki 1200); 12. Steenbergen/Steenbergen (NL, LCR-ADM); 13. Rope/Lawrence (GB, Ireson-Suzuki 1200); 14. Liechti/Locher (CH, LCR-Swissauto), at 2 laps; 15. Stirrat/English (GB, Windle-Honda), at 5 laps. 15 finishers.

Fastest lap: Klaffenböck/Hänni (A/CH, LCR-HRM-Honda), 1'37"619 (149.724 km/h).

(*): The race was run in two legs because of a stoppage for the accident involving Hall/Wood (GB, Ireson-Suzuki). Therefore the combined gaps down for Lovelock/Hibberd (GB, LCR-Suzuki 1200) is more than the time for one lap.

1st August - Europe - Brands Hatch

Pole position (superpole): Webster/James (GB, LCR-Suzuki 1200), 1'30"608 (167.707 km/h).

Fastest lap in qualifying: Abbott/Biggs (GB, Windle-Honda), 1'30"760 (167.426 km/h).

1. Abbott/Biggs (GB, Windle-Honda), 23 laps in 35'50"491 (162.520 km/h); 2. Klaffenböck /Hänni (A/CH, LCR-HRM-Honda), at 12"123; 3. Schlosser/Hauser (CH, LCR-Swissauto), at 31"418; 4. Guy/Peach (GB, LCR-Swissauto), at 38"141; 5. Skene/Skene (GB, Baker-Suzuki 1200), at 1 lap(*); 6. Soutar/Hopkinson (AUS/GB, LCR-ADM); 7. Bertschi/Wäfler (CH, LCR-Suzuki 1200); 8. Fleury/Fleury (NZ, LCR-TFR); 9. Hanquet/Legräve (B, LCR-Suzuki 1200); 10. Hall/Wood (GB, Ireson-Suzuki 1200), at 2 laps; 11. Steenbergen/Steenbergen (NL, LCR-ADM); 12. Rope/Lawrence (GB, Ireson-Suzuki 1200); 13. Liechti/Locher (CH, LCR-Swissauto), at 4 laps; 14. Stirrat/English (GB, Windle-Honda); 15. Phillips/Pocklincton (GB, Windle-Yamaha). 15 finishers.

Fastest lap: Abbott/Biggs (GB, Windle-Honda), 1'31"595 (165.899 km/h).

(*): Steinhausen/Schmidt (D, LCR-Suzuki 1200) crossed the line in fifth place, but were excluded from the race for using fuel which did not comply with the regulations.

29th August - Austria - A1-Ring

Pole position (superpole): Webster/James (GB, LCR-Suzuki 1200), 1'36"515 (161.098 km/h).

Fastest lap in qualifying: Webster/James

(GB, LCR-Suzuki 1200), 1'36"546 (161.046 km/h).

1. Webster/James (GB, LCR-Suzuki 1200), 23 laps in 47'36"234 (125.204 km/h); 2. Klaffenböck/Hänni (A/CH, LCR-HRM-Honda), at 0"240; 3. Muldoon/Woodhead (GB, LCR-ADM), at 36"762; 4. Steinhausen /Schmidt (D, LCR-Suzuki 1200), at 1'18"814; 5. Hauzenberger/Madaras (A, LCR-Suzuki 1200), at 1'37"476; 6. Gray/Pointer (GB, LCR-ADM), at 1'57"674; 7. Fleury/Fleury (NZ, LCR-TFR), at 2'01"439; 8. Hanquet/Legräve (B, LCR-Suzuki 1200), at 2'03"041; 9. Guy/Peach (GB, LCR-Swissauto), at 2'05"112; 10. Liechti/Locher (CH, LCR-Swissauto), at 1 lap; 11. Soutar/Hopkinson (AUS/GB, LCR-ADM); 12. Steenbergen/Steenbergen (NL, LCR-ADM); 13. Stirrat/English (GB, Windle-Honda); 14. Rope/Lawrence (GB, Ireson-Suzuki 1200). 14 finishers.

Fastest lap: Klaffenböck/Hänni (A/CH, LCR-HRM-Honda), 2'00"303 (129.243 km/h).

5th September - The Netherlands - Assen

Pole position (superpole): Webster/James (GB, LCR-Suzuki 1200), 2'09"000 (168.809 km/h).
Fastest lap in qualifying: Abbott/Biggs (GB, Windle-Honda), 2'10"148 (167.320 km/h).

1. Webster/James (GB, LCR-Suzuki 1200), 16 laps in 35'38"484 (162.929 km/h); 2. Abbott/Biggs (GB, Windle-Honda), at 16"414; 3. Klaffenböck/Hänni (A/CH, LCR-HRM-Honda), at 17"400; 4. Muldoon/Woodhead (GB, LCR-ADM), at 1'08"611; 5. Van Gils/Van Gils (NL, LCR-Suzuki 1200), at 1'47"092; 6. Verweijmeren/Kruip (NL, LCR-Suzuki 1200), at 2'01"315; 7. Gray/Pointer (GB, LCR-ADM), at 2'16"241; 8. Steinhausen/Schmidt (D, LCR-Suzuki 1200), at 2'46"574; 9. GÑllros/Berglund (S, LCR-NGK), at 1 lap; 10. Hanquet/Legräve (B, LCR-Suzuki 1200); 11. Rope/Lawrence (GB, Ireson-Suzuki 1200); 12. Stirrat/Aubrey (GB, Windle-Honda); 13. Talens/Kappert (NL, LCR-Suzuki 1200); 14. Steenbergen/Steenbergen (NL, LCR-ADM); 15. Bertschi/Wäfler (CH,

LCR-Suzuki 1200). 15 finishers.
Fastest lap: Webster/James (GB, LCR-Suzuki), 2'11"730 (165.310 km/h).

12th September - Germany - Hockenheim

Pole position (superpole): Webster/James (GB, LCR-Suzuki 1200), 2'09"211 (189.234 km/h).
Fastest lap in qualifying: Webster/James (GB, LCR-Suzuki 1200), 2'09"233 (189.202 km/h).

1. Webster/James (GB, LCR-Suzuki 1200), 14 laps in 30'29"498 (187.110 km/h); 2. Abbott/Biggs (GB, Windle-Honda), at 0"375; 3. Klaffenböck/Hänni (A/CH, LCR-HRM-Honda), at 28"010; 4. Steinhausen/Schmidt (D, LCR-Suzuki 1200), at 55"366; 5. Van Gils/Van Gils (NL, LCR-Suzuki 1200), at 2'08"199; 6. Hanquet/Legräve (B, LCR-Suzuki 1200), at 2'16"319; 7. Eilers/Eilers (D, LCR-Suzuki 1200), at 2'16"913; 8. Whittington/Laidlow (GB, LCR-Honda), at 2'17"631; 9. Muldoon/Woodhead (GB, LCR-ADM), at 1 lap; 10. Reuter/Kölsch (D,

LCR-Suzuki 1200); 11. Rope/Lawrence (GB, Ireson-Suzuki 1200); 12. Steenbergen /Steenbergen (NL, LCR-ADM); 13. Soutar /Hopkinson (AUS/GB, LCR-ADM); 14. Stirrat/Aubrey (GB, Windle-Honda). 14 finishers.

Fastest lap: Abbott/Biggs (GB, Windle-Honda), 2'09"276 (189.139 km/h).

Final classification

1. S. Webster/D. James	GB		LCR-Suzuki 1200	190
2. K. Klaffenböck/A. Hänni	A/CH		LCR-HRM-Honda	179
3. S. Abbott/J. Biggs	GB		Windle-Honda	139
4. M. Schlosser/D. Hauser	CH		LCR-Swissauto	81
5. S. Soutar/T. Hopkinson	AUS/GB		LCR-ADM	66

6. Muldoon/Woodhead (GB, LCR-ADM), 65; 7. Gray/Pointer (GB, LCR-ADM), 59; 8. Steinhausen/Schmidt (D, LCR-Suzuki 1200), 57; 9. Guy/Peach (GB, LCR-Swissauto), 57; 10. Hanquet/Legräve (B, LCR-Suzuki 1200), 51; 11. Steenbergen/Steenbergen (NL, LCR-ADM), 43; 12. Fleury/Fleury (NZ, LCR-TFR), 39; 13. Liechti/Locher (CH, LCR-Swissauto), 32; 14. Bertschi/Wäfler (CH, LCR-Suzuki 1200), 29; 15. Rope/Lawrence (GB, Ireson-Suzuki 1200), 28; 16. Van Gils/Van Gils (NL, LCR-Suzuki 1200), 22; 17. Whittington/Laidlow (GB, LCR-Honda), 21; 18. Hall/Wood (GB, Ireson-Suzuki 1200), 21; 19. Janssen/Van Kessel (NL, LCR-Swissauto), 20; 20. Lovelock/Hibberd (GB, LCR-Suzuki 1200), 18; 21. Stirrat/Aubrey (GB, Windle-Honda), 18; 22. Eilers/Eilers (D, LCR-Suzuki 1200), 16; 23. Gällros/Berglund (S, LCR-NGK), 16; 24. Galbiati/Sala (I, LCR-Suzuki 1200), 13; 25. Schröder/Helbig (CH/D, LCR-Honda), 13; 26. Hauzenberger/Madaras (A, LCR-Suzuki 1200), 11; 27. Skene/Skene (GB, Baker-Suzuki 1200), 11; 28. Van De Velde/Gries (B/D, LCR-Suzuki 1200), 11; 29. Verweijmeren/Kruip (NL, LCR-Suzuki 1200), 10; 30. Fagan/Rous (AUS, LCR-Kawasaki), 9; 31. Pickett/Pickett (AUS, LCR-Kawasaki), 8; 32. Phillips/Pocklincton (GB, Windle-Yamaha), 8; 33. Reuter/Kölsch (D, LCR-Suzuki 1200), 6; 34. Ozimo/Armanino (I, LCR-Suzuki 1200), 4; 35. Spence/Winders (AUS, LCR-Kawasaki), 4; 36. Talens/Kappert (NL, LCR-Suzuki 1200), 3. 36 classified.

European Championship

125 cc

<u>Champion:</u> **Klaus Nöhles (D, Honda). Born on 12th December 1976, at Hamsel/Germany.**
<u>First race:</u> **1995.**
<u>First GP:</u> **Germany 1997 (125).**
<u>Career highlights:</u> **19th ADAC Junior Cup (Suzuki) in 1996; 50th 125 European Championship, 3rd 125 European Championship (Honda) in 1997; 2nd 125 European Championship, 3rd 125 German Championship (Honda) in 1998; 30th 125 World Championship, 125 European Championship, 4th 125 German Championship (Honda) in 1999.**

11th April - Vallelunga - Italy
1. R. Chiarello (I, Aprilia), 19 laps in 27'34"834 (133.09km/h); 2. K. Nöhles (D, Honda), at 0"138; 3. M. Tresoldi (CH,Honda), at 0"903; 4. M. Petrini (I, Aprilia), at 4"595; 5. M.Stief (D, Honda), at 26"384; 6. A. De Angelis (RSM, Honda), at 31"929; 7. M. Masetti (I, Honda), at 33"461; 8. W. De Angelis (RSM, Honda), at 34"252; 9. J. Smrz (CZ, Honda), at 34"527; 10. A. Kariger (D, Aprilia), at 37"289; 11. J. Hules (CZ, Italjet), at 39"677; 12. A. Narduzzi (I, Honda), at 46"114; 13. K. Irsara (I, Honda), at 48"099; 14. P. Ebner (A, Honda), at 48"657; 15. G. Talmacsi (H, Honda), at 48"806.
<u>Fastest lap:</u> G. Caffiero(I, Aprilia), 1'25"842 (135.038 km/h).

2nd May - Assen - The Netherlands
1. K. Nöhles (D, Honda), 18 laps in 27'16"247 (154.965 km/h); 2. M. Petrini (I, Aprilia), at 3"848; 3. M. Stief (D, Honda), at 3"882; 4. J. Hules (CZ, Italjet), at 3"935; 5. R. Chiarello (I, Aprilia), at 25"706; 6. W. De Angelis (RSM, Honda), at 25"892; 7. J. Petit (F, Honda), at 26"737; 8. G. Caffiero (I, Aprilia), at 26"801; 9. D. Tocca (I, Honda), at 26"906; 10. L. Lanzi (I,Aprilia), at 27"534; 11. P. Ebner (A, Honda), at 27"664; 12. M. Masetti (I, Honda), at 30"737; 13. H. Koopman (NL, Honda), at 35"173; 14. W. Van Leuwen (NL, Honda), at 40"975; 15. F. De Marco (I, Aprilia), at 41"449.
<u>Fastest lap:</u> K. Nöhles (D,Honda), 1'29"773 (156.915 km/h).

30th May - Hungaroring - Hungary
1. K. Nöhles (D, Honda), 16 laps in 29'07"52 (130.914 km/h); 2. R. Chiarello (I, Aprilia), at 5"49; 3. W. De Angelis (RSM, Honda), at 9"26; 4. J. Hules (CZ, Italjet), at 10"42; 5. A. De Angelis (RSM, Honda), at 11"71; 6. A. Magda (H, Aprilia), at 12"04; 7. M. Stief (D, Honda), at 18"25; 8. J. Smrz (CZ, Honda), at 18"78; 9. J. Müller (D, Honda), at 19"26; 10. F. De Marco (I, Aprilia), at 22"73; 11. R. Romboli (I, Honda), at 23"17; 12. F. Lai (I, Honda), at 23"56; 13. L. Lanzi (I, Aprilia), at 28"58;14. M. Petrini (I, Aprilia), at 28"83; 15. M. Bisconti (I,Honda), at 39"29.
<u>Fastest lap:</u> J. Hules (CZ, Italjet), 1'48"21.

20th June - Rijeka - Croatia
1. K. Nöhles (D, Honda), 18 laps in 28'28"646 (158.070 km/h); 2. D. Giugovaz (I, Aprilia), at 5"935; 3. M. Petrini (I,Aprilia), at 25"575; 4. J. Hules (CZ, Italjet), at 25"657; 5. J. Müller (D, Honda), at 31"200; 6. F. Lai (I, Honda), at 33"413; 7. R. Chiarello (I, Aprilia), at 36"586; 8. A. De Angelis (RSM,Honda), at 36"798; 9. L. Lanzi (I, Aprilia), at 36"853; 10. W. De Angelis (RSM, Honda), at 36"968; 11. R. Romboli (I, Honda), at 37"420; 12. M. Bisconti (I, Honda), at 39"314; 13. M. Tresoldi (CH, Honda), at 39"355; 14. S. Aliscioni (I, Aprilia), at 54"184;15. G. Talmacsi (H, Honda), at 54"267.
<u>Fastest lap:</u> D.Giugovaz (I, Aprilia), 1'33"901 (159.794 km/h).

25th July - Most - Czech Republic
1. K. Nöhles (D, Honda), 18 laps in 29'02"102 (154.291 km/h); 2. J. Hules (CZ, Italjet), at 2"620; 3. A. De Angelis (RSM, Honda), at 5"240; 4. M. Petrini (I, Aprilia), at 5"253; 5. W. De Angelis (RSM, Honda), at 5"419; 6. M. Tresoldi (CH, Honda), at 11"785; 7. L. Lanzi (I, Aprilia), at 19"881; 8. R. Chiarello (I, Aprilia), at 19"911; 9. M. Bisconti (I, Honda), at 36"901; 10. J. Smrz (CZ, Honda), at 45"129; 11. J. Schmidt (D, Honda), at 52"456; 12. A. Magda (H, Aprilia), at 52"687; 13. I. Kalab (CZ,Honda), at 1'02"949; 14. J. Di Salvo (USA, Honda), at 1'03"097; 15. E. Nigon (F, Yamaha), at 1'03"115.
<u>Fastest lap:</u> K.Nöhles (D, Honda), 1'35"716 (156.012 km/h).

3rd October - Braga - Portugal
1. K. Nöhles (D, Honda), 21 laps in 28'18"666 (136.357 km/h); 2. D. Giugovaz (I, Aprilia), at 3"077; 3. J. Hules (CZ, Italjet), at 5"201; 4. M. Petrini (I, Aprilia), at 17"092; 5. R. Chiarello (I, Aprilia), at 17"267; 6. M. Bisconti (I, Honda), at 17"944; 7. M. Tresoldi (CH, Honda), at 23"187; 8. C. Cipriani (I, Aprilia), at 32"145; 9. J. Smrz (CZ, Honda), at 32"735; 10. M.-N. Roznizam (MAL, Honda), at 38"355; 11. J. Leite (P, Honda), at 41"015; 12. E. Bataille (AND, Aprilia), at 45"031; 13. E. Leardini (I, Aprilia), at 55"472; 14. L. Bedog (SLO, Honda), at 1'19"586; 15. P. Henriques (P, Yamaha), at 1'20"988.
<u>Fastest lap:</u> K.Nöhles (D, Honda), 1'19"732 (136.357 km/h).

10th October - Cartagena - Spain
1. K. Nöhles (D, Honda), 22 laps in 37'01"394 (123.901 km/h); 2. D. Giugovaz (I, Aprilia), at 8"961; 3. M. Bisconti (I, Honda), at 23"112; 4. J. Müller (D, Honda), at 23"363; 5. R. Chiarello (I, Aprilia), at 23"654; 6. M. Petrini (I, Aprilia), at 24"629;7. J. Smrz (CZ, Honda), at 25"515; 8. W. De Angelis (RSM, Honda), at 25"614; 9. J. Hules (CZ, Italjet), at 26"220; 10. P. Hafenegger (D, Honda), at 27"920; 11. M. Tresoldi (CH, Honda), at 28"216; 12. L. lanzi (I, Aprilia), at 39"930; 13. M.-N. Rozniman (MAL, Honda), at 46"470; 14. M. Bottalico (I, Aprilia), at 38"800; 15. B. Pagnoni (I, Honda), at 48"872.
<u>Fastest lap:</u> D. Giugovaz (I, Aprilia), 1'39"827.

Final classification

1. Klaus Nöhles	D	Honda	170 points
2. Riccardo Chiarello	I	Aprilia	95
3. Marco Petrini	I	Aprilia	87

4. J. Hules (CZ, Italjet), 87; 5. D. Giugovaz (I, Aprilia), 60;6. W. De Angelis (RSM, Honda), 59; 7. A. De Angelis (RSM, Honda),45; 8. M. Tresoldi (CH, Honda), 43; 9. M. Bisconti (I, Honda),38; 10. M. Stief (D, Honda), 36; 11. J. Müller (D, Honda), 31;12. J. Smrz (CZ, Honda), 30; 13. L. Lanzi (I, Aprilia), 29; 14.F. Lai (I, Honda), 14; 15. A. Magda (H, Aprilia), 14; 16. M. Masetti (I, Honda), 13; 17. R. Romboli (I, Honda), 10; 18. J. Petit (F, Honda), 9; 19. M.-N. Rosnizam (MAL, Honda), 9; 20. C. Cipriani (I, Aprilia), 8; 21. G. Caffiero (I, Aprilia), 8; 22. D.Tocca (I, Honda), 7; 23. J. Smrz (CZ, Honda), 7; 24. F. De Marco (I, Aprilia), 7; 25. P. Ebner (A, Honda), 7; 26. P. Hafenegger (D, Honda), 6; 27. A. Kariger (D, Aprilia), 6; 28. J. Leite (P,Honda), 5; 29. J. Schmidt (D, Honda), 5; 30. E. Bataille (AND, Aprilia), 4; 31. A. Nardozzi (I, Aprilia), 4; 32. E. Leardini (I, Aprilia), 3; 33. I. Kalab (CZ, Honda), 3; 34. H. Koopman (NL,Honda), 3; 35. K. Irsara (I, Honda), 3; 36. M. Bottalico (I, Aprilia), 2; 37. L. Nedog (SLO, Honda), 2; 38. J. Di Salvo (USA,Honda), 2; 39. S. Aliscioni (I, Aprilia), 2; 40. W. Van Leeuwen (NL, Honda), 2; 41. G. Talmacsi (H, Honda), 2; 42. B. Pagnoni (I,Honda), 1; 43. P. Henriques (P, Yamaha), 1; 44. E. Nigon (F,Yamaha), 1. 44 finishers.

◁ *Klaus Nöhles.*

Karl Harris. ▷

Supersport

<u>Champion:</u> **Sébastien Le Grelle (B, Suzuki).**
<u>Career highlights:</u> **11th Supersport European Championship (Suzuki) in1998; Supersport European Champion (Suzuki) in 1999.**

7th March - Le Mans - France
1. E. Mahé (F, Yamaha), 18 laps in 32'44"442 (142.007 km/h); 2. S. Scheschowitsch (D, Suzuki), at 7"351; 3. J.-Y. Mounier (F, Kawasaki), at 16"532; 4. J.-F. Cortinovis (F, Kawasaki), at 16"621; 5. S. Hole Nielsen (DK, Yamaha), at 29"125; 6. S. Le Grelle (B, Suzuki), at 32"259; 7. K. Verstraeten (NL, Suzuki), at 37"968; 8. B. Stey (F, Honda), at 38"804; 9. A. Giachino (I, Suzuki), at 41"469; 10. B. Jerzenbeck (D, Suzuki), at 52"132; 11. G. Giabbani (F, Kawasaki), at 57"263; 12. O. Fernandez-Albentosa (E, Honda), at 59"814; 13. H. Van Beek (NL, Yamaha), at 1'05"995;14. J.-M. Martin Vazquez (E, Honda), at 1'09"695; 15. K. Poensgen (D, Suzuki), at 1'09"905.
<u>Fastest lap:</u> E. Mahé (F,Yamaha), 1'48"010 (143.487 km/h).

11th April - Vallelunga - Italy
1. S. Le Grelle (B, Suzuki), 25 laps in 36'35"737 (131.983km/h); 2. A. Corradi (I, Kawasaki), at 0"56; 3. S. Di Marco (I, Yamaha), at 0"71; 4. A. Giachino (I, Suzuki), at 3"42; 5. A. Vitellaro (I, Yamaha), at 23"19; 6. S. Hole Nielsen (DK, Yamaha), at 23"64; 7. L.-E. Lamustrom (S, Suzuki), at 25"28; 8. A. Escobar Valenzuela (E, Honda), at 25"81; 9. G. Carnevale (I, Suzuki), at 27"00; 10. B. Jerzenbeck (D, Suzuki), at 27"13; 11. J. Liroström(S, Suzuki), at 29"95; 12. I. Arnoldi (I, Suzuki), at 37"18; 13. E. Wilding (A, Honda), at 39"30; 14. O. Bernhard (D, Suzuki), at 42"60; 15. A. Kopp (D, Yamaha), at 43"94.
<u>Fastest lap:</u> S. Di Marco (I, Yamaha), 1'27"013 (133.221 km/h).

2nd May - Assen - The Netherlands
1. M. Pajic (NL, Kawasaki), 24 laps in 35'15"545 (159.809km/h); 2. H. Van Beek (NL, Yamaha), at 3"373; 3. L. Tijssen (NL, Suzuki), at 18"851; 4. S. Hole Nielsen (DK, Yamaha), at 26"106;5. A. Giachino (I, Suzuki), at 26"486; 6. S. Le Grelle (B, Suzuki), at 30"995; 7. P. Engdahl (S, Yamaha), at 31"054; 8. J.-M. Vazquez (E, Honda), at 32"909; 9. D.-S. Sundby (N, Suzuki), at 38"193; 10. S. Folkesson (S, Suzuki), at 42"668; 11. K. Jennes (B, Kawasaki), at 48"596; 12. M. Van Den Bulk (NL, Yamaha), at 50"353; 13. A. Kopp (D, Yamaha), at 1'05"670; 14. E. Bosma (NL,Yamaha), at 1'05"901; 15. G. Carnevale (I, Suzuki), at 1'06"242.
<u>Fastest lap:</u> H. Van Beek (NL, Yamaha), 1'27"276 (161.405km/h).

30th May - Hungaroring - Hungary
1. S. Scheschowitsch (D, Suzuki), 22 laps in 40'20"48 (129.960km/h); 2. A. Escobar Valenzuela (E, Honda), at 12"63; 3. S. LeGrelle (B, Suzuki), at 14"76; 4. S. Hole Nielsen (DK, Yamaha), at 18"24; 5. A. Giachino (I, Suzuki), at 39"94; 6. J.-M. Vazquez (E, Honda), at 43"92; 7. P. Dudas (H, Suzuki), at 49"52; 8. M. Balaz (SLO, Ducati), at 1'03"11; 9. L. Halaska (H, Yamaha), at 1'06"40; 10. J. Hudecek (CZ, Ducati), at 1'22"92; 11. B.Vitezslav (CZ, Honda); 12. M. Weinand (B, Yamaha), at 1 lap; 13. Z. Iglar (H, Kawasaki). 13 finishers.
<u>Fastest lap:</u> S.Scheschowitsch (D, Suzuki), 1'48"61.

20th June - Rijeka - Croatia
1. S. Scheschowitsch (D, Suzuki), 22 laps in 35'23"095 (155.483km/h); 2. S. Le Grelle (B, Suzuki), at 1"172; 3. F. Brugnara (I, Suzuki), at 2"063; 4. S. Hole Nielsen (DK, Yamaha), at 16"553; 5. O. Bernhard (D, Suzuki), at 16"554; 6. K. Verstraeten (NL, Suzuki), at 29"891; 7. A. Kopp (D, Yamaha), at 47"078; 8. L. Aljinovic (CR, Suzuki), at 47"539; 9. A. Escobar-Valenzuela (E,Honda), at 56"680; 10. M. Balaz (SLO, Ducati), at 56"879; 11. A. Giachino (I, Suzuki), at 1'07"511; 12. R. Henry (B, Suzuki), at 1'13"479; 13. L. Tijssen (NL, Suzuki), at 1'13"630; 14. U. Bua (I, Yamaha), at 1'13"999; 15. R. Livi (I, Ducati), at 1 lap.
<u>Fastest lap:</u> S. Scheschowitsch (D, Suzuki), 1'34"880 (158.145 km/h).

25th July - Most - Czech Republic
1. S. Hole Nielsen (DK, Yamaha), 22 laps in 35'22"146 (154.807km/h); 2. A. Giachino (I, Suzuki), at 2"199; 3. T. Paillot (F, Suzuki), at 10"139; 4. O. Bernhard (D, Suzuki), at 10"770; 5. J. Boesveld (NL, Kawasaki), at 16"668; 6. V. Bican (CZ, Honda), at 19"256; 7. S. Le Grelle (B, Suzuki), at 39"263; 8. L. Tijssen (NL, Suzuki), at 39"814; 9. O. Lelek (CZ, Honda), at 40"069; 10.T. Fritzsche (D, Kawasaki), at 46"807; 11. M. Van Den Bulk (NL, Honda), at 58"570; 12. R. Henry (B, Suzuki), at 1'05"204; 13. T. Foukal (CZ, Yamaha), at 1'05"289; 14. P. Ouda (CZ, Honda), at 1'05"557; 15. K. Prager (CZ, Honda), at 1 lap.
<u>Fastest lap:</u> A. Giachino (I, Suzuki), 1'35"405 (156.521 km/h).

Final classification

1. Sébastien Le Grelle	B	Suzuki	111 points
2. Stefan Scheschowtsch	D	Suzuki	110
3. Soren Hole Nielsen	DK	Yamaha	103

4. A. Giachino (I, Suzuki), 67; 5. A. Escobar Valenzuela (E, Honda), 40; 6. M. Tey Salas (E, Honda), 29; 7. O. Bernhard (D, Suzuki), 28; 8. L. Tijssen (NL, Suzuki), 27; 9. J.-M. MartinVazquez (E, Honda), 27; 10. G. Scudeler (BR, Honda), 25; 11. M.Pajic (NL, Kawasaki), 25; 12. E. Mahé (F, Yamaha), 25; 13. F.Brugnara (I, Suzuki), 24; 14. H. Van Beek (NL, Yamaha), 23; 15. A. Corradi (I, Kawasaki), 20; 16. K. Verstraeten (NL, Suzuki),20; 17. S. Folkesson (S, Suzuki), 18; 18. M. Stief (D, Yamaha),16; 19. E. Gavira (E, Suzuki), 16; 20. T. Paillot (F, Suzuki),16; 21. S. Di Marco (I, Yamaha), 16; 22. J.-Y. Mounier (F, Kawasaki), 16; 23. M. Balaz (CZ, Ducati), 14; 24. E. Ullastres(E, Yamaha), 13; 25. F. Teixeira (P, Honda), 13; 26. J.-F. Cortinovis (F, Kawasaki), 13; 27. A. Kopp (D, Yamaha), 13; 28. B. Jerzenbeck (D, Suzuki), 12; 29. J. Boesveld (NL, Kawasaki), 11; 30. A. Vitellaro (I, Yamaha), 11; 31. R. Reigoto (P, Kawasaki),10; 32. V. Bican (CZ, Honda), 10; 33. G. Carnevale (I, Suzuki),10; 34. P. Dudas (H, Suzuki), 9; 35. P. Engdahl (S, Yamaha), 9;36. L.-E. Lanustrom (S, Suzuki), 9; 37. M. Van Den Bulk (NL, Honda), 9; 38. L. Teixeira (P, Honda), 8; 39. L. Aljinovic (CRO, Suzuki), 8; 40. B. Stey (F, Honda), 8; 41. R. Henry (B, Suzuki),8; 42. F. Riquelme (E, Yamaha), 7; 43. T. Pereira (P, Suzuki), 7; 44. O. Lelek (CZ, Honda), 7; 45. L. Halaska (H, Yamaha), 7; 46. D.-S. Sundby (N, Suzuki), 7; 47. O. Fernandez Albentosa (E,Suzuki), 7; 48. I. Sanchez Alvarez (E, Yamaha), 6; 49. M. Oliveira (P, Yamaha), 6; 50. T. Fritzsche (D, Kawasaki), 6; 51. J. Hudecek (CZ, Ducati), 6; 52. B. Vitzslav (CZ, Honda), 5; 53. K. Jennes (B, Kawasaki), 5; 54. J. Lindström (S, Suzuki), 5; 55. G. Giabbani (F, Kawasaki), 5; 56. M. Luque (E, Suzuki), 4; 57. M.Weinand (B, Yamaha), 4; 58. I. Arnoldi (I, Suzuki), 4; 59. T. Fouxal (CZ, Yamaha), 3; 60. Z. Iglar (H, Kawasaki), 3; 61. E. Wilding (A, Honda), 3; 62. P. Ouda (CZ, Honda), 2; 63. U. Bua (I,Yamaha), 2; 64. E. Bosma (NL, Yamaha), 2; 65. A. Lindström (S,Suzuki), 1; 66. K. Prager (CZ, Honda), 1; 67. R. Livi (I,Ducati), 1; 68. K. Poensgen (D, Suzuki), 1. 68 finishers.

3rd October - Braga - Portugal
1. G. Scudeler (BR, Honda), 27 laps in 36'13"162 (135.077km/h); 2. S. Scheschowitsch (D, Suzuki), at 13"744; 3. E. Gavira (E, Suzuki), at 17"445; 4. F. Teixeira (P, Honda), at 17"594; 5. S. Le Grelle (B, Suzuki), at 17"728; 6. R. Reigoto (P, Kawasaki), at 33"497; 7. S. Hole Nielsen (DK, Yamaha), at 35"373; 8. L.Teixeira (P, Honda), at 35"589; 9. T. Pereira (P, Suzuki), at 40"034; 10. M. Oliveira (P, Yamaha), at 42"897; 11. A. Escobar-Valenzuela (E, Honda), at 43"270; 12. M. Tey Salas (E, Honda), at 43"412; 13. S. Folkesson (S, Suzuki), at 1'03"441; 14. J.-M. Martin Vazquez (E, Honda), at 1'10"641; 15. K. Verstraeten (NL, Suzuki), at 1'16"474.
<u>Fastest lap:</u> G. Scudeler (BR, Honda), 1'18"736.

10th October - Cartagena - Spain
1. M. Tey Salas (E, Honda), 24 laps in 40'20"681 (124.210km/h); 2. S. Scheschowitsch (D, Suzuki), at 13"420; 3. M. Stief (D, Yamaha), at 27"595; 4. E. Ullastres (E, Yamaha), at 27"888;5. S. Hore Nielsen (DK, Yamaha), at 28"416; 6. S. Le Grelle (B, Suzuki), at 29"381; 7. S. Folkesson (S, Suzuki), at 33"691; 8. F. Brugnara (I, Suzuki), at 34"917; 9. F. Riquelme (E, Yamaha), at 36"065; 10. I. Sanchez (E, Yamaha), at 46"544; 11. J.-M. Martin Vasquez (E, Honda), at 57"188; 12. M. Luque (E, Suzuki), at 1'07"199; 13. O. Fernandez (E, Suzuki), at 1'11"384; 14. G. Carnevale (I, Suzuki), at 1'11"425; 15. A. Lindström (S, Suzuki), at 1'19"307.
<u>Fastest lap:</u> M. Tey Salas (E, Honda),1'40"059.

250 cc

Champion: Ivan Clementi (I, Aprilia). Born on 18th January 1975, at Montegiorgio.
First race: 1991.
First GP: Madrid, 1998 (250).
Career highlights: Winner 125 Gilera Trophy in 1992; 125 Sport-Production Italian Champion (Aprilia) in 1995; 41st 125 European Championship (Aprilia) in 1996; 10th 250 European Championship (Aprilia) in 1997; 28th 250 World Championship, 6th 250 European Championship, 5th 250 Italian Championship (Yamaha) in 1998; 250 European Champion, 250 Italian Champion (Aprilia) in 1999.

11th April - Vallelunga - Italy
1. I. Clementi (I, Aprilia), 22 laps in 31'06"940 (136.699km/h); 2. M. Baldinger (D, TSR-Honda), at 9"719; 3. V. Philippe (F, Honda), at 13"875; 4. F. Cotti (I, Yamaha), at 16"134; 5. I. Mengozzi (I, Yamaha), at 17"679; 6. J. Robinson (GB, Honda), at 21"837; 7. D. Ribalta Bosch (E, Yamaha), at 36"043; 8. A.Romagnoli (I, Honda), at 40"727; 9. G. Rizmayer (H, Honda), at 44"548; 10. A. Debon Lacorre (E, Honda), at 48"441; 11. I. Bonilla (E, Honda), at 1'00"448; 12. R. Markink (NL, Aprilia), at 1'00"602; 13. R. Filart (NL, Honda), at 1'04"182; 14. H. Van DeLagemaat (NL, Honda), at 1'04"727; 15. U. Bolterauer (A, Honda), at 1'05"552.
Fastest lap: I. Clementi (I, Aprilia),1'23"885 (138.189 km/h).

2nd May - Assen - The Netherlands
1. I. Clementi (I, Aprilia); 2. J. Robinson (GB, Honda), at 1"026; 3. R. Markink (NL, Aprilia), at 6"046; 4. A. Coates (GB, Honda), at 9"081; 5. I. Mengozzi (I, Yamaha), at 26"885; 6. G. Rizmayer (H, Honda), at 26"928; 7. D. Ribalta Bosch (E, Yamaha), at 26"953; 8. F. Cotti (I, Yamaha), at 27"498; 9. A. Visscher (NL, Aprilia), at 30"427; 10. M. Baldinger (D, TSR-Honda), at 30"428; 11. V. Philippe (F, Honda), at 32"285; 12. A. Romein(NL, Honda), at 45"678; 13. R. Filart (NL, Honda), at 45"727; 14. H. Van De Lagemaat (NL, Honda), at 45"757; 15. U. Bolterauer (A, Honda), at 53"521.

30th May - Hungaroring - Hungary
1. I. Clementi (I, Aprilia), 18 laps in 32'02"09 (133.902km/h); 2. J. Robinson (GB, Honda), at 1"91; 3. M. Baldinger (D,TSR-Honda), at 10"55; 4. G. Rizmayer (H, Honda), at 13"03; 5. F. Cotti (I, Yamaha), at 15"82; 6. I. Mengozzi (I, Yamaha), at 16"23; 7. S. Yuzi (MAL, Honda), at 21"29; 8. V. Philippe (F,Honda), at 21"43; 9. A. Visscher (NL, Aprilia), at 28"49; 10. M. Witzeneder (A, Honda), at 42"96; 11. R. Rous (CZ, Honda), at 45"13; 12. D. Brockmann (D, Honda), at 46"32; 13. C. Manna (I, Aprilia), at 1'01"20; 14. I. Bonilla (E, Honda), at 1'02"08; 15. H. Van De Lagemaat (NL, Honda), at 1'02"22.
Fastest lap: I. Clementi (I, Aprilia), 1'45"43.

20th June - Rijeka - Croatia
1. M. Baldinger (D, TSR-Honda), 20 laps in 33'06"686 (151.054km/h); 2. V. Philippe (F, Honda), at 5"164; 3. G. Rizmayer (H,Honda), at 10"210; 4. I. Clementi (I, Aprilia), at 15"916; 5. F. Cotti (I, Yamaha), at 49"275; 6. V. Castka (SLO, Honda), at 57"810; 7. I. Mengozzi (I, Yamaha), at 1'03"444; 8. R. Markink (NL, Aprilia), at 1'03"759; 9. A. Visscher (NL, Aprilia), at 1'09"259; 10. M. Selmar (DK, Yamaha), at 1'22"033; 11. I. Bonilla (E, Honda), at 1'31"643; 12. H. Van De Lagemaat (NL,Honda), at 1'36"543; 13. D. Brockmann (D, Honda), at 1'50"921;14. U. Bolterauer (A, Honda), at 2'04"088; 15. R. Heierli (CH,Aprilia), at 2'06"488.
Fastest lap: I. Clementi (I,Aprilia), 1'31"074 (164.754 km/h).

25th July - Most - Czech Republic
1. I. Clementi (I, Aprilia), 20 laps in 31'02"772 (160.329km/h); 2. M. Baldinger (D, TSR-Honda), at 9"843; 3. S. Yuzi (MAL,Honda), at 16"064; 4. V. Philippe (F, Honda), at 16"686; 5. I. Mengozzi (I, Yamaha), at 22"584; 6. A. Visscher (NL, Aprilia), at 25"095; 7. J. Robinson (GB, Honda), at 30"926; 8. R. Markink (NL, Aprilia), at 46"724; 9. J. Da Costa (F, Honda), at 46"730;10. M. Witzeneder (A, Honda), at 59"778; 11. H. Van De Lagemaat (NL, Honda), at 1'07"268; 12. R. Rous (CZ, Honda), at 1'07"621;13. U. Hasager (DK, Honda), at 1 lap; 14. J. Ten Napel (NL,Honda); 15. S. Coopman (B, Honda).
Fastest lap: I.Clementi (I, Aprilia), 1'31"430 (163.325 km/h).

3rd October - Braga - Portugal
1. M. Baldinger (D, TSR-Honda), 24 laps in 31'31"095 (137.577km/h); 2. G. Rizmayer (H, Honda), at 10"055; 3. V. Philippe (F, Honda), at 12"521; 4. I. Clementi (I, Aprilia), at 12"737; 5. J. Robinson (GB, Honda), at 13"841; 6. D. Ribalta Bosch (E, Yamaha), at 24"084; 7. R. Wilimi (SF, Honda), at 55"193; 8. R. Markink (NL, Aprilia), at 56"258; 9. H. Van De Lagemaat (NL, Honda), at 1'07"306; 10. G. Lucchetti (I, Yamaha), at 1'12"858; 11. J. Blok (NL, Honda), at 1 lap; 12. R. Rous (CZ, Honda); 13. U. Hasager (DK, Honda); 14. T. North (S, Honda); 15. A.-D. Nacher (E,Honda).
Fastest lap: J. Robinson (GB, Honda), 1'16"336.

10th October - Cartagena - Spain
1. M. Baldinger (D, TSR-Honda), 23 laps in 38'04"903 (126.108km/h); 2. I. Bonilla (E, Honda), at 3"088; 3. D. Tomas Perez (E, Honda), at 3"188; 4. I. Clementi (I, Aprilia), at 3"578; 5. A. Molina (E, Honda), at 4"865; 6. D. Ribalta Bosch (E, Yamaha), at 5"965; 7. J. Robinson (GB, Honda), at 13"382; 8. S. Yuzy (MAL,Honda), at 20"307; 9. V. Philippe (F, Honda), at 18"733; 10. I. Silva (E, Honda), at 23"902; 11. J. Da Costa (F, Honda), at 30"056; 12. C. Gemmel (D, Honda), at 36"590; 13. D. Ortega (E,Honda), at 40"241; 14. V. Castka (SLO, Honda), at 44"739; 15. J. Perez (E, Honda), at 45"182.
Fastest lap: S. Yuzy (MAL, Honda), 1'37"797.

Final classification

1. Mike Baldinger	D	TSR-Honda	138 points
2. Ivan Clementi	I	Aprilia	131
3. Vincent Philippe	F	Honda	87

4. J. Robinson (GB, Honda), 80; 5. G. Rizmayer (H, Honda), 67; 6. I. Menguzzi (I, Yamaha), 54; 7. R. Markink (NL, Aprilia), 44; 8. F. Cotti (I, Yamaha), 44; 9. D. Ribalta Bosch (E, Yamaha), 40;10. I. Bonilla (E, Honda), 32; 11. S. Yuzi (MAL, Honda), 34; 12. A. Visscher (NL, Aprilia), 32; 13. H. Van De Lagemaat (NL,Honda), 22; 14. D.-T. Perez (E, Aprilia), 16; 15. A. Coates (GB, Honda), 16; 16. A. Molina Fuentes (E, Honda), 13; 17. J. Da Costa (F, Honda), 13; 18. R. Rous (CZ, Honda), 13; 19. V. Castka (CZ,Honda), 12; 20. M. Witzeneder (A, Honda), 12; 21. R. Wilimi (SF,Honda), 9; 22. A. Romagnoli (I, Honda), 8; 23. I. Silva (E, Honda), 7; 24. D. Brockmann (D, Honda), 7; 25. R. Filart (NL,Honda), 7; 26. G. Lucchetti (I, Yamaha), 6; 27. M. Selmar (DK,Yamaha), 6; 28. A. Debon Latorre (E, Honda), 6; 29. U. Hasager (DK, Honda), 6; 30. J. Blok (NL, Honda), 5; 31. A. Romein (NL,Honda), 5; 32. U. Bolterauer (A, Honda), 5; 33. C. Gemmel (D, Honda), 4; 34. D. Ortega (E, TSR-Honda), 3; 35. C. Manna (I, Aprilia), 3; 36. T. North (S, Honda), 2; 37. J. Ten Napel (NL,Honda), 2; 38. J. Perez (E, Honda), 1; 39. A.-D. Nacher (E,Honda), 1; 40. S. Coopman (B, Honda), 1; 41. R. Heierli (CH,Honda), 1. 41 finishers.

△ *Ivan Clementi.*

Superstock

Champion: Karl Harris (GB, Suzuki). Born on 21st October 1979, at Ferryby/Yorkshire/Great Britain.
First race: 1995.
Career highlights: 28th Supersport European Championship (Honda) in 1998; 20th Supersport World Championship, 10th Supersport British Championship, Superstock European Champion (Suzuki) in 1999.

2nd May - Donington - Great Britain
1. D. Jefferies (GB, Yamaha), 15 laps in 25'10"053; 2. M. Corrigan (GB, Yamaha), at 3"736; 3. S. Smith (GB, Yamaha), at 11"795; 4. I. Duffus (GB, Yamaha), at 16"893; 5. P. Graves(GB, Yamaha), at 16"970; 6. K. Harris (GB, Suzuki), at 32"983; 7. M. Fisette (B, Suzuki), at 37"730; 8. H. Whitby (GB, Honda), at 38"226; 9. J. Morley (GB, Suzuki), at 38"318; 10. P. Notman (GB, Yamaha), at 49"633; 11. D. Higgins (GB,Yamaha), at 50"839; 12. J. Ellison (GB, Honda), at 1'02"900; 13. E. Burgess (GB, Ducati), at 1'10"234; 14. G. Byrne (GB, Yamaha), at 1'10"466; 15. D. Tosolini (I, Yamaha), at 1'13"996.
Fastest lap: M. Corrigan (GB, Yamaha), 1'39"663 (145.281km/h).

16th May - Albacete - Spain
1. D. Oliver (E, Aprilia), 14 laps in 23'15"678 (127.799 km/h); 2. D. Tosolini (I, Yamaha), at 13"646; 3. D. Duchêne (D, Kawasaki), at 20"193; 4. J. Ellison (GB, Honda), at 20"565; 5. P. Notman (GB, Yamaha), at 26"323; 6. R. Fabbroni (I, Honda), at 26"530; 7. I. Sanchez (E, Yamaha), at 27"045; 8. R. Loscos (E,Yamaha), at 48"013; 9. S. Jond (F, Suzuki), at 52"744; 10. D. Spriet (B, Suzuki), at 52"862; 11. N. Carlberg (S, Suzuki), at1'36"456. 11 finishers.
Fastest lap: D. Oliver (E,Aprilia), 1'38"329 (129.569 km/h).

30th May - Monza - Italy
1. V. Scatola (I, Yamaha), 9 laps in 17'24"511 (178.981km/h); 2. I. Sala (I, Yamaha), at 0"112; 3. D. Oliver (E, Aprilia), at 12"077; 4. D. Messori (I, Kawasaki), at 13"079; 5. M. Fissette (B, Suzuki), at 15"515; 6. M. Rigamonti (I, Yamaha), at 15"570; 7. P. Notman (GB, Yamaha), at 18"675; 8. D. Tosolini (I, Yamaha), at 18"837; 9. F. Pellizzon (I, Aprilia), at 19"213; 10. F. Chiarelli (I, Yamaha), at 22"221; 11. M. Temporali (I, Honda), at 24"491; 12. F. Foret (F, Yamaha), at 34"098; 13. D. Duchêne (D, Kawasaki), at 41"168; 14. R. Fabbroni (I, Honda), at 43"197; 15. J. Ellison (GB, Honda), at 49"873.
Fastest lap: F. Foret (F, Yamaha), 1'54"329 (181.686km/h).

13th June - Nürburgring - Germany
1. D. Oliver (E, Aprilia), 11 laps in 20'05"451 (149.668 km/h); 2. K. Harris (GB, Suzuki), at 2'393; 3. P. Notman (GB, Yamaha), at 3"281; 4. D. Tosolini (I, Yamaha), at 10"886; 5. K. Poensgen (D, Suzuki), at 16"251; 6. D. Duchêne (D, Kawasaki), at 18"393; 7. S. Casaer (B, Yamaha), at 18"984; 8. F. Jond (F, Suzuki), at 19"039; 9. S. Jond (F, Suzuki), at 19"239; 10. T. Van Wezemael (B,Kawasaki), at 24"302; 11. J. Ellison (GB, Honda), at 24"673;12. R. Fabbroni (I, Honda), at 1'07"592; 13. I. Sanchez (E,Yamaha), at 1'11"797; 14. N. Carlberg (S, Suzuki), at 1 lap.14 finishers.
Fastest lap: P. Notman (GB, Yamaha),1'48"241 (151.528 km/h).

27th June - Misano - Italy
1. I. Sala (I, Yamaha), 12 laps in 20'26"218 (143.034 km/h);2. K. Harris (GB, Suzuki), at 9"183; 3. D. Oliver (E, Aprilia), at13"104; 4. M. Temporali (I, Honda), at 14"939; 5. F. Pellizzon (I, Aprilia), at 20"415; 6. D. Tosolini (I, Yamaha), at 22"109;7. F. Jond (F, Suzuki), at 22"469; 8. I. Sanchez (E, Yamaha), at 30"170; 9. M. Fissette (B, Suzuki), at 30"893; 10. P. Notman (GB, Yamaha), at 32"792; 11. R. Fabbroni (I, Honda), at 33"342;12. L. Aljinovic (CR, Suzuki), at 34"796; 13. D. Duchêne (D, Kawasaki), at 37"242; 14. K. Jennes (D, Yamaha), at 45"639;15. R. Leonetti (I, Suzuki), at 46"495.
Fastest lap: I. Sala (I, Yamaha), 1'40"954 (144.778 km/h).

1st August - Brands Hatch - Great Britain
1. D. Jefferies (GB, Yamaha), 12 laps in 18'42"492 (162.449km/h); 2. K. Harris (GB, Suzuki), at 4"331; 3. P. Graves (GB,Yamaha), at 4"472; 4. S. Brogan (GB, Yamaha), at 14"550; 5. G.Scott (GB, Yamaha), at 17"158; 6. R. Read (GB, Yamaha), at 21"737; 7. D. Oliver (E, Aprilia), at 21"888; 8. I. Duffus (GB,Yamaha), at 22"527; 9. A. Buckingham (GB, Yamaha), at 22"796; 10. F. Williamson (GB, Aprilia), at 23"646; 11. M. Fissette (B, Suzuki), at 34"026; 12. P. Notman (GB, Yamaha), at 34"092; 13. F. Jond (F, Suzuki), at 35"979; 14. S. Jond (F, Suzuki), at 36"610; 15. D. Duchêne (D, Kawasaki), at 36"674.
Fastest lap: D. Jefferies (GB, Yamaha), 1'32"786 (163.770km/h).

Final classification

1. Karl Harris	GB	Suzuki	189
2. Daniel Oliver	E	Aprilia	154
3. Daniele Tosolini	I	Yamaha	95

4. M. Fissette (B, Suzuki), 79; 5. P. Notman (GB, Yamaha), 78; 6.D. Duchêne (D, Kawasaki), 60; 7. F. Pellizzon (I, Aprilia), 57;8. S. Jond (F, Suzuki), 53; 9. F. Jond (F, Suzuki), 51; 10. S. Brogan (GB, Honda), 48; 11. J. Ellison (GB, Honda), 44; 12. S.Casaer (B, Yamaha), 41; 13. M. Bauer (A, Kawasaki), 30; 14. R. Fabbroni (I, Honda), 30; 15. K. Poensgen (D, Suzuki), 28; 16. I. Sanchez (E, Yamaha), 28; 17. M. Temporalli (I, Honda), 25; 18. N. Carlberg (S, Suzuki), 24; 19. K. Reilly (GB, Yamaha), 20; 20. J.Morley (GB, Suzuki), 19; 21. K. Vleugels (B, Suzuki), 17; 22. J. Bordoy (E, Yamaha), 13; 23. D. Johnson (GB, Honda), 11; 24. R. Jetschko (A, Honda), 11; 25. B. Steinmetz (D, Yamaha), 10; 26. F. Chiarelli (I, Yamaha), 10; 27. G. Byrne (GB, Yamaha), 10; 28. R. Loscos (E, Yamaha), 8; 29. A. Notman (GB, Honda), 7; 30. O. Four (F, Suzuki), 6; 31. L. Quigley (GB, Yamaha), 4; 32. S. Suzzi (I,Suzuki), 4; 33. A. Bonecchi (I, Yamaha), 4; 34. B. Jerzenbeck (D,Suzuki), 3; 35. A. Goebel (D, Honda), 4; 36. M. Van Kleef (NL,Yamaha), 2; 37. B. Veneman (NL, Yamaha), 2. 37 finishers

29th August - A1-Ring - Austria
1. M. Bauer (A, Kawasaki), 12 laps in 23'14"069 (133.839 km/h); 2. S. Jond (F, Suzuki), at 22"846; 3. M. Fissette (B, Suzuki), at 26"598; 4. K. Harris (GB, Suzuki), at 30"115; 5. S. Casaer (B,Yamaha), at 37"289; 6. K. Jennes (B, Yamaha), at 41"003; 7. F. Pellizzon (I, Aprilia), at 41"119; 8. K. Reilly (GB, Yamaha), at 49"790; 9. R. Jetschko (A, Honda), at 55"408; 10. K. Vleugels (B, Yamaha), at 55"794; 11. O. Four (F, Suzuki), at 56"149; 12. D. Tosolini (I, Yamaha), at 1'01"151; 13. P. Notman (GB, Yamaha), at 1'02"073; 14. D. Oliver (E, Aprilia), at 1'23"480; 15. J. Bordoy (E, Yamaha), at 1'26"951.
Fastest lap: M. Bauer(A, Kawasaki), 1'54"792 (135.448 km/h).

5th September - Assen - The Netherlands
1. K. Harris (GB, Suzuki), 9 laps in 20'10"522 (161.903 km/h); 2. D. Jefferies (GB, Yamaha), at 3"576; 3. D. Oliver (E, Aprilia), at 11"586; 4. S. Brogan (GB, Honda), at 24"052; 5. R. Read (GB, Yamaha), at 27"154; 6. D. Tosolini (I, Yamaha), at 27"261; 7. K. Jennes (B, Yamaha), at 27"351; 8. D. Johnson (GB, Honda), at 31"204; 9. B. Steinmetz (D, Yamaha), at 31"261;10. S. Jond (F, Suzuki), at 31"502; 11. S. Casaer (B, Yamaha), at 33"927; 12. F. Jond (F, Suzuki), at 34"111; 13. K. Poensgen (D, Suzuki), at 47"880; 14. K. Reilly (GB, Yamaha), at 48"458; 15. T.Van Wezemael (B, Kawasaki), at 48"632.
Fastest lap: K.Harris (GB, Suzuki), 2'12"315 (164.579 km/h).

12th September - Hockenheim - Germany
1. K. Harris (GB, Suzuki), 8 laps in 17'31"263 (186.071 km/h); 2. F. Pellizzon (I, Aprilia), at 3"124; 3. D. Tosolini (I,Yamaha), at 3"620; 4. M. Wauters (B, Kawasaki), at 14"444; 5. D. Duchêne (D, Kawasaki), at 14"728; 6. S. Brogan (GB, Honda), at 15"418; 7. S. Casaer (B, Yamaha), at 16"323; 8. F. Heidger (D, Aprilia), at 16"755; 9. T. Knieper (D, Yamaha), at 26"943;10. K. Poensgen (D, Suzuki), at 33"757; 11. F. Jond (F, Suzuki), at 33"846; 12. T. Van Wezemael (B, Kawasaki), at 34"291; 13. J. Bordoy (E, Yamaha), at 35"064; 14. K. Vleugels (B, Suzuki), at 36"415; 15. N. Carlberg (S, Suzuki), at 59"719.
Fastest lap: K. Harris (GB, Suzuki), 2'08"904 (189.685 km/h).

European Championship

German Championship

125 cc

Champion: Dirk Reissmann (Aprilia). Born on 15th November 1975, in Gersdorf.
First race: 1994. First GP: Germany, 1999 (125).
Career highlights: 2nd ADAC Junior Cup in 1996; 10th 125 German Championship (Yamaha) in 1997; 21st 125 European Championship, 5th 125 German Championship (Honda) in 1998; 125 German Championship (Aprilia) in 1999.

25th April - Zweibrücken
1. Nöhles (Honda); 2. Reissmann (Aprilia); 3. Hafenegger (Honda);-4. Müller (Honda); 5. Stief (Honda); 6. Smrz (CZ, Honda); 7. -Kariger (Aprilia); 8. Schmidt (Honda); 9. Lo Bue (Honda); 10.- Neukircher (Honda); 11. Schneider (Honda); 12. Knöfler (Yamaha);-13. Koch (Honda); 14. Rentzsch (Honda); 15. Toth (H, Honda).

2nd May - Hockenheim
1. Reissmann (Aprilia); 2. Hafenegger (Honda); 3. Müller (Honda);- 4. Kariger (Aprilia); 5. Schneider (Honda); 6. Lo Bue (Honda); 7. -Schmidt (Honda); 8. Boder (Honda); 9. Schöffler (Honda); 10. -Knöfler (Yamaha); 11. Fochler (Honda); 12. Hierl (Honda); 13. -Rentzsch (Honda); 14. Walther (Honda); 15. Götti (CH, Honda).

23rd May - Salzburgring - Austria
1. Nöhles (Honda); 2. Ebner (A, Honda); 3. Müller (Honda); 4. -Reissmann (Aprilia); 5. Lo Bue (Honda); 6. R. Harms (DK, Honda); 7. Toth (H, Honda); 8. Hafenegger (Honda); 9. Kariger (Aprilia); -10. Neukirchen (Honda); 11. Knöfler (Yamaha); 12. Walther -(Honda); 13. Hofer (A, Honda); 14. Eble (Honda); 15. Schneider- (Honda).

6th June - Oschersleben
1. Müller (Honda); 2. Reissmann (Aprilia); 3. Treutlein (Honda); -4. Stief (Honda); 5. Hafenegger (Honda); 6. R. Harms (DK, Honda); -7. Nöhles (Honda); 8. Walther (Honda); 9. Kariger (Aprilia); 10.-Knöfler (Yamaha); 11. Schmidt (Honda); 12. Neukirchner (Honda);-13. Smrz (CZ, Honda); 14. Lo Bue (Honda); 15. Schöffler (Honda).

27th June - Most - Czech Republic
1. Müller (Honda); 2. Smrz (CZ, Honda); 3. Toth (H, Honda); 4.-Treutlein (Honda); 5. Neukirchner (Honda); 6. Eble (Honda); 7.-Knöfler (Yamaha); 8. Kariger (Aprilia); 9. Lo Bue (Honda); 10.- Hierl (Honda); 11. Schmidt (Honda); 12. Walther (Honda); 13. -Boder (Honda); 14. Lailach (Honda); 15. Rentzsch (Honda).

11th July - Brno - Czech Republic
1. Nöhles (Honda); 2. Reissmann (Aprilia); 3. Knöfler (Yamaha); -4. Neukirchner (Honda); 5. Schmidt (Honda); 6. Fochler (Honda); -7. Eble (Honda); 8. Walther (Honda); 9. Hafenegger (Honda); 10.- März (Honda); 11. Müller (Honda); 12. Koch (Honda); 13. Toth (H, -Honda); 14. Rentzsch (Honda); 15. Schneider (Honda).

25th July - Nürburgring
1. Reissmann (Aprilia); 2. Müller (Honda); 3. Hafenegger (Honda); -4. Toth (H, Honda); 5. Treutlein (Honda); 6. Lo Bue (Honda); 7.-Neukirchner (Honda); 8. Hierl (Honda); 9. Lailach (Honda); 10.-Schneider (Honda); 11. März (Honda); 12. Walther (Honda); 13.-Eble (Honda); 14. Koch (Honda); 15. Bosman (NL, Honda).

8th August - Schleiz
1. Hafenegger (Honda); 2. Nöhles (Honda); 3. Reissmann (Aprilia); -4. Stief (Honda); 5. Kariger (Aprilia); 6. Toth (H, Honda); 7.-Smrz (CZ, Honda); 8. Neukirchen (Honda); 9. Treutlein (Honda); -10. Lougher (GB, Honda); 11. Müller (Honda); 12. Götti (CH,- Honda); 13. Boder (Honda); 14. März (Honda); 15. Lo Bue (Honda).

5th September - Lagerlechfeld
1. Nöhles (Honda); 2. Hafenegger (Honda); 3. Reissmann (Aprilia); -4. Treutlein (Honda); 5. Toth (H, Honda); 6. Kariger (Aprilia); -7. Müller (Honda); 8. Neukirchen (Honda); 9. Lo Bue (Honda); 10. -Rentzsch (Honda); 11. Knöfler (Yamaha); 12. Götti (CH, Honda);- 13. Walther (Honda); 14. Hierl (Honda); 15. Boder (Honda).

19th September - Assen - The Netherlands
1. Müller (Honda); 2. Hafenegger (Honda); 3. Toth (H, Honda); 4.-Van Leeuwen (NL, Honda); 5. Timmer (NL, Honda); 6. De Haan (NL, -Honda); 7. Knöfler (Yamaha); 8. März (Honda); 9. Walther (Honda);-10. Schöffler (Honda); 11. Lo Bue (Honda); 12. Eble (Honda); 13. Schneider (Honda); 14. Mols (NL, Honda); 15. Moojman (NL, Honda).

Final classification

1. Dirk Reissmann   Aprilia   155 points
2. Jarno Müller   Honda   154
3. Philipp Hafenegger   Honda   143
4. K. Nöhles (Honda), 129; 5. I. Toth (H, Honda), 79; 6. A. -Kariger (Aprilia), 65; 7. M. Neukirchen (Honda), 65; 8. C.-Treutlein (Honda), 60; 9. R. Knöfler (Yamaha), 60; 10. D. Lo Bue -(Honda), 60; 11. J. Smrz (CZ, Honda), 42; 12. T. Walther (Honda), -40; 13. J. Schmidt (Honda), 38; 14. M. Stief (Honda), 37; 15. A. -Eble (Honda), 28; 16. M. Schneider (Honda), 27; 17. S. März-(Honda), 21; 18. P. Ebner (A, Honda), 20; 19. R. Harms (DK, -Honda), 20; 20. E. Hierl (Honda), 20; 21. S. Fochler (Honda), 15; -22. J. Boder (Honda), 15; 23. F. Schöffler (Honda), 14; 24. K. -Rentzsch (Honda), 14; 25. W. Leeuwen (Honda), 13; 26. R. Timmer -(NL, Honda), 11; 27. H. De Haan (NL, Honda), 10; 28. D. Lailach -(Honda), 9; 29. A. Götti (CH, Honda), 9; 30. F. Koch (Honda), 9; -31. I. Lougher (GB, Honda), 6; 32. G. Hofer (A, Honda), 3; 33. R. -Mols (NL, Honda), 2; 34. P. Moojman (NL, Honda), 1; 35. T. Bosman- (NL, Honda), 1. 35 finishers.

Dirk Reissmann.

Mike Baldinger.

250 cc

Champion: Mike Baldinger (Honda). Born on 10th November 1975, in -Merdingen bei Freiburg.
First race: 1993.
First GP: Germany, 1998 (250).
Career highlights: 6th 125 German Championship (Honda) in 1994; 22nd 125 European Championship, 10th 125 German Championship (Honda) in 1995; 5th 125 German Championship (Honda) in-1996; 34th 125 European Championship, 9th 125 German Championship (Honda) in 1997; 37th 250 World Championship, 9th 250 European Championship, 2nd 250 German Championship (Honda) in 1998; 2nd 250 European Championship, 250 German Champion (Honda) in 1999.

25th April - Zweibrücken
1. Baldinger (Honda); 2. Heidolf (Honda); 3. Harms (DK, Honda); -4. Gemmel (Honda); 5. Bolterauer (A, Honda); 6. Brockmann -(Honda); 7. Stasa (CZ, Aprilia); 8. Petzold (Honda); 9. Lackner- (Honda); 10. Rank (Honda); 11. Hodecker (Honda); 12. Heierli (CH, -Honda); 13. Rizmayer (H, Honda); 14. Witsch (Honda); 15. Rothe-(Honda).

2nd May - Hockenheim
1. Neukirchen (Aprilia); 2. Heidolf (Honda); 3. S. Harms (DK, -Honda); 4. Brockmann (Honda); 5. Hodecker (Honda); 6. Rothe -(Honda); 7. Stasa (CZ, Aprilia); 8. Lackner (Honda); 9. Herrmann- (Honda); 10. Witsch (Honda); 11. A. Göbel (Honda); 12. Blattner -(Honda); 13. Ziegelmann (Honda); 14. R. Göbel (Aprilia). 14 finishers.

23rd May - Salzburgring - Austria
1. Baldinger (Honda); 2. Neukirchen (Aprilia); 3. Stasa (CZ, -Aprilia); 4. Witzeneder (A, Honda); 5. Heidolf (Honda); 6. -Brockmann (Honda); 7. Bolterauer (A, Honda); 8. Gemmel (Honda); -9. S. Harms (DK, Honda); 10. Lackner (Honda); 11. A. Göbel-(Honda); 12. Herrmann (Honda); 13. Witsch (Honda); 14. Rank -(Honda); 15. Berger (Honda).

6th June - Oschersleben
1. Baldinger (Honda); 2. Gemmel (Honda); 3. Neukirchen (Aprilia); -4. Brockmann (Honda); 5. Stasa (CZ, Aprilia); 6. S. Harms (DK,- Honda); 7. Lackner (Honda); 8. Rothe (Honda); 9. Rank (Honda);-10. Hodecker (Honda); 11. A. Göbel (Honda); 12. Petzold (Honda);-13. Heierli (CH, Honda); 14. Langer (Honda); 15. Blatter (CH,-Honda).

27th June - Most - Czech Republic
1. Baldinger (Honda); 2. Stasa (CZ, Aprilia); 3. Heidolf (Honda); -4. Bolterauer (Honda); 5. Harms (DK, Honda); 6. Brockmann -(Honda); 7. Rank (Honda); 8. Petzold (Honda); 9. Lackner- (Honda); 10. Langer (Yamaha); 11. A. Göbel (Honda); 12. Hosaker (DK, Honda); 13. R. Göbel (Aprilia); 14. Blatter (CH, Honda). 14 finishers.

11th July - Brno - Czech Republic
1. Baldinger (Honda); 2. Stasa (CZ, Aprilia); 3. Witzeneder (A, -Honda); 4. Brockmann (Honda); 5. Lackner (Honda); 6. Hodecker -(Honda); 7. Rank (Honda); 8. Bolterauer (Honda); 9. Gemmel- (Honda); 10. A. Göbel (Honda); 11. Rothe (Honda); 12. R. Göbel- (Aprilia); 13. Heierli (CH, Honda); 14. Smees (NL, Honda); 15. -Blatter (CH, Honda).

25th July - Nürburgring
1. Neukirchen (Aprilia); 2. Brockmann (Honda); 3. Heidolf -(Honda); 4. Gemmel (Honda); 5. Stasa (CZ, Aprilia); 6. Rank -(Honda); 7. Harms (DK, Honda); 8. Lackner (Honda); 9. Petzold (Honda); 10. Heierli (CH, Honda); 11. Herrmann (Honda); 12. Rothe -(Honda); 13. A. Göbel (Honda); 14. Blatter (CH, Honda); 15. R.-Göbel (Aprilia).

8th August - Schleiz
1. Baldinger (Honda); 2. Neukirchen (Aprilia); 3. Stasa (CZ, -Aprilia); 4. Brockmann (Honda); 5. Heidolf (Honda); 6. Witzeneder -(A, Honda); 7. Lougher (GB, Honda); 8. Lackner (Honda); 9. Rank -(Honda); 10. A. Göbel (Honda); 11. Hodecker (Honda); 12. Brown -(GB, Honda); 13. Rothe (Honda); 14. Heierli (CH, Honda); 15. -English (GB, Honda).

5th September - Lagerlechfeld
1. Baldinger (Honda); 2. Neukirchen (Aprilia); 3. Heidolf -(Honda); 4. Brockmann (Honda); 5. Stasa (CZ, Aprilia); 6. Lackner -(Honda); 7. Gemmel (Honda); 8. Normann (Honda); 9. Rothe (Honda);- 10. Hodecker (Honda); 11. A. Göbel (Honda); 12. Heierli (CH,-Honda); 13. Petzold (Honda); 14. Ziegelmair (Honda); 15. Igel -(Honda).

19th September - Assen - The Netherlands
1. Neukirchen (Aprilia); 2. Stasa (CZ, Aprilia); 3. Baldinger -(Honda); 4. Gemmel (Honda); 5. Brockmann (Honda); 6. Romein (NL, -Honda); 7. Van De Lagemaat (NL, Honda); 8. Markink (NL, Honda); -9. Heidolf (Honda); 10. Blok (NL, Honda); 11. Lackner (Honda);-12. Geenen (NL, Honda); 13. Rothe (Honda); 14. Hasager (DK, -Honda); 15. Heierli (CH, Honda).

Final classification

1. Mike Baldinger   Honda   191 points
2. Matthias Neukirchen   Aprilia   151
3. Bohumil Stasa (CZ)   Aprilia   134
4. D. Heidolf (Honda), 117; 5. D. Brockmann (Honda), 116; 6. C.-Gemmel (Honda), 83; 7. T. Lackner (Honda), 74; 8. S. Harms (DK,-Honda), 69; 9. N. Rank (Honda), 58; 10. K. Hodecker (Honda), 43;-11. U. Bolterauer (A, Honda), 41; 12. T. Rothe (Honda), 41; 13. -A. Göbel (Honda), 41; 14. M. Witzeneder (A, Honda), 39; 15. D. -Petzold (Honda), 30; 16. R. Heierli (CH, Honda), 23; 17. B. -Herrmann (Honda), 16; 18. R. Göbel (Aprilia), 12; 19. H. Blatter (CH, Honda), 12; 20. A. Witsch (Honda), 11; 21. A. Romein (NL, -Honda), 10; 22. H. Van De Lagemaat (NL, Honda), 9; 23. I. Lougher -(GB, Honda), 9; 24. R. Markink (NL, Honda), 8; 25. J. Blok (NL, -Honda), 6; 26. S. Ziegelmaier (Honda), 5; 27. M. Geenen (NL, -Honda), 4; 28. S. Brown (GB, Honda), 4; 29. G. Ritzmayer (H, -Honda), 3; 30. U. Hasager (DK, Honda), 2; 31. H. Smees (NL, -Honda), 2; 32. L. Langer (Honda), 2; 33. W. Igel (Honda), 1; 34. -G. English (GB, Honda), 1; 35. M. Berger (Honda), 1. 35 finishers.

Supersport

Champion: Markus Barth (Suzuki). Born on 20th April 1972, in - Heidenheim.
First race: 1988.
Career highlights: 6th Supersport German Championship (Suzuki) in - 1998; 39th Supersport World Championship, 90th Endurance World Championship, Supersport German Champion (Suzuki) in 1999.

25th April - Zweibrücken
1. Barth (Suzuki); 2. Penzkofer (Yamaha); 3. Oelschläger-(Suzuki); 4. Körner (Suzuki); 5. Kaufmann (Yamaha); 6. -Scheschowitsch (Suzuki); 7. Nebel (Yamaha); 8. Ehrenberger (Suzuki); 9. Jerzenbeck (Suzuki); 10. Klink (Honda); 11. Sebrich- (Suzuki); 12. Linn (Suzuki); 13. Röthig (Kawasaki); 14. Galinski -(Honda); 15. Maher (Yamaha).

2nd May - Hockenheim
1. Oelschläger (Suzuki); 2. Scheschowitsch (Suzuki); 3. Körner -(Suzuki); 4. Barth (Suzuki); 5. Kaufmann (Yamaha); 6. Ehrenberger -(Suzuki); 7. Friedrich (Ducati); 8. Sebrich (Suzuki); 9. Heydt- (Yamaha); 10. Nebel (Yamaha); 11. Penzkofer (Yamaha); 12. Nickel -(Yamaha); 13. Koller (Honda); 14. Wegscheider (Suzuki); 15. -Jerzenbeck (Suzuki).

23rd May - Salzburgring - Austria
1. Kaufmann (Yamaha); 2. Barth (Suzuki); 3. Oelschläger (Suzuki);- 4. Sebrich (Suzuki); 5. Hinterreiter (A, Yamaha); 6. Koller -(Honda); 7. Welink (Kawasaki); 8. Nebel (Yamaha); 9. Körner- (Suzuki); 10. Haslinger (A, Yamaha); 11. Friedrich (Ducati); 12. -Ott (Kawasaki); 13. Murauer (A, Yamaha); 14. Ehrenberger-(Suzuki); 15. Jerzenbeck (Suzuki).

6th June - Oschersleben
1. Körner (Yamaha); 2. Kaufmann (Yamaha); 3. Scheschowitsch -(Suzuki); 4. Nebel (Yamaha); 5. Barth (Suzuki); 6. Friedrich -(Ducati); 7. Heiler (Yamaha); 8. Penzkofer (Yamaha); 9. Nicke (Yamaha); 10. Jerzenbeck (Suzuki); 11. Galinski (Honda); 12.-Heydt (Yamaha); 13. Ott (Kawasaki); 14. Linn (Suzuki); 15.- Kuttruf (Yamaha).

27th June - Most - Czech Republic
1. Kaufmann (Yamaha); 2. Kaufmann (Yamaha); 3. Barth (Suzuki); 4. Nebel (Yamaha); 5. Oelschläger (Suzuki); 6.-Penzkofer (Yamaha); 7. Körner (Suzuki); 8. Sebrich (Suzuki); 9. Friedrich (Ducati); 10. Ehrenberger (Suzuki); 11. Bernhard -(Suzuki); 12. Borkowsky (Yamaha); 13. Welink (Kawasaki); 14.-Buchner (Suzuki); 15. Folger (Suzuki).

11th July - Brno - Czech Republic
1. Scheschowitsch (Suzuki); 2. Körner (Suzuki); 3. Kaufmann- (Yamaha); 4. Sebrich (Suzuki); 5. Welink (Kawasaki); 6.-Oelschläger (Suzuki); 7. Penzkofer (Yamaha); 8. Barth (Suzuki); -9. Ehrenberger (Suzuki); 10. Friedrich (Ducati); 11. Nickel -(Yamaha); 12. Borkowsky (Yamaha); 13. Maher (GB, Yamaha); 14.- Koller (Honda); 15. Hinterreiter (A, Kawasaki).

25th July - Nürburgring
1. Körner (Suzuki); 2. Barth (Suzuki); 3. Heiler (Yamaha); 4. -Nebel (Yamaha); 5. Oelschläger (Suzuki); 6. Friedrich (Ducati); -7. Buchner (Suzuki); 8. Folger (Suzuki); 9. Penzkofer (Yamaha);-10. Heydt (Yamaha); 11. Nickel (Yamaha); 12. Kuttruf (Yamaha);-13. Seefeldt (Kawasaki); 14. Wegscheider (I, Suzuki); 15. Koller -(Honda).

8th August - Schleiz
1. Oelschläger (Suzuki); 2. Scheschowitsch (Suzuki); 3. Barth -(Suzuki); 4. Heiler (Yamaha); 5. Penzkofer (Yamaha); 6. Kaufmann- (Yamaha); 7. Friedrich (Ducati); 8. Koller (Honda); 9. Buchner -(Suzuki); 10. Ehrenberger (Suzuki); 11. Sebrich (Suzuki); 12. -Bernhard (Suzuki); 13. Folger (Suzuki); 14. Tijssen (NL, Suzuki);-15. Körner (Suzuki).

5th September - Lagerlechfeld
1. Barth (Suzuki); 2. Oelschläger (Suzuki); 3. Heiler (Yamaha); -4. Kaufmann (Yamaha); 5. Körner (Suzuki); 6. Scheschowitsch -(Suzuki); 7. Nebel (Yamaha); 8. Sebrich (Suzuki); 9. Penzkofer -(Yamaha); 10. Buchner (Suzuki); 11. Welink (Kawasaki); 12.- Wegscheider (Suzuki); 13. Folger (Suzuki); 14. Heydt (Yamaha);-15. Koller (Honda).

19th September - Assen - The Netherlands
1. Oelschläger (Suzuki); 2. Heiler (Yamaha); 3. Barth (Suzuki); -4. Scheschowitsch (Suzuki); 5. Friedrich (Ducati); 6. Stief -(Yamaha); 7. Körner (Suzuki); 8. Ehrenberger (Suzuki); 9. Nebel (Yamaha); 10. Penzkofer (Yamaha); 11. Folger (Suzuki); 12. -Schulten (Suzuki); 13. Wegscheider (Suzuki); 14. Tijssen (NL, -Suzuki); 15. Welink (Kawasaki).

Final classification

1. Markus Barth   Suzuki   162 points
2. Jürgen Oelschläger   Suzuki   159
3. Stefan Scheschowitsch   Suzuki   139

4. T. Körner (Suzuki), 135; 5. H. Kaufmann (Yamaha), 126; 6. R. -Penzkofer (Yamaha), 83; 7. S. Nebel (Yamaha), 78; 8. A. Heiler -(Yamaha), 74; 9. A. Friedrich (Ducati), 67; 10. S. Sebrich (Suzuki), 60; 11. C. Ehrenberger (Suzuki), 47; 12. M. Welink -(Kawasaki), 29; 13. P. Koller (Honda), 25; 14. E. Buchner -(Suzuki), 24; 15. H. Nickel (Yamaha), 21; 16. A. Folger (Suzuki);17. H. Heydt (Yamaha), 19; 18. B. Jerzenbeck (Suzuki), 15; 19. T.-Hinterreiter (A, Yamaha/Kawasaki), 12; 20. M. Wegscheider -(Suzuki), 11; 21. M. Stief (Yamaha), 10; 22. O. Bernhard -(Suzuki), 9; 23. F. Borkowsky (Yamaha), 8; 24. M. Galinski -(Honda), 7; 25. A. Ott (Kawasaki), 7; 26. F. Haslinger (Yamaha),- 6; 27. T. Klink (Honda), 6; 28. F. Linn (Suzuki), 6; 29. T. -Kuttruf (Yamaha), 5; 30. M. Schulten (Suzuki), 4; 31. R. Maher -(IRL, Yamaha), 4; 32. L. Tijssen (NL, Suzuki), 4; 33. R. Seefeldt -(Kawasaki), 3; 34. R. Murauer (A, Yamaha), 3; 35. T. Röthig -(Kawasaki), 3. 35 finishers.

△
Markus Barth.

German Championship

△
Roger Kellenberger

△
Christer Lindholm.

Pro Superbike

Champion: Christer Lindholm (S, Yamaha). Born on 27th July -1966, in Ekero/Sweden.
First race: 1987.
Career highlights: 31st TT Formula One World Championship, TT Formula One Swedish Champion, Superbike Swedish Champion (Suzuki) in -1989; 42nd Endurance FIM Cup (Honda), 8th Superbike European Championship, Superbike Swedish Champion (Suzuki) in 1990; 45th Superbike World Championship, 2nd Superbike European Championship (Yamaha) in 1991; 14th Superbike World Championship, Superbike Swedish Champion (Yamaha) in 1992; 9th Superbike World Championship, 2nd Superbike European Championship (Yamaha) in 1993; 30th Superbike World Championship -(Yamaha) in 1994; 21st Endurance World Championship, 2nd Pro superbike German Championship (Yamaha) in 1995; 16th Superbike World Championship, Pro Superbike German Champion (Ducati) in 1996; 34th Superbike World Championship, 6th Endurance World Championship, Superbike German Champion (Yamaha) in 1997; 28th Endurance World Championship, 3rd Superbike German in 1998; 42nd Superbike World Championship, 24th Endurance World Championship, Pro Superbike German Champion (Yamaha) in 1999.

2nd May - Hockenheim
Race I: 1. Lindholm (S, Yamaha); 2. Meklau (A, Ducati); 3. -Schmid (Kawasaki); 4. McCarthy (AUS, Suzuki); 5. R. Kellenberger -(CH, Honda); 6. Schulten (Suzuki); 7. Kitsch (Kawasaki); 8. Fritz -(Kawasaki); 9. Heidger (Ducati); 10. Manz (Suzuki); 11. Brikey -(Kawasaki); 12. Wolfsteiner (A, Kawasaki); 13. Bax (Ducati); 14. -Stather (Suzuki); 15. Krumme (Kawasaki).
Race II: 1. Lindholm (S, Yamaha); 2. Meklau (A, Ducati); 3. -Schmid (Kawasaki); 4. R. Kellenberger (CH, Honda); 5. McCarthy -(AUS, Suzuki); 6. Schulten (Suzuki); 7. Heidger (Ducati); 8.- Leuthard (CH, Kawasaki); 9. Rudroff (Suzuki); 10. Stüsser- (Kawasaki); 11. Manz (Suzuki); 12. Künzi (CH, Kawasaki); 13. -Fritz (Kawasaki); 14. Brikey (Kawasaki); 15. Wolfsteiner (A,- Kawasaki).

23rd May - Salzburgring - Austria
Race I: 1. Meklau (A, Ducati); 2. Lindholm (S, Yamaha); 3. -Schulten (Suzuki); 4. Schmid (Kawasaki); 5. Ekerold (SA, -Kawasaki); 6. McCarthy (AUS, Suzuki); 7. Brikey (Kawasaki); 8. Leuthard (CH, Kawasaki); 9. Schneider (Kawasaki); 10. Wolfsteiner -(A, Kawasaki); 11. Camlek (SLO, Yamaha); 12. Dimperl (Ducati);-13. Kainz (A, Ducati); 14. Truninger (CH, Honda); 15. Künzi -(CH, Kawasaki).
Race II: 1. Meklau (A, Ducati); 2. Schulten (Suzuki); 3. -Lindholm (S, Yamaha); 4. Schmid (Kawasaki); 5. McCarthy (AUS,- Suzuki); 6. Bussei (I, Suzuki); 7. Morrison (GB, Yamaha); 8. Ekerold (SA, Kawasaki); 9. Rudroff (Suzuki); 10. Brikey -(Kawasaki); 11. Dimperl (Ducati); 12. Leuthard (CH, Kawasaki);-13. Fritz (Kawasaki); 14. Wolfsteiner (A, Kawasaki); 15.-Schneider (Kawasaki).

6th June - Oschersleben
Race I: 1. Schmid (Kawasaki); 2. Lindholm (S, Yamaha); 3. -Morrison (GB, Yamaha); 4. Bussei (I, Suzuki); 5. Ekerold (SA, -Kawasaki); 6. Meklau (A, Ducati); 7. McCarthy (AUS, Suzuki); 8. Kitsch (Kawasaki); 9. Kiok (Honda); 10. Leuthard (CH, Kawasaki);-11. Platacis (Kawasaki); 12. Dimperl (Ducati); 13. Talmon-Gros -(Suzuki); 14. Künzi (CH, Kawasaki); 15. Stather (Suzuki).
Race II: 1. Meklau (A, Ducati); 2. Lindholm (S, Yamaha); 3.-Schmid (Kawasaki); 4. Morrison (Yamaha); 5. Bussei (Suzuki); 6.-Ekerold (SA, Kawasaki); 7. Schulten (Suzuki); 8. Rudroff (Suzuki); 9. McCarthy (AUS, Suzuki); 10. Fritz (Kawasaki); 11. -Künzi (CH, Kawasaki); 12. Stüsser (Kawasaki); 13. Dimperl -(Ducati); 14. Bax (Ducati); 15. Kitsch (Kawasaki).

27th June - Most - Czech Republic
Race I: 1. Lindholm (S, Yamaha); 2. Meklau (A, Ducati); 3. -McCarthy (AUS, Suzuki); 4. Morrison (GB, Yamaha); 5. Schmid -(Kawasaki); 6. Schulten (Suzuki); 7. Bussei (I, Suzuki); 8.- Dimperl (Ducati); 9. Heidger (Ducati); 10. Kitsch (Kawasaki); 11.-Bursa (CZ, Kawasaki); 12. Schneider (Kawasaki); 13. Camlek (SLO,-Yamaha); 14. Stüsser (Kawasaki); 15. Manz (Kawasaki).
Race II: 1. Lindholm (S, Yamaha); 2. Meklau (A, Ducati); 3. -Bussei (I, Suzuki); 4. Schmid (Kawasaki); 5. Morrison (GB,- Yamaha); 6. Dimperl (Ducati); 7. Ekerold (SA, Kawasaki); 8. McCarthy (AUS, Suzuki); 9. Heidger (Ducati); 10. Bursa (CZ,-Kawasaki); 11. Kitsch (Kawasaki); 12. Brikey

Final classification

1. Christer Lindholm   (S)   Yamaha   271 points
2. Andreas Meklau   (A)   Ducati   250
3. Jochen Schmid   Kawasaki   156
4. K. McCarthy (AUS, Suzuki), 124; 5. B. Morrison (GB, Yamaha),-116; 6. G. Bussei (I, Suzuki), 91; 7. M. Schulten (Suzuki), 85;-8. J. Ekerold (SA, Kawasaki), 83; 9. F. Heidger (Ducati), 55; 10. -P. Leuthard (CH, Kawasaki), 51; 11. H.-J. Brikey (Kawasaki), 46; -12. W. Dimperl (Ducati), 45; 13. H. Kitsch (Kawasaki), 33; 14. E. -Korpiaho (SF, Kawasaki), 32; 15. M. Rudroff (Suzuki), 31; 16. W.- Fritz (Kawasaki), 30; 17. R. Kellenberger (CH, Honda), 24; 18. G.-Stüsser (Kawasaki), 21; 19. M. Manz (Suzuki/Kawasaki), 21; 20. C.-Schneider (Kawasaki), 16; 21. J. Wolfsteiner (A, Kawasaki), 13; -22. C. Künzi (CH, Kawasaki), 12; 23. M. Bursa (CZ, Kawasaki), 11; -24. H. Platacis (Kawasaki), 11; 25. M. Ober (Honda), 8; 26. B. Camlek (SLO, Yamaha), 8; 27. M. Kiok (Honda), 7; 28. J. Berner -(SF, Kawasaki), 5; 29. R. Prang (DK, Yamaha), 5; 30. W. Bax -(Ducati), 5; 31. R. Talmon-Gros (Suzuki), 4; 32. M. Kainz (A, -Kawasaki), 3; 33. U.-M. Stather (Suzuki), 3; 34. S. Trunninger (CH, Honda); 35. W. Krumme (Kawasaki), 1; 36. A. John (Kawasaki),-1. 36 finishers.

(Kawasaki); 13. -Fritz (Kawasaki); 14. Schneider (Kawasaki); 15. Stüsser - (Kawasaki).

11th July - Pannoniaring - Hungary
Race I: 1. Lindholm (S, Yamaha); 2. Meklau (A, Ducati); 3. -Morrison (GB, Yamaha); 4. Schmid (Kawasaki); 5. Ekerold (SA,- Kawasaki); 6. Bussei (I, Suzuki); 7. McCarthy (AUS, Suzuki); 8.Heidger (Ducati); 9. Dimperl (Ducati); 10. Brikey (Kawasaki); 11. -Leuthard (CH, Kawasaki); 12. Rudroff (Suzuki); 13. Manz -(Kawasaki); 14. Platacis (Kawasaki); 15. Talmon-Gros (Suzuki).
Race II: 1. Lindholm (S, Yamaha); 3. Meklau (A, Ducati); 3. -Morrison (GB, Yamaha); 4. Bussei (I, Suzuki); 5. McCarthy (AUS,- Suzuki); 6. Ekerold (SA, Kawasaki); 7. Heidger (Ducati); 8. Brikey (Kawasaki); 9. Schmid (Kawasaki); 10. Leuthard (CH, -Kawasaki); 11. Rudroff (Suzuki); 12. Manz (Kawasaki); 13. -Platacis (Kawasaki); 14. Schneider (Kawasaki); 15. John- (Kawasaki).

25th July - Nürburgring
Race I: 1. Lindholm (S, Yamaha); 2. Meklau (A, Ducati); 3. -Korpiaho (SF, Kawasaki); 4. Ekerold (SA, Kawasaki); 5. Morrison -(GB, Yamaha); 6. Schulten (Suzuki); 7. McCarthy (AUS, Suzuki); 8. -Ober (Honda); 9. Leuthard (CH, Kawasaki); 10. Fritz (Kawasaki);-11. Berner (SF, Kawasaki); 12. Kitsch (Kawasaki); 13. Stüsser- (Kawasaki); 14. Prang (DK, Yamaha); 15. Platacis (Kawasaki).
Race II: 1. Meklau (A, Ducati); 2. Lindholm (S, Yamaha); 3. -Korpiaho (SF, Kawasaki); 4. Schmid (Kawasaki); 5. Morrison (GB, -Yamaha); 6. McCarthy (AUS, Suzuki); 7. Bussei (I, Suzuki); 8.-Heidger (Ducati); 9. Leuthard (CH, Kawasaki); 10. Brikey -(Kawasaki); 11. Stüsser (Kawasaki); 12. Dimperl (Ducati); 13.- Prang (DK, Yamaha); 14. Manz (Kawasaki); 15. Fritz (Kawasaki).

500 cc

Champion: Jörg Schöllhorn (ROC Yamaha). Born on 5th January 1964, in Bad Wursch.
Career highlights: 2nd 250 German Championship in 1994 (Aprilia); 3rd 500 German Championship in 1996 (ROC Yamaha); 4th 500 German Championship (ROC Yamaha) in 1997; 500 German Champion (ROC Yamaha) in 1999.

25th April - Zweibrücken
1. Schöllhorn (ROC Yamaha); 2. Frommknecht (Honda); 3. Stoll (Yamaha); 4. Albrecht (Yamaha); 5. Krachowitzer (Suzuki); 6. Strasser (ROC Yamaha); 7. Guigas (Roll-Yamaha); 8. Spalteholz (Harris-Yamaha); 9. Haarmann (Roll-Yamaha); 10. Raab (Yamaha).

2nd May - Hockenheim
1. Schöllhorn (ROC Yamaha); 2. Stoll (Yamaha); 3. Strasser (ROC-Yamaha); 4. Lehmann (Yamaha); 5. Frommknecht (Honda); 6. Albrecht -(Yamaha); 7. Guigas (Roll-Yamaha); 8. Plaschka (Suzuki); 9. Raab- (Yamaha); 10. Mendel (Yamaha).

6th June - Oschersleben
1. Schöllhorn (ROC Yamaha); 2. Frommknecht (Honda); 3. Strasser -(ROC Yamaha); 4. Stoll (Yamaha); 5. Nowack (Yamaha); 6. Mendel- (Yamaha); 7. Albrecht (Yamaha); 8. Becker (Yamaha); 9. Plaschka- (Suzuki); 10. Spalteholz (Harris-Yamaha).

20th June - Colmar-Berg - Luxembourg
1. Schöllhorn (ROC Yamaha); 2. Frommknecht (Honda); 3. Stoll -(Yamaha); 4. Nowack (Yamaha); 5. Mendel (Yamaha); 6. Plaschka- (Suzuki); 7. Spalteholz (Yamaha); 8. Krachowitzer (Suzuki); 9.- Becker (Yamaha); 10. Eckert (Yamaha).

27th June - Most - Czech Republic
1. Schöllhorn (ROC Yamaha); 2. Frommknecht (Honda); 3. Strasser -(ROC Yamaha); 4. Albrecht (Yamaha); 5. Spalteholz (Yamaha); 6.-Lehmann (Yamaha); 7. Mendel (Yamaha); 8. Rahn (HSS); 9.-Krachowitzer (Suzuki); 10. Elstner (Honda).

25th July - Nürburgring
1. Schöllhorn (ROC Yamaha); 2. Schmassmann (CH, ROC Yamaha); 3. -Strasser (ROC Yamaha); 4. Becker (Harris-Yamaha); 5. Lehmann- (Yamaha); 6. Plaschka (Suzuki); 7. Stoll (Harris-Yamaha); 8.-Guigas (Roll-Yamaha); 9. Rahn (HSS); 10. Spalteholz -(Harris-Yamaha).

15th August - Oschersleben
1. Schöllhorn (ROC Yamaha); 2. Lehmann (Yamaha); 3. Strasser (ROC-Yamaha); 4. Becker (Harris-Yamaha); 5. Rahn (HSS); 6. Nowak -(Yamaha); 7. Guigas (Roll-Yamaha); 8. Krachowitzer (Suzuki); 9.-Zanowski (Yamaha); 10. Albrecht (Yamaha).

29th August - Straubing
1. Schöllhorn (ROC Yamaha); 2. Schmassmann (CH, ROC Yamaha); 3.- Plaschka (Kawasaki); 4. Strasser (ROC Yamaha); 5. Becker -(Harris-Yamaha); 6. Nowak (Yamaha); 7. Spalteholz- (Harris-Yamaha); 8. Moritz (Yamaha); 9. Zarnowski (Yamaha); 10.- Lehmann (Yamaha).

5th Septembrer - Lagerlechfeld
1. Schöllhorn (ROC Yamaha); 2. Schmassmann (CH, ROC Yamaha); 3. -Frommknecht (Honda); 4. Strasser (ROC Yamaha); 5. Plaschka- (Kawasaki); 6. Rahn (HSS); 7. Albrecht (Yamaha); 8. Moritz- (Yamaha); 9. Lehmann (Yamaha); 10. Krachowitzer (Suzuki).

12th September - Frohburg
1. Frommknecht (Honda); 2. Schöllhorn (ROC Yamaha); 3. Strasser -(ROC Yamaha); 4. Becker (Harris-Yamaha); 5. Krachowitzer- (Suzuki); 6. Zarnowski (Yamaha); 7. Lehmann (Yamaha); 8. Guigas- (Roll-Yamaha); 9. Mendel (Bischoff V2); 10. Herrmann (Honda).

Final classification

1. Jörg Schöllhorn — ROC Yamaha — 245 points
2. Siegfrid Frommknecht — Honda — 132
3. Egon Strasser — ROC Yamaha — 132
4. O. Lehmann (Yamaha), 76; 5. Stoll (Harris-Yamaha), 74; 6. -W.-R. Becker (Harris-Yamaha), 65; 7. J. Plaschka (Kawasaki), 62;-8. N. Schmassmann (CH, ROC Yamaha); 9. L. Albrecht (Yamaha), 60;-9. 60; 10. J. Krachowitzer (Suzuki), 54; 11. A. Spalteholz -(Yamaha), 54; 12. M. Guigas (Roll-Yamaha), 50; 13. M. Rahn (HSS),- 46; 14. S. Nowack (Yamaha), 44; 15. R. Mendel (Bischoff V2), 43;-16. D. Zarnowski (Yamaha), 33; 17. M.-W. Koch (Honda), 29; 18. H.- Eckert (Yamaha), 20; 19. A. Moritz (Yamaha), 16; 20. F. Haarmann -(Yamaha), 16; 21. G. Elstner (Suzuki), 14; 22. A. Raab (Yamaha),-13; 23. J. Van der Elsen (Suzuki), 9; 24. J. Herrmann (Honda), 8;-25. R. Born (Yamaha), 6; 26. K.-U. Henneberg (Yamaha), 4; 27. G. Weber (Yamaha), 3; 28. G. Düro (Suzuki), 3. 28 finishers.

Jörg Schöllhorn.

Jörg Steinhausen /Frank Schmidt.

Side-cars

Champions: Jörg Steinhausen/Frank Schmidt (LCR-Suzuki 1200). Born on 31st May 1970.
Career highlights: 20th Side-Cars World Cup in 1997; 13th Side-Cars World Cup, ISRA Cup Winners (LCR-Suzuki) in 1998; 8th Side-Cars World Cup, Side-Cars German Champions (LCR-Suzuki) in 1999.

25th April - Zweibrücken
1. Steinhausen/Schmidt (LCR-Suzuki); 2. Van De Velde/Kolloch-(B/D, LCR-Suzuki); 3. Eilers/Eilers (LCR-Suzuki); 4. -Hemmerling/Schwegler (LCR); 5. Roscher/Gries (LCR-Suzuki); 6.- Häberli/Sauter (CH, LCR); 7. Hauzenberger/Madaras (A,-LCR-Suzuki); 8. Veltjens/Hildebrand (LCR); 9. Reuter/Kölsch-(Suzuki); 10. Schneider/Engelmann (LCR-Kawasaki).

23rd May - Salzburgring - Austria
1. Klaffenböck/Hänni (A/CH, LCR-HRM-Honda); 2. Steinhausen/Parzer-(LCR-Suzuki); 3. Van De Velde/Kolloch (B/D, LCR-Suzuki); 4. -Schneider/Engelmann (LCR-Kawasaki); 5. Hauzenberger/Madaras (A,-LCR-Suzuki); 6. Eilers/Eilers (LCR-Suzuki); 7.Veltjens/Hildebrand (LCR-Suzuki); 8. Kieser/Sanapo (CH,-Kawasaki); 9. Häberli/Sauter (CH, LCR-Suzuki); 10. R. Kutschke/L.-Kutschke (LCR-Honda).

6th June - Oschersleben
1. Steinhausen/Parzer (D/A, LCR-Suzuki); 2. Klaffenböck/Hänni-(A/CH, LCR-HRM-Honda); 3. Roscher/Gries (LCR-Suzuki); 4.- Kohlmann/Anderle (LCR-Honda); 5. Reuter/Kölsch (LCR-Suzuki); 6.- Hauzenberger/Madaras (A, LCR-Suzuki); 7. Häberli/Sauter (CH, -LCR-Suzuki); 8. Van De Velde/Kolloch (B/D, LCR-Suzuki); 9. -Schneider/Engelmann (LCR-Kawasaki); 10. Eilers/Eilers-(LCR-Suzuki).

20th June - Colmar Berg - Luxembourg
1. Klaffenböck/Hänni (A/CH, LCR-HRM-Honda); 2. Steinhausen/Parzer-(D/A, LCR-Suzuki); 3. Van De Velde/Kolloch (B/D, LCR-Suzuki); 4. -Eilers/Eilers (LCR-Suzuki); 5. Hauzenberger/Madaras (A, -LCR-Suzuki); 6. Veltjens/Hildebrand (LCR-Suzuki); 7.Häberli/Sauter (CH, LCR-Suzuki); 8. Hemmerling/Schwegler-(LCR-Yamaha); 9. Becker/Abel (LCR-Suzuki); 10. R. Kutschke/L.-Kutschke (LCR-Honda).

25th July - Nürburgring
1. Klaffenböck/Hänni (A/CH, LCR-HRM-Honda); 2. Van De-Velde/Kolloch (B/D, LCR-Suzuki); 3. Kohlmann/Anderle (LCR-Honda);-4. Reuter/Kölsch (LCR-Suzuki); 5. Hemmerling/Schwegler-(LCR-Yamaha); 6. Eilers/Eilers (LCR-Suzuki); 7. Roscher/Gries-(LCR-Suzuki); 8. Schneider/Engelmann (LCR-Kawasaki); 9. R. -Kutschke/L. Kutschke (LCR-Honda); 10. Kieser/Sanapo (CH,-Seymaz-Kawasaki).

8th August - Schleiz
1. Steinhausen/Schmidt (LCR-Suzuki); 2. Van De Velde/Kolloch-(B/D, LCR-Suzuki); 3. Klaffenböck/Hänni (A/CH, LCR-HRM-Honda); 4.-Reuter/Kölsch (LCR-Suzuki); 5. Eilers/Eilers (LCR-Suzuki); 6.-Hauzenberger/Madaras (A, LCR-Suzuki); 7. Hemmerling/Schwegler (Yamaha); 8. Kohlmann/Anderle (LCR-Honda); 9. Veltjens/Hildebrand-(LCR-Suzuki); 10. Becker/Abel (LCR-Suzuki).

5th September - Lagerlechfeld
1. Van De Velde/Kolloch (B/D, LCR-Suzuki); 2. Steinhausen/Schmidt-(LCR-Suzuki); 3. Kohlmann/Anderle (LCR-Honda); 4. -Hemmerling/Schwegler (LCR-Yamaha); 5. Eilers/Eilers (LCR-Suzuki);- 6. Roscher/Gries (LCR-Suzuki); 7. Reuter/Kölsch (LCR-Suzuki); 8. Veltjens/Hildebrand (LCR); 9. Häberli/Sauter (CH, LCR-Suzuki);-10. R. Kutschke/Jäger (LCR-Honda).

19th September - Assen - The Netherlands
1. Klaffenböck/Hänni (A/CH, LCR-HRM-Honda); 2.-Steinhausen/Schmidt (LCR-Suzuki); 3. Eilers/Eilers (LCR-Suzuki);-4. Kohlmann/Anderle (LCR-Honda); 5. Reuter/Kölsch (LCR-Suzuki);- 6. Hemmerling/Schwegler (Yamaha); 7. Häberli/Sauter (CH, -LCR-Suzuki); 8. Göttlich/Backmann (LCR-Suzuki); 9.-Schneider/Engelmann (LCR-Kawasaki); 10. R. Kutschke/L. Kutschke-(LCR-Honda).

26th September - Oschersleben
1. Klaffenböck/Hänni (A/CH, LCR-HRM-Honda); 2. Webster/James (GB,-LCR-Suzuki); 3. Hauzenberger/Parzer (A, LCR-Suzuki); 4.-Eilers/Eilers (LCR-Suzuki); 5. Steinhausen/Schmidt (LCR-Suzuki);-6. Roscher/Gries (LCR-Suzuki); 7. Becker/Abel (LCR-Suzuki); 8. Häberli/Schrag (CH/D, LCR-Suzuki); 9. Arabin/Lotz (LCR-Honda);-10. Schneider/Engelmann (LCR-Kawasaki).

Final classification

1. Jörg Steinhausen/ Frank Schmidt — LCR-Suzuki — 168 points
2. Klaus Klaffenböck/ Adolf Hänni (A/CH) — LCR-HRM-Honda — 161
3. Daniel Van De Velde/ Andreas Kolloch (B/D) — LCR-Suzuki — 125
4. Eilers/Eilers (LCR-Suzuki), 103; 5.-Hauzenberger/Madaras/Parzer (A, LCR-Suzuki), 71; 6. Reuter/Kölsch-(LCR-Suzuki), 69; 7. Hemmerling/Schwegler (Yamaha), 68; 8. Kohlmann/Anderle (LCR-Honda), 66; 9. Roscher/Gries (LCR-Suzuki),-60; 10. Häberli/Sauter/Schrag (CH/CH/D, LCR-Suzuki), 60; 11.-Schneider/Engelmann (LCR-Kawasaki), 54; 12. Becker/Abel-(LCR-Suzuki), 50; 13. R. Kutschke/L. Kutschke/Jäger (LCR-Honda),-47; 14. Veltjens/Hildebrand (LCR), 44; 15. Arabin/Lotz-(LCR-Honda), 28; 16. Göttlich/Backmann (LCR-Suzuki), 21; 17. -Kiser/Sanapo (CH, Kawasaki), 17; 18. Pohl/Hereth (LCR-Suzuki),-16; 19. Hug/Kubli (CH, SMS-Suzuki), 8; 20. Baer/Lotter/Stodola-(CH/CH/D, Yamaha), 6; 21. Kurt Hock/Kasel/Kuno Hock (Honda), 4;-22. U. Kutschke/T. Kutschke (LCR-Honda), 3; 23.-Källen/Langschandel (BSR), 2; 24. Steiner/Koloska (CH, Suzuki),-2; 25. Stofel/Schrag (LCR), 1. 25 finishers.

French Championship

125 cc

Champion: Jimmy Petit (Honda). Born on 27th February 1980, in - Champigny.
First GP: France, 1998 (125).
Career highlights: 26th 125 European Championship, 3rd 125 French Championship (Honda) in 1998; 18th 125 European Championship, 125 French Champion, 125 French «National» Champion (Honda) in 1999.

7th March - Le Mans
1. De Puniet (Aprilia); 2. J. Petit (Honda); 3. Duterne (Honda);- 4. Dubray (Honda); 5. Louiset (Honda); 6. Nigon (Honda); 7. -Jouret (Honda); 8. Lougassi (Honda); 9. Lefort (Aprilia); 10. Marchand (Honda); 11. Gregoire (Honda); 12. Rebuttini (Honda);-13. Palacios (Honda); 14. Guintoli (Aprilia); 15. Servaes- (Honda).

28th March - Magny-Cours
1. Terrier (Honda); 2. Lefort (Aprilia); 3. Louiset (Honda); 4. -Dubray (Honda); 5. Lougassi (Honda); 6. Rebuttini (Honda); 7. -Guintoli (Aprilia); 8. Palacios (Honda); 9. Marchand (Honda); 10.-Sueur (Pacific Bike); 11. Chêne (Honda); 12. Gregoire (Honda);-13. Krzyzanowski (Honda); 14. Maingret (Honda); 15. Enjolras- (Honda).

18th April - Albi
1. J. Petit (Honda); 2. Terrier (Honda); 3. Duterne (Honda); 4.-Lefort (Aprilia); 5. Dubray (Honda); 6. Lougassi (Honda); 7. -Louiset (Honda); 8. Guintoli (Aprilia); 9. Rebuttini (Honda); 10.- Sueur (Pacific Bike); 11. Krzyzanowski (Honda); 12. Servaes-(Honda); 13. Marchand (Honda); 14. Palacios (Honda); 15. Enjolras -(Honda).

25th April - Nogaro
1. Dubray (Honda); 2. Lefort (Aprilia); 3. Lougassi (Honda); 4.-Nigon (Yamaha); 5. Duterne (Honda); 6. Terrier (Honda); 7. Dubray -(Honda); 8. Guintoli (Aprilia); 9. Rebuttini (Honda); 10. Servaes- (Honda); 11. Krzyzanowski (Honda); 12. Marchand (Honda); 13. -Enjolras (Honda); 14. Maingret (Honda); 15. Palacios (Honda).

9th May - Carole
1. J. Petit (Honda); 2. Duterne (Honda); 3. Nigon (Yamaha); 4. -Dubray (Honda); 5. Terrier (Honda); 6. Rebuttini (Honda); 7.- Lagrive (Honda); 8. Servaes (Honda); 9. Giuntoli (Aprilia); 10.- Jouret (Honda); 11. Enjolras (Honda); 12. Sueur (Pacific Bike);-13. Guignat (Honda); 14. Krzyzanowski (Honda); 15. Maingret -(Honda).

16th May - Le Vigeant
1. J. Petit (Honda); 2. Guintoli (Aprilia); 3. Terrier (Honda); -4. Nigon (Yamaha); 5. Lagrive (Honda); 6. Servaes (Honda); 7.- Duterne (Honda); 8. Jouret (Honda); 9. Krzyzanowski (Honda); 10.-Enjolras (Honda); 11. Rebuttini (Honda); 12. Sueur (Pacific-Bike); 13. Gregoire (Honda); 14. Guignat (Honda); 15. Burdin -(Honda).

20th June - L,denon
1. Duterne (Honda); 2. Terrier (Honda); 3. J. Petit (Honda); 4.-Guintoli (Aprilia); 5. Lefort (Aprilia); 6. Servaes (Honda); 7. -Krzyzanowski (Honda); 8. Dubray (Honda); 9. Sueur (Pacific Bike);- 10. Louiset (Honda); 11. Jouret (Honda); 12. Gregoire (Honda);-13. Rebuttini (Honda); 14. Marchand (Honda); 15. Doublet (Honda).

27th June - Le Castellet
1. Dubray (Honda); 2. Duterne (Honda); 3. Nigon (Yamaha); 4.-Terrier (Honda); 5. Krzyzanowski (Honda); 6. Jouret (Honda); 7.-Louiset (Honda); 8. Sueur (Pacific Bike); 9. Rebuttini (Honda);-10. Marchand (Honda); 11. Enjolras (Honda); 12. Guignat (Honda);-13. Burdin (Honda); 14. Defortescu (Honda); 15. Palacios (Honda).

3rd October - Carole
1. Krzyzanowski (Honda); 2. Terrier (Honda); 3. J. Petit (Honda); -4. Dubray (Honda); 5. Guintoli (Aprilia); 6. Lefort (Aprilia); 7.- Marchand (Honda); 8. Palacios (Honda); 9. Rebbutini (Honda); 10.- Defortescu (Honda).

Final classification

1. Jimmy Petit	Honda	152 points
2. Frédéric Terrier	Honda	135
3. Stéphane Duterne	Honda	117

4. E. Dubray (Honda), 105; 5. G. Lefort (Aprilia), 81; 6. S.-Guintoli (Aprilia), 78; 7. Nigon (Yamaha), 68; 8. D. Krzyzanowski- (Honda), 67; 9. K. Rebbutini (Honda), 57; 10. H. Louiset (Honda),- 51.

Jimmy Petit.

Vincent Philippe.

250 cc

Champion: Vincent Philippe. Born in 11th January 1978, in Trépot. First race: 1992.
First GP: France, 1997 (125).
Career highlights: 12th French Yamaha Cup in 1993; 8th French Yamaha Cup in 1994; 16th 125 French Championship (9th -"national"), 125 Hillclimbs French Champion in 1996; 7th 125 French Championship (3rd "national"), 125 Hillclimbs French Champion in 1997; 9th 250 European Championship, 250 French Champion (Honda) in 1998; 3rd 250 European Championship, 250 French Champion (Honda) in 1999.

7th March - Le Mans
1. Philippe (Honda); 2. Mizera (Honda); 3. Mora (Aprilia); 4.-Metro (Honda); 5. Monneret (Yamaha); 6. Vecchioni (Yamaha); 7.-Raphanaud (RTT); 8. Detot (Honda); 9. Bousiges (Honda); 10. -Raffeau (Aprilia); 11. Martin (Honda); 12. Vacherie (Honda); 13- Stefani (Honda). 13 finishers.

28th March - Magny-Cours
1. Philippe (Honda); 2. Mora (Aprilia); 3. Mizera (Honda); 4. -Vecchioni (Yamaha); 5. Fouloi (Aprilia); 6. Monneret (Yamaha); 7.- Detot (Honda); 8. Stableau (Honda); 9. Chauchot (Yamaha); 10.- Bousiges (Honda); 11. Maizeret (Honda); 12. Raphanaud (RTT); 13.-Vacherie (Honda); 14. Laurentz (Yamaha); 15. Stefani (Honda).

18th April - Albi
1. Philippe (Honda); 2. Da Costa (Honda); 3. Detot (Honda); 4.-Mora (Aprilia); 5. Metro (Honda); 6. Monneret (Yamaha); 7.-Stableau (Honda); 8. Bousiges (Honda); 9. Vacherie (Honda); 10.-Raffeau (Aprilia); 11. Maizeret (Honda). 11 finishers.

25th April - Nogaro
1. Philippe (Honda); 2. Mizera (Honda); 3. Metro (Honda); 4.-Vecchioni (Yamaha); 5. Monneret (Yamaha); 6. Stableau (Honda); 7. -Segues (Honda); 8. Falcone (Honda); 9. Raffeu (Aprilia); 10.- Chauchot (Yamaha); 11. Bousiges (Honda); 12. Fouloi (Aprilia);- 13. Vacherie (Honda); 14. Mora (Aprilia); 15. Maizeret (Honda).

9th May - Carole
1. Philippe (Honda); 2. Mora (Aprilia); 3. Da Costa (Honda); 4. -Mizera (Honda); 5. Vecchioni (Yamaha); 6. Metro (Honda); 7. Detot- (Honda); 8. Fouloi (Aprilia); 9. Monneret (Yamaha); 10. Falcone- (Honda); 11. Stableau (Honda); 12. Chauchot (Yamaha); 13.-Maizeret (Honda); 14. Bousiges (Honda); 15. Vacherie (Honda).

16th May - Le Vigeant
1. Philippe (Honda); 2. Da Costa (Honda); 3. Mizera (Honda); 4. -Vecchioni (Yamaha); 5. Monneret (Yamaha); 6. Fouloi (Aprilia); 7.-Stableau (Honda); 8. Maizeret (Honda); 9. Mora (Aprilia); 10.- Raffeau (Aprilia); 11. Raphanaud (RTT); 12. Chauchot (Yamaha);-13. Vacherie (Honda); 14. Detot (Honda); 15. Martin (Honda).

20th June - Lédenon
1. Mora (Aprilia); 2. Vecchioni (Yamaha); 3. Mizera (Honda); 4.-Detot (Honda); 5. Da Costa (Honda); 6. Bousiges (Honda); 7.-Maizeret (Honda); 8. Fouloi (Aprilia); 9. Martinez (Honda); 10.- Chauchot (Yamaha); 11. Vacherie (Honda); 12. Boyer (Yamaha). 12- finishers.

27th June - Le Castellet
1. Philippe (Honda); 2. Mora (Aprilia); 3. Da Costa (Honda); 4. -Mizera (Honda); 5. Fouloi (Aprilia); 6. Vecchioni (Yamaha); 7.- Falcone (Honda); 8. Maizeret (Honda); 9. Bousiges (Honda); 10.- Raffeau (Aprilia); 11. Vacherie (Honda); 12. Chauchot (Yamaha);-13. Lechaix; 14. Boyer (Yamaha); 15. Dagas.

3rd October - Carole
1. Mora (Aprilia); 2. Mizera (Honda); 3. Dussauge (Fulgur); 4.-Vecchioni (Yamaha); 5. Fouloi (Aprilia); 6. Chauchot (Yamaha); 7.-Falcone (Honda); 8. Martin (Honda); 9. Raphanaud (RTT); 10.- Lamour (Yamaha).

Final classification

1. Vincent Philippe	Honda	175 points
2. Hervé Mora	Aprilia	146
3. Eric Mizera	Honda	134

4. B. Vecchioni (Yamaha), 103; 5. J. Da Costa (Honda), 83; 6. D.Fouloi (Aprilia), 63; 7. P. Monneret (Yamaha), 60; 8. P. Detot(Honda), 57; 9. Metro (Honda), 50; 10. Bousiges (Honda), 45.

French Championship

Supersport

Champion: Eric Mahé. Born on 2nd July 1970, in Senlis.
First race: 1992.
Career highlights: 3rd French Honda Cup in 1992; 140th Endurance World Championship, 9th Supersport European Championship, 2nd Supersport French Championship (Honda) in 1993; 9th Supersport European Championship, 2nd Supersport French Championship (Yamaha) in 1994; 11th Thunderbike Trophy, 10th Supersport French Championship (Honda) in 1995; 21st Endurance World Championship, 6th Thunderbike Trophy, 5th Supersport French Championship (Yamaha) in 1996; 29th Endurance World Championship, 16th Supersport World Cup, 11th Supersport French Championship (Yamaha) in 1997; 20th Endurance World Championship, 9th Supersport French Championship (Suzuki) in 1998; 12th Supersport European Championship, Supersport French Championship (Yamaha) in 1999.

7th March - Le Mans
1. Mahé (Yamaha); 2. Van Den Bossche (Suzuki); 3. Dobé (Suzuki); 4. Scarnato (Kawasaki); 5. Holon (Kawasaki); 6. Muteau (Ducati);-7. Charpentier (Honda); 8. Cortinovis (Kawasaki); 9. Mounier -(Kawasaki); 10. Muscat (Ducati); 11. Stey (Honda); 12. Destoop (Honda); 13. Morillon (Yamaha); 14. Sohier (Yamaha); 15.-Guezennec (Yamaha).

28th March - Magny-Cours
1. Mahé (Yamaha); 2. Muscat (Ducati); 3. Dobé (Suzuki); 4. -Scarnato (Kawasaki); 5. Paillot (Suzuki); 6. Holon (Kawasaki); 7.- Mounier (Kawasaki); 8. Muteau (Ducati); 9. Morillon (Yamaha); 10.- Gomez (Honda); 11. Stey (Honda); 12. Thomas (Yamaha); 13. -Rousseau (Kawasaki); 14. Destoop (Honda); 15. Poulle (Honda).

18th April - Albi
1. Mahé (Yamaha); 2. Muteau (Ducati); 3. Gomez (Honda); 4. -Scarnato (Kawasaki); 5. Holon (Kawasaki); 6. Muscat (Ducati); 7.- Paillot (Suzuki); 8. Dobé (Suzuki); 9. Thomas (Yamaha); 10. Stey- (Honda); 11. Sohier (Yamaha); 12. Rousseau (Kawasaki); 13. Lethin -(Honda); 14. Mounier (Kawasaki); 15. Poulle (Honda).

25th April - Nogaro
1. Scarnato (Kawasaki); 2. Van Den Bossche (Suzuki); 3. Muscat -(Ducati); 4. Holon (Kawasaki); 5. Cazade (Yamaha); 6. Paillot- (Suzuki); 7. Muteau (Ducati); 8. Morillon (Yamaha); 9. Dobé (Suzuki); 10. Stey (Honda); 11. Cortinovis (Kawasaki); 12. Thomas(Yamaha); 13. Rousseau (Kawasaki); 14. Giabbani (Kawasaki); 15. -Destoop (Honda).

9th May - Carole
1. Van Den Bossche (Suzuki); 2. Mahé (Yamaha); 3. Holon -(Kawasaki); 4. Morillon (Yamaha); 5. Muscat (Ducati); 6. Brian -(Honda); 7. Giabbani (Kawasaki); 8. Cortinovis (Kawasaki); 9.- Muteau (Ducati); 10. Dobé (Suzuki); 11. Guérin (Honda); 12. -Rousseau (Kawasaki); 13. Destoop (Honda); 14. Chenais (Yamaha);-15. Sohier (Yamaha).

16th May - Le Vigeant
1. Van Den Bossche (Suzuki); 2. Muscat (Ducati); 3. Mahé -(Yamaha); 4. Paillot (Suzuki); 5. Holon (Kawasaki); 6. Morillon- (Yamaha); 7. Mounier (Kawasaki); 8. Stey (Honda); 9. Cortinovis -(Kawasaki); 10. Rousseau (Kawasaki); 11. Dobé (Suzuki); 12.-Thomas (Yamaha); 13. Giabbani (Kawasaki); 14. Guérin (Honda); 15.- Destoop (Honda).

20th June - Lédenon
1. Van Den Bossche (Suzuki); 2. Mahé (Yamaha); 3. Scarnato -(Kawasaki); 4. Paillot (Suzuki); 5. Holon (Kawasaki); 6. Stey- (Honda); 7. Sohier (Yamaha); 8. Muteau (Ducati); 9. Cortinovis- (Kawasaki); 10. Gomez (Honda); 11. Rousseau (Kawasaki); 12.-Thomas (Yamaha); 13. Morillon (Yamaha); 14. Mounier (Kawasaki);-15. Destoop (Honda).

27th June - Le Castellet
1. Mahé (Yamaha); 2. Paillot (Suzuki); 3. Scarnato (Kawasaki); 4.-Holon (Kawasaki); 5. Morillon (Yamaha); 6. Cortinovis (Kawasaki); -7. Muscat (Ducati); 8. Mounier (Kawasaki); 9. Stey (Honda); 10.-Sohier (Yamaha); 11. Thomas (Yamaha); 12. Guérin (Honda); 13. Rousseau (Kawasaki); 14. Destoop (Honda); 15. Fourcadet.

3rd October - Carole
1. Muscat (Ducati); 2. Muteau (Ducati); 3. Van Den Bossche -(Suzuki); 4. Paillot (Suzuki); 5. Stey (Honda); 6. Morillon- (Yamaha); 7. Destoop (Honda); 8. Rousseau (Kawasaki); 9. Giabbani-(Kawasaki); 10. Dobé (Suzuki).

Final classification

1. Eric Mahé	Yamaha	156 points
2. Arnaud Van Den Bossche	Suzuki	131
3. David Muscat	Ducati	111

4. S. Scarnato (Kawasaki), 96; 5. T. Paillot (Suzuki), 89; 6. L.Holon (Kawasaki), 86; 7. G. Muteau (Ducati), 82; 8. P. Dobé(Suzuki), 64; 9. D. Morillon (Yamaha), 62; 10. B. Stey (Honda),53.

△
Eric Mahé.

French Championship

Stocksport

Champion: Bernard Cazade. Born on 30th July 1967, in La Reole.
First race: 1987.
First GP: Japan 1992 (250).
Career highlights: 2nd French Kawasaki Cup in 1989; 61st Endurance FIM Cup, 3rd 250 French "national" Championship (Honda) in 1990; 31st 250 European Championship, 2nd 250 French Championship, 250 French "national" Champion (Honda) in 1991; 35th 250 IRTA ranking (Honda) in 1992; 4th 250 European Championship, 14th 250 Spanish "open" Championship, 250 French Champion (Honda) in 1993; 21st 250 European Championship (Honda) in 1994; 18th Endurance World Championship (Honda) in 1995; 43rd Endurance World Championship, 30th Thunderbike Trophy (Honda) in 1996; 25th Superbike French Championship (Honda) in 1997; 5th Superbike/Stockbike French Championship (Yamaha) in 1998; Stockbike French Champion, 4th Superbike French Championship (Yamaha) in 1999.

7th March - Le Mans
1. Foret (Yamaha); 2. Cazade (Yamaha); 3. Holon (Kawasaki); 4. -Ulmann (Kawasaki); 5. Sebileau (Kawasaki); 6. Nogueira- (Kawasaki); 7. Braut (Yamaha); 8. Bonhuil (Kawasaki); 9. Guinand- (Yamaha); 10. Neff (Yamaha); 11. Mouzin (Yamaha); 12. Bocquet -(Yamaha); 13. Crassous (Yamaha); 14. Jolivet (Kawasaki); 15.- Sevault (Yamaha).

28th March - Magny-Cours
1. Foret (Yamaha); 2. Ulmann (Kawasaki); 3. Sebileau (Kawasaki); -4. Moreira (Kawasaki); 5. Cazade (Yamaha); 6. Braut (Yamaha); 7.- Bonhuil (Kawasaki); 8. Mouzin (Yamaha); 9. Neff (Yamaha); 10.- Rogier (Yamaha); 11. Crassous (Yamaha); 12. Guinand (Yamaha); 13.-Di Marino (Yamaha); 14. Loustalet (Yamaha); 15. Bocquet (Yamaha).

18th April - Albi
1. Cazade (Yamaha); 2. Holon (Kawasaki); 3. Sebileau (Kawasaki);-4. Foret (Yamaha); 5. Ulmann (Kawasaki); 6. Guinand (Yamaha); 7. -Braut (Yamaha); 8. Bonhuil (Kawasaki); 9. Boutin (Yamaha); 10.-Ciciliani (Yamaha); 11. Bocquet (Yamaha); 12. Di Marino (Yamaha);-13. Herriberry (Yamaha); 14. Huvier (Yamaha); 15. Emonnet -(Yamaha).

25th April - Nogaro
1. Holon (Kawasaki); 2. Ulmann (Kawasaki); 3. Sebileau- (Kawasaki); 4. Cazade (Yamaha); 5. Foret (Yamaha); 6. Braut- (Yamaha); 7. Bonhuil (Kawasaki); 8. Crassous (Yamaha); 9. Mouzin -(Yamaha); 10. Guinand (Yamaha); 11. Boutin (Yamaha); 12. Beaumont -(Yamaha); 13. Bocquet (Yamaha); 14. Servol (Yamaha); 15. Di-Marino (Yamaha).

9th May - Carole

1. Cazade (Yamaha); 2. Holon (Kawasaki); 3. Ulmann (Kawasaki); 4.-Crassous (Yamaha); 5. Foret (Yamaha); 6. Neff (Yamaha); 7. -Nogueira (Suzuki); 8. Mouzin (Yamaha); 9. Servol (Yamaha); 10.- Boutin (Yamaha); 11. Bocquet (Yamaha); 12. Notte (Yamaha); 13. -Agogue (Yamaha); 14. Beaumont (Yamaha); 15. Roch (Yamaha).

16th May - Le Vigeant
1. Cazade (Yamaha); 2. Braut (Yamaha); 3. Foret (Yamaha); 4.-Sebileau (Kawasaki); 5. Neff (Yamaha); 6. Holon (Kawasaki); 7.-Ulmann (Kawasaki); 8. Guinand (Yamaha); 9. Bonhuil (Kawasaki);-10. Boutin (Yamaha); 11. Mouzin (Yamaha); 12. Di Marino (Yamaha);-13. Herriberry (Yamaha); 14. Notte (Yamaha); 15. Colaisseau- (Yamaha).

20th June - Lédenon
1. Holon (Kawasaki); 2. Cazade (Yamaha); 3. Foret (Yamaha); 4.-Neff (Yamaha); 5. Sebileau (Kawasaki); 6. Ulmann (Kawasaki); 7. -Bonhuil (Kawasaki); 8. Mouzin (Yamaha); 9. Boutin (Yamaha); 10.- Ciciliani (Yamaha); 11. Lacroix (Ducati). 11 finishers.

27th June - Le Castellet
1. Holon (Kawasaki); 2. Cazade (Yamaha); 3. Braut (Yamaha); 4.-Neff (Yamaha); 5. Bonhuil (Kawasaki); 6. Crassous (Yamaha); 7.-Foret (Yamaha); 8. Mouzin (Yamaha); 9. Loustalet; 10. Boutin-(Yamaha); 11. Ciciliani (Yamaha); 12. Colaisseau (Yamaha); 13. -Herriberry (Yamaha); 14. Lacroix (Ducati); 15. Martin.

3rd October - Carole
1. Sebileau (Yamaha); 2. Cazade (Yamaha); 3. Ulmann (Kawasaki); -4. Holon (Kawasaki); 5. Bonhuil (Kawasaki); 6. Foret (Yamaha).

Final classification

1. Bernard Cazade   Yamaha 161 points
2. Fabien Foret   Yamaha 120
3. Bertrand Sebileau   Kawasaki 110
4. O. Ulmann (Kawasaki), 104; 5. L. Holon (Kawasaki), 102.

Jean-Pierre Jeandat

▽

Superbike

Champion: Jéhan D'Orgeix. Born on 30th April 1963.
First GP: Spain, 1993 (500).
Career highlights: 2nd French Kawasaki Cup in 1990; 15th Endurance World Championship, 2nd Superbike French Championship (Kawasaki) in 1991; 21st Superbike World Championship, 4th Superbike French Championship (Kawasaki) in 1992; 16th 500 IRTA ranking (Yamaha) in 1993; 26th Endurance World Championship (Suzuki) in 1994; 5th Endurance World Championship, 6th Supersport European Championship, Supersport French Champion (Kawasaki) in 1995; 19th Endurance World Championship, 4th Supersport French Championship (Kawasaki) in 1996; 8th Endurance World Championship, Supersport French Champion, 19th Superbike French Championship (Kawasaki) in 1997; 5th Endurance World Championship, Supersport French Championship (Kawasaki) in 1998; Endurance World Championship, Superbike French Champion in 1999 (Suzuki).

7th March - Le Mans
1. D'Orgeix (Suzuki); 2. Scarnato (Kawasaki); 3. Jeandat (Honda);-4. Foret (Yamaha); 5. Protat (Ducati); 6. Cazade (Yamaha); 7. -Holon (Kawasaki); 8. Ulmann (Kawasaki); 9. Sebileau (Kawasaki);-10. Haquin (Kawasaki); 11. Nogueira (Kawasaki); 12. Braut -(Yamaha); 13. Bonhuil (Kawasaki); 14. Guinand (Yamaha); 15. Neff- (Yamaha).

28th March - Magny-Cours
1. D'Orgeix (Suzuki); 2. Delétang (Yamaha); 3. Protat (Ducati); -4. Foret (Yamaha); 5. Ulmann (Kawasaki); 6. Sebileau (Kawasaki);-7. Moreira (Kawasaki); 8. Cazade (Yamaha); 9. Braut (Yamaha); 10.-Bonhuil (Kawasaki); 11. Mouzin (Yamaha); 12. Neff (Yamaha); 13. -Rogier (Yamaha); 14. Crassous (Yamaha).

18th April - Albi
1. D'Orgeix (Suzuki); 2. Guyot (Kawasaki); 3. Cazade (Yamaha); 4.-Holon (Kawasaki); 5. Sebileau (Kawasaki); 6. Foret (Yamaha); 7.-Fernandez (Kawasaki); 8. Neff (Yamaha); 9. Ulmann (Kawasaki); 10.-Guinand (Yamaha); 11. Braut (Yamaha); 12. Bonhuil (Kawasaki); 13.Maisto (Ducati); 14. Boutin (Yamaha); 15. Ciciliani (Yamaha).

25th April - Nogaro
1. D'Orgeix (Suzuki); 2. Holon (Kawasaki); 3. Protat (Ducati); 4.-Fernandez (Kawasaki); 5. Ulmann (Kawasaki); 6. Sebileau-(Kawasaki); 7. Cazade (Yamaha); 8. Foret (Yamaha); 9. Braut- (Yamaha); 10. Guyot (Kawasaki); 11. Bonhuil (Kawasaki); 12. -Crassous (Yamaha); 13. Neff (Yamaha); 14. Marzloff (Kawasaki);-15. Mouzin (Yamaha).

9th May - Carole
1. Protat (Ducati); 2. D'Orgeix (Suzuki); 3. Cazade (Yamaha); 4.-Fernandez (Kawasaki); 5. Holon (Kawasaki); 6. Ulmann (Kawasaki); -7. Braut (Yamaha); 8. Sebileau (Kawasaki);-10. Crassous (Yamaha); 11. Foret (Yamaha); 12. Neff (Yamaha); 13. Nogueira (Suzuki); 14. Mouzin (Yamaha); 15. Guinand (Yamaha).

16th May - Le Vigeant
1. Protat (Ducati); 2. D'Orgeix (Suzuki); 3. Cazade (Yamaha); 4.-Braut (Yamaha); 5. Foret (Yamaha); 6. Sebileau (Kawasaki); 7.-Neff (Yamaha); 8. Holon (Kawasaki); 9. Mulot (Ducati); 10. Ulmann-(Kawasaki); 11. Guinand (Yamaha); 12. Bonhuil (Kawasaki); 13.- Boutin (Yamaha); 14. Mouzin (Yamaha); 15. Di Marino (Yamaha).

20th June - Lédenon
1. Protat (Ducati); 2. D'Orgeix (Suzuki); 3. Holon (Kawasaki); 4. -Mulot (Ducati); 5. Cazade (Yamaha); 6. Foret (Yamaha); 7. Neff -(Yamaha); 8. Fernandez (Kawasaki); 9. Sebileau (Kawasaki); 10.-Ulmann (Kawasaki); 11. Bonhuil (Kawasaki); 12. Mouzin (Yamaha);-13. Boutin (Yamaha); 14. Ciciliani (Yamaha); 15. Lacroix-(Yamaha).

27th June - Le Castellet
1. Delétang (Yamaha); 2. D'Orgeix (Suzuki); 3. Holon (Kawasaki);-4. Mulot (Ducati); 5. Cazade (Yamaha); 6. Braut (Yamaha); 7. Neff -(Yamaha); 8. Fernandez (Kawasaki); 9. Bonhuil (Kawasaki); 10.- Crassous (Yamaha); 11. Foret (Yamaha); 12. Mouzin (Yamaha); 13.Marzloff (Kawasaki); 14. Loustalet; 15. Boutin (Yamaha).

3rd October - Carole
1. D'Orgeix (Suzuki); 2. Fernandez (Kawasaki); 3. Moreira -(Kawasaki); 4. Cazade (Yamaha); 5. Ulmann (Kawasaki); 6. Holon- (Kawasaki); 7. D'Orgeix (Suzuki); 8. Nogueira (Suzuki); 9.-Bonhuil (Kawasaki); 10. Foret (Yamaha).

Final classification

1. Jéhan D'Orgeix — Suzuki — 160 points
2. Frédéric Protat — Ducati — 118
3. Ludovic Holon — Kawasaki — 95
4. B. Cazade (Yamaha), 93; 5. B. Sebileau (Kawasaki), 80; 6.Fernandez (Kawasaki), 71; 7. Foret (Yamaha), 71; 8. Ulmann(Kawasaki), 64; 9. Braut (Yamaha), 55; 10. Delétang (Yamaha).

△
Jéhan D'Orgeix.

Side-cars

Champions: Hansen/Soares (LCR-Suzuki).

7th March - Le Mans
1. Tuauden/Gougaud (LCR-Suzuki); 2. Hansen/Soares (LCR-Suzuki);-3. Pirroutet/Greffet (LCR-Suzuki); 4. Joron/Virey (LCR-Suzuki); 5.-Le Bail/Gouger (Auto-Moto); 6. Mercier/Gelot (LCR-Suzuki); 7.-Delannoy/Renoud Grapin (Pascut); 8. Lambert/Vannier (Seymaz); 9. Morio/Jehanno (Seymaz); 10. Puissant/Bizette (Honda); 11.-Hachet/Trigent (Yamaha); 12. Martin/Brunet (LCR-Suzuki); 13. -J.-C. Voilque/M. Voilque (Suzuki); 14. Babin/Babin(Seymaz-Suzuki). 14 finishers.

28th March - Magny-Cours
1. Hansen/Soares (LCR-Suzuki); 2. Joron/Virey (LCR-Suzuki); 3. -Pirroutet/Greffet (LCR-Suzuki); 4. Le Bail/Gouger (Auto-Moto); 5.-Heriot/S. Voilque (LCR-Suzuki); 6. Michon/Sicard (LCR-Suzuki); 7.- Mercier/Gelot (LCR-Suzuki); 8. Delannoy/Renoud Grapin (Pascut);-9. J.-C. Voilque/M. Voilque (Suzuki); 10. Niogret/Goncalves-(LCR); 11. Martin/Brunet (LCR-Suzuki); 12. Babin/Babin-(Seymaz-Suzuki); 13. Pilatt/Perion (LCR-Suzuki); 14.-Peugeot/Peugeot (Suzuki). 14 finishers.

18th April - Albi
1. Hansen/Soares (LCR-Suzuki); 2. Le Bail/Gouger (Auto-Moto) 3.-Heriot/S. Voilque (LCR-Suzuki); 4. Joron/Virey (LCR-Suzuki); 5.-Michon/Sicard (LCR-Suzuki); 6. Lacroix/Michel (LCR-Honda); 7.-J.-C. Voilque/M. Voilque (Suzuki); 8. Brunzazzi/Berger-(Bellasi-Suzuki); 9. Guigue/Legrand (LCR-Suzuki); 10.-Niogret/Goncalves (LCR). 10 finishers.

25th April - Nogaro
1. Hansen/Soares (LCR-Suzuki); 2. Heriot/S. Voilque (LCR-Suzuki);-3. Joron/Virey (LCR-Suzuki); 4. Le Bail/Gouger (Auto-Moto); 5.-Michon/Sicard (LCR-Suzuki); 6. Niogret/Goncalves (LCR); 7. J.-C.-Voilque/M. Voilque (Suzuki); 8. Lambert/Vannier (Seymaz); 9.- Dureau/Roux (Seymaz-Suzuki); 10. Guigue/Legrand (LCR-Suzuki); 11.-Martin/Brunet (LCR-Suzuki); 12. Coulaud/Dupuis (Seymaz). 12- finishers.

9th May - Carole
1. Hansen/Soares (LCR-Suzuki); 2. Tuauden/Gougaud (LCR-Suzuki);-3. Heriot/S. Voilque (LCR-Suzuki); 4. Joron/Virey (LCR-Suzuki);-5. Michon/Sicard (LCR-Suzuki); 6. Le Bail/Gouger (Auto-Moto); 7.-Niogret/Goncalves (LCR); 8. Mercier/Gelot (LCR-Suzuki); 9. Lambert/Vannier (Seymaz); 10. Montagnier/Poitou (Kawasaki); 11.-Artman-Guérin/Bertex (LCR-Suzuki); 12. J.-C. Voilque/M. Voilque-(Suzuki); 13. Delannoy/Renoud Grapin (Pascut); 14. Martin/Brunet-(LCR-Suzuki); 15. Puisant/Bizette (Honda).

16th May - Le Vigeant
1. Hansen/Soares (LCR-Suzuki); 2. Joron/Virey (LCR-Suzuki); 3. -Heriot/S. Voilque (LCR-Suzuki); 4. Michon/Sicard (LCR-Suzuki); 5.-Delannoy/Renoud Grapin (Pascut); 6. Lambert/Vannier (Seymaz); 7.-Morio/Jehanno (Seymaz); 8. Martin/Brunet (LCR-Suzuki); 9.Puissant/Bizette (Honda); 10. Guigue/Legrand (LCR-Suzuki); 11.-Dureau/Roux (Seymaz-Suzuki); 12. Coulaud/Dupuis (Seymaz); 13.-Tuauden/Gougaud (LCR-Suzuki). 13 finishers.

20th June - Lédenon
1. Michon/Sicard (LCR-Suzuki); 2. Niogret/Goncalves (LCR); 3.-Delannoy/Renoud Grapin (Pascut); 4. Guigue/Legrand (LCR-Suzuki); -5. Brunzazzi/Berger (Bellasi-Suzuki); 6. Martin/Brunet-(LCR-Suzuki); 7. Lambert/Vannier (Seymaz); 8. Montagnier/Poitou-(Kawasaki). 8 finishers.

27th June - Le Castellet
1. Hansen/Soares (LCR-Suzuki); 2. Lambert/Vannier (Seymaz); 3. - Minguet/Babin; 4. Joron/Virey (LCR-Suzuki); 5. Niogret/Goncalves (LCR); 6. Michon/Sicard (LCR-Suzuki); 7. Delannoy/Renoud Grapin-(Pascut); 8. Guigue/Legrand (LCR-Suzuki); 9. Martin/Brunet-(LCR-Suzuki). 9 finishers.

3rd October - Carole
1. Hansen/Soares (LCR-Suzuki); 2. Joron/Virey (LCR-Suzuki); 3. -Michon/Sicard (LCR-Suzuki); 4. Le Bail/Gouger (Auto-Moto); 5.-Lambert/Carr_re (Seymaz); 6. Baer/Portal; 7. Mercier/Thomassier (LCR-Suzuki); 8. Minguet/Babin; 9.-Delannoy/Coulaud (Pascut); 10. Niogret/Goncalves (LCR).

Final classification

1. Hansen/Soares — LCR-Suzuki — 175 points
2. Joron/Virey — LCR-Suzuki — 115
3. Michon/Sicard — LCR-Suzuki — 92
4. Le Bail/Gouger (Auto-Moto), 80; 5. Heriot/Voilque(LCR-Suzuki), 79; 6. Lambert/Vannier/Carrère (Seymaz), 73; 7.Niogret/Goncalvez (LCR), 65; 8. Delannoy/Renoud Grapin/Coulaud(Pascut), 61; 9. Tuauden/Gougaud (LCR-Suzuki), 48; 10.Martin/Brunet (LCR-Suzuki), 41.

125 cc

The champion: Darren Barton (Honda). Born on 12th November 1974, in Blackburn. First race: 1992. First GP: Great Britain, 1994 (125).
Career highlights: 7th 125 British Championship in 1994; 21st 125 World Championship, 30th 125 Spanish open Championship, 125 British Champion (Yamaha) in 1995; 22nd 125 World Championship (Aprilia) in 1996; 29th 125 World Championship (Honda) in 1997; 9th 125 British Championship (Honda) in 1998; 125 British Champion (Honda) in 1999.

28th March - Brands Hatch
1. Jennings (Honda); 2. Patrickson (Honda); 3. Barton (Honda); 4. Green (Honda); 5. Palmer (Honda); 6. Morris (Honda); 7. Pearson (Honda); 8. Notman (Honda); 9. Mateer (Honda); 10. Tibble (Honda); 11. P. Robinson (Honda); 12. L. Haslam (Honda); 13. Davies (Honda); 14. Gray (Honda); 15. Owens (Honda).

5th April - Thruxton
1. Jennings (Honda); 2. Green (Honda); 3. Barton (Honda); 4. Patrickson (Honda); 5. Lougher (Honda); 6. Ford-Dunn (Honda); 7. L. Haslam (Honda); 8. Palmer (Honda); 9. Tibble (Honda); 10. P. Robinson (Honda); 11. Morris (Honda); 12. Pearson (Honda); 13. Notman (Honda); 14. Goodall (Honda); 15. Sawford (Honda).

25th April - Oulton Park
1. Barton (Honda); 2. Patrickson (Honda); 3. Jennings (Honda); 4. L. Haslam (Honda); 5. Green (Honda); 6. Lougher (Honda); 7. Palmer (Honda); 8. Goodall (Honda); 9. Morris (Honda); 10. Tibble (Honda); 11. Burns (Honda); 12. Wilcox (Honda); 13. Owens (Honda); 14. P. Robinson (Honda); 15. Sawford (Honda).

9th May - Snetterton
1. Patrickson (Honda); 2. Green (Honda); 3. L. Haslam (Honda); 4. Jennings (Honda); 5. Burns (Honda); 6. Ford-Dunn (Honda); 7. Morris (Honda); 8. Notman (Honda); 9. Robinson (Honda); 10. Pearson (Honda); 11. Davies (Honda); 12. Topham (Honda); 13. Sawford (Honda); 14. Laverty (Honda); 15. Gray (Honda).

31st May - Donington Park
1. Burns (Honda); 2. Barton (Honda); 3. Patrickson (Honda); 4. Jennings (Honda); 5. L. Haslam (Honda); 6. Ford-Dunn (Honda); 7. Green (Honda); 8. Falls (Honda); 9. K. Robinson (Honda); 10. Morris (Honda); 11. Goodall (Honda); 12. Gray (Honda); 13. Mateer (Honda); 14. Sproston (Honda); 15. Notman (Honda).

20th June - Silverstone
1. L. Haslam (Honda); 2. Barton (Honda); 3. Patrickson (Honda); 4. P. Robinson (Honda); 5. Jennings (Honda); 6. Goodall (Honda); 7. Palmer (Honda); 8. K. Robinson (Honda); 9. Morris (Honda); 10. Wilcox (Honda); 11. Ford-Dunn (Honda); 12. Sproston (Honda); 13. Pearson (Honda); 14. Davies (Honda); 15. Mateer (Honda).

18th July - Oulton Park
1. Green (Honda); 2. L. Haslam (Honda); 3. Barton (Honda); 4. Burns (Honda); 5. Patrickson (Honda); 6. K. Robinson (Honda); 7. Disalvo (Honda); 8. Goodall (Honda); 9. Laverty (Honda); 10. Lougher (Honda); 11. Pearson (Honda); 12. Sproston (Honda); 13. Owens (Honda); 14. Norman (Honda); 15. Saxelby (Honda).

8th August - Knockhill
1. Burns (Honda); 2. Barton (Honda); 3. Green (Honda); 4. Patrickson (Honda); 5. Goodall (Honda); 6. K. Robinson (Honda); 7. L. Haslam (Honda); 8. Palmer (Honda); 9. Ford-Dunn (Honda); 10. P. Robinson (Honda); 11. Laverty (Honda); 12. Mateer (Honda); 13. Morris (Honda); 14. Elkin (Honda); 15. Tibble (Honda).

15th August - Mallory Park
1. Burns (Honda); 2. L. Haslam (Honda); 3. Patrickson (Honda); 4. Ford-Dunn (Honda); 5. Goodall (Honda); 6. Palmer (Honda); 7. Laverty (Honda); 8. K. Robinson (Honda); 9. Barton (Honda); 10. Elkin (Honda); 11. Sproston (Honda); 12. Mateer (Honda); 13. P. Robinson (Honda); 14. Davies (Honda); 15. Saxelby (Honda).

30th August - Cadwell Park
1. Barton (Honda); 2. Green (Honda); 3. Burns (Honda); 4. Patrickson (Honda); 5. Tibble (Honda); 6. Goodall (Honda); 7. Elkin (Honda); 8. K. Robinson (Honda); 9. Ford-Dunn (Honda); 10. L. Haslam (Honda); 11. Palmer (Honda); 12. Morris (Honda); 13. Topham (Honda); 14. Pearson (Honda); 15. Sproston (Honda).

19th September - Brands Hatch
1. Burns (Honda); 2. Barton (Honda); 3. Green (Honda); 4. Patrickson (Honda); 5. Jennings (Honda); 6. Tibble (Honda); 7. Goodall (Honda); 8. Falls (Honda); 9. Elkin (Honda); 10. Ford-Dunn (Honda); 11. Palmer (Honda); 12. Lougher (Honda); 13. K. Robinson (Honda); 14. Topham (Honda); 15. P. Robinson (Honda).

26th September - Donington Park
1. Tibble (Honda); 2. Barton (Honda); 3. Patrickson (Honda); 4. L. Haslam (Honda); 5. Ford-Dunn (Honda); 6. P. Robinson (Honda); 7. Martin (Honda); 8. Lougher (Honda); 9. Palmer (Honda); 10. K. Robinson (Honda); 11. Saxelby (Honda); 12. Lindsay (Honda); 13. R. Haslam (Honda); 14. Laverty (Honda); 15. Murphy (Honda).

Final classification

1. Darren Barton	Honda	205
2. Steve Patrickson	Honda	192
3. Alan Green	Honda	150

4. C. Burns (Honda), 145; 5. L. Haslam (Honda), 142; 6. P. Jennings (Honda), 103; 7. M. Ford-Dunn (Honda), 80; 8. J. Goodall (Honda), 75; 9. C. Palmer (Honda), 73; 10. K. Tibble (Honda), 67; 11. K. Robinson (Honda), 61; 12. P. Robinson (Honda), 54; 13. G. Morris (Honda), 51; 14. I. Lougher (Honda), 40; 15. J. Pearson (Honda), 29; 16. C. Elkin (Honda), 25; 17. M. Laverty (Honda), 25; 18. A. Notman (Honda), 22; 19. D. Mateer (Honda), 19; 20. J. Falls (Honda), 17; 21. C. Sproston (Honda), 16; 22. M. Davies (Honda), 12; 23. M. Wilcox (Honda), 10; 24. C. Topham (Honda), 10; 25. C. Martin (Honda), 9; 26. J. Disalvo (Honda), 9; 27. R. Saxelby (Honda), 8; 28. C. Gray (Honda), 7; 29. R. Haslam (Honda), 7; 30. S. Owens (Honda), 7; 31. A. Sawford (Honda), 5; 32. D. Lindsay (Honda), 4; 33. D. Murphy (Honda), 1. 33 finishers.

250 cc

The champion: John McGuiness. Born on 16th April 1972, in Morecambe. First race: 1991. First GP: Great Britain, 1997 (250).
Career highlights: ACU Clubmans Champion (Kawasaki) in 1991; 10th 250 British Championship (Honda) 1996; 35th 250 World Championship (Aprilia) in 1997; 4th 250 British Championship, 29th 500 World Championship (Honda) in 1998; 250 British Champion (Honda) in 1999.

28th March - Brands Hatch
1. J. Robinson (Honda); 2. McGuiness (Honda); 3. S. Sawford (Aprilia); 4. A. Coates (Honda); 5. L. Jackson (Honda); 6. Stead (Honda); 7. Edwards (TSR-Honda); 8. May (Aprilia); 9. Lee (Yamaha); 10. Jones (Honda); 11. Bennett (Honda); 12. Nutt (Honda); 13. Clarke (Honda); 14. Hopper (Honda); 15. G. Haslam (Honda).

5th April - Thruxton
1. Norval (SA, Honda); 2. McGuiness (Honda); 3. J. Robinson (Honda); 4. Lee (Yamaha); 5. G. Haslam (Honda); 6. L. Jackson (Honda); 7. G. Jackson (Honda); 8. May (Aprilia); 9. Davis (Honda); 10. Payten (AUS, Honda); 11. Hutchinson (Honda); 12. Tunstall (Honda); 13. Stead (Honda); 14. Bennett (Honda); 15. S. Sawford (Aprilia).

25th April - Oulton Park
1. McGuiness (Honda); 2. Norval (SA, Honda); 3. J. Robinson (Honda); 4. Jones (Honda); 5. A. Coates (Honda); 6. G. Haslam (Honda); 7. Clarke (Honda); 8. May (Aprilia); 9. Tunstall (Honda); 10. Lee (Yamaha); 11. L. Jackson (Honda); 12. Stead (Honda); 13. Hincks (Honda); 14. Summerfield (Honda); 15. Thompson (Honda).

9th May - Snetterton
1. J. Robinson (Honda); 2. McGuiness (Honda); 3. Norval (SA, Honda); 4. A. Coates (Honda); 5. G. Haslam (Honda); 6. Lee (Yamaha); 7. Sawford (Aprilia); 8. Clarke (Honda); 9. Jackson (Honda); 10. Thompson (Honda); 11. Hopper (Honda); 12. Swain (Honda); 13. Marshall (Honda); 14. Grinling (Honda); 15. Thomas (Honda).

31st May - Donington Park
1. A. Coates (Honda); 2. McGuiness (Honda); 3. Norval (SA, Honda); 4. Clarke (Honda); 5. L. Jackson (Honda); 6. Tunstall (Honda); 7. G. Haslam (Honda); 8. Levy (Honda); 9. Thompson (Honda); 10. Marshall (Honda); 11. Swain (Honda); 12. Edwards (Honda); 13. May (Aprilia); 14. Bennett (Honda); 15. Nutt (Honda).

20th June - Silverstone
1. Norval (SA, Honda); 2. McGuiness (Honda); 3. Sawford (Aprilia); 4. Jones (Honda); 5. Clarke (Honda); 6. Thompson (Honda); 7. L. Jackson (Honda); 8. G. Haslam (Honda); 9. Lee (Yamaha); 10. Thomas (Honda); 11. Swain (Honda); 12. G. Jackson (Honda); 13. Hutchinson (Honda); 14. Summerfield (Honda); 15. Cowie (Honda).

18th July - Oulton Park
1. A. Coates (Honda); 2. L. Jackson (Honda); 3. McGuiness (Honda); 4. Jones (Honda); 5. Davis (Honda); 6. Sawford (Aprilia); 7. Clarke (Honda); 8. Tunstall (Honda); 9. May (Aprilia); 10. Thompson (Honda); 11. Bennett (Honda); 12. Ellison (Honda); 13. Walker (Aprilia); 14. Bishop (Honda); 15. Swain (Honda).

8th August - Knockhill
1. J. Robinson (Honda); 2. A. Coates (Honda); 3. McGuiness (Honda); 4. Smart (Aprilia); 5. Sawford (Aprilia); 6. Clarke (Honda); 7. Davis (Honda); 8. L. Jackson (Honda); 9. Thompson (Honda); 10. Norval (SA, Honda); 11. G. Haslam (Honda); 12. G. Jackson (Honda); 13. Ellison (Honda); 14. Bennett (Honda); 15. Tunstall (Honda).

15th August - Mallory Park
1. J. Robinson (Honda); 2. A. Coates (Honda); 3. McGuiness (Honda); 4. Jones (Honda); 5. Davis (Honda); 6. G. Jackson (Honda); 7. G. Haslam (Honda); 8. Tunstall (Honda); 9. Ellison (Honda); 10. Johnson (Honda); 11. Thompson (Honda); 12. Sawford (Aprilia); 13. Levy (Honda); 14. Clarke (Honda); 15. Swain (Honda).

30th August - Cadwell Park
1. J. Robinson (Honda); 2. McGuiness (Honda); 3. Jones (Honda); 4. G. Haslam (Honda); 5. Clarke (Honda); 6. Ellison (Honda); 7. A. Coates (Honda); 8. Sawford (Aprilia); 9. Tunstall (Honda); 10. Gourlay (Honda); 11. Bennett (Honda); 12. May (Aprilia); 13. Herzburg (Yamaha); 14. Walker (Aprilia); 15. English (Honda).

19th September - Brands Hatch
1. J. Robinson (Honda); 2. McGuiness (Honda); 3. A. Coates (Honda); 4. G. Haslam (Honda); 5. Ellison (Honda); 6. Clarke (Honda); 7. Jones (Honda); 8. Tunstall (Honda); 9. Edwards (TSR-Honda); 10. M. Coates (Honda); 11. Gourlay (Honda); 12. Ramsay (Honda); 13. G. Jackson (Honda); 14. Bishop (Honda); 15. Levy (Honda).

26th September - Donington Park
1. McGuiness (Honda); 2. Jones (Honda); 3. A. Coates (Honda); 4. Ellison (Honda); 5. Clarke (Honda); 6. Ramsay (Honda); 7. Gourlay (Honda); 8. Bennett (Honda); 9. G. Jackson (Honda); 10. Levy (Honda); 11. Tunstall (Honda); 12. Walker (Aprilia); 13. Nutt (Honda); 14. Brown (Honda); 15. Bishop (Honda).

Final classification

1. John McGuiness	Honda	238
2. Jamie Robinson	Honda	182
3. Adrian Coates	Honda	168

4. S. Norval (SA, Honda), 108; 5. P. Jones (Honda), 103; 6. A. Clarke (Honda), 97; 7. G. Haslam (Honda), 90; 8. S. Sawford (Aprilia), 75; 9. L. Jackson (Honda), 74; 10. T. Tunstall (Honda), 58; 11. D. Ellison (Honda), 48; 12. G. Jackson (Honda), 44; 13. G. Lee (Yamaha), 43; 14. S. Thompson (Honda), 42; 15. J. Davis (Honda), 38; 16. G. May (Aprilia), 38; 17. I. Bennett (Honda), 29; 18. S. Edwards (TSR-Honda), 20; 19. L. Gourlay (Honda), 20; 20. T. Levy (Honda), 18; 21. P. Stead (Honda), 17; 22. F. Swain (Honda), 16; 23. C. Ramsay (Honda), 14; 24. S. Smart (Aprilia), 13; 25. A. Marshall (Honda), 9; 26. M. Walker (Aprilia), 9; 27. A. Hutchinson (Honda), 8; 28. M. Nutt (Honda), 8; 29. D. Thomas (Honda), 7; 30. L. Hopper (Honda), 7; 31. M. Coates (Honda), 6; 32. D. Johnson (Honda), 6; 33. M. Payten (AUS, Honda), 6; 34. C. Bishop (Honda), 5; 35. S. Summerfield (Honda), 4; 36. M. Herzburg (Yamaha), 3; 37. H. Hincks (Honda), 3; 38. S. Brown (Honda), 2; 39. R. Grinling (Honda), 2; 40. G. English (Honda), 1; 41. D. Cowie (Honda), 1. 41 finishers.

Supersport

The champion: John Crawford (Suzuki). Born on 18th February 1969, in Coatbridge. First race: 1988.
Career highlights: 2nd Scottish Open Championship (Suzuki) in 1989; 600 Scottish Champion (Yamaha) in 1990; 2nd Scottish Regal Championship in 1994; 42nd Thunderbike Trophy, 5th Supersport British Championship (Honda) in 1995; 4th Supersport British Championship (Kawasaki) in 1996; 4th Supersport British Championship (Suzuki) in 1997; Supersport British Champion (Suzuki) in 1998; 32nd Supersport World Championship, Supersport British Champion (Suzuki) in 1999.

28th March - Brands Hatch
1. Plater (Honda); 2. Muggeridge (AUS, Honda); 3. Crawford (Suzuki); 4. Moodie (Honda); 5. Pallot (Honda); 6. Simpson (Honda); 7. Thomas (Yamaha); 8. Richards (Yamaha); 9. Frost (Honda); 10. Mendes (Yamaha); 11. Coulter (IRL, Honda); 12. K. Harris (Suzuki); 13. McCallen (Yamaha); 14. Wickens (Yamaha); 15. Ramsay (Honda).

5th April - Thruxton
1. Crawford (Suzuki); 2. Plater (Honda); 3. Thomas (Yamaha); 4. Muggeridge (AUS, Honda); 5. Moodie (Honda); 6. Simpson (Honda); 7. Richards (Yamaha); 8. Horner (Honda); 9. Coulter (IRL, Honda); 10. Graves (Yamaha); 11. Pallott (Honda); 12. K. Harris (Suzuki); 13. Chapman (Suzuki); 14. Byrne (Honda); 15. McCallen (Yamaha).

25th April - Oulton Park
1. Crawford (Suzuki); 2. Moodie (Honda); 3. Brown (Honda); 4. Simpson (Honda); 5. Wickens (Yamaha); 6. K. Harris (Suzuki); 7. McCallen (Yamaha); 8. Richards (Yamaha); 9. Plater (Honda); 10. Mendes (Yamaha); 11. Byrne (Honda); 12. Borley (Honda); 13. Graves (Yamaha); 14. Pallott (Honda); 15. Ramsay (Honda).

9th May - Snetterton
1. Crawford (Suzuki); 2. Frost (Honda); 3. Moodie (Honda); 4. Plater (Honda); 5. Muggeridge (AUS, Honda); 6. Thomas (Yamaha); 7. Borley (Honda); 8. Nowland (Honda); 9. Smith (Kawasaki); 10. Pallott (Honda); 11. K. Harris (Suzuki); 12. Crockford (Suzuki); 13. Quigley (Suzuki); 14. Chapman (Suzuki); 15. Horner (Honda).

31st May - Donington Park
1. Crawford (Suzuki); 2. Plater (Honda); 3. Thomas (Yamaha); 4. Moodie (Honda); 5. Richards (Yamaha); 6. Brown (Honda); 7. Nowland (Honda); 8. Horner (Honda); 9. Borley (Honda); 10. Wickens (Yamaha); 11. Morley (Suzuki); 12. Pallott (Honda); 13. Jennings (Honda); 14. Chapman (Suzuki); 15. Tinsley (Honda).

20th June - Silverstone
1. Moodie (Honda); 2. Richards (Yamaha); 3. Brown (Honda); 4. Muggeridge (AUS, Honda); 5. Morley (Suzuki); 6. Borley (Honda); 7. Crawford (Suzuki); 8. Graves (Yamaha); 9. K. Harris (Suzuki); 10. Tinsley (Honda); 11. Wickens (Yamaha); 12. Pallott (Honda); 13. Plater (Honda); 14. Jennings (Honda); 15. Ramsay (Honda).

18th July - Oulton Park
1. Crawford (Suzuki); 2. Moodie (Honda); 3. K. Harris (Suzuki); 4. Plater (Honda); 5. Richards (Yamaha); 6. Thomas (Yamaha); 7. Borley (Honda); 8. Wickens (Yamaha); 9. Muggeridge (AUS, Honda); 10. Pallott (Honda); 11. Ellison (Honda); 12. Crockford (Suzuki); 13. Brogan (Suzuki); 14. Mendes (Yamaha); 15. Graves (Yamaha).

8th August - Knockhill
1. Moodie (Honda); 2. Crawford (Suzuki); 3. Plater (Honda); 4. Richards (Yamaha); 5. Muggeridge (AUS, Honda); 6. Brown (Honda); 7. Borley (Honda); 8. Thomas (Yamaha); 9. Graves (Yamaha); 10. Coulter (IRL, Yamaha); 11. Jennings (Honda); 12. K. Harris (Suzuki); 13. Horner (Honda); 14. Ramsay (Honda); 15. Brogan (Honda).

15th August - Mallory Park
1. Plater (Honda); 2. Muggeridge (AUS, Honda); 3. Crawford (Suzuki); 4. Moodie (Honda); 5. Richards (Yamaha); 6. Byrne (Honda); 7. Nowland (Honda); 8. Coulter (IRL, Yamaha); 9. K. Harris (Suzuki); 10. Graves (Yamaha); 11. Borley (Honda); 12. Wickens (Yamaha); 13. Horner (Honda); 14. Brogan (Honda); 15. Ellison (Honda).

30th August - Cadwell Park
1. Plater (Honda); 2. Crawford (Suzuki); 3. Muggeridge (AUS, Honda); 4. Moodie (Honda); 5. Richards (Yamaha); 6. Thomas (Yamaha); 7. Wickens (Yamaha); 8. Borley (Honda); 9. Brown (Honda); 10. Horner (Honda); 11. Tinsley (Honda); 12. Whitby (Honda); 13. Jennings (Honda); 14. Nowland (Honda); 15. Johnson (Honda).

19th September - Brands Hatch
1. Moodie (Honda); 2. Crawford (Suzuki); 3. Plater (Honda); 4. Coulter (IRL, Yamaha); 5. Borley (Honda); 6. Muggeridge (AUS, Honda); 7. Brown (Honda); 8. Thomas (Yamaha); 9. Richards (Yamaha); 10. Whitby (Honda); 11. Sebileau (F, Honda); 12. Tinsley (Honda); 13. Stroud (NZ, Kawasaki); 14. Beaumont (Honda); 15. Crockford (Suzuki).

26th September - Donington Park
1. Plater (Honda); 2. Muggeridge (AUS, Honda); 3. Crawford (Suzuki); 4. Jefferies (Yamaha); 5. Thomas (Yamaha); 6. Coulter (IRL, Yamaha); 7. Borley (Honda); 8. Wickens (Yamaha); 9. Whitby (Honda); 10. Nowland (Honda); 11. Tinsley (Honda); 12. Crockford (Suzuki); 13. Brogan (Honda); 14. Breslin (Honda); 15. Horner (Honda).

Final classification

1. John Crawford	Suzuki	242
2. Steve Plater	Honda	208
3. Jim Moodie	Honda	194

4. K. Muggeridge (AUS, Honda), 141; 5. G. Richards (Yamaha), 109; 6. D. Thomas (Yamaha), 98; 7. P. Borley (Honda), 81; 8. P. Brown (Honda), 68; 9. S. Wickens (Yamaha), 53; 10. K. Harris (Suzuki), 52; 11. W. Coulter (IRL, Honda/Yamaha), 49; 12. A. Pallott (Honda), 38; 13. W. Nowland (Honda), 34; 14. I. Simpson (Honda), 33; 15. P. Graves (Yamaha), 31; 16. M. Horner (Honda), 31; 17. R. Frost (Honda), 27; 18. A. Tinsley (Honda), 22; 19. S. Byrne (Honda), 17; 20. H. Whitby (Honda), 17; 21. J. Morley (Suzuki), 16; 22. F. Mendes (Yamaha), 14; 23. J. Crockford (Suzuki), 14; 24. D. Jefferies (Yamaha), 13; 25. P. McCallen (Yamaha), 13; 26. P. Jennings (Honda), 13; 27. S. Brogan (Honda), 9; 28. J. Chapman (Suzuki), 8; 29. S. Smith (Kawasaki), 7; 30. J. Ellison (Honda), 6; 31. B. Sebileau (F, Honda), 5; 32. C. Ramsay (Honda), 5; 33. L. Quigley (Suzuki), 4; 34. A. Stroud (NZ, Kawasaki), 3; 35. D. Beaumont (Honda), 2; 36. P. Breslin (Honda), 2; 37. D. Johnson (Honda), 1. 37 finishers.

Superbike

The champion: Troy Bayliss (AUS, Ducati). Born on 30th March 1969, in Taree/New South Wales. First GP: Australia, 1997 (250).
Career highlights: 6th Supersport 600 Australian Championship in 1993; 6th Supersport 600 Australian Championship in 1994; 2nd Supersport 600 Australian Championship in 1995; 2nd "2+4" Superbike Australian Championship, 3rd "Shell" Superbike Australian Championship in 1996; 27th 250 World Championship, 20th Superbike World Championship, 2nd "2+4" Superbike Australian Championship, 2nd "Shell" Superbike Australian Championship (Suzuki) in 1997; 40th Superbike World Championship, 8th Superbike British Championship (Ducati) in 1998; Superbike British Champion (Ducati) in 1999.

28th March - Brands Hatch
Race I: 1. Hodgson (Ducati); 2. Walker (Kawasaki); 3. Reynolds (Ducati); 4. Bayliss (AUS, Ducati); 5. Haydon (Suzuki); 6. Emmett (Ducati); 7. MacKenzie (Yamaha); 8. Hislop (Kawasaki); 9. Young (Yamaha); 10. Heal (Kawasaki); 11. Wood (Kawasaki); 12. Craggill (AUS, Suzuki); 13. Giles (Kawasaki); 14. Ashton (Yamaha); 15. Bailey (Suzuki).
Race II: 1. Haydon (Suzuki); 2. Walker (Kawasaki); 3. Hodgson (Ducati); 4. Reynolds (Ducati); 5. Emmett (Ducati); 6. Hislop (Kawasaki); 7. Bayliss (AUS, Ducati); 8. Young (Yamaha); 9. Heal (Kawasaki); 10. Craggill (AUS, Suzuki); 11. Wood (Kawasaki); 12. Giles (Kawasaki); 13. Ashton (Yamaha); 14. Smith (Yamaha); 15. Nottingham (Yamaha).

5th April - Thruxton
Race I: Race I: 1. Bayliss (AUS, Ducati); 2. Haydon (Suzuki); 3. Walker (Kawasaki); 4. Hislop (Kawasaki); 5. Reynolds (Ducati); 6. Emmett (Ducati); 7. Young (Yamaha); 8. Wood (Kawasaki); 9. Craggill (AUS, Suzuki); 10. Crockford (Kawasaki); 11. Sampson (Yamaha); 12. Hodson (Kawasaki); 13. Jones (Kawasaki); 14. Nottingham (Yamaha); 15. Hipwell (Suzuki).
Race II: 1. Haydon (Suzuki); 2. Walker (Kawasaki); 3. Bayliss (AUS, Ducati); 4. Hislop (Kawasaki); 5. Hodgson (Ducati); 6. MacKenzie (Yamaha); 7. Young (Yamaha); 8. Wood (Kawasaki); 9. Craggill (AUS, Suzuki); 10. Sampson (Yamaha); 11. Giles (Kawasaki); 12. Jones (Kawasaki); 13. Smith (Yamaha); 14. Hodson (Kawasaki); 15. D. Harris (Yamaha).

25th April - Oulton Park
Race I: 1. Bayliss (AUS, Ducati); 2. Emmett (Ducati); 3. Walker (Kawasaki); 4. Hodgson (Ducati); 5. MacKenzie (Yamaha); 6. Craggill (AUS, Suzuki); 7. Hislop (Kawasaki); 8. Young (Yamaha); 9. Giles (Kawasaki); 10. Wood (Kawasaki); 11. Heal (Kawasaki); 12. Sampson (Yamaha); 13. Ashton (Yamaha); 14. Nottingham (Yamaha); 15. Hodson (Kawasaki).
Race II: 1. Bayliss (AUS, Ducati); 2. Haydon (Suzuki); 3. Reynolds (Ducati); 4. Walker (Kawasaki); 5. Hodgson (Ducati); 6. MacKenzie (Yamaha); 7. Craggill (AUS, Suzuki); 8. Young (Yamaha); 9. Giles (Kawasaki); 10. Hislop (Kawasaki); 11. Heal (Kawasaki); 12. Wood (Kawasaki); 13. Emmett (Ducati); 14. Nottingham (Yamaha); 15. Smith (Yamaha).

9th May - Snetterton
Race I: 1. Reynolds (Ducati); 2. Bayliss (AUS, Ducati); 3. Hodgson (Ducati); 4. Walker (Kawasaki); 5. Hislop (Kawasaki); 6. MacKenzie (Yamaha); 7. Haydon (Suzuki); 8. Craggill (Suzuki); 9. Emmett (Ducati); 10. Giles (Kawasaki); 11. Young (Yamaha); 12. Heal (Kawasaki); 13. Nottingham (Yamaha); 14. Ashton (Yamaha); 15. D. Harris (Yamaha).
Race II: 1. Bayliss (AUS, Ducati); 2. Reynolds (Ducati); 3. Walker (Kawasaki); 4. Hodgson (Ducati); 5. Hislop (Kawasaki); 6. Emmett (Ducati); 7. MacKenzie (Yamaha); 8. Haydon (Suzuki); 9. Craggill (AUS, Suzuki); 10. Giles (Kawasaki); 11. Young (Yamaha); 12. Heal (Kawasaki); 13. Wood (Kawasaki); 14. Ashton (Yamaha); 15. Nottingham (Yamaha).

31st May - Donington Park
Race I: 1. Haydon (Suzuki); 2. Walker (Kawasaki); 3. Hodgson (Ducati); 4. Emmett (Ducati); 5. Craggill (AUS, Suzuki); 6. Heal (Kawasaki); 7. Sampson (Yamaha); 8. Nottingham (Yamaha); 9. Wood (Kawasaki); 10. Stringer (Yamaha); 11. Ashton (Yamaha); 12. D. Harris (Yamaha); 13. Smith (Yamaha); 14. Jones (Kawasaki); 15. Redgate (Kawasaki).
Race II: 1. Reynolds (Ducati); 2. Haydon (Suzuki); 3. Hodgson (Ducati); 4. Walker (Kawasaki); 5. MacKenzie (Yamaha); 6. Bayliss (AUS, Ducati); 7. Craggill (AUS, Suzuki); 8. Emmett (Ducati); 9. Hislop (Kawasaki); 10. Young (Yamaha); 11. Heal (Kawasaki); 12. Stringer (Yamaha); 13. Redgate (Kawasaki); 14. Sampson (Yamaha); 15. Nottingham (Yamaha).

20th June - Silverstone
Race I: 1. Bayliss (AUS, Ducati); 2. Reynolds (Ducati); 3. Hodgson (Ducati); 4. Emmett (Ducati); 5. MacKenzie (Yamaha); 6. Craggill (AUS, Suzuki); 7. Byrne (Kawasaki); 8. Hislop (Kawasaki); 9. Heal (Kawasaki); 10. Wood (Kawasaki); 11. Sampson (Yamaha); 12. Nottingham (Yamaha); 13. Jones (Kawasaki); 14. D. Harris (Yamaha); 15. Marks (Yamaha).
Race II: 1. Bayliss (AUS, Ducati); 2. Walker (Kawasaki); 3. Reynolds (Ducati); 4. Hodgson (Ducati); 5. MacKenzie (Yamaha); 6. Craggill (AUS, Suzuki); 7. Emmett (Ducati); 8. Byrne (Kawasaki); 9. Young (Yamaha); 10. Hislop (Kawasaki); 11. Sampson (Yamaha); 12. Wood (Kawasaki); 13. Redgate (Kawasaki); 14. D. Harris (Yamaha); 15. Nottingham (Yamaha).

18th July - Oulton Park
Race I: 1. Reynolds (Ducati); 2. Emmett (Ducati); 3. Hodgson (Ducati); 4. Haydon (Suzuki); 5. Bayliss (Ducati); 6. Young (Yamaha); 7. Byrne (Kawasaki); 8. Craggill (Suzuki); 9. Heal (Kawasaki); 10. Vincent (Kawasaki); 11. Giles (Kawasaki); 12. Wood (Kawasaki); 13. Nottingham (Yamaha); 14. Sampson (Yamaha); 15. D. Harris (Yamaha).
Race II: 1. Emmett (Ducati); 2. Bayliss (Ducati); 3. Reynolds (Ducati); 4. Hodgson (Ducati); 5. Haydon (Suzuki); 6. Walker (Kawasaki); 7. Craggill (Suzuki); 8. Byrne (Kawasaki); 9. Vincent (Kawasaki); 10. Giles (Kawasaki); 11. Wood (Kawasaki); 12. Sampson (Yamaha); 13. Nottingham (Yamaha); 14. Marks (Yamaha); 15. Hodson (Kawasaki).

8th August - Knockhill
Race I: 1. Emmett (Ducati); 2. Walker (Kawasaki); 3. Haydon (Suzuki); 4. MacKenzie (Yamaha); 5. Reynolds (Ducati); 6. Craggill (AUS, Suzuki); 7. Giles (Kawasaki); 8. Bayliss (AUS, Ducati); 9. Heal (Kawasaki); 10. Wood (Kawasaki); 11. Vincent (Kawasaki); 12. Sampson (Yamaha); 13. Young (Yamaha); 14. Nottingham (Yamaha); 15. D. Harris (Yamaha).
Race II: 1. Reynolds (Ducati); 2. MacKenzie (Yamaha); 3. Walker (Kawasaki); 4. Emmett (Ducati); 5. Giles (Kawasaki); 6. Young (Yamaha); 7. Craggill (AUS, Suzuki); 8. Heal (Kawasaki); 9. Sampson (Yamaha); 10. Blackley (Kawasaki); 11. Bennett (Kawasaki); 12. Hodson (Kawasaki); 13. Nottingham (Yamaha); 14. Wilson (Honda). 14 classés.

15th August - Mallory Park
Race I: 1. Haydon (Suzuki); 2. Emmett (Ducati); 3. Walker (Kawasaki); 4. Bayliss (AUS, Ducati); 5. Hodgson (Ducati); 6. Reynolds (Ducati); 7. MacKenzie (Yamaha); 8. Giles (Kawasaki); 9. Craggill (AUS, Suzuki); 10. Heal (Kawasaki); 11. Blackley (Kawasaki); 12. Young (Yamaha); 13. Wood (Kawasaki); 14. Sampson (Yamaha); 15. Nottingham (Yamaha).
Race II: 1. Reynolds (Ducati); 2. Bayliss (AUS, Ducati); 3. Walker (Kawasaki); 4. Emmett (Ducati); 5. Haydon (Suzuki); 6. Hodgson (Ducati); 7. MacKenzie (Yamaha); 8. Young (Yamaha); 9. Craggill (AUS, Suzuki); 10. Giles (Kawasaki); 11. Llewellyn (Kawasaki); 12. Blackley (Kawasaki); 13. Nottingham (Yamaha); 14. Sampson (Yamaha); 15. Wood (Kawasaki).

30th August - Cadwell Park
Race I: 1. Walker (Kawasaki); 2. Hodgson (Ducati); 3. Reynolds (Ducati); 4. Bayliss (AUS, Ducati); 5. Hislop (Yamaha); 6. Emmett (Ducati); 7. Haydon (Suzuki); 8. Craggill (AUS, Suzuki); 9. MacKenzie (Yamaha); 10. Giles (Kawasaki); 11. Heal (Kawasaki); 12. Sampson (Yamaha); 13. Blackley (Kawasaki); 14. D. Harris (Yamaha); 15. Hodson (Kawasaki).
Race II: 1. Bayliss (AUS, Ducati); 2. Walker (Kawasaki); 3. Reynolds (Ducati); 4. Hislop (Yamaha); 5. Hodgson (Ducati); 6. Emmett (Ducati); 7. MacKenzie (Yamaha); 8. Craggill (AUS, Suzuki); 9. Haydon (Suzuki); 10. Llewellyn (Kawasaki); 11. Heal (Kawasaki); 12. Sampson (Yamaha); 13. Giles (Kawasaki); 14. Ashton (Yamaha); 15. Hodson (Kawasaki).

19th September - Brands Hatch
Race I: 1. Walker (Kawasaki); 2. Bayliss (AUS, Ducati); 3. Hodgson (Ducati); 4. Hislop (Yamaha); 5. MacKenzie (Yamaha); 6. Reynolds (Ducati); 7. Haydon (Suzuki); 8. Craggill (AUS, Suzuki); 9. Llewellyn (Kawasaki); 10. Heal (Kawasaki); 11. Byrne (Kawasaki); 12. Giles (Kawasaki); 13. Blackley (Kawasaki); 14. Ashton (Yamaha); 15. Crockford (Suzuki).
Race II: 1. Reynolds (Ducati); 2. Emmett (Ducati); 3. Bayliss (AUS, Ducati); 4. Hodgson (Ducati); 5. MacKenzie (Yamaha); 6. Hislop (Yamaha); 7. Craggill (AUS, Suzuki); 8. Haydon (Suzuki); 9. Byrne (Kawasaki); 10. Heal (Kawasaki); 11. Giles (Kawasaki); 12. Young (Yamaha); 13. Sampson (Yamaha); 14. Blackley (Kawasaki); 15. Ashton (Yamaha).

26th September - Donington Park
Race I: 1. Walker (Kawasaki); 2. MacKenzie (Yamaha); 3. Reynolds (Ducati); 4. Hislop (Yamaha); 5. Byrne (Kawasaki); 6. Bayliss (AUS, Ducati); 7. Haydon (Suzuki); 8. Young (Yamaha); 9. Heal (Kawasaki); 10. Craggill (AUS, Suzuki); 11. Marks (Yamaha); 12. Hodson (Kawasaki); 13. Berner (SF, Kawasaki); 14. Crockford (Suzuki); 15. Scott (Honda).
Race II: 1. Hodgson (Ducati); 2. Bayliss (AUS, Ducati); 3. Emmett (Ducati); 4. Craggill (AUS, Suzuki); 5. Hislop (Yamaha); 6. Byrne (Kawasaki); 7. MacKenzie (Yamaha); 8. Haydon (Suzuki); 9. Giles (Kawasaki); 10. Walker (Kawasaki); 11. Heal (Kawasaki); 12. Young (Yamaha); 13. Blackley (Kawasaki); 14. Redgate (Suzuki); 15. Scott (Honda).

Final classification

1. Troy Bayliss (AUS)	Ducati	394
2. Chris Walker	Kawasaki	366
3. John Reynolds	Ducati	357

4. N. Hodgson (Ducati), 301; 5. J. Haydon (Suzuki), 289; 6. S. Emmett (Ducati), 286; 7. N. MacKenzie (Yamaha), 210; 8. M. Craggill (AUS, Suzuki), 200; 9. S. Hislop (Kawasaki/Yamaha), 173; 10. P. Young (Yamaha), 123; 11. D. Heal (Kawasaki), 115; 12. P. Giles (Kawasaki), 108; 13. D. Wood (Kawasaki), 75; 14. B. Sampson (Yamaha), 68; 15. S. Byrne (Kawasaki), 67; 16. N. Nottingham (Yamaha), 40; 17. G. Blackley (Kawasaki), 26; 18. D. Ashton (Yamaha), 22; 19. M. Llewellyn (Kawasaki), 18; 20. M. Vincent (Kawasaki), 18; 21. J. Hodson (Kawasaki), 18; 22. D. Harris (Yamaha), 14; 23. P. Jones (Kawasaki), 12; 24. R. Stringer (Yamaha), 10; 25. J. Crockford (Suzuki), 9; 26. D. Redgate (Suzuki), 9; 27. R. Smith (Yamaha), 9; 28. S. Marks (Yamaha), 8; 29. R. Bennett (Kawasaki), 5; 30. J. Berner (SF, Kawasaki), 3; 31. K. Wilson (Honda), 2; 32. G. Scott (Honda), 2; 33. D. Bailey (Suzuki), 1; 34. C. Hipwell (Suzuki), 1. 34 finishers.

Italy Championship

125 cc

The champion: Fabrizio De Marco (Aprilia). Born on 24th April 1981, at Roma.
First race: 1997.
Career highlights: Winner Aprilia Challenge 125 in 1998; 24th 125 European Championship, 125 GP Italian Champion (Aprilia) in 1999.

21st March - Varano
1. De Marco (Aprilia); 2. Caffiero (Aprilia); 3. Hules (CZ, Italjet)(*); 4. Tocca (Honda); 5. W. De Angelis (RSM, Honda); 6. Bisconti (Honda); 7. Iommi (Yamaha); 8. Magnani (Aprilia); 9. Pagnoni (Honda); 10. Donelli (Rumi); 11. Aliscioni (Aprilia); 12. Cipriani (Yamaha); 13. Ramponi (Honda); 14. A. De Angelis (RSM, Honda); 15. Irsara (Honda).

28th March - Misano
1. Goi (Honda); 2. Caffiero (Aprilia); 3. A. De Angelis (RSM, Honda); 4. Petrini (Aprilia); 5. Bisconti (Honda); 6. Lanzi (Aprilia); 7. Fasanella (Honda); 8. Bosio (Aprilia); 9. Aliscioni (Aprilia); 10. Magnani (Aprilia); 11. Irsara (Honda); 12. Donelli (Rumi); 13. Tocca (Honda); 14. Ciavatta (Honda); 15. Di Sante (Aprilia).

12th June - Magione
1. De Marco (Aprilia); 2. Chiarello (Aprilia); 3. Lai (Italjet); 4. Buzzi (Honda); 5. Tocca (Honda); 6. E. Leardini (Aprilia); 7. Aliscioni (Aprilia); 8. Irsara (Honda); 9. Romboli (Honda); 10. Magnani (Aprilia); 11. Gentile (Honda); 12. Hules (CZ, Italjet)(*); 13. Bisconti (Honda); 14. Giugovaz (Aprilia); 15. Lanzi (Aprilia).

27th June - Binetto
1. A. De Angelis (RSM, Honda); 2. W. De Angelis (RSM, Honda); 3. De Marco (Aprilia); 4. Chiarello (Aprilia); 5. Buzzi (Honda); 6. Tocca (Honda); 7. Lai (Italjet); 8. Petrini (Aprilia); 9. Irsara (Honda); 10. Bisconti (Honda); 11. Aliscioni (Aprilia); 12. Angeloni (Honda); 13. Raimondi (Honda); 14. Berta (Honda); 15. Tonini (Aprilia).

29th August - Misano
1. Lai (Italjet); 2. Petrini (Aprilia); 3. Chiarello (Aprilia); 4. W. De Angelis (RSM, Honda); 5. A. De Angelis (RSM, Honda); 6. Bisconti (Honda); 7. Tocca (Honda); 8. Pistoni (Rumi); 9. Stern (SLO, Aprilia)(*); 10. Zappa (Mancini); 11. Tonini (Aprilia); 12. Romboli (Honda); 13. Buzzi (Honda); 14. Tallevi (Honda); 15. Raimondi (Honda).

(*): Hules (CZ, Italjet) and Stern (SLO, Aprilia) are not eligible for points counting towards the Italian Championship.

Final classification

1. Fabrizio De Marco	Aprilia	66 points
2. Alex De Angelis (RSM)	Honda	55
3. Fabrizio Lai	Italjet	50

4. R. Chiarello (Aprilia), 49; 5. W. De Angelis (RSM, Honda), 46; 6. D. Tocca (Honda), 46; 7. M. Petrini (Aprilia), 41; 8. G. Caffiero (Aprilia), 40; 9. M. Bisconti (Honda), 38; 10. A. Buzzi (Honda), 28; 11. S. Aliscioni (Aprilia), 27; 12. I. Goi (Honda), 25; 13. K. Irsara (Honda), 22; 14. C. Magnani (Aprilia), 21; 15. L. Lanzi (Aprilia), 12; 16. R. Romboli (Honda), 12; 17. J. Donelli (Rumi), 11; 18. E. Leardini (Aprilia), 10; 19. A. Iommi (Yamaha), 10; 20. D. Fasanella (Honda), 9; 21. C. Pistoni (Rumi), 8; 22. S. Bosio (Aprilia), 8; 23. B. Pagnoni (Honda), 8; 24. M. Tonini (Aprilia), 8; 25. A. Zappa (Mancini), 7; 26. F.-A. Gentile (Honda), 6; 27. C. Cipriani (Yamaha), 5; 28. M. Raimondi (Honda), 5; 29. M. Angeloni (Honda), 4; 30. S. Ramponi (Honda), 4; 31. T. Tallevi (Honda), 3; 32. D. Giugovaz (Aprilia), 3; 33. A. Berta (Honda), 2; 34. D. Ciavatta (Honda), 2; 35. N. Di Sante (Aprilia), 1. 35 finishers.

(*): the four best scores of each rider are taken into account.

250 cc

The champion: Ivan Clementi (Aprilia). Born on 18th January 1975, in Montegiorgio.
First race: 1991.
First GP: Madrid, 1998 (250).
Career highlights: Winner Gilera 125 Trophy in 1992; Italian 125 Sport-Production Champion (Aprilia) in 1995; 41st 125 European Championship (Aprilia) in 1996; 10th 250 European Championship (Aprilia) in 1997; 28th 250 World Championship, 6th 250 European Championship, 5th 250 Italian Championship (Yamaha) in 1998; 250 European Champion, 250 Italian Champion (Aprilia) in 1999.

21st March - Varano
1. Pennese (Aprilia); 2. Clementi (Aprilia); 3. Cotti (Yamaha); 4. Sabbatucci (Yamaha); 5. Ronzoni (Yamaha); 6. Morselli (TSR-Honda); 7. Copertini (Aprilia); 8. Porto (Yamaha); 9. Vitali (Honda). 9 finishers.

28th March - Misano
1. Fiorillo (Aprilia); 2. Cotti (Yamaha); 3. Stasa (CZ, Aprilia)(*); 4. Di Stefano (Honda); 5. Sabbatucci (Yamaha); 6. Isola (Yamaha); 7. Ronzoni (Yamaha); 8. Ferrari (Aprilia); 9. Morselli (TSR-Honda); 10. Vitali (Honda). 10 finishers.

12th June - Magione
1. Clementi (Aprilia); 2. Cotti (Yamaha); 3. Pennese (Aprilia)(**); 4. Sabbatucci (Yamaha); 5. Ragni (Honda); 6. Morselli (TSR-Honda); 7. Ronzoni (Yamaha); 8. Bricchi (Yamaha); 9. Biondi (Honda); 10. Vitali (Honda); 11. Porto (Yamaha); 12. Isola (Yamaha). 12 finishers.
(**): Pennese (Aprilia) was goven a 30 second penalty for having jumped the start.

27th June - Binetto
1. Clementi (Aprilia); 2. Pennese (Aprilia); 3. Cotti (Yamaha); 4. Lucchetti (Aprilia); 5. Ronzoni (Yamaha); 6. Isola (Yamaha); 7. Morselli (TSR-Honda); 8. Vitali (Honda). 8 finishers.

29th August - Misano
1. Mengozzi (Yamaha); 2. Cotti (Yamaha); 3. Pennese (Aprilia); 4. Morselli (TSR-Honda); 5. Clementi (Aprilia); 6. Sirianni (Yamaha)(*); 7. Goretti (Yamaha); 8. Sabbatucci (Yamaha); 9. Vida (H, Yamaha)(*); 10. Ronzoni (Yamaha); 11. Vitali (Honda); 12. Fabiani (Honda); 13. Isola (Yamaha); 14. Hudovernik (SLO, Yamaha)(*); 15. Porto (Yamaha).

(*): Stasa (CZ, Aprilia), Sirianni (Yamaha), Vida (H, Yamaha) and Hudovernik (SLO, Yamaha) are not eligibée for points for the Italian Championship.

Final classification

1. Ivan Clementi	Aprilia	81 points
2. Stefano Pennese	Aprilia	77
3. Filippo Cotti	Yamaha	76

4. R. Sabbatucci (Yamaha), 48; 5. M. Morselli (TSR-Honda), 42; 6. J. Ronzoni (Yamaha), 41; 7. T. Isola (Yamaha), 30; 8. O. Vitali (Honda), 29; 9. I. Mengozzi (Yamaha), 25; 10. G. Fiorillo (Aprilia), 25; 11. D. Porto (Yamaha), 17; 12. S. Di Stefano (Honda), 16; 13. G. Lucchetti (Aprilia), 13; 14. M. Ragni (Honda), 11; 15. G. Goretti (Yamaha), 10; 16. C. Biondi (Honda), 10; 17. F. Ferrari (Aprilia), 9; 18. M. Copertini (Aprilia), 9; 19. A. Bricchi (Yamaha), 8; 20. F. Fabiani (Honda), 6. 20 finishers.

(*): the four best scores of each rider are taken into account.

Supersport

The champion: Norino Brignola (Bimota). Born on 7th December 1972, in Roma.
Career highlights: 44th 125 European Championship, 26th 125 Spanish open Championship (Aprilia) in 1995; 600 Sport-Production Italian Champion (Bimota) in 1998; 45th Supersport World Championship, Supersport Italian Champion (Bimota) in 1999.

25th April - Misano
1. Ianuzzo (Yamaha); 2. Teneggi (Ducati); 3. Brignola (Bimota); 4. Pasini (Ducati); 5. Briguet (CH, Suzuki)(*); 6. Monaco (Ducati); 7. Conforti (Kawasaki); 8. Mariottini (Kawasaki); 9. Antonelli (Yamaha); 10. Migliorati (Suzuki); 11. Messori (Kawasaki); 12. Mazzali (Yamaha); 13. Pini (Ducati); 14. Bastianini (Ducati); 15. Carpani (Ducati).
(*): Yves Briguet (CH, Suzuki) is not eligible for points.

9th May - Misano
1. Brignola (Bimota); 2. Teneggi (Ducati); 3. Mariottini (Kawasaki); 4. Nobles (Honda); 5. Vitellaro (Yamaha); 6. Marchini (Honda); 7. Borciani (Honda); 8. Bastianini (Ducati); 9. Messori (Kawasaki); 10. Pasini (Ducati); 11. Antonelli (Yamaha); 12. Foti (Ducati); 13. Zappa (Suzuki); 14. Villa (Ducati); 15. Mazzali (Yamaha).

18th July - Imola
1. Panichi (Bimota); 2. Iannuzzo (Yamaha); 3. Teneggi (Ducati); 4. Pini (Ducati); 5. Mazzali (Yamaha); 6. Pasini (Ducati); 7. Conforti (Kawasaki); 8. Zappa (Suzuki); 9. Furlan (Ducati); 10. Villa (Ducati); 11. Mariottini (Kawasaki); 12. Colombo (Ducati); 13. Brugnara (Suzuki); 14. Bastianini (Ducati); 15. Tomassoni (Yamaha).

19th September - Mugello
1. Tortoroglio (Ducati); 2. Brignola (Bimota); 3. Iannuzzo (Yamaha); 4. Panichi (Bimota); 5. Risitano (Kawasaki); 6. Borciani (Yamaha); 7. Teneggi (Ducati); 8. Antonelli (Yamaha); 9. Foti (Ducati); 10. Brugnara (Suzuki); 11. Arnoldi (Suzuki); 12. Pasini (Ducati); 13. Villa (Yamaha); 14. Colombo (Ducati); 15. Chert (Kawasaki).

26th September - Vallelunga
1. Brignola (Bimota); 2. Tortoroglio (Ducati); 3. Panichi (Bimota); 4. Teneggi (Ducati); 5. Brugnara (Suzuki); 6. Risitano (Kawasaki); 7. Borciani (Yamaha); 8. Zappa (Suzuki); 9. Pasini (Ducati); 10. Bartolini (Ducati); 11. Temporali (Honda); 12. Romanelli (Ducati); 13. Fabbroni (Honda); 14. Conti (Kawasaki); 15. Montegrande (Yamaha).

Final classification

1. Norino Brignola	Bimota	86 points
2. Roberto Teneggi	Ducati	69
3. Vittorio Iannuzzo	Yamaha	61

4. R. Panichi (Bimota), 54; 5. W. Tortoroglio (Ducati), 45; 6. L. Pasini (Ducati), 35; 7. C. Mariottini (Kawasaki), 30; 8. M. Borciani (Yamaha/Honda), 29; 9. M. Risitano (Kawasaki), 21; 10. I. Antonelli (Yamaha), 21; 11. F. Brugnara (Suzuki), 20; 12. A. Zappa (Suzuki), 20; 13. L. Conforti (Kawasaki), 18; 14. A. Mazzali (Yamaha), 17; 15. L. Pini (Ducati), 16; 16. A. Vitellaro (Yamaha), 13; 17. T.-A. Nobles (Honda), 13; 18. E.-F. Bastianini (Ducati), 13; 19. D. Messori (Kawasaki), 13; 20. S. Foti (Ducati), 12; 21. G. Villa (Ducati/Yamaha), 12; 22. M. Marchini (Honda), 11; 23. F. Monaco (Ducati), 10; 24. F. Furlan (Ducati), 7; 25. V. Bartolini (Honda), 6; 26. C. Migliorati (Suzuki), 6; 27. M. Colombo (Ducati), 6; 28. M. Temporali (Honda), 5; 29. I. Arnoldi (Suzuki), 5; 30. G. Romanelli (Ducati), 4; 31. R. Fabbroni (Honda), 3; 32. S. Conti (Kawasaki), 2; 33. A. Montegrande (Yamaha), 1; 34. L. Chert (Kawasaki), 1; 35. A. Tomassoni (Yamaha), 1; 36. I. Bellezza (Ducati), 1; 37. F. Carpani (Ducati), 1. 37 finishers.

(*): the four best scores of each rider are taken into account.

Superbike

The champion: Paolo Casoli (Ducati). Born on 18th August 1965, in Castelnuovo Monti.
First race: 1982.
First GP: Italie, 1984 (125).
GP wins: 1 (125).
First GP win: Portugal (Jarama) 1987 (125).
Career highlights: 8th 125 European Championship (MBA) in 1984; 3rd 125 European Championship (MBA), Superbike Italisn Champion in 1985; 14th 125 World Championship (MBA) in 1986; 3rd 125 World Championship (AGV) in 1987; 44th 250 World Championship (Garelli) in 1988; 35th 250 World Championship (Honda) in 1989; 17th 250 World Championship, 2nd 250 Italian Championship (Yamaha) in 1990; 10th 250 World Championship (Yamaha) in 1991; 21st 250 World Championship, 2nd 250 Italian Championship (Yamaha) in 1992; 26th 250 World Championship (Gilera) in 1993; 13th Superbike World Championship (Yamaha) in 1994; 16th Superbike World Championship, Superbike Italian Champion (Yamaha) in 1995; 14th Superbike World Championship, Superbike Italian Champion (Ducati) in 1996; 1st Supersport World Cup, Supersport Italian Champion (Ducati) in 1997; 4th Supersport World Cup (Ducati) in 1998; 14th Supersport World Championship, Superbike Italian Champion (Ducati) in 1999.

25th April - Misano
The race was cancelled after a fatal accident, when Claudio Carotti lost his life in the supersport event.

9th May - Misano
1. Casoli (Ducati); 2. Assirelli (Yamaha); 3. Blora (Ducati); 4. Bartolini (Suzuki); 5. Accornero (Suzuki); 6. Di Maso (Kawasaki); 7. Pezzoni (Suzuki); 8. Marchetti (Ducati); 9. Malvini (Ducati); 10. Dondi (Ducati); 11. Berti (Suzuki); 12. Leonetti (Ducati); 13. Suozzo (Yamaha); 14. Bosio (Ducati); 15. Giorgi (Suzuki).

18th July - Imola
1. Casoli (Ducati); 2. Assirelli (Yamaha); 3. Di Maso (Kawasaki); 4. Pezzoni (Suzuki); 5. Boccelli (Ducati); 6. Marchetti (Ducati); 7. Bosetti (Ducati); 8. Berti (Suzuki); 9. Giorgi (Suzuki); 10. Montini (Yamaha); 11. Caspon (Ducati); 12. Leonetti (Ducati); 13. Stoppa (Suzuki); 14. Chiapello (Kawasaki); 15. Angeloni (Suzuki).

19th September - Mugello
1. Casoli (Ducati); 2. Gramigni (Yamaha); 3. Di Maso (Kawasaki); 4. Assirelli (Yamaha); 5. Cantalupo (Ducati); 6. Bosetti (Ducati); 7. Bartolini (Suzuki); 8. Bocelli (Ducati); 9. Montini (Yamaha); 10. Macias (COL, Ducati); 11. Marchetti (Ducati); 12. Preussler (CH, Kawasaki); 13. Velez (Ducati); 14. Maran (Kawasaki); 15. Chiapello (Kawasaki).

26th September - Vallelunga
1. Casoli (Ducati); 2. Blora (Ducati); 3. Di Maso (Kawasaki); 4. Scatola (Yamaha); 5. Bartolini (Suzuki); 6. Boccelli (Ducati); 7. Assirelli (Yamaha); 8. Bosetti (Ducati); 9. Pezzoni (Suzuki); 10. Macias (COL, Ducati); 11. Marchetti (Ducati); 12. Bosio (Ducati); 13. Leonetti (Ducati); 14. Giorgi (Suzuki); 15. Montini (Yamaha).

Final classification

1. Paolo Casoli	Ducati	100 points
2. Redamo Assirelli	Yamaha	62
3. Ferdinando Di Maso	Kawasaki	58

4. P. Blora (Ducati), 36; 5. V. Bartolini (Suzuki), 33; 6. L. Pezzoni (Suzuki), 32; 7. D. Marchetti (Ducati), 30; 8. M. Boccelli (Ducati), 29; 9. P. Bosetti (Ducati), 27; 10. A. Gramigni (Yamaha), 20; 11. V. Montini (Yamaha), 15; 12. B. Scatola (Yamaha), 13; 13. M. Berti (Suzuki), 13; 14. R. Leonetti (Ducati), 12; 15. G. Cantalupo (Ducati), 11; 16. M. Accornero (Suzuki), 11; 17. M. Giorgi (Suzuki), 11; 18. R. Bosio (Ducati), 8; 19. P. Malvini (Ducati), 7; 20. F. Caspon (Ducati), 7; 21. P. Dondi (Ducati), 6; 22. E. Chiapello (Kawasaki), 6; 23. G. Maran (Kawasaki), 5; 24. D. Stoppa (Suzuki), 3; 25. A. Suozzo (Yamaha), 3; 26. A. Rossi (Ducati), 1; 27. C. Angeloni (Suzuki), 1. 27 finishers.

(*): the four best scores are taken into account.

125 Sport-Production

The champion: Danilo Azzolini (Aprilia).

21ˢᵗ March - Varano
1. Alfonsi (Aprilia); 2. Castellani (Aprilia); 3. E. Leardini (Aprilia); 4. Manzari (Aprilia); 5. Orioli (Cagiva); 6. Azzolini (Aprilia); 7. Fusto (Honda); 8. Perlini (Aprilia); 9. Tesori (Aprilia); 10. Calonaci (Aprilia); 11. Segoni (Aprilia); 12. Ricci (Aprilia); 13. Petrucci (Aprilia); 14. Papucci (Aprilia); 15. Sigolo (Aprilia).

28th March - Misano
1. L. Leardini (Aprilia); 2. E. Leardini (Aprilia); 3. Manzari (Aprilia); 4. Castellani (Aprilia); 5. Menghi (Aprilia); 6. Orioli (Cagiva); 7. Perlini (Aprilia); 8. Tonini (Aprilia); 9. Azzolini (Aprilia); 10. Ricci (Aprilia); 11. Zena (Aprilia); 12. Petrucci (Cagiva); 13. Boccoloni (Aprilia); 14. Barboni (Aprilia); 15. Ranaldi (Aprilia).

25th April - Misano
1. Azzolini (Aprilia); 2. Alfonsi (Aprilia); 3. Perlini (Aprilia); 4. E. Leardini (Aprilia); 5. Colnaci (Aprilia); 6. L. Leardini (Aprilia); 7. Manzari (Aprilia); 8. Menghi (Aprilia); 9. Tricomi (Aprilia); 10. Ricci (Aprilia); 11. Diotallevi (Aprilia); 12. Zena (Aprilia); 13. Bottalico (Aprilia); 14. Segoni (Aprilia); 15. Tonini (Aprilia).

9th May - Misano
1. Azzolini (Aprilia); 2. Manzari (Aprilia); 3. Bottalico (Aprilia); 4. Menghi (Aprilia); 5. Tonini (Aprilia); 6. Perlini (Aprilia); 7. Diotallevi (Aprilia); 8. Segoni (Aprilia); 9. Zamponi (Aprilia); 10. Papucci (Aprilia); 11. Sabatini (Aprilia); 12. Ranaldi (Aprilia); 13. Rossi (Aprilia); 14. Dionisi (Aprilia); 15. Alfonsi (Aprilia).

13ᵗʰ June - Magione
1. Alfonsi (Aprilia); 2. Menghi (Aprilia); 3. Azzolini (Aprilia); 4. E. Leardini (Aprilia); 5. Zena (Aprilia); 6. Manzari (Aprilia); 7. Diotallevi (Aprilia); 8. Papucci (Aprilia); 9. Castellani (Aprilia); 10. Perlini (Aprilia); 11. Tonini (Aprilia); 12. Zocchi (Aprilia); 13. Rinaldi (Aprilia); 14. Vergoni (Aprilia); 15. Tricomi (Aprilia).

27ᵗʰ June - Binetto
1. Manzari (Aprilia); 2. Azzolini (Aprilia); 3. Menghi (Aprilia); 4. E. Leardini (Aprilia); 5. Bottalico (Aprilia); 6. Orioli (Cagiva); 7. Papucci (Aprilia); 8. Zocchi (Aprilia); 9. Musilli (Cagiva); 10. Giordani (Aprilia); 11. Caiterzi (Yamaha). 11 finishers.

18ᵗʰ July - Imola
1. Alfonsi (Aprilia); 2. Azzolini (Aprilia); 3. Segoni (Aprilia); 4. Diotallevi (Aprilia); 5. Orioli (Cagiva); 6. Menghi (Aprilia); 7. Bartolini (Aprilia); 8. Fusto (Aprilia); 9. Perlini (Aprilia); 10. Cherti (Aprilia); 11. Menculini (Aprilia); 12. Zamponi (Aprilia); 13. Ranaldi (Aprilia); 14. Petrucci (Aprilia); 15. Fara (Cagiva).

28ᵗʰ August - Misano
1. Perlini (Aprilia); 2. Alfonsi (Aprilia); 3. Azzolini (Aprilia); 4. E. Leardini (Aprilia); 5. Menghi (Aprilia); 6. Segoni (Aprilia); 7. Manzari (Aprilia); 8. Orioli (Cagiva); 9. Zamponi (Aprilia); 10. Tonini (Aprilia); 11. Papucci (Aprilia); 12. Conti (Aprilia); 13. Ranaldi (Aprilia); 14. Zudic (H, Aprilia); 15. Gennari (Aprilia).

19ᵗʰ September - Mugello
1. Azzolini (Aprilia); 2. Alfonsi (Aprilia); 3. Lanzi (Aprilia); 4. Perlini (Aprilia); 5. Manzari (Aprilia); 6. E. Leardini (Aprilia); 7. L. Leardini (Aprilia); 8. Castellani (Aprilia); 9. Menghi (Aprilia); 10. Gennari (Aprilia); 11. Papucci (Aprilia); 12. Vergoni (Aprilia); 13. Orioli (Cagiva). 14. Zena (Aprilia); 15. Bosco (Aprilia).

26ᵗʰ September - Vallelunga
1. Lanzi (Aprilia); 2. Segoni (Aprilia); 3. Alfonsi (Aprilia); 4. Azzolini (Aprilia); 5. E. Leardini (Aprilia); 6. Manzari (Aprilia); 7. Perlini (Aprilia); 8. Calonaci (Aprilia); 9. Bartolini (Aprilia); 10. Sementilli (Aprilia); 11. Zena (Aprilia); 12. Papucci (Aprilia); 13. Chinucci (Aprilia); 14. Minchella (Aprilia); 15. Ricci (Aprilia).

Final classification

1. Danilo Azzolini   Aprilia   160 points
2. Lorenzo Alfonsi   Aprilia   152
3. Nunzio Felice Manzari   Aprilia   114
4. E. Leardini (Aprilia), 99; 5. P. Perlini (Aprilia), 97; 6. O. Menghi (Aprilia), 96; 7. L. Segoni (Aprilia), 61; 8. L. Orioli (Cagiva), 53; 9. S. Castellani (Aprilia), 48; 10. L. Leardini (Aprilia), 44; 11. L. Lanzi (Aprilia), 41; 12. A. Papucci (Aprilia), 39; 13. L. Diotallevi (Aprilia), 36; 14. G. Tonini (Aprilia), 32; 15. M. Bottalico (Aprilia), 30; 16. M. Zena (Aprilia), 27; 17. D. Calonaci (Aprilia), 25; 18. S. Zamponi (Aprilia), 18; 19. C. Fusto (Aprilia), 17; 20. A. Ricci (Aprilia), 17; 21. S. Bartolini (Aprilia), 16; 22. S. Ranaldi (Aprilia), 14; 23. E. Zocchi (Aprilia), 12; 24. F. Petrucci (Cagiva), 9; 25. R. Tricomi (Aprilia), 8; 26. D. Gennari (Aprilia), 8; 27. C. Musilli (Cagiva), 7; 28. M. Tesori (Aprilia), 7; 29. M. Sementilli (Aprilia), 6; 30. L. Chert (Aprilia), 6; 31. F. Giordani (Aprilia), 6; 32. M. Vergoni (Aprilia), 6; 33. S. Mencolini (Aprilia), 5; 34. A. Caiterzi (Yamaha), 5; 35. R. Sabatini (Aprilia), 5; 36. P. Conti (Aprilia), 4; 37. P. Chinucci (Aprilia), 3; 38. A. Rossi (Aprilia), 3; 39. G. Boccolini (Aprilia), 3; 40. A. Minchella (Aprilia), 2; 41. I. Dionisi (Aprilia), 2; 42. C. Barboni (Aprilia), 2; 43. S. Bosco (Aprilia), 1; 44. F. Fabrizi (Aprilia), 1; 45. A. Fara (Cagiva), 1; 46. L. Sigolo (Aprilia), 1. 46 finishers.

(*): the eight best scores od each rider are taken into account.

600 Sport-Production

The champion: Maurizio Prattichizzo (Yamaha).

21ˢᵗ March - Varano
1. Prattichizzo (Yamaha); 2. Corradi (Kawasaki); 3. Belletti (Ducati); 4. Cruciani (Ducati); 5. Antonello (Yamaha); 6. Temporali (Honda); 7. Valia (Honda); 8. Di Marco (Yamaha); 9. Carlacci (Yamaha); 10. Berta (Honda); 11. Giordani (Ducati); 12. Guareschi (Yamaha); 13. Caini (Honda); 14. Romanelli (Ducati); 15. D'Amico (Yamaha).

28th March - Misano
1. Corradi (Kawasaki); 2. Pizzagalli (Ducati); 3. Cruciani (Ducati); 4. Antonello (Yamaha); 5. Belletti (Ducati); 6. Pratichizzo (Yamaha); 7. Carlacci (Yamaha); 8. Giachino (Suzuki); 9. Tondini (Kawasaki); 10. Projetto (Kawasaki); 11. Melone (Yamaha); 12. Nannelli (Suzuki); 13. Valia (Honda); 14. Capriotti (Suzuki); 15. Temporali (Honda).

25th April - Misano
The race was cancelled after a fatal accident, when Claudio Carotti lost his life in the supersport event.

9th May - Misano
1. Pizzagalli (Ducati); 2. Antonello (Yamaha); 3. Pratichizzo (Yamaha); 4. Di Marco (Yamaha); 5. Corradi (Kawasaki); 6. Carlacci (Yamaha); 7. Belletti (Ducati); 8. Vizziello (Yamaha); 9. Mauri (Kawasaki); 10. Tondini (Kawasaki); 11. Valia (Honda); 12. Cruciani (Ducati); 13. Guareschi (Yamaha); 14. Ruggiero (Kawasaki); 15. Berta (Kawasaki).

13ᵗʰ June - Magione
1. Carlacci (Yamaha); 2. Di Marco (Yamaha); 3. Cruciani (Ducati) 4. Valia (Honda); 5. Antonello (Yamaha); 6. Pratichizzo (Yamaha); 7. Tondini (Kawasaki); 8. Pizzagalli (Ducati); 9. Vizziello (Yamaha); 10. Guareschi (Yamaha); 11. Romanelli (Ducati); 12. Lopez (Suzuki); 13. Melone (Yamaha); 14. Ruggiero (Kawasaki); 15. Manici (Honda).

27ᵗʰ June - Binetto
1. Cruciani (Ducati); 2. Carlacci (Yamaha); 3. Valia (Honda); 4. Corradi (Kawasaki); 5. Vizzielo (Yamaha); 6. Guareschi (Yamaha); 7. Tondini (Kawasaki); 8. Di Marco (Yamaha); 9. Melone (Yamaha); 10. Nannelli (Suzuki); 11. Nocetti (Yamaha); 12. Ruggiero (Kawasaki); 13. Pizzagalli (Ducati); 14. Rossi (Yamaha). 14 finishers.

18ᵗʰ July - Imola
1. Corradi (Kawasaki); 2. Antonello (Yamaha); 3. Pizzigalli (Ducati); 4. Valia (Honda); 5. Di Marco (Yamaha); 6. Nocetti (Yamaha); 7. Ruggiero (Kawasaki); 8. Guareschi (Yamaha); 9. Iommi (Kawasaki); 10. Nannelli (Suzuki); 11. Manici (Honda); 12. Melone (Yamaha); 13. Mauri (Kawasaki); 14. Mancuso (Yamaha); 15. Caini (Honda).

29ᵗʰ August - Misano
1. Pratichizzo (Yamaha); 2. Cruciani (Ducati); 3. Proietto (Kawasaki); 4. Manici (Kawasaki); 5. Guareschi (Yamaha); 6. Nannelli (Suzuki); 7. D'Amico (Yamaha); 8. Caini (Honda); 9. Antonello (Yamaha); 10. Di Marco (Yamaha); 11. Ruggiero (Kawasaki); 12. Corradi (Kawasaki); 13. Iommi (Kawasaki); 14. Belletti (Ducati); 15. Carlacci (Yamaha).

19ᵗʰ September - Mugello
1. Pratichizzo (Yamaha); 2. Carlacci (Yamaha); 3. Belletti (Ducati); 4. Valia (Honda); 5. Tondini (Kawasaki); 6. Proietto (Kawasaki); 7. Guareschi (Yamaha); 8. Nocetti (Yamaha); 9. Manici (Honda); 10. Melone (Yamaha); 11. Mauri (Kawasaki); 12. Ricci (Suzuki); 13. Romanelli (Ducati); 14. Ciaroni (Suzuki); 15. Pasini (Yamaha).

26ᵗʰ September - Vallelunga
1. Pratichizzo (Yamaha); 2. Carlacci (Yamaha); 3. Valia (Honda); 4. Guareschi (Yamaha); 5. Belletti (Ducati); 6. Pizzagalli (Ducati); 7. Cruciani (Ducati); 8. Corradi (Kawasaki); 9. Ruggiero (Kawasaki); 10. Tondini (Kawasaki); 11. Antonello (Yamaha); 12. Mauri (Kawasaki); 13. Rossi (Yamaha); 14. Ricci (Suzuki); 15. Galie (Suzuki).

Final classification

1. Maurizio Prattichizzo   Yamaha   136 points
2. Antonio Carlacci   Yamaha   136
3. Stefano Cruciani   Ducati   103
4. A. Corradi (Kawasaki), 101; 5. A. Valia (Honda), 86; 6. R. Antonello (Yamaha), 83; 7. A. Pizzagalli (Ducati), 79; 8. D. Di Marco (Yamaha), 65; 9. R. Belletti (Ducati), 65; 10. G. Guareschi (Yamaha), 63; 11. M. Tondini (Kawasaki), 48; 12. J. Proietto (Kawasaki), 32; 13. S. Ruggiero (Kawasaki), 28; 14. G. Vizziello (Yamaha), 26; 15. A. Manici (Honda), 25; 16. G. Nannelli (Suzuki), 25; 17. A. Melone (Yamaha), 24; 18. E. Nocetti (Yamaha), 22; 19. L. Mauri (Kawasaki), 18; 20. M. Temporali (Honda), 11; 21. F.-L. Caimi (Honda), 11; 22. G. Romanelli (Ducati), 10; 23. D. D'Amico (Yamaha), 10; 24. A. Iommi (Kawasaki), 9; 25. A. Giachino (Suzuki), 8; 26. A. Berta (Honda/Kawasaki), 7; 27. R. Ricci (Suzuki), 6; 28. G. Giordani (Ducati), 5; 29. E. Rossi (Yamaha), 5; 30. V. Lopez (Suzuki), 4; 31. F. Ciaroni (Suzuki), 2; 32. F. Capriotti (Suzuki), 2; 33. G. Galie (Suzuki), 1; 34. E. Pasini (Yamaha), 1; 35. A. Mancuso (Yamaha), 1. 35 finishers.

(*): the eight best scores of each rider are taken into account.

Ivan Clementi.

Norino Brignola.

Paolo Casoli.

Supersport

4th April - Lédenon - France
Race I: 1. Stamm (Kawasaki); 2. Jaggi (Honda); 3. Duss- (Ducati); 4. Leibundgut (Honda); 5. Mäder -(Yamaha); 6. Mäder -(Yamaha); 7. Schmaus (D, Suzuki); 8. Hagmann (Yamaha); 9. Hauser-(Honda) 10. Häfeli (Kawasaki); 11. Kessler (Ducati); 12. Keist (Yamaha); 13. M. Bachmann (Ducati); 14. Burkhalter (Honda); 15.- Giger (Yamaha).
Race II: 1. Stamm (Kawasaki); 2. Jaggi (Honda); 3. R. Bachmann- (Honda); 4. Leibundgut (Honda); 5. Hauser -(Ducati); 7. Häfeli (Kawasaki); 8. Keist (Yamaha); 9. Kilchenmann- (Honda) 10. Burkhalter (Honda); 11. Mäder (Yamaha); 12. Schmaus- (D, Suzuki); 13. Duss (Ducati); 14. Hagmann (Yamaha); 15. Giger -(Yamaha).

15th May - Oschersleben - Germany
Race I: 1. Körner (D, Suzuki); 2. Ott (D, Kawasaki); 3. R. -Bachmann (Honda); 4. Hagmann (Yamaha); 5. Leibundgut (Honda); 6. -Kessler (Ducati); 7. Trauffer (Ducati); 8. Stamm (Kawasaki); 9. -M. Bachmann (Ducati); 10. Rumpel (Kawasaki); 11. Burkhalter-(Honda). 11 finishers.
Race II: 1. Körner (D, Suzuki); 2. Stamm (Kawasaki); 3. Lang -(Yamaha); 4. Leibundgut (Honda); 5. Hagmann (Yamaha); 6. Mäder- (Yamaha); 7. Cosson (Honda); 8. Rumpel (Kawasaki); 9. Schelbert -(D, Yamaha); 10. Kessler (Ducati); 11. Keist (Yamaha); 12. M. Bachmann (Ducati); 13. Burkhalter (Honda). 13 finishers.

4th July - Boécourt - La Caquerelle
Race I: 1. Papaux (Kawasaki); 2. Krummenacher (Honda); 3. Stamm- (Kawasaki); 4. Jaggi (Honda); 5. Hauser (Honda); 6. Hagmann- (Yamaha); 7. Leibundgut (Honda); 8. Keist (Yamaha); 9. Cosson- (Yamaha); 10. Mäder (Yamaha); 11. Kessler (Ducati); 12.-Kilchenmann (Honda); 13. Bachmann (Ducati); 14. Schmid -(Kawasaki); 15. Burkhalter (Honda).
Race II: 1. Stamm (Kawasaki); 2. Krummenacher (Honda); 3.-Papaux (Kawasaki); 4. Jaggi (Honda); 5. Hauser (Honda); 6.-Hagmann (Yamaha); 7. Leibundgut (Honda); 8. Cosson (Yamaha); 9. -Mäder (Yamaha); 10. Keist (Yamaha); 11. Kessler (Ducati); 12. -Bachmann (Ducati); 13. Schmid (Kawasaki); 14. Kilchenmann- (Honda); 15. Burkhlater (Honda).

11th July - Magny-Cours - France
Race I: 1. Jaggi (Honda); 2. Mäder (Yamaha); 3. Duss (Ducati); -4. Leibundgut (Honda); 5. Hagmann (Yamaha); 6. Kessler (Ducati);-7. Keist (Yamaha); 8. Häfeli (Kawasaki); 9. Kilchenmann (Honda);-10. Bachmann (Honda); 11. Schmid (Kawasaki); 12. Burkhalter (Honda); 13. Hauser (Honda); 14. Stamm (Kawasaki); 15. Cosson -(Yamaha).
Race II: 1. Jaggi (Honda); 2. Mäder (Yamaha); 3. Hagmann- (Yamaha); 4. Stamm (Kawasaki); 5. Duss (Ducati); 6. Hauser -(Honda); 7. Häfeli (Kawasaki); 8. Keist (Yamaha); 9. Kilchenmann- (Honda); 10. Bachmann (Honda); 11. Schmid (Kawasaki); 12.-Burkhalter (Honda); 13. Kessler (Ducati); 14. Leibundgut (Honda);-15. Cosson (Yamaha).

18th July - Châtel-Saint-Denis - Les Paccots
1. Papaux (Kawasaki); 2. Krummenacher (Honda); 3. Hauser (Honda); -4. Knecht (Suzuki); 5. Jaggi (Honda); 6. Stamm (Kawasaki); 7.-Mäder (Yamaha); 8. Kilchenmann (Honda); 9. Keist (Yamaha); 10.- Hagmann (Yamaha); 11. M. Bachmann (Ducati). 11 finishers.

30th-31st October - Lédenon - France
Race I: 1. Hagmann (Yamaha); 2. Jaggi (Honda); 3. Stamm- (Kawasaki); 4. Mäder (Yamaha); 5. Leibundgut (Honda); 6. Hauser- (Honda); 7. Keist (Yamaha); 8. Knecht (Suzuki); 9. Lang (Yamaha);-10. Kessler (Ducati); 11. Rollier (Suzuki); 12. Häfeli -(Kawasaki); 13. Cosson (Yamaha); 14. Burkhalter (Honda); 15. R. - Bachmann (Honda). 18 finishers.
Race II: 1. Stamm (Kawasaki); 2. Jaggi (Honda); 3. Portmann (Yamaha); 4. Leuthard (Ducati); 5. Mäder (Yamaha); 6. R. Bachmann- (Honda); 7. Leibundgut (Honda); 8. Hauser (Honda); 9. Lang- (Yamaha); 10. Keist (Yamaha); 11. Knecht (Suzuki); 12. Cosson -(Yamaha); 13. Kessler (Ducati); 14. Häfeli (Kawasaki); 15. M. -Bachmann (Ducati).

Final classification

1. Claude-Alain Jaggi	Honda	196
2. Roman Stamm	Kawasaki	192
3. Ueli Mäder	Yamaha	150

4. Hagmann (Yamaha), 131; 5. Leibundgut (Honda), 113; 6. Hauser -(Honda), 84; 7. Keist (Yamaha), 78; 8. Kessler (Ducati), 74; 9.- Papaux (Kawasaki), 66; 10. Krummenacher (Honda), 60.

Hillclimbs FMS Cup: 1. Papaux (Kawasaki), 66; 2. -Krummenacher (Honda), 60; 3. Stamm (Kawasaki), 51.

△
Claude-Alain Jaggi.

Kilian Lütolf

Stocksport élite

4th April - Lédenon - France
Race I: 1. Peter (Honda); 2. Lütolf (Yamaha); 3. Bitzi (Honda);-4. Lehmann (Yamaha); 5. Bärtsch (Yamaha); 6. Joliat (Yamaha); 7. -Kunz (Honda); 8. Bühler (Kawasaki). 8 finishers.
Race II: 1. Peter (Honda); 2. Lütolf (Yamaha); 3. Bitzi -(Honda); 4. Lehmann (Yamaha); 5. Bärtsch (Yamaha); 6. Joliat -(Yamaha); 7. Rindlisbacher (Kawasaki); 8. Bühler (Kawasaki); 9. Kunz (Honda). 9 finishers.

15th May - Oschersleben - Germany
Race I: 1. Bitzi (Honda); 2. Lehmann (Yamaha); 3. Lütolf -(Yamaha); 4. Joliat (Yamaha); 5. Kunz (Honda). 5 finishers.
Race II: 1. Lütolf (Yamaha); 2. Bärtsch (Yamaha); 3. Bitzi -(Honda); 4. Kunz (Honda); 5. Lehmann (Yamaha). 5 finishers.

4th July - Boécourt - La Caquerelle
Race I: 1. Lütolf (Yamaha); 2. Joliat (Yamaha); 3. Bitzi -(Honda); 4. Bärtsch (Yamaha); 5. Lehmann (Yamaha); 6. Jantz- (Kawasaki); 7. Kunz (Honda); 8. Bühler (Kawasaki). 8 finishers.
Race II: 1. Lütolf (Yamaha); 2. Joliat (Yamaha); 3. Bitzi -(Honda); 4. Bärtsch (Yamaha); 5. Lehmann (Yamaha); 6. Jantz -(Kawasaki); 7. Bühler (Kawasaki); 8. Kunz (Honda). 8 finishers.

11th July - Magny-Cours - France
Race I: 1. Lütolf (Yamaha); 2. Jantz (Kawasaki); 3. Bärtsch-(Yamaha); 4. Lehmann (Yamaha); 5. Bitzi (Honda); 6. Bühler-(Kawasaki); 7. Joliat (Yamaha); 8. Kunz (Honda). 8 finishers.

Race II: 1. Lütolf (Yamaha); 2. Jantz (Kawasaki); 3. Bärtsch-(Yamaha); 4. Lehmann (Yamaha); 5. Bitzi (Honda); 6. Joliat -(Yamaha); 7. Bühler (Kawasaki); 8. Kunz (Honda). 8 finishers.

18th July - Châtel-Saint-Denis - Les Paccots
1. Joliat (Yamaha); 2. Lütolf (Yamaha); 3. Jantz (Kawasaki); 4.-Lehmann (Yamaha); 5. Bitzi (Honda); 6. Bühler (Yamaha); 7.-Bärtsch (Yamaha). 7 finishers.

30th-31st October - Lédenon - France
Race I: 1. Jantz (Kawasaki); 2. Bärtsch (Yamaha); 3. Keiser -(Yamaha); 4. Lehmann (Yamaha); 5. Hafner (Yamaha).
Race II: 1. Jantz (Kawasaki); 2. Keiser (Yamaha); 3. Lehmann -(Yamaha); 4. Bärtsch (Yamaha); 5. Bitzi (Honda); 6. Hafner- (Yamaha).

Final classification

1. Kilian Lütolf	Yamaha	201
2. Roger Jantz	Kawasaki	166
3. Jakob Bärtsch	Yamaha	154

4. Bitzi (Honda), 151; 5. Lehmann (Yamaha), 136; 6. Joliat -(Yamaha), 117; 7. Kunz (Honda), 91; 8. Bühler (Kawasaki), 77; 9. -Peter (Honda), 50; 10. Keiser (Yamaha), 36.
Hillclimbs FMS Cup: 1. Lütolf (Yamaha), 70; 2. Joliat -(Yamaha), 65; 3. Bitzi (Honda), 43.

Stocksport "rookie"

4th April - Lédenon - France
Race I: 1. Carrard (Yamaha); 2. Büchler (Yamaha); 3. Wegmann -(Honda). 3 finishers.
Race II: 1. Büchler (Yamaha); 2. Wegmann (Honda); 3. Carrard -(Yamaha). 3 finishers.

15th May - Oschersleben - Germany
Race I: 1. Carrard (Yamaha); 2. Wegmann (Honda); 3. Büchler- (Yamaha). 3 finishers.
Race II: 1. Carrard (Yamaha); 2. Büchler (Yamaha); 3. Wegmann -(Honda). 3 finishers.

11th July - Magny-Cours - France
Race I: 1. Carrard (Yamaha); 2. Wegmann (Honda); 3. Büchler -(Yamaha). 3 finishers.

Race II: 1. Carrard (Yamaha); 2. Büchler (Yamaha); 3. Wegmann-(Honda). 3 finishers.

30th-31st October - Lédenon - France
Race I: 1. Carrard (Yamaha); 2. Büchler (Yamaha); 3. Wegmann -(Honda). 3 finishers.
Race II: 1. Carrard (Yamaha); 2. Büchler (Yamaha); 3. Wegmann- (Honda). 3 finishers.

Final classification

1. Head Carrard	Yamaha	225
2. Armin Büchler	Yamaha	197
3. Martina Wegmann	Honda	172

△
Head Carrard.

Monobike

4th April - Lédenon - France
Race I: 1. Götz (KTM); 2. Kausch (Honda); 3. Bechtiger (MuZ); -4. Ott (D, Kawasaki); 5. Sczogiel (D, Sczogiel); 6. Egli (MuZ);- 7. Klötzli (MuZ); 8. Ziegler (KTM); 9. Knecht (MuZ); 10. Hauser -(Honda); 11. Kägi (MuZ). 11 finishers.
Race II: 1. Götz (KTM); 2. Kausch (Honda); 3. Knecht (MuZ); 4. -Bechtiger (MuZ); 5. Egli (MuZ); 6. Hauser (Honda); 7. Ott (D, -Kawasaki); 8. Sczogiel (D, Sczogiel); 9. Kägi (MuZ); 10. Ziegler-(KTM); 11. Klötzli (MuZ). 11 finishers.

15th May - Oschersleben - Germany
Race I: 1. Bergfeld (D, KTM); 2. Sczogiel (D, Honda); 3. Kausch- (Honda); 4. Schmidt (D, Honda); 5. Hauser (Honda); 6. Delling (D, -MuZ); 7. Schäfer (D, MuZ); 8. Voss (D, KTM). 8 finishers.
Race II: 1. Knecht (MuZ); 2. Hauser (Honda); 3. Sczogiel (D, -Honda); 4. Bergfeld (D, KTM); 5. Bitterlin (Barigo-Rotax); 6.-Egli (MuZ); 7. Kausch (Honda); 8. Delling (D, MuZ); 9. Schäfer- (D, MuZ); 10. Voss (D, KTM). 10 finishers.

4th July - Boécourt - La Caquerelle
Race I: 1. Egli (MuZ); 2. Klötzli (MuZ); 3. Daehler (RST); 4.- Haag (Yamaha); 5. Knecht (MuZ); 6. Götz (KTM); 7. Sczogiel (D, -Honda); 8. Bechtiger (MuZ); 9. Knauer (Honda); 10. Duc (Husqvarna); 11. Vuilleumier (Yamaha). 11 finishers.
Race II: 1. Daehler (RST); 2. Egli (MuZ); 3. Knecht (MuZ); 4.-Klötzli (MuZ); 5. Haag (Yamaha); 6. Bechtiger (MuZ); 7. Götz-(KTM); 8. Sczogiel (D, Honda); 9. Knauer (Honda); 10. Duc (Husqvarna); 11. Vuilleumier (Yamaha). 11 finishers.

11th July - Magny-Cours - France
Race I: 1. Kausch (Honda); 2. Sczogiel (D, Honda); 3. Egli -(MuZ); 4. Bechtiger (MuZ); 5. Knecht (MuZ); 6. Knauer (Honda); 7.-Bodiment (MuZ); 8. Pieussergues (F, Honda). 8 finishers.
Race II: 1. Knecht (MuZ); 2. Pieussergues (F, Honda); 3. Kausch -(Honda); 4. Sczogiel (D, Honda); 5. Bechtiger (MuZ); 6. Knauer- (Honda); 7. Egli (MuZ). 7 finishers.

18th July - Châtel-Saint-Denis - Les Paccots
1. Daehler (RST); 2. Klötzli (MuZ); 3. Egli (MuZ); 4. Bechtiger -(MuZ); 5. Haag (Yamaha); 6. Knecht (MuZ); 7. Kägi (MuZ). 7 finishers.

30th-31st October - Lédenon - France
Race I: 1. Gautschi (Kawasaki); 2. Devoyon (Honda); 3. Kausch -(Honda); 4. Monti; 5. Hauser (Honda); 6. De Haese (Honda); 7. -Knecht (MuZ); 8. Egli (MuZ); 9. Faurel; 10. Statuto (Honda); 11.-Klötzli (MuZ); 12. Pépin (Honda); 13. Bechtiger (MuZ); 14. Haag -(Yamaha); 15. Riboulet (Honda). 20 finishers.
Race II: 1. Kausch (Honda); 2. Monti; 3. Devoyon (Honda); 4.-Gautschi (Kawasaki); 5. Knecht (MuZ); 6. Hauser (Honda); 7.-Statuto (Honda); 8. Pépin (Honda); 9. Klötzli (MuZ); 10. Riboulet -(Honda); 11. Bechtiger (MuZ); 12. Knauer (Honda); 13. Haag- (Yamaha); 14. Altherr (KTM); 15. Hotz (KTM). 19 finishers.

Final classification

1. Rolf Knecht	MuZ	151
2. Fritz Egli	MuZ	132
3. Thomas Bechtiger	MuZ	121

4. Klötzli (MuZ), 84; 5. Hauser (Honda), 82; 6. Götz (KTM), 69; -7. Haag (Yamaha), 40; 8. Gautschi (Kawasaki), 38; 9. Knauer -(Honda), 28; 10. Debrunner (Husaberg), 18.
Hillclimbs FMS Cup: 1. Egli (MuZ), 61; 2. Klötzli (MuZ),-53; 3. Knecht (MuZ), 37.

Jean-Luc Papaux.

Rolf Knecht.

Fun

4th April - Lédenon - France
Race I: 1. Hauri (Ducati) 2. Tschudin (Honda); 3. Sager -(Suzuki); 4. Maier (D, Kawasaki); 5. Sonderer (Kawasaki); 6.- Fries (Ducati); 7. Kiok (D, Honda); 8. Bitzi (Honda); 9. Hauser (Yamaha); 10. Schneider (Kawasaki).
Race II: 1. Tschudin (Honda); 2. Hauri (Ducati); 3. Sager -(Suzuki); 4. Sonderer (Kawasaki); 5. Kiok (D, Honda); 6. Bitzi -(Honda); 7. Schneider (Kawasaki); 8. Erdin (Yamaha); 9. Bigler (Suzuki); 10. Schopf (Aprilia).

15th May - Oschersleben - Germany
Race I: 1. Schnyder (Ducati); 2. Hauri (Ducati); 3. Sager -(Suzuki); 4. Waldmeier (Yamaha); 5. Biber (Ducati); 6. Sonderer -(Kawasaki); 7. Bitzi (Honda); 8. Hauser (Yamaha); 9. Fries (Ducati); 10. Merk (D, Yamaha).
Race II: 1. Schnyder (Ducati); 2. Hauri (Ducati); 3. Sager- (Suzuki); 4. Waldmeier (Yamaha); 5. Biber (Ducati); 6. Engeli -(Ducati); 7. Sonderer (Kawasaki); 8. Hauser (Yamaha); 9. Fries (Ducati); 10. Bitzi (Honda).

11th July - Magny-Cours - France
Race I: 1. Hauri (Ducati); 2. Hangartner (Honda); 3. Bitzi -(Honda); 4. Sperandio (Yamaha); 5. Beyeler (Suzuki); 6. Fries-(Ducati); 7. Aregger (Ducati); 8. Lötscher (Suzuki); 9. Erdin (Yamaha); 10. Dreier (Honda).
Race II: 1. Schorderet (Honda); 2. Hauri (Ducati); 3. Weder -(Yamaha); 4. Hangartner (Honda); 5. Sperandio (Yamaha); 6. Bantle- (Yamaha); 7. Neyeler (Suzuki); 8. Bitzi (Honda); 9. Aregger- (Ducati); 10. Erdin (Yamaha).

30th-31st October - Lédenon - France
Race I: 1. Schwegler (Kawasaki); 2. Hofmann (Kawasaki); 3. -Beyeler (Suzuki); 4. Lütolf (Yamaha); 5. Leuthard (Ducati); 6. -Hangartner (Suzuki); 7. Sonderer (Kawasaki); 8. Alma (Suzuki); 9. -Blau (Kawasaki); 10. Fries (Ducati); 11. Bitzi (Honda); 12. Erdin -(Yamaha); 13. Bigler (Suzuki); 14. Bantle (Yamaha); 15. Doetsch -(Honda).
Race II: 1. Hofmann (Kawasaki); 2. Schwegler (Kawasaki); 3. -Beyeler (Suzuki); 4. Sonderer (Kawasaki); 5. Fries (Ducati); 6.-Bantle (Yamaha); 7. Alma (Suzuki); 8. Lütolf (Yamaha); 9. Hangartner (Honda); 10. Bitzi (Honda); 11. Bigler (Suzuki); 12. -Omlor (Suzuki); 13. Balmer (Kawasaki); 14. Erdin (Yamaha); 15. -Leeman (Honda).

Side-Cars

4th July - Boécourt - La Caquerelle
Race I: 1. Liechti/Locher (LCR-BRM); 2. Schopfer/Schopfer-(Kawasaki); 3. Bruchez/Bruchez (Suzuki). 3 finishers.
Race II: 1. Liechti/Locher (LCR-BRM); 2. Schopfer/Schopfer-(Kawasaki); 3. Bruchez/Bruchez (Suzuki). 3 finishers.

18th July - Châtel-Saint-Denis - Les Paccots
1. Schlosser/Hauser (LCR-BRM); 2. Liechti/Locher (LCR-BRM). 2- finishers.

Oldtimer - Solo - 1949

4th July - Boécourt - La Caquerelle
Race I: 1. Rutz (Rudge 500); 2. Müller (Scott 498); 3. Jaberg -(Motosacoche); 4. Jud (Rudge 500); 5. Rümmel (Rudge); 6. Burri -(BSA); 7. Frauchiger (Moto Guzzi). 7 finishers.
Race II: 1. Jud (Rudge 500); 2. Rutz (Rudge 500); 3. Frauchiger -(Moto Guzzi); 4. Burri (BSA); 5. Rümmel (Rudge). 5 finishers.

18th July - Châtel-Saint-Denis - Les Paccots
1. Frauchiger (Moto Guzzi); 2. Jud (Rudge 500); 3. Kaufmann -(Condor); 4. Burri (BSA); 5. Jaberg (Motosacoche); 6. Rümmel -(Rudge); 7. Rutz (Rudge 500); 8. Hürlimann (Motosacoche); 9.-Blatter (DKW). 9 finishers.

Final classification

1. Bernadette Jud	Rudge	58 points
2 . Jakob Rutz	Rudge	54
3 . Paul Frauchiger	Moto Guzzi	50

4. Burri (Gilera), 36; 5. Rümmel (Rudge), 32; 6. Jaberg (Motosacoche), 27; 7. Müller (Scott 498), 20; 8. Kaufmann (Condor), 16; 9. Hürlimann (Mtosacoche), 8; 10. Blatter (DKW), 7. 10 classés.

Oldtimer - Solo + 1948

4th July - Boécourt - La Caquerelle
Race I: 1. Allamand (Ducati); 2. Schnider (Honda); 3. Hage -(BSA); 4. Kormann (Aermacchi); 5. Charrière (Norton); 6. M. -Baggenstos (Suzuki); 7. Graf (Norton Manx); 8. Rlethig (Kawasaki); 9. Liechti (Triumph); 10. Kaufmann (Honda); 11.-Biscaini (Weston); 12. Züger (BSA); 13. Blanchard (Ducati); 14.-Kunz (Ducati); 15. Pfister (Norton).
Race II: 1. H. Baggenstos (Suzuki); 2. Larice (Ducati); 3. -Kormann (Aermacchi); 4. Schnider (Honda); 5. Allamand (Ducati); -6. Züger (BSA); 7. Kunz (Ducati); 8. Liechti (Triumph); 9. M. Baggenstos (Suzuki); 10. Heiz (Vincent); 11. Hage (BSA); 12.-Charrière (Norton); 13. Kaufmann (Honda); 14. Blanchard (Ducati);-15. Zürcher (Triumph).

18th July - Châtel-Saint-Denis - Les Paccots
1. Schnider (Honda); 2. Zürcher (Triumph); 3. Mischeler (BSA); 4.-Kleiner (Triumph); 5. Bellon (Honda); 6. Pierre (Suzuki); 7. -Blanchard (Ducati); 8. Rüegg (Honda); 9. Johner (Honda); 10. Kunz- (Ducati); 11. Coche (F, Honda); 12. Baudat (Honda); 13. Röthig -(Kawasaki); 14. Schwendimann (Moto Morini); 15. Kaufmann (Honda).

Final classification

1. Heinz Schnider	Honda	58
2. Daniel Allamand	Ducati	36
3. Heinz Kormann	Aermacchi	29

4. H. Baggenstos (Suzuki), 25; 5. Hage (BSL), 23; 6. Zürcher-(Triumph), 21; 7. Larice (Ducati), 20; 8. Kunz (Ducati), 20; 9. -M. Baggenstos (Suzuki), 17; 10. Mischler (Terrot), 16; 11.- Blanchard (Ducati), 16; 12. Liechti (Triumph) et Röthig -(Kawasaki), 15; 14. Charrière (Norton), 15; 15. Züger (BSA), 14; -16. Kaufmann (Egli-Honda), 14; 17. Kleiner (Triumph), 13; 18.-Rüegg (Honda), 10; 19. Graf (Norton), 9; 20. Coche (F, Honda), 8; -21. Heiz (Vincent) et Schwendimann (Morini), 6; 23. Biscaini -(Norton), 5; 24. Federli (Ducati), 4; 25. Graf (Yamaha), 3; 26.-Pfister (Norton) et Sern (Ducati), 1. 27 finishers.

Bernadette Jud.

Oldtimers Side-Cars

4th July - Boécourt - La Caquerelle
Race I: 1. Stamm/Müller (Suzuki); 2. Saudan/Stiefel (Triumph); -3. Müller/Landolf (BMW); 4. Flück/Zünd (Suzuki); 5. G. -Ruckstuhl/Epprecht (BMW Kneeler); 6. Lemp/Lemp (Norton); 7. Kulmer/Franz (BMW); 8. U. Ruckstuhl/Dinten (BSA Hornet); 9.-Eichhorn/Schaechtele (D, BMW); 10. Fankhauser/Fankhauser-(Suzuki); 11. Sonnay/Sauteur (Suzuki); 12. Baur/Grossen (BMW). 12 finishers.
Race II: 1. Fankhauser/Fankhauser (Suzuki); 2. Lemp/Lemp -(Norton); 3. Stamm/Müller (Suzuki); 4. Müller/Landolf (BMW); 5.-U. Ruckstuhl/Dinten (BSA Hornet); 6. Eichhorn/Schaechtele (D, -BMW); 7. Fässler/Fässler (BMW); 8. G. Ruckstuhl/Epprecht (BMW- Kneeler); 9. Baur/Grossen (BMW); 10. Flück/Zünd (Suzuki); 11. -Kulmer/Franz (BMW).

18th July - Châtel-Saint-Denis - Les Paccots
1. G. Ruckstuhl/Epprecht (BMW Kneeler); 2. Brönnimann/Pfister-(BSA); 3. Fässler/Fässler (BMW); 4. Flück/Zünd (Suzuki); 5. -Bärtschi/Frankauser (Windle); 6. U. Ruckstuhl/Dinten (BSA Hornet);-7. Belon/Mottier (BMW); 8. Todeschini/Todeschini (Kawasaki); 9. Bezon/Bonzon (Suzuki); 10. Clerc/Mai (Yamaha); 11.-Fankhauser/Fankhauser (Suzuki); 12. Stamm/Müller (Suzuki); 13. -Saudan/Stiefel (Triumph); 14. Lemp/Lemp (Norton); 15. Müller/Landolt (BMW).

Final classification

1. René Stamm — Suzuki — 47
2. Georg Ruckstuhl — BMW — 44
3. Fritz Fankhauser — Suzuki — 38
4. Lemp (Norton), 34; 5. Flück (Suzuki), 33; 6. Müller (BMW), 32; -7. U. Ruckstuhl (BSA), 29; 8. Saudan (Triumph), 25; 9. Fässler-(BMW), 25; 10. Brönnimann (BSA), 20; 11. Eichhorn (D, BMW), 17;-12. Kulmer (BMW), 15; 13. Bärtschi (Windle), 11; 14. Todeschini -(Kawasaki), 9; 15. Bezon (Suzuki), 8; 16. Sonnay (Suzuki), 7. 16- finishers.

△
Head Carrard.

Supermotard Prestige

16th May - Büron
Race I: 1. Ott (D, RST); 2. Duchêne (F, Kawasaki); 3. Götz-(KTM); 4. Müller (Yamaha); 5. Trinkner (F, Honda); 6. Künzel (D,- Husqvarna); 7. Zachmann (Suzuki); 8. Singele (Husqvarna); 9. -Rosenblatt (F, Kawasaki); 10. Bantli (Yamaha); 11. Widmer- (Vertemati); 12. P. Möri (Yamaha); 13. Baumann (Honda); 14. -Gautschi (KTM); 15. Bosonnet (Husqvarna).
Race II: 1. Ott (D, RST); 2. Duchêne (F, Kawasaki); 3. Müller- (Yamaha); 4. Künzel (D, Husqvarna); 5. Trinkner (D, Honda); 6. -Widmer (Vertemati); 7. Zachmann (Suzuki); 8. Singele (Husqvarna); -9. Burgherr (KTM); 10. Walch (F, Yamaha); 11. Rosenblatt (F, Kawasaki); 12. P. Möri (Yamaha); 13. J. Möri (Yamaha); 14. Oehri -(Yamaha); 15. Baumann (Honda).

13th June - Buochs
Race I: 1. Ott (D, RST); 2. Duchêne (F, Kawasaki); 3. Müller -(Yamaha); 4. Künzel (Husqvarna); 5. B. Gautschi (KTM); 6. Widmer- (Vertemati); 7. Götz (KTM); 8. Bantli (Yamaha); 9. Schäfer -(Husqvarna); 10. Burgherr (KTM); 11. P. Möri (Yamaha); 12. Zachmann (Suzuki); 13. Baumgartner (Yamaha); 14. Johler (D,-Husqvarna); 15. Rosenblatt (F, Kawasaki).
Race II: 1. Ott (D, RST); 2. B. Gautschi (KTM); 3. Müller -(Yamaha); 4. Götz (KTM); 5. Widmer (Vertemati); 6. Duchêne- (Kawasaki); 7. Burgherr (KTM); 8. Zachmann (Suzuki); 9. Bantli (Yamaha); 10. Schäfer (Husqvarna); 11. Rosenblatt (F, Kawasaki);-12. J. Möri (Yamaha); 13. Chételat (Monnier); 14. Fischer -(Husqvarna); 15. Marti (Yamaha).

11th July - Bern
Race I: 1. Duchêne (F, Kawasaki); 2. B. Gautschi (KTM); 3. -Müller (Yamaha); 4. Götz (KTM); 5. Zachmann (Suzuki) 6. Oehri -(Yamaha); 7. Bantli (Yamaha); 8. Singele (Husqvarna); 9. Walther -(Yamaha); 10. Brenzikofer (Husqvarna); 11. Gysi (KTM); 12. -Burgherr (KTM); 13. J. Möri (Yamaha); 14. Rosenblatt (F,-Kawasaki); 15. Johler (D, Husqvarna).
Race II: 1. Ott (D, RST); 2. Duchêne (F, Kawasaki); 3. Künzel -(D, Husqvarna); 4. Götz (KTM); 5. B. Gautschi (KTM); 6. Müller- (Yamaha); 7. Oehri (Yamaha); 8. Zachmann (Suzuki); 9. Bantli -(Yamaha); 10. Burgherr (KTM); 11. Rosenblatt (F, Kawasaki); 12. -Mezard (CCM); 13. Walther (Yamaha); 14. Schäfer (Husqvarna); 15. -Brenzikofer (Husqvarna).

15th August - Eschenbach
Race I: 1. Müller (Yamaha); 2. Duchêne (F, Kawasaki); 3.- Salvador (F, KTM); 4. B. Gautschi (KTM); 5. Götz (KTM); 6. Künzel- (D, Husqvarna); 7. Bantli (Yamaha); 8. Zachmann (Suzuki); 9.- Singele (Husqvarna); 10. Baumgartner (Yamaha); 11. Koch (Yamaha);-12. Walther (Yamaha); 13. Gysi (KTM); 14. Johler (Husqvarna); 15. -Mézard (CCM).
Race II: 1. Ott (D, RST); 2. Duchêne (F, Kawasaki); 3. Müller-(Yamaha); 4. B. Gautschi (KTM); 5. Salvador (F, KTM); 6. Zachmann -(Suzuki); 7. Baumgartner (Yamaha); 8. Künzel (D, Husqvarna); 9. -Bantli (Yamaha); 10. Singele (Husqvarna); 11. Freidig (KTM); 12. -Chételat (Monnier); 13. Schäfer (Husqvarna); 14. Rosenblatt (F, -Kawasaki); 15. Oehri (Yamaha).

26th September - Thoune
Race I: 1. Müller (Yamaha); 2. B. Gautschi (KTM); 3. Duchêne-(F, Kawasaki); 4. Götz (KTM); 5. Künzel (D, Husqvarna); 6. -Zachmann (Suzuki); 7. Bantli (Yamaha); 8. Oehri (Yamaha); 9. Baumgartner (Yamaha); 10. Schäfer (Husqvarna); 11. Walther -(Yamaha); 12. Singele (Husqvarna); 13. Freidig (KTM); 14. Marti -(Yamaha); 15. Alpsteg (Yamaha).
Race II: 1. Götz (KTM); 2. Künzel (D, Husqvarna); 3. Duchêne- (F, Kawasaki); 4. Müller (Yamaha); 5. Bantli (Yamaha); 6. Oehri -(Yamaha); 7. B. Gautschi (KTM); 8. Walther (Yamaha); 9. Zachmann- (Suzuki); 10. Rosenblatt (F, Kawasaki); 11. Schäfer (Husqvarna); 12. Singele (Husqvarna); 13. Marti (Yamaha); 14. Klötzli (MuZ);-15. Baumgartner (Yamaha).

10th October - Frauenfeld
Race I: 1. Ott (D, RST); 2. B. Gautschi (KTM); 3. Götz (KTM); -4. Duchêne (F, Kawasaki); 5. Müller (Yamaha); 6. Bantli (Yamaha);-7. Zachmann (Suzuki); 8. Oehri (Yamaha); 9. Singele (Husqvarna);-10. Johler (D, Husqvarna); 11. Bosonnet (Husqvarna); 12. -Rosenblatt (F, Kawasaki); 13. Marti (Yamaha); 14. Weinmann- (Yamaha); 15. Körner (D, Husqvarna).
Race II: 1. Ott (D, RST); 2. B. Gautschi (KTM); 3. Götz (KTM);- 4. Duchêne (F, Kawasaki); 5. Müller (Yamaha); 6. Bantli (Yamaha);-7. Zachmann (Suzuki); 8. Mézard (CCM); 9. Klötzli (MuZ); 10. -Singele (Husqvarna); 11. Oehri (Yamaha); 12. Wolff (Husaberg);-13. Johler (Husqvarna); 14. Gonthier (Husqvarna); 15. Gysi (KTM).

Final classification

1. Daniel Müller — Yamaha — 173
2. Beat Gautschi — KTM — 144
3. Marcel Götz — KTM — 137
4. S. Zachmann (Suzuki), 102; 5. R. Bantli (Yamaha), 93; 6. P.-Singele (Husqvarna), 58; 7. R. Oeri (Yamaha), 53; 8. S. Widmer -(Vertemati), 36; 9. M. Burgherr (KTM), 32; 10. G. Schäfer (Husqvarna), 29; 11. R. Walther (Yamaha), 27; 12. R. Baumgartner -(Yamaha), 26; 13. P. Möri (Yamaha), 13; 14. J. Möri (Yamaha), 10;-15. R. Gysi (KTM), 9; 16. T. Klötzli (MuZ), 9; 17. K. Marti -(Yamaha), 9; 18. H. Freidig (KTM), 8; 19. R. Chételat (Monnier),-7; 20. W. Brenzikofer (Husqvarna), 7; 21. R. Bosonnet (HVA), 6;- 22. E. Koch (Yamaha), 5; 23. B. Baumann (Honda), 4; 24. P.-Fischer (Husqvarna), 2; 25. P. Gonthier (Husqvarna), 2; 26. H.-Weinmann (Yamaha), 2; 27. M. Alpsteg (Yamaha), 1. 27 finishers.

Supermotard Challenger

16th May - Büron
1. Muff (Suzuki); 2. Freidig (KTM); 3. Chételat (Monnier); 4.-Hueber (F, Yamaha); 5. Fässler (Yamaha); 6. Senn (Yamaha); 7.- Röder (D, Honda); 8. Duc (Husqvarna); 9. Marti (Yamaha); 10.- Walzer (KTM); 11. Favre (VOR); 12. Weinmann (Yamaha); 13. Bucher -(Vertemati); 14. Stricker (KTM); 15. Studer (KTM).

13th June - Buochs
1. Walther (Yamaha); 2. Kägi (MuZ); 3. Stricker (KTM); 4. Stulz -(KTM); 5. Fässler (Yamaha); 6. Oehri (Yamaha); 7. Rais (KTM); 8.-Cesini (MuZ); 9. Nyffeler (Husaberg); 10. A. Gautschi (Husqvarna); 11. Schmid (Husaberg); 12. Altherr (KTM); 13. -Metzger (Husqvarna); 14. Philipona (Husaberg); 15. Kaufmann- (KTM).

11th July - Bern
1. Hostettler (MuZ); 2. Koch (Yamaha); 3. P. Möri (Yamaha); 4. -Baumgartner (Yamaha); 5. Senn (Yamaha); 6. Duc (Husqvarna); 7. -Bühler (KTM); 8. Rais (KTM); 9. Nyffeler (Husaberg); 10. Kägi- (MuZ); 11. Dähler (RST-Kawasaki); 12. Kurz (Yamaha); 13. Kaufmann- (KTM); 14. Reusser (Yamaha); 15. Iten (Monnier).

15th August - Eschenbach
1. Voser (KTM); 2. Lamarchand (F, KTM); 3. Kägi (MuZ); 4. Sauvain -(Yamaha); 5. Fässler (Yamaha); 6. Fischer (Husqvarna); 7. Senn -(Yamaha); 8. Elliker (Yamaha); 9. Gonthier (Husqvarna); 10.- Baumann (Honda); 11. Muff (Suzuki); 12. Klötzli (MuZ); 13. Stulz -(KTM); 14. Kaufmann (KTM); 15. Philippona (Husaberg).

26th September - Thoune
1. Stulz (KTM); 2. Dähler (RST-Kawasaki); 3. P. Möri (Yamaha); 4.-Schmid (Husaberg); 5. Hostettler (MuZ); 6. Kägi (MuZ); 7. Muff -(Suzuki); 8. Elliker (Yamaha); 9. Voser (KTM); 10. Kaufmann -(KTM); 11. A. Gautschi (Husqvarna); 12. Senn (Yamaha); 13. Cesini -(MuZ); 14. Rais (KTM); 15. Hehli (Yamaha).

10th October - Frauenfeld
1. Stulz (KTM); 2. Baumann (Honda); 3. Rais (KTM); 4. Kaufmann -(Husqvarna); 5. Schmid (Husaberg); 6. Wirth (Yamaha); 7. Hehli -(Yamaha); 8. Graf (F, KTM); 9. A. Gautschi (Husqvarna); 10. Haag -(Yamaha); 11. Bucher (Vertemati); 12. Zünd (KTM); 13. Fässler (Yamaha); 14. Ganz (Yamaha); 15. Senn (Yamaha).

Final classification

1. Thomas Stulz — KTM — 56
2. Livio Kägi — MuZ — 48
3. Hans Fässler — Yamaha — 36
4. W. Senn (Yamaha), 35; 5. P. Muff (Suzuki), 34; 6. Y. Rais -(KTM), 34; 7. E. Hostettler (MuZ), 31; 8. P. Möri (Yamaha), 30; -9. R. Schmid (Husaberg), 29; 10. P. Voser (KTM), 27; 11. B. -Baumann (Honda), 23; 12. N. Dähler (RST), 22; 13. R. Walther -(Yamaha), 20; 14. Y. Duc (Husqvarna), 18; 15. A. Gautschi -(Husqvarna), 18; 16. E. Koch (Yamaha), 17; 17. H. Freidig (KTM),-17; 18. S. Lamarchand (F, KTM), 17; 19. C. Stricker (KTM), 17; -20. W. Elliker (Yamaha), 16; 21. R. Chételat (Monnier), 15; 22. -R. Nyffeler (Husaberg), 14; 23. R. Baumgartner (Yamaha), 13; 24. -P. Kaufmann (Husqvarna), 13; 25. N. Sauvain (Yamaha), 13; 26. M.-Hueber (F, Yamaha), 13; 27. S. Kaufmann (KTM), 12; 28. P. Cesini -(MuZ), 11; 29. P. Fischer (Husqvarna), 10; 30. A. Hehli (Yamaha),-10; 31. R. Oehri (Yamaha), 10; 32. R. Wirth (Yamaha), 10; 33. T. -Röder (D, Honda), 9; 34. A. Bühler (KTM), 9; 35. R. Graf (F, -KTM), 8; 36. R. Bucher (Vertemati), 8; 37. P. Gonthier -(Husqvarna), 7; 38. K. Marti (Yamaha), 7; 39. P. Walzer (KTM), 6; -40. E. Haag (Yamaha), 6; 41. B. Favre (VOR), 5; 42. H. Weinmann- (Yamaha), 4; 43. N. Zünd (KTM), 4; 44. G. Altherr (KTM), 4; 45. -P. Kurz (Yamaha), 4; 46. T. Klötzli (MuZ), 4; 47. A. Metzger (D, -Husqvarna), 3; 48. T. Philipona (Husaberg), 3; 49. U. Reusser- (Yamaha), 2; 50. R. Ganz (Yamaha), 2; 51. J. Iten (Monnier), 1;-52. R. Studer (KTM), 1. 52 finishers.

Supermotard Fun

16th May - Büron
1. Nef (KTM); 2. Oesch (RST); 3. Filli (KTM); 4. F. Müller (KTM);- 5. Wiederkehr (Husqvarna); 6. C. Müller (Husaberg); 7. Egli -(Yamaha); 8. Sonner (KTM); 9. Harr (Honda); 10. Marty (KTM); 11.- Keller (Husqvarna); 12. Dummermuth (RST); 14.-Bösch (Suzuki); 15. Frey (Vertemati).

13th June - Buochs
1. Filli (KTM); 2. Gsell (Husqvarna); 3. Jenny (Yamaha); 4. C.- Müller (Husaberg); 5. Weibel (Yamaha); 6. Harr (Honda); 7.- Hasler (KTM); 8. Keller (Husqvarna); 9. Scheidegger (Honda); 10.- Gallina (Yamaha); 11. Steiner (BMW); 12. Allenbach (KTM); 13. -Durrer (KTM); 14. Jenni (Yamaha); 15. Schmid (Yamaha).

11th July - Bern
1. Filli (KTM); 2. Sonner (KTM); 3. C. Müller (Husaberg); 4. -Murer (Husqvarna); 5. Hasler (KTM); 6. Frey (Vertemati); 7. Gsell -(Husqvarna); 8. Gallina (Yamaha); 9. Scheidegger (Honda); 10. -Dummermuth (RST); 11. Bolliger (Yamaha) 12. Allemann (KTM); 13.- Hess (KTM); 14. Scherrer (Husqvarna); 15. Grangier (KTM).

15th August - Eschenbach
1. Filli (KTM); 2. Gsell (Husqvarna); 3. C. Müller (Husaberg); 4.-Sonner (KTM); 5. Gallina (Yamaha); 6. Scheidegger (Honda); 7. -Dummermuth (RST); 8. De Bell (Husqvarna); 9. Bösch (Suzuki); 10.- Hasler (KTM); 11. Harr (Honda); 12. Salzmann (Monnier); 13.- Bolliger (Yamaha); 14. Hess (KTM); 15. Wiederkehr (Husqvarna).

26th September - Thoune
1. Oesch (RST); 2. S. Steiner (Yamaha); 3. Gsell (Husqvarna); 4. -Wüthrich (Yamaha); 5. De Bell (Husqvarna); 6. Bösch (Suzuki); 7. -Keller (Husqvarna); 8. Wiederkehr (Husqvarna); 9. Egli (Yamaha);-10. P. Steiner (KTM); 11. Meier (Honda); 12. Allenbach (KTM); 13. Scheidegger (Honda); 14. Vogel (Vertemati); 15. Bärenfaller- (Yamaha).

10th October - Frauenfeld
1. Gsell (Husqvarna); 2. C. Müller (Husaberg); 3. Keller -(Husqvarna); 4. Sonner (KTM); 5. Oesch (RST); 6. Bärenfaller -(Yamaha); 7. Widmer (Kawasaki); 8. Bolliger (Yamaha); 9. Hess- (KTM); 10. Scheidegger (Honda); 11. Weibel (Husqvarna); 12. De -Bell (Husqvarna); 13. Wiederkehr (Husqvarna); 14. Egli (Yamaha);-15. Hasler (KTM).

Supermotard Youngster

16th May - Büron
Race I: 1. Allemann (Yamaha); 2. Aggeler (Yamaha); 3. Känel- (Yamaha); 4. Heierli (Honda); 5. Blöchliger (KTM); 6. Imgüt- (Sachs); 7. Dubois (Sachs); 8. Lanz (Yamaha); 9. Baumann (Yamaha);-10. Gorgiev (Sachs).
Race II: 1. Känel (Yamaha); 2. Allemann (Yamaha); 3. Blöchliger -(KTM); 4. Heierli (Honda); 5. Imgüt (Sachs); 6. Dubois (Sachs); -7. Aggeler (Yamaha); 8. Gorgiev (Sachs); 9. Lanz (Yamaha); 10.-Baumann (Yamaha).

13th June - Buochs
1. Allemann (Yamaha); 2. Känel (Yamaha); 3. Blöchliger (KTM); 4. -Aggeler (Yamaha); 5. Heierli (Honda); 6. Gorgiev (Sachs); 7. -Imgüt (Sachs); 8. Dubois (Sachs); 9. Lanz (Yamaha); 10. Wittwer- Yamaha).

11th July - Bern
Race I: 1. Allemann (Yamaha); 2. Blöchliger (KTM); 3. Aggeler -(Yamaha); 4. Imgüt (Sachs); 5. Forestier (Husqvarna); 6. Heierli -(Honda); 7. Gorgiev (Sachs); 8. Wittwer (Yamaha); 9. Baumann -(Yamaha); 10. Held (KTM).
Race II: 1. Allemann (Yamaha); 2. Blöchliger (KTM); 3. Heierli -(Honda); 4. Aggeler (Yamaha); 5. Gorgiev (Sachs); 6. Imgüt- (Sachs); 7. Lanz (Yamaha); 8. Baumann (Yamaha); 9. Wittwer (Yamaha); 10. Held (KTM).

15th August - Eschenbach
Race I: 1. Allemann (Yamaha); 2. Känel (Yamaha); 3. Imgüt- (Sachs); 4. Aggeler (Yamaha); 5. Lanz (Yamaha); 6. Blöchliger-(KTM); 7. Heierli (Honda); 8. Gorgiev (Sachs); 9. Dubois (Sachs);-10. Baumann (Yamaha).
Race II: 1. Känel (Yamaha); 2. Allemann (Yamaha); 3. Imgüt- (Sachs); 4. Lanz (Yamaha); 5. Heierli (Honda); 6. Blöchliger- (KTM); 7. Dubois (Sachs); 8. Gorgiev (Sachs); 9. Aggeler (Yamaha); 10. Baumann (Yamaha).

26th September - Thoune
Race I: 1. Allemann (Yamaha); 2. Imgüt (Sachs); 3. Aggeler -(Yamaha); 4. Heierli (Honda); 5. Känel (Yamaha); 6. Blöchliger- (KTM); 7. Lanz (Yamaha); 8. Baumann (Yamaha); 9. Wittwer (Yamaha); 10. Aeschbacher (Yamaha).
Race II: 1. Allemann (Yamaha); 2. Aggeler (Yamaha); 3. Heierli -(Honda); 4. Blöchliger (KTM); 5. Känel (Yamaha); 6. Lanz -(Yamaha); 7. Imgüt (Sachs); 8. Wittwer (Yamaha); 9. Dubois (Sachs); 10. Baumann (Yamaha).

10th October - Frauenfeld
Race I: 1. Allemann (Yamaha); 2. Aggeler (Yamaha); 3. Känel -(Yamaha); 4. Blöchliger (KTM); 5. Lanz (Yamaha); 6. Imgüt- (Sachs); 7. Heierli (Honda); 8. Gorgiev (Sachs); 9. Dubois- (Sachs); 10. Forestier (Husqvarna).
Race II: 1. Allemann (Yamaha); 2. Aggeler (Yamaha); 3. Känel -(Yamaha); 4. Blöchliger (KTM); 5. Imgüt (Sachs); 6. Heierli -(Honda); 7. Lanz (Yamaha); 8. Forestier (Husqvarna); 9. Dubois (Sachs); 10. Wittwer (Yamaha).

Final classification

1. Luc Allemann	Yamaha	214
2. Michael Aggeler	Yamaha	153
3. Franz Blöchliger	KTM	144

4. S. Känel (Yamaha), 141; 5. R. Imgüt (Sachs), 130; 6. A.-Heierli (Honda), 129; 7. R. Lanz (Yamaha), 99; 8. D. Dubois -(Sachs), 73; 9. G. Gorgiev (Sachs), 71; 10. S. Baumann (Yamaha), -69; 11. E. Wittwer (Yamaha), 56; 12. D. Forestier (Husqvarna), -25; 13. L. Held (KTM) and M. Weiersmüller (Kawasaki), 16; 15. R. -Aeschbacher (Yamaha), 10. 15 finishers.

Supermotard Women

16th May - Büron
Race I: 1. Stöckli (Yamaha); 2. Berglas (Husaberg); 3. -Scheidegger (Honda); 4. Stiner (Husaberg); 5. Hofmann (Kawasaki); -6. Gasser (KTM); 7. Aufdenblatten (Suzuki); 8. Graf (Suzuki); 9. -Zimmermann (KTM); 10. Klöti (Yamaha).
Race II: 1. Stöckli (Yamaha); 2. Berglas (Husaberg); 3. -Klöti (Yamaha); 4. Stöckli (Husaberg); 5. Stiner (Husaberg); 6. -Gasser (KTM); 7. Hofmann (Kawasaki); 8. Aufdenblatten (Suzuki); -9. Zimmermann (KTM); 10. Graf (Suzuki).

13th June - Buochs
1. Stöckli (Yamaha); 2. Berglas (Husqvarna); 3. Scheidegger -(Honda); 4. Bethke (KTM); 5. Klöti (Yamaha); 6. Hofmann- (Kawasaki); 7. Arnet (Husberg); 8. Gasser (KTM); 9. Stiner (Husqvarna); 10. Aufdenblatten (Suzuki).

11th July - Bern
Race I: 1. Stöckli (Yamaha); 2. Berglas (Husaberg); 3. -Scheidegger (Husaberg); 4. Rieser (Husqvarna); 5. Hofmann -(Kawasaki); 6. Stiner (Husaberg); 7. Zimmermann (KTM); 8. Aufdenblatten (Suzuki); 9. Sahli (KTM); 10. Graf (Suzuki).
Race II: 1. Rieser (Husqvarna); 2. Stöckli (Yamaha); 3. Berglas -(Husaberg); 4. Scheidegger (Husaberg); 5. Stiner (Husaberg); 6. -Gasser (KTM); 7. Zimmermann (KTM); 8. Aufdenblatten (Suzuki); 9.-Sahli (KTM); 10. Graf (Suzuki).

15th August - Eschenbach
Race I: 1. Hediger (KTM); 2. Scheidegger (Husaberg); 3. Berglas -(Husaberg); 4. Stiner (Husaberg); 5. Zimmermann (KTM); 6. Stöckli -(Yamaha); 7. Hofmann (Kawasaki); 8. Aufdenblatten (Suzuki); 9. -Sahli (KTM); 10. Rieser (Husqvarna).
Race II: 1. Stöckli (Yamaha); 2. Hediger (KTM); 3. Berglas -(Husaberg); 4. Scheidegger (Husaberg); 5. Hofmann (Kawasaki); 6. -Stiner (Kawasaki); 7. Gasser (Husaberg); 8. Zimmermann (KTM); 9. Sahli -(KTM); 10. Aufdenblatten (Suzuki).

26th September - Thoune
Race I: 1. Stöckli (Yamaha); 2. Scheidegger (Honda); 3. Stiner -(Husaberg); 4. Gasser (KTM); 5. Schmutz (KTM); 6. Sahli (KTM); 7. -Aufdenblatten (Suzuki); 8. Hofmann (Kawasaki); 9. Graf (Suzuki);-10. Zimmermann (KTM).
Race II: 1. Stöckli (Yamaha); 2. Scheidegger (Honda); 3. Rieser -(Husqvarna); 4. Hofmann (Kawasaki); 5. Stiner (Husaberg); 6. -Gasser (KTM); 7. Schmutz (KTM); 8. Zimmermann (KTM); 9. Sahli -(KTM); 10. Aufdenbatten (Suzuki).

10th October - Frauenfeld
Race I: 1. Hediger (KTM); 2. Stöckli (Yamaha); 3. Rieser -(Husqvarna); 4. Bethke (KTM); 5. Scheidegger (Honda); 6. Stiner -(Husaberg); 7. Gasser (KTM); 8. Sahli (KTM); 9. Kyburz (Suzuki);-10. Graf (Suzuki).
Race II: 1. Hediger (KTM); 2. Stöckli (Yamaha); 3. Scheidegger -(Honda); 4. Rieser (Husqvarna); 5. Bethke (KTM); 6. Stiner -(Husaberg); 7. Gasser (KTM); 8. Sahli (KTM); 9. Kyburz (Suzuki);-10. Zimmermann (KTM).

US-Championship

250 cc

<u>The Champion:</u> Chuck Sorensen (Yamaha). Born on 14th August 1972, in Santa Clara/California.
<u>Races record:</u> 26th in US 250 Championship 1992; 21st in US 250 Championship 1993; 2nd in US 250 Championship (Yamaha) 1994; 3rd in US 250 Championship (Yamaha) 1995; 17th in US 250 Championship, 30th in US Supersport 750 Championship (Honda) 1997; 3rd in US 250 Championship (Yamaha) 1998; US 250 Champion (Yamaha) 1999.

7th March - Daytona
1. L. Lavado (VEN, Yamaha); 2. McGuiness (GB, Honda); 3. Esser (BMW); 4. Sorensen (Aprilia); 5. D. King (Honda); 6. Gilbert (Yamaha); 7. K. King (Yamaha); 8. Vos (NL, Aprilia); 9. Lee (Honda); 10. Richardson (Honda); 11. Leggitt (Yamaha); 12. Quintero (Honda); 13. Stephens (Yamaha); 14. France (Honda); 15. Kanie (Yamaha).

21st March - Phoenix
1. Sorensen (Yamaha); 2. Terranova (Yamaha); 3. Cubbage (Yamaha); 4. D. King (Honda); 5. Vos (NL, Yamaha); 6. K. King (Yamaha); 7. Esser (Honda); 8. Ulrich (Yamaha); 9. Sorbo (Yamaha); 10. Quintero (Honda); 11. L. Roberts (Yamaha); 12. King (Yamaha); 13. Jensen (Aprilia); 14. Lind (Yamaha); 15. France (Honda).

18th April - Willow Springs
1. Sorensen (Yamaha); 2. Salaverria (Aprilia); 3. Terranova (Yamaha); 4. Ienatsch (Yamaha); 5. Cubbage (Yamaha); 6. Ulrich (Yamaha); 7. K. King (Yamaha); 8. Sorbo (Yamaha); 9. Esser (Honda); 10. Vos (NL, Honda); 11. Georges (Yamaha); 12. Melneciuc (Honda); 13. Candelaria (Yamaha); 14. Lind (Yamaha); 15. Jeffery (NZ, Honda).

25th April - Sears Point
1. Sorensen (Yamaha); 2. Salaverria (Aprilia); 3. Terranova (Yamaha); 4. Leggitt (Honda); 5. K. King (Yamaha); 6. Sorbo (Yamaha); 7. Ulrich (Yamaha); 8. Vos (NL, Honda); 9. Marchini (Honda); 10. France (Honda); 11. De Groot (Honda); 12. Cubbage (Yamaha); 13. Jeffery (NZ, Honda); 14. Esser (Honda); 15. Candelaria (Yamaha).

2nd May - Laguna Seca
1. Terranova (Yamaha); 2. Q. King (Yamaha); 3. Sands (Yamaha); 4. Ienatsch (Aprilia); 5. Salaverria (Aprilia); 6. Sorensen (Yamaha); 7. Melneciuc (Honda); 8. Griffiths (Yamaha); 9. D. King (Honda); 10. Reeser (Yamaha); 11. France (Honda); 12. Esser (Honda); 13. Georges (Yamaha); 14. K. King (Yamaha); 15. Jeffery (NZ, Honda).

6th June - Road Atlanta
1. Sorensen (Yamaha); 2. Sands (Yamaha); 3. Ulrich (Yamaha); 4. D. King (Honda); 5. Q. King (Yamaha); 6. Sorbo (Yamaha); 7. Quintero (Honda); 8. Melneciuc (Honda); 9. Himmelsbach (Yamaha); 10. Lind (Yamaha); 11. Staeopoli (Honda); 12. Grier (Honda); 13. Bonner (Yamaha); 14. France (Honda); 15. Worthington (Aprilia).

13th June - Road America
1. Sands (Yamaha); 2. Renfrow (Honda); 3. Sorensen (Yamaha); 4. K. King (Yamaha); 5. Stephens (Honda); 6. D. King (Honda); 7. Ulrich (Yamaha); 8. Himmelsbach (Yamaha); 9. Melneciuc (Honda); 10. Quintero (Honda); 11. Maloney (Yamaha); 12. Worthington (Aprilia); 13. MacKay (Yamaha); 14. Doe (Yamaha); 15. Lind (Yamaha).

20th June - Loudon
1. D. King (Honda); 2. Ulrich (Yamaha); 3. Wood (Yamaha); 4. Q. King (Yamaha); 5. Vos (NL, Yamaha); 6. Sorbo (Yamaha); 7. Staropoli (Honda); 8. Quintero (Honda); 9. Iannarelli (Yamaha); 10. France (Honda); 11. Bonner (Yamaha); 12. Reynolds (Yamaha); 13. Zajac (Yamaha); 14. Rios (Yamaha); 15. Anderson (Yamaha).

18th July - Lexington
1. Sorensen (Yamaha); 2. Renfrow (Honda); 3. D. King (Honda); 4. Ulrich (Yamaha); 5. Vos (NL, Honda); 6. Himmelsbach (Yamaha); 7. Esser (Honda); 8. Q. King (Yamaha); 9. Sorbo (Yamaha); 10. Melneciuc (Honda); 11. Bonner (Yamaha); 12. Stephens (Honda); 13. France (Honda); 14. Quintero (Honda); 15. Lind (Yamaha).

1st August - Brainerd
1. Sorensen (Yamaha); 2. Hale (Honda); 3. D. King (Honda); 4. Esser (Honda); 5. Ulrich (Yamaha); 6. Sorbo (Yamaha); 7. Lind (Yamaha); 8. Melneciuc (Honda); 9. Vos (NL, Honda); 10. Himmelsbach (Yamaha); 11. Stephens (Honda); 12. France (Honda); 13. Staropoli (Honda); 14. Quintero (Honda); 15. Jensen (Aprilia).

19th September - Fontain
1. Sands (Yamaha); 2. Sorensen (Yamaha); 3. Q. King (Yamaha); 4. Leggitt (Honda); 5. D. King (Honda); 6. Esser (Honda); 7. Vos (NL, Honda); 8. K. King (Yamaha); 9. Melneciuc (Honda); 10. Ulrich (Yamaha); 11. Renfrow (Honda); 12. L. Roberts (Yamaha); 13. France (Honda); 14. Sorbo (Yamaha); 15. Jensen (Aprilia).

Final classification

1. Chuck Sorensen	Yamaha	340
2. Derek King	Honda	263
3. Chris Ulrich	Yamaha	243

4. Q. King (Yamaha), 237; 5. J. Vos (NL, Honda), 203; 6. E. Sorbo (Yamaha), 200; 7. G. Esser (Honda), 198; 8. J. France (Honda), 194; 9. R. Quintero (Honda), 169; 10. P. Melneciuc (Honda), 154; 11. B. Lind (Yamaha), 136; 12. R. Sands (Yamaha), 135; 13. G. Terranova (Yamaha), 126; 14. K. King (Yamaha), 105; 15. W. Himmelsbach (Yamaha), 96; 16. A. Salaverria (Aprilia), 93; 17. R. Renfrow (Honda), 91; 18. C. Jensen (Aprilia), 90; 19. J. Bonner (Yamaha), 88; 20. R. Staropoli (Honda), 85. 96 classified.

Supersport 600

<u>The Champion:</u> Nicky Hayden. Born on 30th July 1981, in Owensboro/Kentucky.
<u>Races record:</u> 4th US Supersport 600 Championship, 4th US Supersport 750 Championship (Suzuki) 1998; US Supersport 600 Champion, 22nd US Superbike Championship, 2nd US Formula Xtreme Championship (Honda) 1999.

5th March - Daytona
1. Mi. DuHamel (CAN, Honda); 2. K. Roberts (Honda); 3. Hacking (Yamaha); 4. N. Hayden (Honda); 5. Yates (Kawasaki); 6. Hayes (Suzuki); 7. Oliver (Yamaha); 8. Rapp (Suzuki); 9. Harrington (Kawasaki); 10. Marmor (Kawasaki); 11. Mori (J, Yamaha); 12. T. Hayden (Yamaha); 13. Pridmore (Suzuki); 14. Barnes (Yamaha); 15. Cornwell (Honda).

21st March - Phoenix
1. N. Hayden (Honda); 2. Hacking (Yamaha); 3. T. Hayden (Yamaha); 4. Alexander (Suzuki); 5. Yates (Kawasaki); 6. Crevier (CAN, Suzuki); 7. Oliver (Yamaha); 8. Pridmore (Suzuki); 9. Harrell (Yamaha); 10. Harrington (Kawasaki); 11. Hayes (Suzuki); 12. K. Roberts (Honda); 13. Kipp (Suzuki); 14. Rapp (Suzuki); 15. Zemke (Suzuki).

18th April - Willow Springs
1. T. Hayden (Yamaha); 2. Hacking (Yamaha); 3. Yates (Kawasaki); 4. N. Hayden (Honda); 5. Hayes (Suzuki); 6. Oliver (Yamaha); 7. Crevier (CAN, Suzuki); 8. K. Roberts (Honda); 9. Zemke (Suzuki); 10. Kipp (Suzuki); 11. Kowalski (Honda); 12. Parriott (Honda); 13. Martin (Kawasaki); 14. E. Bostrom (Honda); 15. Mi. DuHamel (CAN, Honda).

25th April - Sears Point
1. N. Hayden (Honda); 2. Mi. DuHamel (CAN, Honda); 3. Yates (Kawasaki); 4. K. Roberts (Honda); 5. Crevier (CAN, Suzuki); 6. T. Hayden (Yamaha); 7. Pridmore (Suzuki); 8. Parriott (Honda); 9. Kipp (Yamaha); 10. Hayes (Suzuki); 11. Oliver (Yamaha); 12. Rapp (Suzuki); 13. E. Bostrom (Honda); 14. Mori (J, Yamaha); 15. Zemke (Suzuki).

2nd May - Laguna Seca
1. T. Hayden (Yamaha); 2. Crevier (CAN, Suzuki); 3. Buckmaster (AUS, Suzuki); 4. Hacking (Yamaha); 5. Oliver (Yamaha); 6. E. Bostrom (Honda); 7. Rapp (Suzuki); 8. N. Hayden (Honda); 9. Pridmore (Suzuki); 10. Mi. DuHamel (CAN, Honda); 11. Wasson (Suzuki); 12. Kovarick (Suzuki); 13. Doran (Honda); 14. Mori (J, Yamaha); 15. Kowalski (Honda).

6th June - Road Atlanta
1. N. Hayden (Honda); 2. T. Hayden (Yamaha); 3. Hacking (Yamaha); 4. Yates (Kawasaki); 5. Hayes (Suzuki); 6. Oliver (Yamaha); 7. Crevier (CAN, Suzuki); 8. Rapp (Suzuki); 9. K. Roberts (Honda); 10. E. Bostrom (Honda); 11. Pridmore (Suzuki); 12. Kowalski (Honda); 13. Harrell (Yamaha); 14. Kipp (Suzuki); 15. Sands (Yamaha).

13th June - Road America
1. Hacking (Yamaha); 2. N. Hayden (Honda); 3. T. Hayden (Yamaha); 4. K. Roberts (Honda); 5. E. Bostrom (Honda); 6. Crevier (CAN, Suzuki); 7. Hayes (Suzuki); 8. Rapp (Suzuki); 9. Mori (J, Yamaha); 10. Pridmore (Suzuki); 11. Graves (Yamaha); 12. Kowalski (Honda); 13. Zemke (Suzuki); 14. Parriott (Honda); 15. R.-L. Hayden (Suzuki).

20th June - Loudon
1. N. Hayden (Honda); 2. Yates (Kawasaki); 3. T. Hayden (Yamaha); 4. Hacking (Yamaha); 5. Crevier (CAN, Suzuki); 6. Hayes (Suzuki); 7. E. Bostrom (Honda); 8. K. Roberts (Honda); 9. Rapp (Suzuki); 10. Hopkins (Suzuki); 11. Pridmore (Suzuki); 12. Parriott (Honda); 13. Gill (Kawasaki); 14. Kipp (Suzuki); 15. Buckmaster (AUS, Suzuki).

10th July - Laguna Seca
1. T. Hayden (Yamaha); 2. Hacking (Yamaha); 3. K. Roberts (Honda); 4. E. Bostrom (Honda); 5. N. Hayden (Honda); 6. Pridmore (Suzuki); 7. Yates (Kawasaki); 8. Crevier (CAN, Suzuki); 9. Parriott (Honda); 10. Hayes (Suzuki); 11. Rapp (Suzuki); 12. Zemke (Suzuki); 13. Kowalski (Honda); 14. Graves (Yamaha); 15. R.-L. Hayden (Suzuki).

Final classification

1. Nicky Hayden	Honda	372
2. Tommy Hayden	Yamaha	364
3. Kurtis Roberts	Honda	300

4. J. Hacking (Yamaha), 285; 5. A. Yates (Kawasaki), 268; 6. J.-K. Hayes (Suzuki), 267; 7. S. Crevier (CAN, Suzuki), 262; 8. S. Rapp (Suzuki), 236; 9. E. Bostrom (Honda), 226; 10. J. Pridmore (Suzuki), 221; 11. B. Parriott (Honda), 195; 12. T. Kipp (Suzuki), 192; 13. R. Oliver (Yamaha), 169; 14. S. Kowalski (Honda), 161; 15. J. Zemke (Suzuki), 138; 16. D. Buckmaster (AUS, Suzuki), 132; 17. Mi. DuHamel (CAN, Honda), 115; 18. P. Harrell (Yamaha), 108; 19. J. Gill (Kawasaki), 99; 20. T. Mori (J, Yamaha), 76. 122 classified.

18th July - Lexington
1. N. Hayden (Honda); 2. T. Hayden (Yamaha); 3. K. Roberts (Honda); 4. Yates (Kawasaki); 5. E. Bostrom (Honda); 6. Hayes (Suzuki); 7. Pridmore (Suzuki); 8. Hopkins (Suzuki); 9. Kipp (Suzuki); 10. Rapp (Suzuki); 11. Gill (Kawasaki); 12. Buckmaster (AUS, Suzuki); 13. Parriott (Honda); 14. Zemke (Suzuki); 15. Wood (Kawasaki).

1st August - Brainerd
1. Hacking (Yamaha); 2. K. Roberts (Honda); 3. N. Hayden (Honda); 4. Hayes (Suzuki); 5. T. Hayden (Yamaha); 6. Parriott (Honda); 7. Kipp (Suzuki); 8. Kowalski (Honda); 9. Pridmore (Suzuki); 10. Buckmaser (AUS, Suzuki); 11. Crevier (CAN, Suzuki); 12. Rapp (Suzuki); 13. Zemke (Suzuki); 14. E. Bostrom (Honda); 15. Wood (Kawasaki).

19th September - Fountain
1. Yates (Kawasaki); 2. T. Hayden (Yamaha); 3. K. Roberts (Honda); 4. Crevier (CAN, Suzuki); 5. N. Hayden (Honda); 6. E. Bostrom (Honda); 7. Rapp (Suzuki); 8. Kipp (Suzuki); 9. Buckmaster (AUS, Suzuki); 10. Oliver (Yamaha); 11. Parriott (Honda); 12. Hayes (Suzuki); 13. Harrell (Yamaha); 14. R.-L. Hayden (Suzuki); 15. Junge (Kawasaki).

Supersport 750

<u>The Champion:</u> Tom Kipp. Born on 17th November 1968, in Willoughby/Ohio.
<u>Races record:</u> 41st US Supersport 600 Championship 1987; 18th US Superbike Championship 1988; 8th US Superbike Championship, 23rd US Supersport 750 Championship, 6th US Supersport 600 Championship 1989; 45th World Superbike Championship, 6th US Superbike Championship (Yamaha) 1990; 31st World Superbike Championship, 10th US Superbike Championship, 18th US Supersport 750 Championship, 2nd US Supersport 600 Championship (Yamaha), 115e World Endurance Championship (Suzuki) 1991; 6th US Superbike Championship, 22nd US Supersport 750 Championship, US Supersport 600 Champion (Honda) 1992; 20th US Superbike Championship, 13th US Supersport 600 Championship 1993; 12th US Superbike Championship, US Supersport 750 Champion 1994; 38th World Superbike Championship, 3rd US Superbike Championship, US Supersport 750 Champion (Yamaha) 1995; 3rd US Supersport 750 Championship (Yamaha) 1996; 33rd World Superbike Championship, 7th US Superbike Championship, 7th US Supersport 600 Championship (Yamaha) 1997; 6th US Superbike Championship (Ducati) 1998; US Supersport 750 Champion, 12th US Supersport 600 Championship (Suzuki) 1999.

5th March - Daytona
1. Hayes (Suzuki); 2. Moore (Suzuki); 3. Kipp (Suzuki); 4. Lopez (Suzuki); 5. Alexander (Suzuki); 6. Bowman (Suzuki); 7. Gibbs (Suzuki); 8. Randolph (Suzuki); 9. Zemke (Suzuki); 10. T. Hayden (Yamaha); 11. Ma. DuHamel (CAN, Suzuki); 12. Haskovec (Suzuki); 13. Harrington (Kawasaki); 14. Henning (Suzuki); 15. Jacobi (Suzuki).

20th March - Phoenix
1. Kipp (Suzuki); 2. Alexander (Suzuki); 3. T. Hayden (Yamaha); 4. Moore (Suzuki); 5. Cicotto (Suzuki); 6. Haskovec (Suzuki); 7. Randolph (Suzuki); 8. Hayes (Suzuki); 9. Haner (Suzuki); 10. Harrington (Kawasaki); 11. Ma. DuHamel (CAN, Suzuki); 12. Bowman (Suzuki); 13. Clarke (Suzuki); 14. Parriott (Honda); 15. Jacobi (Suzuki).

18th April - Willow Springs
1. Kipp (Suzuki); 2. Zemke (Suzuki); 3. Moore (Suzuki); 4. T. Hayden (Yamaha); 5. Alexander (Suzuki); 6. Lopez (Suzuki); 7. Hayes (Suzuki); 8. Ma. DuHamel (CAN, Suzuki); 9. Bowman (Suzuki); 10. Adams (Suzuki); 11. Parriott (Honda); 12. Randolph (Suzuki); 13. Chase (Suzuki); 14. Doran (Honda); 15. Short (Suzuki).

25th April - Sears Point
1. Kipp (Suzuki); 2. T. Hayden (Yamaha); 3. Randolph (Suzuki); 4. Parriott (Honda); 5. Moore (Suzuki); 6. Zemke (Suzuki); 7. Lopez (Suzuki); 8. Bowman (Suzuki); 9. Ma. DuHamel (CAN, Suzuki); 10. Gill (Suzuki); 11. Haskovec (Suzuki); 12. Foster (Kawasaki); 13. Hayes (Suzuki); 14. Sneyd (Honda); 15. Rayborn (Suzuki).

2nd May - Laguna Seca
1. Kipp (Suzuki); 2. Moore (Suzuki); 3. Alexander (Suzuki); 4. T. Hayden (Yamaha); 5. Bowman (Suzuki); 6. Ma. DuHamel (Suzuki); 7. Hayes (Suzuki); 8. Parriott (Honda); 9. Doran (Honda); 10. Henning (Suzuki); 11. Zemke (Suzuki); 12. Acree (Suzuki); 13. Rayborn (Suzuki); 14. Prussiano (Suzuki); 15. Chase (Suzuki).

6th June - Road Atlanta
1. Kipp (Suzuki); 2. Lopez (Suzuki); 3. Zemke (Suzuki); 4. Moore (Suzuki); 5. R.-L. Hayden (Suzuki); 6. Ma. DuHamel (Suzuki); 7. Barnes (Suzuki); 8. Alexander (Suzuki); 9. T. Hayden (Yamaha); 10. Buckmaster (AUS, Suzuki); 11. Prussiano (Suzuki); 12. Rose (Suzuki); 13. Randolph (Suzuki); 14. Jacobi (Suzuki); 15. Wilson (Suzuki).

13th June - Road America
1. Lopez (Suzuki); 2. Zemke (Suzuki); 3. Kipp (Suzuki); 4. Moore (Suzuki); 5. Bowman (Suzuki); 6. Buckmaster (AUS, Suzuki); 7. Alexander (Suzuki); 8. R.-L. Hayden (Suzuki); 9. Ma. DuHamel (CAN, Suzuki); 10. Hayes (Suzuki); 11. T. Hayden (Yamaha); 12. Randolph (Suzuki); 13. Rankin (Suzuki); 14. Parriott (Honda); 15. Clarke (Suzuki).

20th June - Loudon
1. Lopez (Suzuki); 2. Zemke (Suzuki); 3. Bowman (Suzuki); 4. Buckmaster (AUS, Suzuki); 5. Hopkins (Suzuki); 6. Randolph (Suzuki); 7. Moore (Suzuki); 8. Alexander (Suzuki); 9. Parriott (Honda); 10. Ma. DuHamel (CAN, Suzuki); 11. R.-L. Hayden (Suzuki); 12. Chouinard (Suzuki); 13. Gill (Kawasaki); 14. Haskovec (Suzuki); 15. Silva (Kawasaki).

Final classification

1. Tom Kipp	Suzuki	344
2. Jake Zemke	Suzuki	288
3. Jimmy Moore	Suzuki	274

4. G. Lopez (Suzuki), 247; 5. Ma. DuHamel (CAN, Suzuki), 247; 6. J. Randolph (Suzuki), 234; 7. J. Bowman (Suzuki), 228; 8. T. Hayden (Yamaha), 214; 9. B. Parriott (Honda), 186; 10. R. Alexander (Suzuki), 183; 11. D. Buckmaster (AUS, Suzuki), 150; 12. J.-K. Hayes (Suzuki), 147; 13. J. Jacobi (Suzuki), 128; 14. J. Gill (Kawasaki), 119; 15. R.-L. Hayden (Suzuki), 118; 16. S. Clarke (Suzuki), 100; 17. V. Haskovec (Suzuki), 96; 18. G. Henning (Suzuki), 79; 19. J. Haner (Suzuki), 70; 20. D. Duprey (Suzuki), 65. 127 classified.

18th July - Lexington
1. T. Hayden (Yamaha); 2. Zemke (Suzuki); 3. Kipp (Suzuki); 4. Gill (Kawasaki); 5. Randolph (Suzuki); 6. Ma. DuHamel (CAN, Suzuki); 7. Parriott (Honda); 8. Moore (Suzuki); 9. Jacobi (Suzuki); 10. Doerfler (Suzuki); 11. Hopkins (Suzuki); 12. Henning (Suzuki); 13. McGrath (Suzuki); 14. Bowman (Suzuki); 15. Roeder (Yamaha).

1st August - Brainerd
1. Buckmaster (AUS, Suzuki); 2. Lopez (Suzuki); 3. Zemke (Suzuki); 4. Bowman (Suzuki); 5. Kipp (Suzuki); 6. Randolph (Suzuki); 7. R.-L. Hayden (Suzuki); 8. Ma. DuHamel (CAN, Suzuki); 9. Parriott (Honda); 10. Jacobi (Suzuki); 11. Jensen (Yamaha); 12. Wood (Kawasaki); 13. Clarke (Suzuki); 14. Mennenga (Suzuki); 15. Fryer (Yamaha).

19th September - Fountain
1. Kipp (Suzuki); 2. Buckmaster (AUS, Suzuki); 3. Zemke (Suzuki); 4. Bowman (Suzuki); 5. Randolph (Suzuki); 6. Clarke (Suzuki); 7. Lopez (Suzuki); 8. Moore (Suzuki); 9. R.-L. Hayden (Suzuki); 10. Ma. DuHamel (CAN, Suzuki); 11. Chouinard (Suzuki); 12. Haner (Suzuki); 13. Duprey (Suzuki); 14. Hart (Suzuki); 15. Burke (Suzuki).

◁ *Steve Goddard*

▷ *Steve Goddard*

Superbike

The Champion: Mathew Mladin. Born on 10th March 1972, in Camden/Australia. First race: 1991. First GP: Australie, 1993 (500).
Races record: Australian 80 "flat track" Champion 1981; Australian Motocross 80 Champion 1982; Australian 250 Production Champion (Suzuki) 1991; 27th World Superbike Championship, Australian Superbike Champion (Kawasaki) 1992; 13th 500 World Championship (Cagiva) 1993; 37th World Superbike Championship (Kawasaki) 1994; 35th World Superbike Championship, 2nd Australian Superbike Championship (Kawasaki) 1995; 4th US Superbike Championship (Suzuki) 1996; 3rd US Superbike Championship (Suzuki) 1997; 3rd US Superbike Championship (Suzuki) 1998; US Superbike Champion (Suzuki) 1999.

7th March - Daytona
1. Mi. DuHamel (CAN, Honda); 2. Mladin (AUS, Suzuki); 3. Oliver (Yamaha); 4. B. Bostrom (Ducati); 5. Rapp (Suzuki); 6. Pridmore (Suzuki); 7. Yates (Kawasaki); 8. Chandler (Kawasaki); 9. Pegram (Ducati); 10. Wait (Ducati); 11. Gobert (AUS, Ducati); 12. Barnes (Yamaha); 13. Cicotto (Suzuki); 14. Mizdal (Suzuki); 15. Moe (Kawasaki).

21st March - Phoenix
1. Gobert (AUS, Ducati); 2. Mladin (AUS, Suzuki); 3. B. Bostrom (Ducati); 4. Picotte (CAN, Harley-Davidson); 5. Hacking (Yamaha); 6. Pridmore (Suzuki); 7. Pegram (Suzuki); 8. Mi. DuHamel (CAN, Honda); 9. Oliver (Yamaha); 10. Smith (Harley-Davidson); 11. Crevier (CAN, Suzuki); 12. Wait (Ducati); 13. Chandler (Yamaha); 14. Yates (Suzuki); 15. Greaves (Suzuki).

18th April - Willow Springs
1. Pegram (Ducati); 2. B. Bostrom (Ducati); 3. Hacking (Yamaha); 4. Mladin (AUS, Suzuki); 5. Rapp (Suzuki); 6. Pridmore (Suzuki); 7. Oliver (Yamaha); 8. Wait (Ducati); 9. E. Bostrom (Honda); 10. Crevier (CAN, Suzuki); 11. Chandler (Kawasaki); 12. N. Hayden (Honda); 13. Yates (Kawasaki); 14. Russell (Harley-Davidson); 15. Martin (Kawasaki).

25th April - Sears Point
1. Mladin (AUS, Suzuki); 2. Chandler (Kawasaki); 3. Picotte (CAN, Harley-Davidson); 4. Yates (Kawasaki); 5. Gobert (AUS, Ducati); 6. Mi. DuHamel (CAN, Honda); 7. Hacking (Yamaha); 8. E. Bostrom (Honda); 9. Rapp (Suzuki); 10. Pegram (Ducati); 11. B. Bostrom (Ducati); 12. Russell (Harley-Davidson); 13. Randolph (Suzuki); 14. Short (Suzuki); 15. Greaves (Suzuki).

2nd May - Laguna Seca
1. Gobert (AUS, Ducati); 2. Mladin (AUS, Suzuki); 3. Chandler (Kawasaki); 4. Yates (Kawasaki); 5. Mi. DuHamel (CAN, Honda); 6. B. Bostrom (Ducati); 7. Crevier (CAN, Suzuki); 8. Oliver (Yamaha); 9. E. Bostrom (Honda); 10. Pegram (Ducati); 11. Pridmore (Suzuki); 12. Hacking (Yamaha); 13. Wait (Ducati); 14. Rapp (Suzuki); 15. Moore (Suzuki).

6th June - Road Atlanta
Course I: 1. Gobert (AUS, Ducati); 2. B. Bostrom (Ducati); 3. Hacking (Yamaha); 4. Oliver (Yamaha); 5. Mi. DuHamel (CAN, Honda); 6. Mladin (AUS, Suzuki); 7. Pridmore (Suzuki); 8. E. Bostrom (Honda); 9. Wait (Ducati); 10. Rapp (Suzuki); 11. Pegram (Ducati); 12. Crevier (CAN, Suzuki); 13. Yates (Kawasaki); 14. Ma. DuHamel (CAN, Suzuki); 15. Mizdal (Suzuki).
Course II: 1. Gobert (AUS, Ducati); 2. B. Bostrom (Ducati); 3. Mladin (AUS, Suzuki); 4. Yates (Kawasaki); 5. Crevier (CAN, Suzuki); 6. Pegram (Ducati); 7. E. Bostrom (Honda); 8. Chandler (Kawasaki); 9. Barnes (Suzuki); 10. McGrath (Suzuki); 11. Randolph (Suzuki); 12. Ma. DuHamel (Suzuki); 13. Mizdal (Suzuki); 14. Deatherage (Suzuki); 15. Pridmore (Suzuki).

13th June - Road America
1. Gobert (AUS, Ducati); 2. B. Bostrom (Ducati); 3. Hacking (Yamaha); 4. Chandler (Kawasaki); 5. Mladin (AUS, Suzuki); 6. E. Bostrom (Honda); 7. N. Hayden (Honda); 8. Rapp (Suzuki); 9. Pridmore (Suzuki); 10. Yates (Kawasaki); 11. Picotte (CAN, Harley-Davidson); 12. Pegram (Ducati); 13. Moore (Suzuki); 14. Bowman (Suzuki); 15. Clarke (Suzuki).

20th June - Loudon
1. Chandler (Kawasaki); 2. B. Bostrom (Ducati); 3. Gobert (AUS, Ducati); 4. Mladin (AUS, Suzuki); 5. Hacking (Yamaha); 6. E. Bostrom (Honda); 7. Crevier (CAN, Suzuki); 8. Picotte (CAN, Harley-Davidson); 9. Pegram (Ducati); 10. Pridmore (Suzuki); 11. Russell (Harley-Davidson); 12. Rapp (Suzuki); 13. Bowman (Suzuki); 14. Randolph (Suzuki); 15. Moore (Suzuki).

18th July - Lexington
1. Chandler (Kawasaki); 2. Mladin (AUS, Suzuki); 3. Pridmore (Suzuki); 4. E. Bostrom (Honda); 5. Picotte (CAN, Harley-Davidson); 6. Crevier (CAN, Suzuki); 7. Yates (Kawasaki); 8. Pegram (Ducati); 9. Gobert (AUS, Ducati); 10. B. Bostrom (Ducati); 11. Miller (Yamaha); 12. Greaves (Suzuki); 13. Ma. DuHamel (CAN, Suzuki); 14. Deatherage (Suzuki); 15. Grigg (Kawasaki).

1st August - Brainerd
1. B. Bostrom (Ducati); 2. Mladin (AUS, Suzuki); 3. Gobert (AUS, Ducati); 4. E. Bostrom (Honda); 5. Pegram (Ducati); 6. Hacking (Yamaha); 7. Pridmore (Suzuki); 8. N. Hayden (Honda); 9. Crevier (CAN, Suzuki); 10. Chandler (Kawasaki); 11. Rapp (Suzuki); 12. Yates (Kawasaki); 13. Randolph (Suzuki); 14. Moore (Suzuki); 15. Deatherage (Suzuki).

19th September - Fountain
1. Chandler (Kawasaki); 2. Picotte (CAN, Harley-Davidson); 3. N. Hayden (Honda); 4. Mladin (AUS, Suzuki); 5. B. Bostrom (Ducati); 6. Crevier (CAN, Suzuki); 7. Pegram (Ducati); 8. Smith (Ducati); 9. Wait (Ducati); 10. Russell (Harley-Davidson); 11. Hacking (Yamaha); 12. E. Bostrom (Honda); 13. Rapp (Suzuki); 14. Williams (Kawasaki); 15. Oliver (Yamaha).

Final classification

1. Mathew Mladin	Suzuki	361
2. Ben Bostrom	Ducati	351
3. Anthony Gobert	Ducati	315

4. D. Chandler (Kawasaki), 307; 5. L. Pegram (Ducati), 283; 6. J. Pridmore (Suzuki), 243; 7. E. Bostrom (Honda), 237; 8. A. Yates (Kawasaki), 234; 9. J. Hacking (Yamaha), 230; 10. S. Crevier (CAN, Suzuki), 220; 11. S. Rapp (Suzuki), 204; 12. P. Picotte (CAN, Harley-Davidson), 178; 13. R. Oliver (Yamaha), 162; 14. Ma. DuHamel (CAN, Suzuki), 161; 15. M. Wait (Ducati), 148; 16. Mi. DuHamel (CAN, Honda), 141; 17. J. Randolph (Suzuki), 137; 18. D. Mizdal (Suzuki), 132; 19. J. Bowman (Suzuki), 106; 20. S. Russell (Harley-Davidson), 100. 76 classified.

Formula Xtreme

The Champion: Kurtis Roberts. Born on 17th November 1978, in Turlock/California. First race: 1991. First GP: Malaysia, 1997 (250).
Races record: 34th Spanish 250 open Championship (Yamaha) 1994; 20th Spanish 250 open Championship (Yamaha) 1995; 12th European 250 open Championship (Yamaha) 1996; 2nd US 250 Championship, 11th US Supersport 600 Championship (Honda) 1998; 3rd US Supersport 600 Championship (Honda) 1998; US Formula Xtreme Champion (Honda) 1999.

20th March - Phoenix
1. K. Roberts (Honda); 2. Hayes (Suzuki); 3. Sullivan (Kawasaki); 4. Greaves (Suzuki); 5. Harrell (Yamaha); 6. Barnes (Yamaha); 7. Sweeney (Honda); 8. Lopez (Suzuki); 9. Voelker (Honda); 10. Call (Suzuki).

18th April - Willow Springs
1. N. Hayden (Honda); 2. K. Roberts (Honda); 3. Hayes (Suzuki); 4. Adams (Suzuki); 5. Miller (Yamaha); 6. Grigg (Kawasaki); 7. Mori (J, Yamaha); 8. Lopez (Suzuki); 9. Hagan (Yamaha); 10. Voelker (Honda).

25th April - Sears Point
1. N. Hayden (Honda); 2. Miller (Yamaha); 3. K. Roberts (Honda); 4. Hayes (Suzuki); 5. Lopez (Suzuki); 6. Short (Suzuki); 7. Hagan (Yamaha); 8. Salaverria (Yamaha); 9. Harrell (Yamaha); 10. Call (Suzuki).

2nd May - Laguna Seca
1. K. Roberts (Honda); 2. Miller (Yamaha); 3. Harrell (Yamaha); 4. Grigg (Kawasaki); 5. Mori (J, Yamaha); 6. Graves (Yamaha); 7. Short (Suzuki); 8. Sullivan (Kawasaki); 9. Salaverria (Yamaha); 10. Lopez (Suzuki).

6th June - Road Atlanta
1. N. Hayden (Honda); 2. Lopez (Suzuki); 3. Hayes (Suzuki); 4. Grigg (Kawasaki); 5. Graves (Yamaha); 6. Mori (J, Yamaha); 7. Miller (Yamaha); 8. Haskovec (Yamaha); 9. Greaves (Suzuki); 10. Szoke (CAN, Honda).

13th June - Road America
1. K. Roberts (Honda); 2. Miller (Yamaha); 3. Graves (Yamaha); 4. Lopez (Suzuki); 5. Hayes (Suzuki); 6. Mori (J, Yamaha); 7. Brotz (Yamaha); 8. Diedrich (Yamaha); 9. Mumford (Yamaha); 10. Mennenga (Suzuki).

20th June - Loudon
1. N. Hayden (Honda); 2. Hayes (Suzuki); 3. Miller (Yamaha); 4. K. Roberts (Honda); 5. Conboy (Yamaha); 6. Mori (J, Yamaha); 7. Mizdal (Suzuki); 8. Brotz (Yamaha); 9. Fischer (Suzuki); 10. Gonyea (Suzuki).

18th July - Lexington
1. N. Hayden (Honda); 2. K. Roberts (Honda); 3. Grigg (Kawasaki); 4. Barnes (Yamaha); 5. Lopez (Suzuki); 6. Szoke (CAN, Honda); 7. Greaves (Suzuki); 8. Bemisderfer (Yamaha); 9. Mrklas (Yamaha); 10. Doerfler (Suzuki).

1st August - Brainerd
1. N. Hayden (Honda); 2. Harrell (Yamaha); 3. Hayes (Suzuki); 4. Graves (Yamaha); 5. K. Roberts (Honda); 6. Lopez (Suzuki); 7. Barnes (Yamaha); 8. Sullivan (Kawasaki); 9. Deatherage (Kawasaki); 10. Brotz (Yamaha).

19th September - Fountain
1. N. Hayden (Honda); 2. Hayes (Suzuki); 3. Miller (Yamaha); 4. Lopez (Suzuki); 5. Taylor (Kawasaki); 6. K. Roberts (Honda); 7. Barnes (Yamaha); 8. Turner (Yamaha); 9. Orlando (Kawasaki); 10. Mizdal (Suzuki).

Final classification

1. Kurtis Roberts	Honda	298
2. Nicky Hayden	Honda	280
3. Joshua-Kurt Hayes	Suzuki	253

4. M. Miller (Yamaha), 241; 5. A.-G. Lopez (Suzuki), 231; 6. R. Greaves (Suzuki), 165; 7. S. Grigg (Kawasaki), 162; 8. C. Brotz (Yamaha), 148; 9. T. Mori (J, Yamaha), 140; 10. P. Harrell (Yamaha), 133; 11. M. Barnes (Yamaha), 120; 12. M. Sullivan (Kawasaki), 112; 13. C. Graves (Yamaha), 107; 14. J.-R. Page (Yamaha), 82; 15. C. Call (Suzuki), 80; 16. V. Voelker (Honda), 80; 17. D. Mizdal (Suzuki), 74; 18. J. Szoke (CAN, Honda), 72; 19. D. Battley (Yamaha), 65; 20. J. Hagan (Yamaha), 64. 96 classified.

Remerciements

Nous remercions tout particulièrement pour leur participation:
- Markus Lehner (adaptation allemande)
- Eric Silberman (adaptation anglaise)
- Josep Viaplana (adaptation espagnole)
et pour la partie statistique, Maurizio Mazzoni (Italie) et Bennie Pinners (Pays-Bas).

Crédit photographique

Toutes les photos sont de Maurice Büla, sauf:
- Roger Lohrer (18, 19, 33, 34, 35, 44b, 135b, 154, 155, 167, 172, 173, 174 et 175)
- Yamaha Racing PR (47b)
- Groupe Métraux PR (68)
- Dorna PR (71a)
- Pan Images (92)

Achevé d'imprimer sur les presses de l'Imprimerie Sézanne, à Bron (69) - France en novembre 1999.